Vasilii Rozano…

# Vasilii Rozanov and the Creation

## The Edenic Vision and the Rejection of Eschatology

By
Adam Ure

BLOOMSBURY
NEW YORK • LONDON • NEW DELHI • SYDNEY

**Bloomsbury Academic**
An imprint of Bloomsbury Publishing Plc

175 Fifth Avenue
New York
NY 10010
USA

50 Bedford Square
London
WC1B 3DP
UK

**www.bloomsbury.com**

First published by Continuum International Publishing Group 2011
Paperback edition first published 2013



**Library of Congress Cataloging-in-Publication Data**
Ure, Adam.
Vasilii Rozanov and the creation: the Edenic vision and the rejection of eschatology/by Adam Ure.
p. cm.
Includes bibliographical references (p. ) and index.
ISBN 978-1-4411-5494-1 (hardback: alk. paper) 1. Rozanov, V. V. (Vasilii Vasil′evich), 1856-1919. 2. Creation. 3. Eschatology. 4. Christianity--Philosophy. 5. Russkaia pravoslavnaia tserkov′--Doctrines. I. Title.
B4259.R694U74 2011
197--dc22

2011008356

ISBN: HB: 978-1-4411-5494-1
PB: 978-1-6235-6816-0

Typeset by Fakenham Prepress Solutions, Fakenham, Norfolk NR21 8NN

# Contents

## Acknowledgements

This book developed from my doctoral thesis completed at the School of Slavonic and East European Studies, University College London, in 2009. My doctorate was only made possible through funding by the Arts and Humanities Research Council, to whom I am very grateful.

During my doctoral research and subsequently I have had the benefit of the advice and help of many excellent scholars, and would like to thank especially my doctoral supervisor Robin Aizlewood, Pamela Davidson, Geoffrey Hosking and Tim Beasley-Murray for their many wise words, Stephen Hutchings and Philip Cavendish for their suggestions particularly after the doctorate was completed, Oliver Smith for many shared interests and the staff at SSEES.

I should also like to express my deep personal gratitude for support, advice and the loan of books to Viktor Sukach, whose help was crucial to the writing of this book. Thanks also to Aleksandr Nikoliukin, Leonid Katsis, and the staff at INION RAN. Also many thanks to Irina Edoshina and the staff at Kostroma State University for their prolonged support.

Some material for this book is adapted from Adam Ure, 'Rozanov and the Coin', *Slavonica*, 16 (April 2010), and used with kind permission from Jekaterina Young and the Slavonica editors.

In addition, some material is adapted from Adam Ure, 'Rozanov, the Creation, and the Rejection of Eschatology', *SEER*, 89 (April 2011) and used with kind permission from Barbara Wyllie and the SEER editorial board.

Also, many, many personal thanks to my family for all their help and patience.

# Introduction

Vasilii Rozanov was one of the most important, original and daring Russian thinkers and writers of the end of the nineteenth and the beginning of the twentieth centuries. He was a towering figure in the philosophical, literary and political environment of his time, and left a major imprint on Russian culture which extends through to the present day. A major influence on thinkers such as Sergii Bulgakov, Berdiaev and Bakhtin, his writing also had a wide-ranging impact on the development of Russian literature, from the Acmeists such as Mandel′shtam, through Formalists such as Shklovskii, Futurists including Khovin and Maiakovskii, to the rebellious traditions of non-official Soviet writers such as Ginzberg and Venedikt Erofeev. His fingerprints also reach far beyond the borders of Russian culture; he had an important role in shaping the development of Western literature through his direct influence on figures of the stature of D.H. Lawrence and Vladimir Nabokov, and since the end of the Soviet Union has been rediscovered in the West as an early exponent of existentialism and phenomenology.

Rozanov's contribution extends beyond the narrow, self-absorbed circles in which many of his peers often appeared to operate. Rozanov played an important role in Russian social, political and religious affairs. Beyond his multitudinous works on philosophy and literature, he bravely challenged the Orthodox Church and its theology, as well as government domestic and foreign policy, social issues, health and the economy. His petitioning led to reform of Russia's marriage and divorce laws, and it is difficult to think of a contemporary Russian thinker, save Lev Tolstoi, who had such a wide-ranging impact on Russia's religious and social conscience. Rozanov corresponded widely with Russian citizens who read his newspaper and magazine articles, often taking up the cause of the disadvantaged. This care for Russia's 'little people' and their everyday problems lends credence to Rozanov's own positioning as a man of the people whose thought emerges from the Russian folk.[1] This distinguishes him (in his own mind as well as that of critics including myself) from the often ethereal concerns of his coevals among the religious intelligentsia.

1 This concern for the importance of religion for ordinary people is also strangely apparent in Bloch's examination of the 'plebeian' element of Biblical exegesis. See Ernst Bloch, *Atheism in Christianity*, trans. by J.T. Swann (London: Verso, 2009), p. 62.

Rozanov's preoccupation with the realities of everyday life for ordinary Russian people, in the context of a new cosmological focus Rozanov injects into Russian Orthodoxy, provides one of the main areas of focus of this book.

Despite his enormous contribution to Russian culture, Rozanov has been generally ignored as one of the most important Russian thinkers and neglected as a topic of academic study. There are many reasons for this. The Soviet regime (although dissuaded by Gor´kii from executing Rozanov) anathematized his memory, no doubt in part following Trotskii's fervent condemnation of his work.[2] Throughout the vast majority of the Soviet period, the academic study of Rozanov was not permitted. The Rozanov archives were generally closed to the public, and publication of his works was not permitted. A few scholars, most notably Viktor Sukach in Moscow, studied Rozanov unofficially, and largely in secret and at significant personal risk. In the West, it was not possible to take full account of Rozanov's sizeable output. The major thinkers who left Russia and bore to the West the new wave of Russian religious thought, including Berdiaev, Sergii Bulgakov, Merezhkovskii and Frank, failed to import with them Rozanov's full significance or acknowledge his influence on their own thought. As Lutokhin noted, Rozanov had no 'school' or disciples, unlike many Russian philosophers or writers.[3] More formal Russian Orthodox thinkers who emigrated, such as Georgii Florovskii or Nikolai Losskii, openly attacked Rozanov as an immoral thinker.[4] Clergymen such as Archimandrite Mikhail (Pavel Semenov) considered Rozanov the Antichrist who pronounced the worst heresies possible.

Secondly, the criticism of Rozanov as unsystematic, by his peers on all sides of the philosophical spectrum, has to some extent set up an

2 L. Trotskii, *Literatura i revoliutsiia* (Moscow: Gosudarstvennoe izdatel´stvo, 1924), pp. 34–5.

3 D.A. Lutokhin, 'Vospominaniia o Rozanove', in *Vasilii Rozanov: Pro et Contra. Lichnost´ i tvorchestvo Vasiliia Rozanova v otsenke russkikh myslitelei i issledovatelei*, ed. by V.A. Fateev, 2 vols (St Petersburg: Izdatel´stvo Russkogo Khristianskogo gumanitarnogo instituta, 1995), I, pp. 193–9 (p. 193).

4 Florovskii considers Rozanov an un-Christian thinker, 'hypnotized by flesh', whose life was 'a chaos of fleeting moments, episodes and flashes'. Georgii Florovskii, *Puti russkogo bogosloviia* (Paris: YMCA Press, 1937), pp. 461–3. Although Losskii acknowledges Rozanov's 'sparks of genius', he points to Rozanov's 'pathological' personality and his 'unhealthy' interest in sex. Nikolai Losskii, *Istoriia russkoi filosofii* (Moscow: Vysshaia Shkola, 1991), pp. 435–6.

unfair reputation of Rozanov which persists today and impedes his acceptance as a 'mainstream' Russian thinker. This has been especially true in the West, with our traditional demand for consistency in philosophy and our predilection for segregating literature from this sphere. Such views are changing, as scholars in the UK and the USA turn to evaluate, broadly speaking, Russian literature as an expression of Russian thought. With the upsurge in interest in Russian philosophy since the beginning of the 1990s, we have become more exposed to a strand of Russian thought which intentionally privileges the spontaneous and the individual over a priori philosophical systems, and the increasing attention devoted to thinkers such as Shestov is testament to this. This book challenges dominant thinking by arguing for a deeper underlying consistency to Rozanov's approach, so far ignored by his most of his critics. Indeed, the development of Rozanov's later writing is a natural fulfilment of his initial work on the realization of potential, making Rozanov a highly honest thinker. In this respect, I concur with Galkovskii's assessment that Rozanov remains fundamentally consistent (a brief adolescent flirting with atheism aside), unlike his peers who are paradoxically considered more schematic even though they changed their outlook profoundly during their careers.[5] (Rozanov himself was critical of many of idealist thinkers, especially Berdiaev, who found their way to speculative religious thought after years spent proclaiming socialism.[6]) In many ways, Rozanov was an extremely single-minded and rigid thinker; Novoselov noted his lack of flexibility, calling him an 'edinomyshlennik';[7] and Bakhtin noted Rozanov for his monological approach to Dostoevskii.[8] Minskii was also highly critical of Rozanov's unwillingness to accept opposing schemes.[9] I suggest that Rozanov, emerging from the Orthodox Church, preserves in many ways a highly dogmatic approach to the truth (although this truth is often a personal

5 Dmitrii Galkovskii, 'Zakruglennyi mir', in *Beskonechnyi tupik*, 2 vols (Moscow: Izdatel′stvo Dmitriia Galkovskogo, 2008), II, pp. 1078–1100 (pp. 1080–1).

6 V.V. Rozanov, 'Nikolai Berdiaev. Smysl tvorchestva. Opyt opravdaniia cheloveka', in *Russkaia mysl′* (Moscow: Algoritm-EKSMO, 2006), pp. 491–7 (p. 496).

7 *Zapiski peterburgskikh Religiozno-filosofskikh sobranii (1901–1903 gg.)*, ed. by S.M. Polovinkin (Moscow: Respublika, 2005), p. 444.

8 M.M. Bakhtin, *Problemy tvorchestva Dostoevskogo* (Kiev: Firm 'Next', 1994), p. 10.

9 *Zapiski peterburgskikh Religiozno-filosofskikh sobranii*, p. 272.

construct). Hence the relative formality with which this book tackles the systematic aspects of Rozanov's religiosity may surprise some readers who are familiar with Rozanov's later and more spontaneous writings, and who might expect a focus on the individual and chaotic. Rozanov imbibes the philosophical current of the time, initiated by Solov´ev, of challenging the Russian Orthodox Church's control of dogma, and in this respect is a highly creative thinker, though ironically he presents his rebellious ideas aggressively with little flexibility or compromise. Novoselov's highly astute critique, which was in fact picked up by other contemporaries, has not yet been fully investigated in Rozanov scholarship.

This underlies the dominating aspect of Rozanov's approach, which is his tendency to assume other systems of thought – be it formal Orthodox tenets or the ideas of other philosophers – and, while dismissing their source, subsequently present such ideas as his own. As I hope to show, the style of Rozanov's theological discourse is itself shaped by the Creation. One of the complexities of Rozanov's thought is the fervency of his attack on the Church for limiting human freedom in its theology, and yet at the same time he preserves the dogmatic nature of Church teaching and presents an alternative truth which is itself often highly inflexible. Rozanov insists that the Russians are by nature 'adogmatic' and long for freedom of faith.[10] However, Solov´ev criticized Rozanov's lack of religious tolerance.[11] Borodaevskii was more succinct when he noted that Rozanov, in rejecting the dogma of the Church, is only trying to replace this with his own dogma.[12] Yet by attacking the Church's authority over doctrine and its relevance to contemporary life, Rozanov helps open up a new type of 'experiential dogmatics', in Florenskii's words, which aims at reconciling dogma with the need for human experience within a contemporary context.

Thirdly, close to the charge of philosophical inconsistency is that of Rozanov's immorality. This was the key point of Trotskii's attack, and during Rozanov's lifetime Struve was also a fervent critic of Rozanov's versatility, which he saw as disingenuous avarice (Struve called Rozanov

---

10 V.V. Rozanov, 'Nashi missionery i mariavitskoe dvizhenie', in *Staraia i molodaia Rossiia: Stat´i i ocherki 1909 g.*, ed. by A.N. Nikoliukin (Moscow: Respublika, 2004), pp. 135–8 (p. 136).

11 V.S. Solov´ev, 'Porfirii Golovlev o svobode i vere', in *Vasilii Rozanov: Pro et Contra*, I, pp. 282–91 (pp. 286–8). Solov´ev touches on an important point in Rozanov, that is his attempt to make the subjective a universal category.

12 *Zapiski peterburgskikh Religiozno-filosofskikh sobranii*, p. 324.

'organically amoral and godless in nature'). Rozanov acquired a notorious reputation for changing his colours in order to sell contradictory articles to rival publications. However, in this book I shall argue that Rozanov's supposed venality can be understood within the context of his broader understanding of the theological value of the family, money and the link between the two. Accusations of anti-Semitism in Rozanov have been harder to handle. Although Rozanov is not culpable for the extreme nationalism that engulfed the world after his death, his ideas of race and the folkish, or even völkisch, attachment to the Earth place him firmly in the wider European movement to provide scientific definitions of ethnicity, as well as more sinister mythologies of *Blut und Boden*. (It is not so much the mythological, but the merging of the mythological with the historical which is of particular concern; although Rozanov's approach is unique, similar movements climaxed with the traumatic events of the 1930s and 1940s.[13]) Few academics have been bold enough to delve in detail into Rozanov's treatment of the Jews, with the notable exception of Mondry, Engelstein and Katsis, and although I do not offer a comprehensive treatment of this subject, I attempt to contextualize aspects of Rozanov's Jewish work within the broader theme of his views on the Creation and the Jewish people's relationship, not to Christianity, but to Egypt.

The fourth point is that Rozanov has typically been considered too distant from the mainstream of Russian thought to be accepted into the canon of Russian thinkers. Rozanov was in many ways an isolated figure, professionally and personally. His desire to be close to the Russian people and to incarnate within himself an expression of the 'Russian idea' distanced him from the intelligentsia, itself esoteric and elitist. Many of his strikingly original but decidedly eccentric ideas are shocking, offensive and difficult to accept, and by all accounts Rozanov the man evoked a similar response. Yet in this book I argue that in many ways Rozanov is a highly typical Russian thinker; paradoxically, it is the manner of his drawing on key traditions of Russian philosophy which places him firmly at the centre of Russian thought. Rozanov's

---

13 Rozanov read and appeared to admire Russian translations of Houston Stewart Chamberlain. For a wider appraisal of the use of pagan mythology in Nazi ideology, see for example Ludwig Lewisohn, 'The Revolt Against Civilization', in *Essays in Context*, ed. by Sandra Fehl Tropp and Ann Pierson D'Angelo (New York/Oxford: Oxford University Press, 2001), pp. 117–25.

revolt against Russian philosophy emerges from his own heritage within those same traditions. His thought is shaped by a profound utopianism and an unshakeable conviction that philosophy can be implemented in Russia to serve the common good. Rozanov shares his adherence to these two key aspects of Russian philosophy with major Russian thinkers, from Chaadaev through Solov′ev to Solzhenitsyn. Indeed, although Rozanov goes out of his way to present himself as very different from the mainstream of Russian thought, he, like practically all the major protagonists of the Silver Age, owes much to the influence of Solov′ev, a debt which Rozanov is often unwilling to concede. (One of the more interesting points around this time is how various thinkers interpreted, modified and continued in their particular fashion the inheritance left by Solov′ev, an area which perhaps lies at the centre of Rozanov's disagreements with Berdiaev.)

## The development of Rozanov's thought

Over two decades have passed since the opening of Rozanov's writing to the public, and academics now enjoy unprecedented access to his work. His output was immense, and his projected (though never realized) complete works would have comprised over 50 volumes.[14] To date, a major proportion of his articles and letters has been reprinted and published, principally with the funding of the Russian government, through the Russian Academy of Sciences' Institute of Scientific Information for Social Sciences (INION RAN) under the leadership of Aleksandr Nikoliukin, and also by Viktor Sukach. However, the publication of a complete works, which would include Rozanov's correspondence, is in no way imminent. The difficulty of transcribing Rozanov's notoriously difficult handwriting and the limited number of scholars who can read his script, as well as the vast amount of his output, have slowed attempts to republish him. (Suvorin had to employ a printer

14 Nikoliukin has located Rozanov's draft plan for a publication of his complete works, reprinted as V.V. Rozanov, 'Plan Polnogo sobraniia sochinenii, sostavlennyi V.V. Rozanovym v 1917 godu', in V.V. Rozanov, *Religiia, filosofiia, kul′tura*, ed. by A.N. Nikoliukin (Moscow: Respublika, 1992), p. 368. The fact that such a document exists appears to debunk the myth, most probably initiated by Siniavskii, that Rozanov did not want to release a complete works.

especially to decipher Rozanov's handwriting.[15]) In addition, academics have also been confronted with the logistical problem of locating much material relating to Rozanov, especially his letters. It is scattered around various state and private archives, and new work is still being uncovered. Rozanov often did not commit his thoughts to notebooks, but would scribble down his ideas on whatever material came to hand, even sometimes on the soles of his slippers. Nevertheless, the republication of his major works means that modern-day scholars are able to appraise the development of his career.[16]

Rozanov was born to a devout Orthodox family in Kostroma and descended from a line of Orthodox believers and clergy; the Rozanov surname was probably adopted by Vasilii's paternal grandfather, who conferred on his son (Rozanov's father) the name of one of his seminary teachers.[17] His uncle was Archbishop of Yaroslavl. Rozanov spent his early years on the banks of the Volga and was steeped in the rural traditions of the area. He maintained a deep affection for Russia's provinces, her rivers and forests, and the religious behaviour which emerged from the people's ties with the Earth. There is something definitely 'kondovyi' (a Russian word which is difficult to translate into English, but which denotes an old-fashioned provincial outlook, and also refers to an attachment to wood) in his attitude to Russian nature. He loved the Volga, calling it the 'Russian Nile', and he wrote frequently about plants, flowers and trees, and the smell of nature. This elemental dimension pervades all of Rozanov's thought (and is the major factor in Berdiaev's critique of Rozanov as an un-Christian thinker).

Another important aspect is the experience of Rozanov's own childhood and how this informs his own utopian vision (an important dimension where I also note his influence on Nabokov). Nikoliukin has examined how Rozanov's memories of provincial life around the Volga helped him construct a mythology of Russian country life and cultivate a religious

15 Tat′iana Rozanova, *Bud′te svetly dukhom (Vospominaniia o V.V. Rozanove)* (Moscow: Blue Apple, 1999), p. 104.

16 Henrietta Mondry, 'Is the End of Censorship in the Former Soviet Union a Good Thing? The Case of Vasily Rozanov', *East European Jewish Affairs*, 32 (2002), 114–20 (p. 115).

17 V.G. Sukach, 'Detskie gody V.V. Rozanova', in *Chteniia, posviashchennye 80-letiiu pamiati V.V. Rozanova*, ed. by Iu.V. Lebedev (Kostroma: Kostromskoi filial Rossiiskogo fonda kul′tury, 1999), pp. 23–38 (p. 24).

relationship with Russian nature.[18] This comes across as the presentation of a golden age associated with Rozanov's childhood. Rozanov was born into an extremely poor family in the small town of Vetluga, around 400 miles northwest of Moscow. His father, a woodsman, died from cold in 1861 after chasing illegal foresters through a river. Rozanov's mother was left to care for the six children on a miserly pension. She died in 1870, leaving the young Vasilii to be taken in by his older brother Nikolai. The two brothers lived in Simbirsk and Nizhny Novgorod, where Vasilii started to read Nekrasov, his first literary love. He also started to read translations of British philosophers, especially Spencer, Bentham and J.S. Mill. Here he experienced a fleeting and teenage interest in atheism, which led to conflict with his conservative older brother. Although this phase quickly passed and gave way to renewed love for Orthodoxy and a deeply critical view of positivism, Rozanov was highly struck by what he saw as the strong ethical emphasis among these British thinkers, and this appears to have had a long-lasting influence on him. The notion that philosophy is tasked to change society, although a common thread running through Russian thinkers, was with Rozanov from an early age.

Tied to his love of nature is the love of the sexual, and Rozanov makes the leap from the universal and schematic to the individual by relying heavily on personal experience. In his later recollections of his childhood, laid out explicitly in letters to friends (the norms and laws of his time censoring publication of such matters), Rozanov lays out that the sensual experience of the person has wider cosmological implications.[19] There is a dominant strand in Christianity, especially in Eastern traditions, that correct worship involves the foregoing of sensual experience and stresses conceptual thought, yet for Rozanov the opposite is the case. Rozanov's

18 Nikoliukin refers to the woods and forests surrounding the Volga, as well as the river itself, which gave rise to the myths and legends which are common in that area. Aleksandr Nikoliukin, *Golgofa Vasiliia Rozanova* (Moscow: Russkii Put′, 1998), p. 17. His mythological vision of his own childhood, and of the natural world which surrounded him in his early years, had a crucial influence on Rozanov. Rozanov recognized that the word 'Kostroma' derived from the name of an ancient Slavic god. V.V. Rozanov, 'Kostroma i kostromichi', in *Staraia i molodaia Rossiia*, pp. 215–18 (p. 216). We note a similar mythologization of nature and youth coincidently in Florenskii, who also had strong family ties to Kostroma. See Avril Pyman, *Pavel Florensky: A Quiet Genius* (New York: Continuum, 2010), p. 59.

19 For a discussion of this see especially Nikolai Boldyrev, *Semia Ozirisa, ili Vasilii Rozanov kak poslednii vetkhozavetnyi prorok* (Cheliabinsk: Ural L.T.D., 2001), p. 23.

faith was underpinned by a feeling for the divine, the direct experience of God which he attempted to conceptualize and justify. Sexual feeling was for Rozanov entirely cosmological. Sex is a completely natural act, but as nature itself is holy, then sexual activity in itself becomes an act of worship. This view remains with Rozanov throughout his life, and the most important element of his project is to reconcile this elemental and pantheistic side of his outlook with his Russian Orthodox heritage.

In 1878, Rozanov left to study at Moscow Imperial University's faculty of philosophy and history. He appears to have admired his lecturers, who included F.I. Buslaev, N.S. Tikhonravov, V.I. Ger′e and V.O. Kliuchevskii. He also read and admired Sergei Solov′ev's celebrated history of Russia, and became well acquainted with the work of the Slavophiles, especially Khomiakov and the Aksakovs. His love for history developed alongside a renewal of his own faith while a student, and brought to his attention the need to reconcile historical experience with the unchanging demands of religion and Scripture. Rozanov accepts historical progress and especially the need to improve society through technological amelioration, but strives to balance this with a deep-seated belief that man's spiritual needs are essentially pre-modern and pre-Christian. Hence one problem Rozanov attempts to overcome is to find a way to allow Russian religious consciousness to engage with history, at the same time striving to prevent history from being seen as involution.

While a student, Rozanov met and fell in love with Apollinariia Suslova, sister to renowned radical feminist and pioneering physician Nadezhda, and former mistress to Dostoevskii. Rozanov and Suslova married in 1880, an ill-fated 'mystical tragedy' in Rozanov's words. Suslova was years older than her husband and apparently tormented him endlessly. When they eventually separated in 1886, Suslova refused to grant Rozanov a divorce, meaning that he had to marry his second wife, Varvara Rudneva, in a secret church ceremony performed in 1891 by a complicit priest. Rozanov was in effect committing bigamy, and his children born to Rudneva were officially illegitimate and unable to take his name. The Church's and the state's failure to recognize the nature of human relationships, that people organically fall in and out of love with each other, and should be permitted to consecrate new relationships with other people, led Rozanov to launch a public campaign against the strict divorce laws governing Orthodox Russians.

His first work, written while still a schoolmaster in Briansk (Rozanov moved there after completing his studies in 1882), was *O ponimanii* (1886), a systematic critique of positivist materialism. Six hundred copies were printed, at Rozanov's own expense, of which hardly any were sold. Although it was received warmly by a handful of minor religious thinkers, such as Sergei Sharapov, or Rozanov's friend the theologian A.I. Uspenskii, it was generally ignored or dismissed. Some critics saw it as a low-rate regurgitation of Hegel, and his teacher colleagues suspected him of having copied it from somewhere.[20] In this work, Rozanov attacks positivist empiricists and attempts a definition of understanding as a means of unlocking the underlying unity of appearances. Rozanov identifies the common origin of all things, in their createdness by God, as the source of this unity, and hence lays the foundation for a future programme which examines the activity involved in the Creation. He relies heavily on Hegel and Slavophile theories on integral knowledge, but what marks this out, and what makes it a crucial starting point for the rest of his work, is his focus on potentiality (realized in the Creation) as a dynamic mediator between the spiritual and the material. For Rozanov, understanding acts as the potentiality of knowledge, joining together disparate aspects of sensual experience with reason in a quasi-sexual union. Certain neo-Kantian influences come out here in Rozanov, as he explains understanding as having an a priori quality that gives unity to the world of appearances.[21] However, Rozanov distinguishes himself from Kant by opening up the possibility for experience to be privileged over rational knowledge, a tendency which comes out more in Rozanov's later works. Rozanov also, leaning on Hegel, lays out a theory of art as a religious act, which also comes out in his future work.

During his time as a provincial schoolmaster, Rozanov expanded his studies to universal philosophies on history and the natural world. In 1890, he published his long essay 'Mesto khristianstva v istorii' and also collaborated with P.D. Pervov, a fellow teacher from the Elets gymnasium, on a translation of the first five books of Aristotle's *Metaphysics* (Rozanov's Greek was poor and his contribution went as far as providing extensive footnotes and his own interpretation of the Greek's philosophy). Rozanov also started to write journalistic articles for various periodicals. During this time, he made the acquaintance of Nikolai Strakhov, who became a close friend, confidant and patron.

20 Valerii Fateev, *S russkoi bezdnoi v dushe: Zhizneopisanie Vasiliia Rozanova* (St Petersburg: Kostroma, 2001), p. 79.

21 V.V. Rozanov, *O ponimanii: Opyt issledovaniia prirody, granits, i vnutrennego stroeniia nauki kak tsel'nogo znaniia*, ed. by V.G. Sukach (Moscow: Tanias, 1996), pp. 15–16.

Strakhov's thought was to have profound influence on Rozanov's own philosophy, especially Strakhov's ability to investigate cultural phenomena through a specifically Russian religious-aesthetic prism. Strakhov's detailed writings on the importance for Russian religious life of figures such as J.S. Mill, Renan and Darwin, his dynamism of thought in extracting Russian themes from foreign subjects, lay the groundwork for Rozanov's later work on the same topics. There is also an important link that Strakhov provides between Rozanov and the highly significant views of Grigor′ev on the organic development of culture. And on a more practical level, Strakhov helped, through his own criticism, establish Rozanov as a writer, with his essay on Rozanov's book on the Grand Inquisitor.[22]

Rozanov had first approached Strakhov for assistance with the publication of his own work, but the orphan quickly developed a strong emotional dependence on the older man. Their relationship started as a correspondence in which Rozanov revealed his burgeoning ideas and intimate problems, to which Strakhov replied with fatherly advice and often stern reprimands. Rozanov even confessed to Strakhov his desire to commit suicide. Strakhov saw Rozanov as chaotic and impetuous, and believed that Rozanov stood too closely under the influence of Dostoevskii. He advised Rozanov to shake off this infatuation, and instead encouraged him to read more Tolstoi, a move which mirrored Strakhov's own beliefs at that time (in many surprising ways, Tolstoi shares parallels with Rozanov, and Rozanov's criticism of the great writer and thinker is a recurring theme in this book). Rozanov later published their letters, along with his correspondence with Leont′ev, in the book *Literaturnye izgnanniki* (first edition 1913), which provides fascinating insight into the early development of Rozanov's thought. In these letters, one notes Rozanov's fascination with pre-Christian societies and their religions, in particular ancient Egypt and the classical world, and here Rozanov lays the seeds for his fleshed-out examination of religiosity which emerges in the first decade of the twentieth century.

22 In his essay, Strakhov picked up on Rozanov's ability to construct general and eternal concepts about Dostoevskii's religiosity from specific points in Dostoevskii's work, a talent which Rozanov would develop throughout his career. See N. Strakhov, 'V. Rozanov. "Legenda o velikom inkvizitore" F.M. Dostoevskogo', in *Bor′ba s zapadom v nashei literature*, 3 vols (Kiev: Tip. I.I. Chokolova, 1898), III, pp. 220–7 (p. 222). Strakhov's significance for the history of Russian culture more widely deserves more academic investigation.

Around 1886, Rozanov also made an epistolary acquaintance with Konstantin Leont´ev, who helped Rozanov consolidate his views on the organic development of culture. (Rozanov also drew on the works of the Russian botanist Sergei Rachinskii and assimilated his biological works into his religious understanding.[23]) The two men never met, though their correspondence is highly important. As I shall argue below, Leont´ev's influence was vital as it forced Rozanov to bring together the religion of the Earth he inherited from the *pochvenniki* with the formal doctrines of the Orthodox Church.

Rozanov first won widespread public recognition with his 1891 work *Legenda o velikom inkvizitore F.M. Dostoevskogo*, published in *Russkii vestnik*. This book was the first major study of Dostoevskii as a religious writer and established the eponymous passage in Dostoevskii's final novel as a 'legend'. In his examination of Dostoevskii and Christianity, Rozanov sides with well-established Slavophile theories on the differences between Orthodoxy, Catholicism and Lutheranism, and various interpretations of individual freedom and religious authority. However, as several critics have noted, the *Legenda* is particularly striking in that Rozanov prioritizes the ethnic basis for each group's religious practices, rather than siding with traditional Slavophiles who argued that different Christian denominations shape national characteristics.[24]

In 1893, Rozanov wrote 'Sumerki prosveshcheniia' (re-published in a compilation of articles under the same name in 1899), an essay highly critical of the education system in Russia, a topic to which he devoted scores of articles throughout his life. In this work, Rozanov laid the foundation for his repeated critique of Russian schools, the dry impersonal nature of teaching and the need to reconfigure the school as an extension of the family. The authorities reacted angrily to this, as a result of which Rozanov was forced to leave the teaching profession. Having secured with the help of Strakhov and Filippov a post in the civil service as College Counsellor, he moved to St Petersburg. In these first years in the imperial capital, Rozanov struggled both financially and in terms of inspiration. This changed in 1899, when he was offered

23 See V.V. Rozanov, 'Serg. Al. Rachinskii. Sbornik statei', in *Iudaizm: Stat´i i ocherki 1898–1901 gg.*, ed. by A.N. Nikoliukin (Moscow: Respublika, 2010), pp. 138–40.

24 This point is made in, among others, Frederick C. Copleston, *Philosophy in Russia: From Herzen to Lenin and Berdyaev* (Tunbridge Wells: Search Press, 1986), p. 198.

a permanent position at Suvorin's *Novoe Vremia*, which he held until 1917. This was the start of an intensely fruitful period, and in the almost 20 years Rozanov worked at *Novoe Vremia*, he produced on average three articles a week for this newspaper alone. In addition, Rozanov was also published, with Suvorin's reluctant approval, in several other periodicals, including *Novyi Put´*, *Russkoe slovo* and even the *Torgovo-promyshlennaia gazeta*. He integrated himself with the *Mir Iskusstva* group, and contributed essays on art to their magazine. In addition, he co-founded the Religious-Philosophical Meetings (which later developed into the Religious-Philosophical Society), where his lectures criticized the doctrine and the detachment of the Orthodox Church, and called for a renewed dialogue between clergy and society and between dogma and experience.

Rozanov took with him that distinct branch of religious thought that tries to incorporate Orthodox principles into the everyday facets of Russian life. Alongside Bukharev, other under-investigated thinkers, such as the economist Sergei Sharapov and the writer Ivan Romanov (better known as Rtsy) drew on these major issues. They looked principally at the family and agrarian economy as a medium by which the values of Orthodoxy could somehow be preserved, while allowing for the technological development of society and the economy. Rozanov's thought is particularly striking in the way it points to the activity of the embodied person as a means of stepping over this. The work and personality of Ivan Romanov also had a particularly deep and lasting influence on Rozanov. The fact that Romanov lived in St Petersburg was one of the factors in Rozanov's decision to move to the capital (although, as Rozanov got to know him better, he developed a more ambivalent relationship towards the elder writer).[25] Fateev provides an account of Rozanov's correspondence with the Petersburg conservatives, including Tertii Filippov, Afanasii Vasil´ev, Nikolai Aksakov and Osip Kablits, in whose circle Rozanov moved in his first years in the capital. Fateev suggests that it was Rozanov's dissatisfaction with these 'undeveloped' Slavophiles that pushed him towards the Symbolist group of the Merezhkovskiis and their allies. Nevertheless, Rozanov harboured a warm relationship with Ivan Romanov, who would be forgotten as a writer without Rozanov's intervention in his life. Rozanov deeply admired Rtsy's writing, which he considered misunderstood and undervalued.

In his early Petersburg days, Rozanov's essays tended to discuss universal philosophical schemes and questions of history, such as

---

25 See Fateev, *S russkoi bezdnoi v dushe*, pp. 129–32, 147–50.

'Pochemu my otkazyvaemsia ot "nasledstva 60–70-kh godov"?' (1891) or 'Krasota v prirode i ee smysl' (1895). However, by the turn of the century, he had started to investigate more personal issues, particularly the attitude of the Russian Church to marriage and the family. In 1901 he released *V mire neiasnogo i nereshennogo* (republished in 1904), which examined the philosophy of the family, and followed this with the 1903 book *Semeinyi vopros v Rossii*, which looked at the practical implications of his theories. He started to examine in depth the Russian Orthodox Church, in books such as *Okolo tserkovnykh sten* (1905) or *Temnyi Lik* (1911). In this period he also turned his attention to pre-Christian religions, devoting scores of articles to Judaism and paganism, such as a series of essays 'Iudaizm', published in *Novyi Put´* in 1903. All these studies were undertaken from the same point of view, that is to discover how the Russians can re-establish their lost connections with the Creation. Therefore Rozanov instils a religious dimension into all his writing, ensuring that it has a metaphysical quality.[26] The way Rozanov's ideas are expressed in his newspaper and magazine articles reveals much about the conflict of religious ideas and public discourse, and the development of Russian journalism (especially Suvorin's contribution) at this time requires further investigation.[27]

Rozanov became more disillusioned with the Church's hostility towards the family, a view which found full expression in his lecture 'O Sladchaishem Iisuse i gor´kikh plodakh mira', delivered to the Religious-Philosophical Society in 1907, in which he attacked Christ for diverting man's attention away from this world, and also in his 1911 book *Liudi lunnogo sveta*, in which he was highly critical of Orthodox asceticism, depicting Christian monasticism as a form of sexual deviancy and relying on the contemporary scientific research of figures such as Richard von Krafft-Ebing and Nikolai Pirogov to support his claims. Between 1910 and 1913, in the wake of the Beilis Affair, Rozanov compiled a series of essays highly critical of the Jews and their supposed use of blood in rituals. *Oboniatel´noe i osiazatel´noe otnoshenie evreev k krovi* (1914) was written with some help from Florenskii (though it is important not to understate Rozanov's responsibility for the project as a whole), but was so aggressive towards the Jews that even the conservative *Novoe Vremia*

26 V.A. Fateev, 'Publitsist s dushoi metafizika i mistika', in *Vasilii Rozanov: Pro et Contra*, I, pp. 5–36 (p. 35).

27 N.Iu. Kazakova, *Filosofiia igry: V.V. Rozanov – Zhurnalist i literaturnyi kritik* (Moscow: Flinta-Nauka, 2001), p. 59.

refused to publish it and only the extremist *Zemshchina* would take it on.[28] As a consequence of this work, Rozanov was driven out of the Religious-Philosophical Society, and many of his erstwhile friends and supporters, most notably Merezhkovskii and Filosofov, turned away from him.

Around the same time, Rozanov turned to a strikingly subjective style of writing, relying on aphorisms, informal spontaneous musings and short descriptions of family life. Many commentators have described this 'Fallen Leaves' genre, or the *Opavshelistika*, as Nietzschian in its influence, though it owes more to the work of Ivan Romanov, who similarly composed books of short passages about the home (as early as 1899 Rozanov had experimented with 'Embriony', a short work of aphorisms). The *Opavshelistika* dominated the last section of his career and includes his most famous works, such as *Uedinennoe* (published in 1912 but immediately confiscated by the censor), *Opavshie list′ia* (two bundles, 1913 and 1915), *Smertnoe* (1913), *Sakharna* (written from 1911 to 1913, but not published in full until 1998), *Mimoletnoe* (written in 1915 but not published until 1994) and *Apokalipsis nashego vremeni* (written in several parts between 1917 and 1918, but not published in full until 2000). In addition, towards the end of his life, Rozanov also started to compile essays on the ancient Egyptians and their reverence for the beginning of the world. His final Egyptian work is striking, as it was composed alongside what many consider Rozanov's masterpiece, his *Apokalipsis*, in which he evaluated the Revolution as a distinctly Russian disaster for which Christ is responsible. The coincidence of beginnings and eschatology, and the way these are managed through writing, will be very important in the final chapters of this book.

While in Petersburg, Rozanov had access to the collections at the Hermitage and the Imperial Museum of Egyptology, through which he developed his interest (which he had held from his student days) in the ancient world. In probing this, Rozanov claims to find the fundamental tenets which lie at the relationship between God and humanity, founded at the beginning of time. Rozanov claims that Egypt is 'the root of everything'. He sees here the key to the original types of worship which he believes are absent in Orthodoxy, and which the Russian Church should restore. Key to this is the Egyptians' understanding of Creation

---

28 Edith W. Clowes, *Fiction's Overcoat: Russian Literary Culture and the Question of Philosophy* (Ithaca: Cornell University Press, 2004), p. 181. *Oboniatel′noe i osiazatel′noe otnoshenie evreev k krovi* has been reprinted in V.V. Rozanov, *Sakharna* (Moscow: Respublika, 1998), pp. 273–413.

and their ability to foster a proper relationship with the divine based on God's creatorship and the physical relationship this entails. Rozanov also engaged a great deal with the Jewish people, and his highly controversial writings have been perhaps the area which has most interested Western scholars since 1991, and in particular Mondry's highly progressive and useful studies.

## Approach of this book

In this book, I argue that Rozanov rejects the doctrine and teachings of the Russian Orthodox Church that focus on its eschatology, that teach that this world is only matter-in-waiting which anticipates the end of time and its eventual transfiguration. The Church's position is made clear in its teaching that Christ's death promises the salvation of humankind, but only at the end of time, and outside earthly experience. Hence Rozanov presents an opposition between our existence now in time, and the Church's speculative promise of a full union with God which can only take place after our deaths. Rozanov, like many of his peers, saw Russian Orthodoxy as unable to present a coherent way of living religiously in this world, though his attempt to reform its teachings comes from within the Church.

Instead, Rozanov argues that our religiosity should be based not on the Crucifixion of Christ, but on the Creation of the Earth by God. This ensures for him the sanctity of the physical. God's work can only be good, but Rozanov provides an original explanation for this by going further, arguing for a sexual Creation of a universe which is consubstantial with the divine. For Rozanov, God gives birth to the cosmos, which then in turn contains Him (the world becomes God's home). This bold pantheism ensures our communion with God within everyday existence, but also permits Rozanov to overcome the division of epistemology and ontology in Hellenic thought which has dogged Russian religious philosophy despite the efforts of its major protagonists. Life, not being, is the subject of Rozanov's inquiry.[29]

29 Rozanov's is a highly important contribution to making philosophy relevant to life. As Berdiaev insists, 'the key idea of Russian philosophy is the idea of the concrete existent, of the underlying real existence which precedes rationalism'. Nikolai Berdiaev, *Russkaia ideia: Osnovnye problemy russkoi mysli XIX veka i nachala XX veka* (Paris: YMCA Press, 1971), p. 267.

Rozanov founds his beliefs firmly in the Old Testament, particularly its narration of the Creation, God's original plans for humanity in Eden and how we cope with our expulsion from Paradise. (It is little wonder that one of the literary works that intrigued him most was Milton's *Paradise Lost*.) Despite the fact that in his early period he provided systematic investigations into the philosophy of the natural world and history (demonstrating his heritage in Strakhov and Danilevskii, whom he often defended from Solov′ev's criticism), it is in his middle period (from the start of his full-time collaboration with *Novoe Vremia* to around 1910) that Rozanov starts to locate this thought in the teachings of the Old Testament. There is no sign that Rozanov ever doubted the reality of the physical world, but the narration of the Creation in the Bible becomes the unquestionable proof for Rozanov's faith that matter enjoys a special relationship with the divine which has its basis in creatorship. Rozanov goes on to build a philosophical framework by which sense experience is explained theologically. Therefore Rozanov provides a neat merging of natural theology with religion as revelation, eschewing the ontological arguments for God that we see, for example, in his friend Florenskii. Like Solov′ev, Rozanov provides a complex merging of Scripture, philosophy, history, natural science and mythology. However, unlike Solov′ev's reliance on the New Testament and the speculative promise of the end, Rozanov instead bases his thought in the Creation and human experience, ensuring the validity of a real religion. It is Rozanov's particular merging of the essence and energies of God, the inevitable result of his pantheistic union of God and the world, which permits Rozanov to present a coincidence of the historical and the religious which often sits more comfortably than that of his peers.

This book begins with an examination of Orthodox teaching on the importance of the Apocalypse as the promise of the final coming of the Kingdom of God. It looks at how this teaching is the basis for Orthodox worship, which re-enacts the Resurrection of Christ as the promise for our future salvation and provides an eschatological foundation to Christian experience. Rozanov then takes the theoretical and practical implications of this, arguing that the Church demands its believers choose between God and the Earth. Rozanov contends that Orthodoxy, privileging the afterlife over this life, in fact encourages its worshippers to look to the end of the world and to seek death. I also examine how Russian speculative religious thinkers attempted to overcome this division of Orthodox experience from historical consciousness by presenting a religious interpretation of history, but which in fact resulted in them presenting history itself as teleological. Rozanov gets round this by focusing on the Creation, and in particular the creative act as providing for the dynamism of the cosmos. The Creation involves the somatization of the divine ideas, which is essentially a sexual act, and humans are obliged to repeat this through their own sexuality.[30] Therefore for Rozanov, sex and childbirth is a religious duty, the supreme act of *imitatio Dei*, the implications of which have been hitherto ignored (for Rozanov, like many religious thinkers, to imitate is to know). This preoccupation with conception and childbirth distinguishes Rozanov from most other thinkers, with the possible exception of Schopenhauer.

This highlights Rozanov's complex attitude towards the Russian Orthodox Church. He does not reject the Church as an institution, but understands it as naturally constituted by the body of the Russian people, whom he loved deeply.[31] Just as all Russians are innately members of this body, linked by a common biology, it is impossible for a non-Russian to be a member of their Church. It is also impossible for Russians to be excommunicated from the Church (Rozanov fervently condemned the Holy Synod for its excommunication of Tolstoi). Here Rozanov is close to a strong tradition in Russia, still potent within the Orthodox Church today, that does not differentiate between Russianness and Orthodoxy. Rozanov is also close to the traditions of the *pochvenniki*, who identified the organic concept of the Russian people as the locus for a national religion. He also shares the *pochvennik's* opposition to the common Slavophile view that the Orthodox Church as an institution naturally expresses a doctrinal truth. There is no sense in his reform that Rozanov wants to destroy the Church per se, but he posits an engagement from within. This is very much a downwards-up approach, launched in the name of the people; it is worth noting Rozanov's deep affection for individual priests, Orthodox church buildings and Orthodoxy's rites and rituals.[32] Gippius describes the simple, almost churchly, character of the

30 V.V. Rozanov, 'Mater′ialy k resheniiu voprosa', in *Semeinyi vopros v Rossii* (Moscow: Respublika, 2004), pp. 195–270 (p. 225).

31 Rozanov's approach is intensely physical and he understands the command to love one's neighbour in a biological manner. George Louis Kline, *Religious and Anti-Religious Thought in Russia* (Chicago: University of Chicago Press, 1968), p. 48.

32 Tareev, one of Rozanov's most astute critiques, notes Rozanov's complex attitude to Orthodoxy: 'A serving priest, dressed in his robes, is necessarily his enemy, but the very same priest, as a family man, would inevitably be his friend.' See M.M. Tareev, 'V.V. Rozanov', in *Vasilii Rozanov: Pro et*

Rozanovs' Petersburg home on Shpalernaia, where priests were frequent visitors.[33] His focus on the theosis of the worshipper, rather than on the kenosis of God, places his thought closer to formal Orthodoxy rather than to the traditions of speculative religious thought. At the same time, Rozanov was accused of not attending church services and seemed to derive greater pleasure from regular meetings with his fellow thinkers (his Sunday evening *jour-fixe* being a weekly highlight of the literary scene).[34] Hence his approach highlights the tension between the dogma of the Church leadership and the experience of contemporary life.

Rozanov's paganistic conclusions mean that he in turn must contend with the nature and activity of Christ, the basis of Chapter 2. This is the most complex aspect of his thought, especially as Rozanov, despite all his attacks on Christ and the established Church, consistently considered himself Orthodox. This was a matter of concern to his peers, especially Berdiaev, who struggled to assimilate Rozanov's essentially pagan elements with his deep affection for the Russian Orthodox Church. This book argues that having located the Creation as the centre of his religiosity, Rozanov then accommodates the historical Christ to this. For Rozanov, Christ's Incarnation and Resurrection are not the key to his worldview, but hold significance merely in their examples of re-enactments of the Creation. I attempt to contextualize Rozanov's attitude towards Christ in the wider search by his peers for non-Christian religions. Always with a focus on the practical implications of worship, I look at Rozanov's work within a religious-philosophical environment which traditionally had a confused Christology. Whereas in Russian religious culture, the nature of the perichoresis of the Trinity traditionally provided a model for the relationship between the idea and the realization of philosophy, Rozanov instead removes Jesus from the centre of his thought and looks primarily at the creative work of God down onto Earth. This in turn has implications for his treatment of the relationship between formal Orthodoxy and Russian creative philosophy more broadly. But Rozanov provides for a unique encounter of faith with

---

*Contra*, II, pp. 52–73 (p. 53). Rozanov correspondingly held a high opinion of Tareev and his expression of personalism in religious consciousness. See V.V. Rozanov, 'Novaia kniga o khristianstve', in *Staraia i molodaia Rossiia*, pp. 9–17.

33 Z.N. Gippius, 'Zadumchivyi strannik: O Rozanove', in *Vasilii Rozanov: Pro et Contra*, I, pp. 143–85 (p. 153).

34 M.M. Prishvin, 'O V.V. Rozanove (Iz "Dnevnika")', in *Vasilii Rozanov: Pro et Contra*, I, pp. 103–31 (p. 117).

the proofs of established philosophy, therefore giving a new perspective on the dialogue between religion and philosophy. Rozanov, following Hegel, insists that religion and philosophy should share the same object of inquiry, and although he does sometimes carve an elevated position for religion, this is not an exclusive place. Rozanov's lack of Christology allows him to present a less antagonistic relationship between theology and philosophy, and in this way he foreshadows the creative work of contemporary scholars such as Khoruzhii.

Having laid out his ideas on the workings of the cosmos and its divine origins, Rozanov looks to practical implications of these, and how the individual relates to the divine Godhead on an everyday basis. The key to this is the activity of the phallus (as symbol and agent) and the potential within it for new life. Sexual activity provides the link between the individual and the cosmological, and the penis demonstrates the reality of our own divinity and the potential for salvation. This becomes the core feature of the Rozanov project. Perhaps more than any other Russian thinker, Rozanov delves into the effects formal religion has had on practically all aspects of Russian life and culture, its politics, social affairs, education, health and art. In his efforts to persuade the Orthodox Church to end its hostility to Russian life, Rozanov looks specifically to the examples of pre-Christian religions, especially ancient Egypt. Rozanov presents a highly subjective and static vision of Egypt, where he suggests religiosity was based on the Creation, and where there was no division between religious doctrine and the people. This Rozanovian image of Egypt, simultaneously historical and mythological, sits alongside his vision of Eden as the ideal state to which humanity should aspire to return. The subjugation of Egypt to Greece and its formal philosophy parallels for Rozanov humankind's decision to revere the Tree of Knowledge rather than the Tree of Life. Rozanov's curious and deeply unsettling examination of the beliefs and practices of Jewish Russians, in Chapter 4, is a consequence of the loss of Paradise. Rozanov studies the Jews only because he believes that they have preserved in contemporary life the secrets of religion which the ancient Hebrews stole from their neighbours. Rozanov suspects that the Jewish household could provide the lessons for the Russians to re-enact Eden, yet his focus on bodily activity as the prime means of religious transmission leads him instead to perverse conclusions.

This book concludes by looking at Rozanov's appreciation of literature as sacred, both in its production and its consumption. The starting point here appears to be Remizov's statement, with which Rozanov concurs, that to write is to pray.[35] The comparison of prayer to writing is common in Christian theology, but in Rozanov's aesthetics and in his religiosity, worship is always practical and essentially sexual. Although Crone presents Rozanov's writing as the sublimation of sex, I contend that Rozanov's literature is in itself an imitation or a repetition of the sex act. For Rozanov, literature should emerge from the Old Testament and extol the virtues of family life and sexual love, and he brings these Biblical aesthetics into practically all his literary critiques. This is clearest in the novel (Rozanov is well aware of the etymology of the word 'roman'), where the entry of the main characters into the book, their appearance as heroes and their loving union, mirrors the Creation of the world.[36] For example, Rozanov interprets the sexual union of Nekhliudov and Katiusha as their return to Eden, a completely different conclusion from Tolstoi himself (for Rozanov, resurrection must always be seen as a rebirth). So Rozanov presents a different appraisal of how theology, especially its eschatological themes, shapes literature. More importantly, it is in the field of literature that Rozanov lays out perhaps most explicitly the way in which humans can continue to re-enact the Creation in their contemporary lives. The Creation, and creativity, permeates all Rozanov's thinking, in that it leads him to shun endings in favour of beginnings. The effort to validate his religiosity means that he reinterprets conclusions not as a demise, but as an opportunity for a new beginning.

This fear of conclusions was made apparent by Rozanov's exposure to Leont´ev. Despite falling somewhat out of fashion after his premature death, Leont´ev was very important in forcing Rozanov to reconsider Russian theories of organic development. Leont´ev believed that all civilizations, as all life, are destined to pass through stages of youthful simplicity, mature complexity, followed by decline and dissolution. Yet for Rozanov, Leont´ev's ideas on organic development are highly pessimistic, as they conclude with deterioration and death. Rozanov modifies Leont´ev by using the Creation as a model which allows for the potential for new life, for new beginnings. It is the aesthetic field where this is made most tangible, and Rozanov cuts across both well-known ideas of organic development and the eschatology of formal Orthodoxy

35 Aleksei Remizov, *Kukkha: Rozanovy pis´ma* (New York: Serebrianyi Vek, 1978), p. 47.

36 V.V. Rozanov, 'Poputnye zametki (O romane)', in *Iudaizm*, pp. 166–7 (p. 166).

to present a much more optimistic focus against a widespread disillusionment with Russian culture.

> Уже Леонтьев более десяти лет назад ощущал это всеобщее кругом разложение и советовал, как политическую программу: «подморозить гниющее». Печальный совет самого пламенного из наших консерваторов, пожалуй, единственного консерватора-идеалиста. Печальный и бессильный совет: он забыл, что ведь не вечная же зима настанет, что на установку вечной зимы не хватит сил ни у какого консерватизма и что как потеплеет, так сейчас же начнется ужасная вонь от разложения. Он, биолог, забыл другое явление, что вырастают чудные орхидеи на гниющих останках старых дерев.
>
> More than ten years ago, Leont′ev felt this all-encompassing decay and advised us, like a political programme: 'Prevent the rot by freezing everything'. Melancholy advice from the most fiery of our conservatives, perhaps our only idealist conservative. Melancholy and impotent advice: he forgot that winter does not last forever, that no conservatism is strong enough to preserve winter forever, and as soon as it warms, the terrible stench of decay starts. A biologist, he forgot the other phenomenon, that wondrous orchids grow from the rotting remains of old trees.[37]

There are of course here ideas of the eternal return which we see in other thinkers, such as Nietzsche or Schelling. But Rozanov here provides for a unique encounter of faith with the proofs of established philosophy, giving a new perspective on the dialogue between formal religion and experience. Hence Rozanov gives particular emphasis to the process of writing itself as evidence of the special relationship between the creative act of God and the created. For Rozanov, literature cannot be detached from the processes that went into composing it. Both reader and writer are joined through artistic effort which is sexual and seminal. Therefore Rozanov's own attempts to write, the dazzling passages of the *Opavshelistika*, are not a break from his earlier, essayistic works, but their fulfilment. Rozanov taught that the potential for creativity must be realized through sexuality, and he demonstrates this himself in the production of books which are designed to inseminate the reader, as it were, and convince them of the need themselves to create.

In his examination of the *Opavshelistika*, Shklovskii's focus on form in effect split the study of Rozanov, both in Russia and the West. Whereas a large proportion of Rozanov criticism is devoted to the content of his

37 V.V. Rozanov, 'Gosudarstvo i obshchestvo', in *Kogda nachal′stvo ushlo...* (Moscow: Respublika, 2005), pp. 38–43 (p. 43).

religious thought, such as Poggioli's 1957 study *Rozanov*,[38] another part, such as Crone's sophisticated 1978 breakdown of the voices within the 'trilogy' of *Uedinennoe* and the two parts of *Opavshie list'ia*, is specifically devoted to the study of Rozanov through the prism of literary theory.[39] This division stands to this day.[40] However, I hope to offer a way of overcoming this by suggesting that it is primarily a Creation-focused religiosity that informs both the style and the content of Rozanov's later writings, and which is the key to reconciling this division in scholarship on his *Opavshelistika*.

Therefore Rozanov provides not so much a philosophical system, but a complex project which is highly reliant on praxis and on its own self-realization. (Rozanov never considered himself a philosopher or a historian, and preferred to refer to himself as a 'publitsist'.) As I intend to examine the manner in which Rozanov attempts to reform the Russian Orthodox Church, this book will rely predominantly on his works which engage with the Church, written generally between 1900 and 1910. He graduates from formal theories on history to a groundbreaking demonstration on how to implement his ideas on the family. He tackles highly disperse themes, but all these revolve around the Creation as the manner in which the divine ideas are realized and how humans should respond. The Creation provides the central event to which all phenomena and earthly events owe their ultimate origin, and Rozanov offers a somewhat Spenglerian view of how aspects of a culture are interrelated. (This book is a rejection to some extent of Florovskii's assertion that Rozanov had no centre.[41]) Rozanov is intent on showing the permanent relevance of humans' physical relationship with God, and therefore, while accepting earthly experience, attempts to mitigate as far as possible against possible dissolution. For this reason, Minskii accused him of 'standing outside philosophy and outside history'.[42] Hence my approach is not an attempt to impose a rigid system onto Rozanov's thought where there is none, but to offer a new explanation for Rozanov's underlying motivations. Berdiaev claimed that Rozanov was deliberately vague,

38 Renato Poggioli, *Rozanov* (London: Bowes & Bowes, 1962).

39 Anna Lisa Crone, *Rozanov and the End of Literature: Polyphony and the Dissolution of Genre in Solitaria and Fallen Leaves* (Würzburg: Jal-Verlag, 1978).

40 Stephen C. Hutchings, *Russian Modernism: The Transfiguration of the Everyday* (Cambridge: Cambridge University Press, 1997), p. 179.

41 Florovskii, p. 461.

42 *Zapiski peterburgskikh Religiozno-filosofskikh sobranii*, p. 318.

often refusing to come to conclusions and thereby forcing the reader to make their own mind up.[43] Therefore this book adopts a largely heuristic and thematic approach, and will treat Rozanov's work synchronically rather than diachronically.

The lack of emphasis on the Creation in Christianity is reflected in the relative scarcity of theological study devoted to this area (as well as in philosophy more broadly). There is a broader sense in scholarship that studies of the Creation have become 'increasingly marginal', especially its cosmological significance.[44] This is particularly the case in Russian Orthodoxy, where the privileging of the New Testament over the Old is especially marked. In Rozanov's time, Russia lacked the sophisticated Biblical exegesis that had developed in Western Europe.[45] This was particularly acute regarding Old Testament hermeneutics, and Rozanov, well aware of this, went out of his way to draw attention to the very few theologians in Russia, such as Georgii Vlastov, who studied Genesis.[46]

Rozanov makes a rare and important contribution to studies of Genesis, especially in preserving the cosmological importance of the Creation. His singular approach is informed by formal Orthodoxy, ancient Greek philosophy and mythology. Importantly, Rozanov remains close to an Aristotelian materialism, in which he insists on examining phenomena not 'in statu quo', but 'in statu agente'.[47] Rozanov, following in the traditions of Aristotle and formal Orthodoxy (as well as most probably being influenced indirectly by Leibniz's examinations of the underlying force holding the material world together), sees the universe in terms of activity rather than being. In fact, in a philosophical tradition which had tended to elevate the importance of Plato and reject Aristotle, Rozanov's reliance on the latter is an unusual contribution (Rozanov

43 N.A. Berdiaev, 'Khristos i mir', in *Vasilii Rozanov: Pro et Contra*, II, pp. 25–40 (p. 26).

44 Terje Stordalen, *Echoes of Eden: Genesis 2–3 and Symbolism of the Eden Garden in Biblical Hebrew Literature* (Leuven: Peeters, 2000), p. 21.

45 Alexander I. Negrov, *Biblical Interpretation in the Russian Orthodox Church* (Tübingen: Mohr Siebeck, 2008), p. 23.

46 V.V. Rozanov, 'Georgii Vlastov. Sviashchennaia letopis′', in *Iudaizm*, pp. 126–8.

47 V.V. Rozanov, 'Predislovie ko vtoromu izdaniiu', in *V mire neiasnogo i nereshennogo* (Moscow: Respublika, 1995), p. 8. Rozanov discusses the meaning of Aristotelian understanding and form in a letter of 15 February 1888 (O.S.) to Strakhov, reprinted in V.V. Rozanov, *Literaturnye izgnanniki. N.N. Strakhov, K.N. Leont′ev* (Moscow: Respublika, 2001), p. 155.

frequently expressed his admiration for Plato, but on closer examination we see that this is because Rozanov interprets Plato in distinct Aristotelian terms). Consequently, his work becomes increasingly dominated by an examination of God's activity (the sexual acts involved in Creation) and correspondingly for the correct type of activity through which we respond to this. This often overrides formal philosophical schemes, as praxis is privileged over formal thought. In his own literature, the act of writing itself becomes key and overshadows to a large extent the content of what is written. Rozanov pre-empts the 'activity turn' in European thought, the shift from the examination of consciousness to that of practice. Like Marx, and like later thinkers such as Heidegger and Husserl, Rozanov investigates praxis as a way to overcome a dissatisfaction with rationalist and empirical thought. Although important work has already been done by Hutchings on the importance of activity in Russian thought,[48] this is an area which warrants further scholarship. Rozanov examines specifically the activity of God and how the human should respond to this. His belief that humanity has already experienced the ideal, has lived in Paradise, prevents his thought from positing a speculative ideal like many of his peers. He also practised his own philosophy; he was perhaps the only one of his peers to cultivate a contented family environment, with plenty of children.

Where as some scholars detach the act of Creation from the ideal of Paradise (the *Paradiesmythus* from *Paradiesvorstellungen*),[49] Rozanov relies on Aristotelian materialism to posit Creation as one act, a seamless relationship between the act of Creation and the ontological perfection of humanity. There can be no detachment of God's activity of Creation and the ideal of Eden. Paradise, humanity's ideal condition, is inextricably linked to God's activity.[50] But this has to be made relevant to contemporary Russian experience. Tareev accused Rozanov of trying to transplant the ancient mandates of religion to contemporary Russian life: 'You want to turn the specific into the general, into the universal; you believe that what happened in Babylon or Palestine happens now in the

48 Hutchings, *Russian Modernism*. The tensions between activity and faith were an issue of concern among Rozanov's peers: Frank and Shestov accused Merezhkovskii of simplifying religion to a desire for political revolution.

49 See Stordalen, pp. 31–3.

50 For Aristotle, the goal of activity is achieved 'by the very fact of activity'. See Alexei Chernyakov, *The Ontology of Time* (Dordrecht: Kluwer Academic, 2002), p. 47.

Russian countryside'.[51] Rozanov here plays his part in a more common aspect of Russian religiosity, the desire to see Biblical events through a national prism; the Society of Slavophiles in 1845 declared solemnly that Adam was a Slav who had lived in Russia.[52] However, for Rozanov, it is the continuing relevance of God's creativity, marked through the symbolism of the phallus, which preserves the physical links between God and humans, and which gives hope that humanity can restore Paradise.

51 Letter to V.V. Rozanov, dated 30 December 1905 (O.S.), NIOR RGB. F. 248. M 3823. Ed. khr. 14, p. 4.

52 According to a letter from F.M. Dostoevskii to his brother Mikhail, 8 October 1845 (O.S). Reprinted in F.M. Dostoevskii, *Polnoe sobranie sochinenii v tradtsati tomakh*, 30 vols (Leningrad: Nauka, 1970-), XXVIII, p. 114.

## Chapter 1

# Creation and Eschatology

In September 1901, Vasilii Rozanov received a letter from one of his readers, identified only as 'S. B-kh from St Petersburg'. 'S. B-kh' thanked Rozanov for his philosophy of the family and his investigations of the spiritual crisis in Russia. The reader staunchly agreed with Rozanov's criticism of the asceticism prevalent in Russian Orthodoxy, the accompanying lack of a feeling for God, and then turned to the reasons for this.

> Начало мира останется вечно тайной для человечества. Но человеку нужно жить, не решив так или иначе этих вопросов: надо же чем-нибудь успокоить свой тревожный ум. Создаются, поэтому, разные космогонические теории образования миров, у каждого по-своему (Моисей и Лаплас). Нам с вами нравится кн. Бытия, как сердечно говорящая о начале мира. Это личное наше дело – что нам больше может нравиться.
>
> The beginning of the world will forever remain a mystery for humanity. But the human must live without having solved these problems one way or another: he needs something to comfort his troubled mind. Therefore people create different cosmological theories about the formation of worlds, each one his own (Moses and Laplace). You and I like the Book of Genesis, which speaks so tenderly of the beginning of the world. This is our personal issue – what could be more pleasing to us?[1]

Rozanov considered this an exceptionally profound analysis, which he shared with 'all his soul'. Somehow, the unknown S. B-kh touches on issues ignored by the rest of Rozanov's contemporaries, but which rest at the centre of his thought; that is the very nature of the Creation of the universe by God, whether the reasons and processes behind this act are accessible to human knowledge, and the implications of the Creation for how humans live. The opposition Rozanov sets up between the Creation and the Apocalypse, the beginning of the world and its end, dominates his entire project. His argument that Russian Orthodoxy privileges the Apocalypse over the Creation leads him to uncover far-reaching consequences for Russian society. However, before we examine the implications of Rozanov's philosophy, it is first important to examine the theological context in which he operated.

---

1 Published in V.V. Rozanov, 'O strastnom v cheloveke nachale', in *Semeinyi vopros v Rossii*, pp. 162–8 (p. 165).

The culmination of Christian history is the Apocalypse and the Second Coming of Christ. This is prefigured in the central event in Christian worship, the Resurrection of Christ, as portrayed in all four gospels and re-enacted through the Eucharist. Christ's sacrifice is portrayed as the renewal of the covenant between God and humanity, overcoming our separation from the divine which results from original sin. Participation in the Eucharist promises an eventual salvation, only outside human time.[2] Therefore, the Apocalypse, and its promise in the Resurrection, takes precedence over other events in Christological activity, including the birth of Christ.[3] It is the Resurrection that allows man to participate in theosis, one the central tenets of Orthodoxy, demonstrated in Athanasius' famous mantra that 'God became man so that man can become God'.[4]

The focus on the end has led to an ambiguity in the way Christianity evaluates the material realm. Christianity teaches that the world is holy, as it was created by God. Yet at the same time, it argues that the physical world is in a state of flux. God and creation are viewed not statically, but in a state of constant movement (kinesis) towards the eschaton. Creation is necessarily defined by this movement, which consists in the fact that matter, and all created beings, are required to fulfil their divine purpose, or logos, i.e. transfiguration at the end of time.[5] Creation is marked by a

---

2 Vassiliadis argues that the Eucharist is the 'sole expression of the church's identity'; but this should be considered a 'glimpse and manifestation of the eighth day'. Therefore in Orthodoxy, he writes, the central event of worship is 'exclusively *eschatological*'. Petros Vassiliadis, *Eucharist and Witness: Orthodox Perspectives on the Unity and Mission of the Church* (Geneva [England]: WCC Publications, 1998), pp. 56–60. I shall return to the Eucharist in the following chapter.

3 A.V. Kartashev, *Tserkov′, Istoriia, Rossiia: Stat′i i vystupleniia* (Moscow: Izdatel′stvo 'Probel', 1996), p. 167. As Vassiliadis notes, the birth of Christ is itself an eschatological event, as this marks the moment where the eschaton enters human history; Christ's coming only has value in terms of His future suffering and Resurrection. Vassiliadis, p. 52.

4 Gustafson examines the consequences of theosis for Russian thought, defining deification as 'the acquisition of immortality, bliss and a superhuman fullness and intensity of life often coupled with a transfiguration of the natural cosmos itself'. Richard F. Gustafson, 'Soloviev's Doctrine of Salvation', in *Russian Religious Thought*, ed. by Judith Deutsch Kornblatt and Richard F. Gustafson (Madison: University of Wisconsin Press, 1996), pp. 31–48 (p. 38).

5 John Meyendorff, *Byzantine Theology: Historical Trends and Doctrinal Themes* (New York: Fordham University Press, 1974), p. 133.

seemingly contradictory double movement of God's manifestation. The descent of the divine to Earth, and God's manifestation in infinite multiplicity, takes place alongside the striving of each object on Earth upwards towards unity.[6] God's activity is seen as His continuing revelation on Earth in the economy of the Son through the Holy Spirit.

> The true purpose of Creation is, therefore, not contemplation of divine essence (which is inaccessible), but communion in divine energy, transfiguration, and transparency to divine action in the world.[7]

Meyendorff continues that the very existence of creation is dependent on this dual activity of God and humanity.[8] Dynamism in the Orthodox tradition is therefore presented as the movement of each created entity towards its divinely set purpose, alongside the simultaneous manifestation of God to the world. Worship in the Orthodox tradition is seen as placing 'emphasis on God as motion – an energy to participate in, rather than a static entity to be figured'.[9] Such teachings permit a division between divine time and human time, human history and a religious eschatology which involves the end of human experience and its final transfiguration as the Kingdom of Heaven. Hence the Orthodox Church posits its earthly task in some way as essentially complete, therefore denying a soteriological meaning to earthly history. At the same time, the Orthodox Church insists that each moment in human time has meaning only in terms of the eschaton. Human experience only has religious significance by continued reference to the Apocalypse.

This is a particularly prominent aspect of Orthodoxy, which insists that all teachings and dogma, including the Liturgy, have already been given by the Church through the guidance of the Holy Spirit and do not require addition or alteration. The Orthodox Church prides itself on adhering to the truths given in the Bible and the first seven Ecumenical Councils (here the first seven church councils up to the Second Council of Nicaea in 787, not including the Apostolic Council of Jerusalem depicted in Acts 15). Here it is distinguished from other churches, including the Roman Catholic Church, which since Nicaea II have permitted under certain circumstances the development of doctrine. This

---

6 C.E. Rolt, *Dionysius the Areopagite on the Divine Names and the Mystical Theology* (Montana: Kessinger, 1992), p. 65.

7 Meyendorff, *Byzantine Theology*, p. 133.

8 Ibid.

9 Hutchings, *Russian Modernism*, p. 30.

highly dogmatic aspect of the Orthodox Church has at various points in its history put it into conflict with modernity, and this is again a crucial aspect for the Russian Church at the start of the twenty-first century. However, the question of modernity became one of the defining aspects of Russian religious thought's engagement with formal Orthodoxy as it grew as an independent force through the nineteenth and early twentieth centuries.

Christ's cosmological influence ensures that Orthodox time has a definitely eschatological content, and the tensions this causes between divine and human time are not easily reconciled. Zizioulas writes that the Orthodox are 'traditionalists', but are also simultaneously 'detached from the problems of history and preoccupied with the "triumphalism" of their liturgy'.[10] This tension presented in Orthodoxy between its eschatology and modernity is one of the key problems facing Rozanov and his peers as they grappled to make the Orthodox experience relevant to their own time.

Despite the fact that there are two aspects to Christ's sacrifice, the Passion and the Resurrection, the message of Christianity is that humanity and the cosmos are imperfect and in need of transfiguration. This sense of the fallenness of the world is mirrored by the necessity of God's humiliation. There is a link here made explicit in Orthodoxy between love and suffering; although Christ is given by God to humanity as an act of *philanthropia*, Orthodox worship highlights 'not just the *suffering humanity* of Christ, but a *suffering God*'.[11] By making deifi-

---

10 Zizioulas concludes that the reconciliation of eschatology and historicity can only be achieved through the Eucharist. He argues that participation in the Eucharist must be an 'epicletic' event, in which history itself does not guarantee salvation; in other words, the Church 'asks to receive from God what she has already received historically in Christ as if she had not received it all'. The Eucharist is a tradition, but at the same time also acts as remembrance of future salvation. Zizioulas concedes that the fact that Orthodox theology has often neglected the role of the Eucharist in mediating between history and the eschaton has meant that it has often been difficult to reconcile the two, leading to an emphasis on eschatology. John D. Zizioulas, *Being as Communion: Studies in Personhood and the Church* (London: Darton, Longmann and Todd 1985), pp. 171–88.

11 Ware examines the importance of the Crucifixion in Orthodoxy and its connection to the Resurrection and insists on the prominence of Resurrection, arguing that 'even Golgotha is a theophany; even on Good Friday the Church sounds a note of Resurrection joy'. Timothy Ware, *The Orthodox Church* (Harmondsworth: Penguin, 1963), pp. 232. Rozanov

cation contingent on the suffering and death of Christ, the Orthodox Church teaches that salvation can only be achieved after our own deaths. Orthodoxy makes a connection between the Apocalypse and our own demise, and therefore the concept of death has gained great importance in Orthodox worship and by extension within Russian culture. This seeming fixation with death is well demonstrated by Nil Sorskii, one of the most revered Russian saints, who warns that we must focus on our own deaths when we pray.

> After Adam's fall, he fell under sickness, subject to every woe. Death entered creation and it overcame us too. But the foreseen death of the Lord and his ineffable wisdom teach us that, by his coming, he overcame the serpent and gave us resurrection, transferring his slaves and servants into life everlasting.
>
> Thus we should keep in mind the thought of our Lord's Second Coming and our resurrection and the Last Judgement, recalling that our Lord taught about these future events found in his Gospel.[12]

Nil Sorskii teaches that the Orthodox must constantly focus on the image of his own grave, directing his attention to life beyond. *Imitatio Christi* certainly plays an important role, as Jesus tells his disciples to abandon their everyday lives, renounce themselves and take up their own crosses (Matthew 16:24). Physical suffering brings us to closer to Christ. Asceticism proves the denial of the body and the rejection of the temptations of Satan. Kartashev writes that before we can achieve our own resurrection we must undergo the torment of life and our own Golgotha.[13]

By eating the flesh of Christ, worshippers are drawn into the body of the Church, also understood as the body of Christ, and thereby engage in communal salvation.[14] The Eucharist is the ultimate sign that life can be identified with being. This life is understood corporately; taking the Host must be performed within a community, as knowledge and communion are identical.[15] To the Orthodox, communal worship is seen

---

would disagree and would argue that the Russian Church tends to prioritize the Passion over the Resurrection; he in fact finds the Orthodox Church guilty of the mistakes of which the Orthodox accuse the Roman Catholic Church.

12 Nil Sorsky, *The Complete Writings*, ed. and trans. by George A. Maloney (New York: Paulist Press, 2003), pp. 93–4.

13 Kartashev, p. 167.

14 Vassiliadis, p. 52.

15 Zizioulas, p. 81.

as a liberation from the biological, genealogical and national categories which divide humans. The Eucharist means that humans are united on a spiritual (horizontal) basis. Christianity marks a shift from the religions which preceded it, especially ancient Egyptian religion and Judaism; in general terms, these pre-Christian religions tend to place greater significance on the genealogical (vertical) connections between men, underlining the vitality of the family, reproduction and generational ties.

An important factor in Orthodoxy is apophatic theology, influenced by the fifth-century writings of the Pseudo-Dionysius. Despite controversy over the platonic nature of his thought, Dionysius was proclaimed 'most Orthodox' by the Lateran Council of 649, and his theories laid the basis for the Eastern Church's mystical theology, influencing theologians such as Maxim the Confessor and Gregory Palamas and also the Russian spiritual revival of the nineteenth century.[16] Dionysius differentiated between positive (cataphatic) and negative (apophatic) theology. The former involves assertions about the nature of God, which provides only an imperfect knowledge of the divine. The latter involves the negation of all that is not God in order to permit our ascent to Him. 'All knowledge has as an object that which is. Now God is beyond all that exists. In order to approach Him it is necessary to deny all that is inferior to Him, that is to say, all which is'.[17]

Dionysius' mysticism presents the ascent to God as involving three stages: purification, illumination, and finally perfection, or theology. This process is intrinsically linked with the movement 'beyond perceptible symbols to their meanings, and then beyond these conceptual meanings to unknowing'.[18] There is nothing on Earth which can help the worshipper achieve knowledge of God. Everything perceived and understood should be left behind. In the initial stages of the ascent to God, it is possible to make affirmative comments, such as likening Him to a 'lion', a 'bear' or the 'sun of righteousness'. However, this cataphatic theology can only apply to the economy of the divine; assertions about God must be denied, until the believer eventually moves beyond concepts.[19] Apophaticism suggests the denial of our body's role

16 Paul Rorem, *Pseudo-Dionysius: A Commentary on the Texts and an Introduction to Their Influence* (New York/Oxford: Oxford University Press, 1993), pp. 3–4.

17 Vladimir Lossky, *The Vision of God*, trans. by Asheleigh Moorhouse (Crestood, New York: St Vladimir's Seminary Press, 1983), p. 25.

18 Rorem, p. 191.

19 T. Timothey, *Dionysius' Mysticism: A Modern Version of the Middle English Translation* (York: 1st Resource, 1990), pp. 4–5.

in salvation.[20] Dionysius uses as an example Moses, who left behind his people to climb Mount Sinai and immerse himself in the blinding cloud of God's presence. Although Dionysius maintains that some degree of relationship between man and the Godhead is possible, as God is the creator of mankind and creatorship implies a degree of relativity, the Orthodox believer is nevertheless confronted by the fact that this relationship cannot involve the essence of God. Any direct communion with God's essence would imply His presence within an earthly object, which is tantamount to pantheism.

Tensions between soul and body, apparent in Dionysius, were also explored by the Patricians. The desert fathers were concerned that the soul could be laden down by bodily worries, and hence they emphasized the denial of physical desires in order to purify the soul. In discussing the development of patristic thought, Zizioulas explains that, prior to the desert fathers, the Graeco-Roman world had not endowed the individual person with any ontological value. The ancient world tended to view the individual only in terms of his broader function within society. In order to give each human an individual worthiness before God, the fathers identified the concept of the person with the idea of the hypostasis. However, they could only achieve this by separating the notion of hypostasis from substance (ousia).[21]

> The basic ontological position of the theology of the Greek Fathers might be set out briefly as follows. No substance or nature exists without person or hypostasis or mode of existence. No person exists without substance or nature, *but* the ontological 'principle' or 'cause' of being – i.e. that which makes a thing to exist – is not the substance or nature but the *person* or hypostasis. Therefore being is traced back not to substance but to person.[22]

The priority of hypostasis over ousia is reflected in Orthodox teaching on the Trinity. This doctrine has far-reaching consequences for the way the body itself is constituted as apocalyptic. Orthodoxy places the personae of the Trinity, and not their substance, as the 'ontological principle' of God.

> Among the Greek Fathers the unity of God, the one God, and the ontological 'principle' or 'cause' of the being and life of God does not consist in the one

20 Ibid., p. 9.
21 Zizioulas, pp. 38–9.
22 Ibid., pp. 41–2.

> substance of God but in the *hypostasis*, that is, *the person of the father*. The one God is not the one substance but the Father, who is the 'cause' both of the generation of the Son and of the procession of the Spirit. Consequently, the ontological 'principle' of God is traced back, once again, to the person.[23]

Zizioulas is discussing the theology of the Greek Fathers, and these arguments have continued in the traditions of the Russian Orthodox Church. By divorcing what it means to have a person from being itself, the Orthodox believer is taught that personhood is distinct from material existence. Zizioulas considers this a liberation of the hypostasis from biology; it is a factor in Orthodoxy's argument that the soul is separate from the body. This separation of person from matter enables the Orthodox to disregard the body's role in soteriology. This anthropology mirrors the Trinitarian doctrine of the Church: God's nature is distinct from, and superior to, His will. The Patricians attempted to underline God's ontological freedom from what He does, and this belief has persisted in Russian Orthodoxy. Meyendorff writes that 'in God the order of nature precedes the order of volitive action'. From this, it follows that God's nature is necessarily separated from the nature of creation.[24] This means that communion with God, according to the Orthodox tradition, can only entail a hypostatic union, as demonstrated by the example of Jesus Christ. The Orthodox Church insists that although we can worship God, there can be no union of substance with Him.[25]

Orthodox doctrines over the separateness of hypostasis and ousia are reflected in the practice of hesychasm, a form of spiritual prayer common in the early ages of Eastern Christianity, which was developed in the thirteenth and fourteenth centuries, and which became more widespread in Russian culture in the eighteenth and nineteenth centuries. This return to a passive, contemplative form of spirituality in Russia was encouraged predominantly by the publication in 1793 of the *Dobrotoliubie*, the Slavonic translation of the *Philokalia* produced by Paisii Velichkovskii, a starets from Mount Athos. The *Philokalia* was a collection of Greek spiritualist writings, composed by the Desert Fathers of the fourth century. Its publication in Russia brought the broader Russian public into contact with a tradition of prayer which had hitherto only really

23 Ibid., pp. 40–1.
24 Meyendorff, *Byzantine Theology*, p. 130.
25 Ibid.

existed in monasteries, and which was to play a dominant role in Russian religious life up to the Revolution and beyond.[26]

Hesychasm rests on the belief that, although God is beyond our world, the human can enter into communion with Him through His energies. These kerygma are likened to the Taboric Light which Jesus presented. They are begotten and not created, and penetrate all created matter.[27] Hesychasm involves attaining a complex ontological state, in which the whole body is transfigured through the enhypostatic light.[28] Hesychasts advocate permanent prayer through which the mind, soul and body are transformed on Earth. The mind should be placed in the heart, thereby ensuring that the worshipper is not distracted by anything earthly, but contemplates exclusively God.[29] Interest in hesychasm was given special impetus in Russia by the appearance in the late nineteenth century of the anonymous *Otkrovennye rasskazy strannika dukhovnomu svoemu ottsu*. This narrates the trials of a young man who is unable to pray, until he is taught hesychasm and the Jesus Prayer. The pilgrim is told by his starets to incorporate the recital of the short prayer ('Jesus Christ, have mercy on me, a sinner') into all aspects of his life. Eventually, the prayer becomes the central aspect of the pilgrim's life, and he is able to banish all other thoughts from his mind.

> I became so accustomed to the prayer that when I stopped praying, even for a brief time, I felt as though something were missing, as if I had lost something. When I began to pray again, I was immediately filled with an inner lightness and joy. If I happened to meet people, I no longer felt any desire to speak with them; I only longed for solitude, to be alone with my prayer.[30]

It is hard to underestimate the reverence held for the *Philokalia* and the importance it took in Orthodox spirituality. For its adherents, the *Philokalia* was the only way to understand Orthodox mysticism. It unlocked the mystical meaning of the Holy Scriptures, and was

---

26 Sergei Hackel, 'Trail and Victory: The Spiritualist Tradition of Modern Russia', in *Christian Spirituality: Post-Reformation and Modern*, ed. by Louis Dupré and Don E. Salies in collaboration with J. Meyendorff (London: SCM, 1990), pp. 458–69 (pp. 458–9).

27 Gregory Palamas, *The Triads*, trans. by Nicholas Gendle, ed. by John Meyendorff (New York: Paulist Press, 1983), pp. 74, 78.

28 Ibid., p. 78.

29 Ibid., p. 49.

30 *The Way of a Pilgrim*, trans. by Olga Savin (Boston/London: Shambhala, 1996), pp. 15–16.

considered the 'necessary viewing lens' through which to see the sun of the Bible.[31] Critics of the hesychast tradition argued that it necessarily leads to a negation of the body and of the world. However, Palamas argued that it does not involve the disincarnation of the mind, as the entire human person, including the body, is transfigured through the Taboric Light, as demonstrated by the Transfiguration of Christ. He argued that the flesh cannot be excluded from prayer, as the Incarnation of Jesus Christ and the role of the sacraments proved that the body had a vital role to play in worship.[32]

In summary, the teachings of the Orthodox Church reveal serious ambiguities in the value of this world, and the way man should relate to matter. Official Orthodox doctrine states that the world is sanctified through divine createdness. The Incarnation of God as Jesus Christ helps explain some elements of Orthodox worship that are intensely physical (in very many cases more so than other Christian denominations), such as rituals, vocal prayer, the use of incense, and icons. However, at the same time, Orthodoxy also presents the world as matter-in-waiting, which will only be fully redeemed at the eschaton. In other words, in terms of the reality of the Kingdom of God, we are confronted with the 'already', and yet at the same time the 'not yet'.[33] As suggested above, it is only through a highly sophisticated explanation of the Eucharist that these competing architectonics of worship can be resolved.

In Orthodox worship, therefore, salvation is essentially eschatological.[34] The world can only be redeemed through the death and Resurrection of Christ, and this is brought onto the personal level; we can only be saved after our own deaths. All Biblical and historical events point towards the final resurrection of humanity at the end of time, and the eschaton takes priority over the Creation of the world, as well as the Incarnation of Christ. It follows that the focus in Orthodoxy on the material only lends an increased apocalyptic fervour to earthly

---

31 Ibid., p. 11.

32 Palamas, p. 88. Rozanov specifically rejects the belief that the *Philokalia* has a physical dimension and asserts that it cannot make incarnate the Word of God. Rozanov sees attempts to revive the *Philokalia* in contemporary Russia as part of the Byzantine restoration within Russian thought, which can only be harmful. See V.V. Rozanov, 'Perstye temy', in *V nashei smute: Stat′i 1908 g. Pis′ma k E.F. Gollerbakhu*, ed. by A.N. Nikoliukin (Moscow: Respublika, 2004), pp. 107–61 (pp. 132–3).

33 Vassiliadis, p. 52.

34 Ibid., p. 99.

experience. For the Orthodox, paradoxically, the reality of salvation after this life was clearly marked in their own body: the practice of hesychasm demonstrates the real possibility of the transfiguration of this world. Billington writes that the Eastern Christians believe in their unique role to bring about the 'final, heavenly kingdom', as 'hesychast mysticism encouraged the Orthodox to believe that such a transformation was an imminent possibility through a spiritual intensification of their own lives – and ultimately of the entire Christian *imperium*'.[35] Therefore to the Orthodox, the body itself is viewed eschatologically. Moreover, as a result of Russian culture's assumption of the apophatic traditions of Byzantine thinkers such as the Pseudo-Dionysius, there is an opposition of epistemology and ontology, as well as a rejection of history, that is first seriously challenged in the nineteenth century by Chaadaev.[36] Such views have serious repercussions for Rozanov's thought. Rozanov can only reconcile the body to earthly experience by arguing that it is naturally holy, without recourse to hesychasm or the Incarnation.

However, it is the ambiguities over the Orthodox evaluation of the material, and the significance of the Creation, which Rozanov exploits in his engagement with the Russian Church. Rozanov believes that the Church only understands the 'omega' of Christianity, but not the 'alpha' of Christianity, and calls for a clear re-evaluation of the Church's attitude towards the world. Moreover, even where the Church's teachings on the value of matter are clear, Rozanov claims that such teachings are not put into practice by the clergy, who display a hostile attitude towards the Russian people, the family and childbirth.

---

35 James Hadley Billington, *The Icon and the Axe: An Interpretive History of Russian Culture* (London: Weidenfeld & Nicolson, 1966), pp. 55–6.

36 See P. Kuznetsov, 'Metafizicheskii Nartsiss i russkoe molchanie: P.Ia. Chaadaev i sud'ba filosofii v Rossii', in *P.Ia. Chaadaev: Pro et Contra. Lichnost' i tvorchestvo Petra Chaadaeva v otsenke russkikh myslitelei i issledovatelei*, ed. by A.A. Ermichev and A.A. Zlatopol'skaia (St Petersburg: Izdatel'stvo Russkogo Khristianskogo gumanitarnogo instituta, 1998), pp. 729–52 (p. 730). Aizlewood has investigated this point and writes: 'earthly historical existence is viewed as essentially already completed, and so in inheriting this tradition Russian consciousness finds itself in a position of extra-historical existence'. See Robin Aizlewood, 'Revisiting Russian Identity in Russian Thought: From Chaadaev to the Early Twentieth Century', *Slavonic and East European Review*, 78 (2000), 20–43 (p. 23).

## Eschatology and history in Russian philosophy

Aspects of formal Orthodox teaching encourage a separation of religious and historical consciousness which can sometimes be different to reconcile. The Orthodox Church considers that its earthly task is largely complete. Scripture is already given, and doctrine and dogma are all already laid out through the first seven Ecumenical Councils. These truths are considered the Revelation of God, they are not subject to alteration or improvement, and must remain unchanged until the end of time. This has presented serious difficulties in the Orthodox Church's attempts to engage with the modern world. For instance, it is worth comparing the Orthodox position with that of the Roman Catholic Church, which in its effort to reinterpret its social mission in the Second Vatican Council (1962–1965) explicitly rejected Patristics as a basis for theological renewal, owing to its disassociation of religious experience from history.

It is hardly surprising that in Russia, some of the most important attempts at dialogue between Church and society took place outside the confines of official Orthodox thinking. It is specifically in the attempt to reconcile the tension between Russian religiosity and the experience of modernity that we might locate the origins of modern Russian religious philosophy in the early nineteenth century.[37] Chaadaev was clearly a utopian thinker, who set out his aim at the start of his Philosophical Letters as the establishment of the Kingdom of God on Earth. Yet this is couched in historical terms, and here he owes much to Schelling's attempt to describe history as the necessary revelation and consummation of the absolute.[38] The historical orientation of Chaadaev's thought is displayed in his Philosophical Letters, where the epistolary method and supposed dialogue with Ekaterina Panova reaffirms the sense of ethical and intellectual development.

In his First Philosophical Letter, Chaadaev argues for the creation of a Russian religious history, the intellectual and moral development of society towards its gradual perfection. These are important themes,

---

37 Berdiaev also argues that independent Russian religious thought was awakened by the problem of history, and thereby touches on the attempt by his peers to reconcile a specifically Russian history with a Russian eschatology. See *Russkaia ideia*, p. 36.

38 For the importance of Schelling, and the apparent rejection of Hegel, in Chaadaev, see I.I. Filippov, 'Legenda russkoi literatury', in *P.Ia. Chaadaev: Pro et Contra*, pp. 331–53 (especially pp. 341–3).

echoed in Solov′ev and Tolstoi, with which Rozanov would later engage. There is certainly a hint of the reproductive, or at least generational, which Chaadaev highlights in terms of the relationship between history and utopia, which emerges later with modifications in Rozanov. Chaadaev believes that historical experience must be incorporated into the cyclical routines of Russian domestic life. It is not enough for Russians to have a history, as their social, moral and intellectual development can only be affirmed by assimilating the ethical sphere into the domestic. (It is this interplay between the progressive and the homely which re-emerges, though with a more sexual dimension, in Rozanov.) For Chaadaev, the lack of a Russian history is demonstrated by the absence of the proper domestic circumstances in which this can be realized: 'Nobody has a definite sphere of existence, nobody has proper habits; nobody has rules for anything. Nobody even has a home life [...] In our families we appear like strangers'.[39] Chaadaev argues that the Russians have become detached from the development of divine reason as it has been expressed in Europe through the generational transmission of human ideas. It is not enough for Russians to create their own history, as such an abstract approach would lack an ethical dimension. Chaadaev argues that for history to become moral, it must be incorporated into the continuing generational patterns of the family, where humanity re-enacts and renews the dogmatic life.

However, though he introduces the issue of history into Russian thought, Chaadaev ends up privileging the intellectual over the familial, thereby bringing into modern Russian philosophy at its inception the precedence of the theoretical. 'One understands nothing of Christianity if one does not realize that Christianity has a purely historical side, which is so essentially part of dogma that it contains, in some way, all the philosophy of Christianity, for it demonstrates what it has done for humans and what it will do for them in the future'.[40] Through history, Christianity for Chaadaev becomes more than simply a philosophy or a system of moral imperatives, but a divine eternal power which acts universally in the mental sphere. It is at this point where Rozanov's thought deviates from Chaadaev's. Although Chaadaev speaks of temporal progress, this is subordinated to the idea of the future perfection of

---

39 P.Ia. Chaadaev, 'Lettres philosophiques adressées à une dame: Lettre première', in *Polnoe sobranie sochinenii i izbrannye pis′ma*, 2 vols (Moscow: Nauka, 1991), I, pp. 86–106 (p. 90).

40 Chaadaev, 'Lettre première', p. 98.

humanity, at the end of time where faith and intellectualism are unified.[41] This proposed Paradise for Chaadaev necessarily cancels out 'the old order': the world as we know it now must be overcome.[42]

Ironically, Rozanov would later imitate Chaadaev's discernment of a person's philosophical principles from their physiognomy; in a 1913 essay devoted to the differences between Chaadaev and Odoevskii, Rozanov appears to draw his conclusions about the former from his portrait, displayed in Gershenzon's first compilation of Chaadaev's works. Rozanov criticizes Chaadaev's features, which smack of an un-Russian aloofness and egotism; he accuses the philosopher of 'a marble-like, cold, and Catholic face'.[43] Rozanov turns the tables on Chaadaev, and argues that it is not Russia, but the philosopher himself who lacks true familial relations: 'It is impossible to imagine "Chaadaev's mother", "Chaadaev's father" or his "dancing sisters".'[44] Rozanov rejects the abstract theoreticism in Chaadaev, his privileging of a universal history over a Russian history. However, despite his dislike of Chaadaev, there are certainly key elements in Rozanov which seem to originate in his predecessor. Firstly, as noted, Chaadaev attempts to assimilate history into the intimate patterns of the domestic. Secondly, Chaadaev, like Rozanov later, rejects the stagnating influence of Byzantine culture on Russian religiosity, and calls for a Western style of theological discourse which is more accepting of modernity.

A slightly different approach to how the Church should incorporate itself into Russian culture was taken by Aleksandr Bukharev (Archimandrite Feodor), a major inspiration for many Russian religious thinkers, including Solov´ev, Florenskii, Tareev and Rozanov. The fact that the word of God became flesh provided Bukharev with the model by which the clergy should accept their ministry to this world.[45] Bukharev insisted that creative work was essential for the Russian Orthodox Church to enter into history. Although he believed

---

41 Ibid.

42 Ibid., p. 99.

43 Rozanov contrasts Chaadaev's egotism and coldness towards Russia with Odoevskii's reciprocated love for the Russian people. See V.V. Rozanov, 'Chaadaev i kn. Odoevskii', in V.V. Rozanov, *Na fundamente proshlogo: Stat´i i ocherki 1913–1915 gg.*, ed. by A.N. Nikoliukin (Moscow: Respublika, 2007), pp. 54–62 (p. 56).

44 Ibid., p. 55.

45 Paul Valliere, *Modern Russian Theology: Bukharev, Solov´ev, Bulgakov: Orthodox Theology in a New Key* (Edinburgh: T&T Clark, 2000), p. 105.

that the Church was the body of Christ, he argued that her work on Earth was not complete, but had to be brought to fruition through ecclesiastical renewal. It was principally through a reengagement with Christ as embodied God, Bukharev believed, that the Church could recover its sacramental relationship to Russian society and overcome its adherence to abstract truth.[46] Rozanov was intrigued and inspired by Bukharev's call on the Church to go out into this world and, unsurprisingly, engaged his widow in an intimate correspondence (it was typical of Rozanov to get closer to the objects of his study by probing at their marital relations). Rozanov discussed the Bukharev Affair, defending the former monk against the criticism of journalist Viktor Askochenskii (Oskoshnyi/Otskochenskii). Rozanov praised Bukharev for his 'fleshiness', his willingness to abandon monkhood to get married, his openness to scientific knowledge and his desire to reinvestigate 'the very nature of the human through the activity of known religious thought'.[47] There is a striking correspondence between Bukharev's insistence on seeing the 'image and likeness of God' in every human, regardless of their religious orientation or ethnic background, and Rozanov's position.[48] The coincidence between both Bukharev and Rozanov is demonstrated by their mutual interest in the Apostle Thomas and the affirmation of his faith through his physical contact with the divine, which highlights the sanctity of worldly existence, of 'the whole earthly and material area with all its complexity'.[49] There can also be little doubt that Bukharev's detailed engagement with Russian literature and its characters as a source of

---

46 A. Bukharev, *Moia apologiia po povodu kriticheskikh otzyvov o knige: o sovremmenykh dukhovnykh potrebnostiakh mysli i zhizni, osobenno russkoi* (Moscow, no given publisher, 1866), pp. 8–9.

47 V.V. Rozanov, 'Askochenskii i Arkhim. Feod. Bukharev', in *Okolo tserkovnykh sten* (Moscow: Respublika, 1999), pp. 241–53 (see especially pp. 245–6).

48 Ibid.

49 Valliere examines this in *Modern Russian Theology*, pp. 53–4. That being said, Bukharev's justification of the value of matter is essentially Christological, whereas for Rozanov the sanctity of the body ultimately derives from the Father's creativity. Rozanov's examination of Thomas hints at a denial of Christ's own importance in favour of a holy fleshiness that comes from the First Person. See 'Sovest´ - otnoshenie k Bogu - otnoshenie k Tserkvi', in *Okolo tserkovnykh sten* (pp. 124–7).

spiritual enlightenment fed into Rozanov's conception of how authors should conceptualize their religious duty.[50]

Nevertheless, there is a sense that, because of Chaadaev and the establishment of a type of philosophical discourse that is essentially historical, modern Russian thought seems to accommodate a powerful sense that the eschaton takes priority over the present moment. The attempt to make Russian religious consciousness historical incorporated into Russian speculative thinking the sense that the Earth in its present condition must be transfigured, hence Berdiaev's close attention to history. Valliere, who delineates traditional neo-patristic thought from the creative approach favoured by the speculative thinkers, notes a corresponding opposition between the emphasis on theosis in formal Orthodoxy, and the focus on kenosis which is more central to the lay religious philosophers.[51] Hence one of the results of the attempt by Russian speculative religious thinkers to make Russian religious consciousness more appropriate to everyday life, was the introduction of a strong eschatological aspect to lay philosophy and the reaffirmation of the limited value of this Earth. Hence Gorodetskaia's claim that humility, even the desire to suffer physically for the sake of salvation, based on Christ's kenosis, has become a national ideal in Russian culture.[52] It is this belief in Russian culture more widely that this Earth is of lesser value than some purported future ideal that inspires Rozanov's concerns.

## Rozanov's Creation

Like the thinkers that inspired him, Rozanov grappled with the problematics of matter, that long-standing dichotomy that Orthodoxy tends to present of 'God *or* the Earth'.[53] Rozanov presents a relationship of creatorship that emphasizes the need for constant activity (similar to Orthodox 'doulia') as a response to the divine. Rozanov insists that the Church should revere the

50 See Bukharev's letters to Gogol′, in which Bukharev examined the religious value of Gogol′'s literary works, presenting concerns which Rozanov would later revisit. Arkhimandrit Feodor, *Tri pis′ma k N.V. Gogoliu* (St Petersburg, no given publisher, 1860).

51 Valliere, *Modern Russian Theology*, p. 14.

52 See Nadejda Gorodetzky, *The Humiliated Christ in Modern Russian Thought* (London: SPCK, 1938), pp. 25–6.

53 This dichotomy is discussed in Frederick C. Copleston, *Russian Religious Philosophy: Selected Aspects* (Tunbridge Wells: Search Press, 1988), p. 92.

world, as its sanctity arises from the fact that it was created by God. This is the key to Rozanov's approach, the divine act of creativity, the motives and processes by which God comes to create the universe.

As he looks increasingly to Scripture to substantiate his thought, Rozanov is drawn naturally to the Old Testament, and especially to its start. The narration of the Creation is the key text in Rozanov's exegesis, and he repeatedly quotes Genesis. Rozanov insists that God did not just create the spiritual world, but also the physical world. The fact that these two dimensions came into being simultaneously proves the sanctity of matter.[54] This demonstrates the sacramental nature of reality which Rozanov assumes from Orthodoxy, but also shows his intent to lend this a justification based on God's creativity.

> Бог сотворил мир невидимый и *видимый*, сотворил бесплотных духов, но и сотворил *тело* Солнца, *тело* растений и животных; и сотворил человека с душой и *телом*. И потому человек создал и церковь душевную и *телесную*. У нас это выразилось в «человеке Божием» и в обрядах. И «осанна» обоим.
>
> God created the world that is unseen and *seen*, created fleshless spirits, but also created the *body* of the Sun, the *body* of plants and animals; and created the human with a soul and a *body*. And therefore the human created the spiritual and the *bodily* church. For us this is expressed in the 'man of God' and in rites. And 'hosanna' to them both.[55]

However, Rozanov is interested in the processes and motivation for God's Creation of the Earth, which in turn informs the way humans should behave and worship. He presents the Creation as a sexual act. Going against formal Orthodox teaching, he suggests that there are two components to the divine, a masculine and a feminine aspect which come together through the divine will to create. Unlike Solov´ev, Rozanov sees God as bisexual, rather than asexual.[56]

---

54 V.V. Rozanov, 'Nebesnoe i zemnoe', in *Okolo tserkovnykh sten*, pp. 156–71 (p. 159).

55 'Novaia kniga o khristianstve', p. 17.

56 Naiman notes that androgyny became the ideal for religious thinkers of the time, particularly Solov´ev and Berdiaev. These tend to understand sexual difference as punishment for the Fall, and here Rozanov is a notable exception. The ideal of androgyny also had wide-ranging consequences in the post-revolutionary years for thinkers who wished to create a new Soviet person. See Eric Naiman, *Sex in Public: The Incarnation of Early Soviet Ideology* (Princeton: Princeton University Press, 1997), especially pp. 34–5, 44–5.

> Когда мир был сотворен, то он, конечно, был цел, «закончен»: но он был *матовый*. Бог (боги) сказал: «Дадим ему *сверкание!*» И сотворили боги – *лицо*.
>
> Я все сбиваюсь говорить по-старому «Бог», когда давно надо говорить *Боги*; ибо ведь их *два*, Эло-*гим*, а не Эло-*ах* (ед. число). Пора оставлять эту навеянную нам богословским недомыслием ошибку. Два Бога – *мужская* сторона Его, и сторона – *женская*. Эта последняя есть та «Вечная Женственность», мировая женственность, о которой начали теперь говорить повсюду. «По образу и подобию Богов (Эло*гим*) сотворенное», все и стало или «мужем», или «женой», «самкой» или «самцом», от яблони и до человека. «Девочки» – конечно, в Отца Небесного, а мальчики – в Матерь Вселенной! Как у людей: дочери – в отца, сыновья – в мать.
>
> When the world was created, of course it was whole, 'finished': but it was *dull*. God (the gods) said: 'Let us give it *splendour*!' And the gods created – *the countenance*. I always make the mistake of saying in the old style 'God', when for a long time we should say *Gods*; for there are *two* of them, Elo-*him*, and not Elo-*ah* (singular form). It is time for us to abandon this error, given to us by theological thoughtlessness. There are two Gods – Its *masculine* aspect, and the *feminine* aspect. This latter aspect is that 'Eternal Feminine', the world's femininity, of which everybody has lately started to speak. 'Created in the image and likeness of the Gods (Elo*him*)', everything became 'a man' or 'a woman', 'male' or 'female', from the apple tree to the human being. 'Girls' of course are the image of the Heavenly Father, and 'boys' – of the Universal Mother! Just as in people – daughters are the image of the father, and sons of the mother.[57]

The Creation presents key problems which he, like many other religious thinkers, have had to overcome. Foremost among these is the possibility that the Creation of a world that is relative to the divine might lead to a disunity of the created realm. Rozanov sides with Plotinus in positing a world which falls into potential disunion at Creation and therefore might suffer from a growing division from God (an opposing stance is taken by Hegel, who argues for a historical movement from multiplicity to unity, and also by Schelling, who insists that God created an imperfect Earth in order to allow for the development of the absolute through its manifestation in life). However, Rozanov overcomes this as we shall see through the consubstantiality of the Earth.

The relationship between the Creation and the eschaton is problematic in readings of Solov´ev. Despite the complexity and inconsistency of Solov´ev's thought, he presents the Creation in physical terms, and this reliance on corporeal terminology must have had some influence on

---

57 Vasilii Rozanov, *Liudi lunnogo sveta: Metafizika khristianstva* (St Petersburg: Prodolzhenie zhizni, 2003), p. 58.

Rozanov. In Lecture Ten of his *Chteniia o Bogochelovechestve*, Solov′ev explains that nature (he notes the etymology of this word and its relation to birth) fell away from God, or all-unity, and joined with the world soul, or Sophia, through a free act which led to multiplicity. Here Solov′ev is close to typical Orthodox thinking over the tension of the potential disharmony of the created world and its anticipation of a future, extra-temporal unification, privileging teleology over origins. Solov′ev expresses in sexual terms this union between 'the divine principle' and Sophia; Sophia is fertilized by the divine and gives birth to the material world.[58] Solov′ev mitigates the importance of the divine principle by describing a long and tortuous process of return to all-unity. It appears that this can only be achieved through a free and conscious overcoming of the human will and subjugation to Divinity. Despite Solov′ev's investigation of the Creation, it appears that this becomes contingent on the future perfection of humanity and the coming of the Kingdom of God. Solov′ev uses distinctly Pauline terminology to present the Church as the body of Christ which 'swallows up' everything weak and earthly at the Apocalypse. The Creation is foreshadowed by the future re-establishment of a unity that can only be achieved outside history.[59] For Solov′ev, humanity is enslaved to the material.[60]

Despite Rozanov's general rejection of the pessimism of Solov′ev's thought, he clearly was heavily influenced by his contemporary; Rozanov is much more Solov′evian than he would like to admit. Rozanov appropriates Solov′ev's use of physical terminology to describe the Creation, though for the former this is more literal. Rozanov's literalism in describing the sexuality of God allows for a direct correlation between divine and human activity through the imitation of creativity. Rozanov argues that it is the specific nature of the divine and sexual Creation that intimately defines the relationship between God and person. Nevertheless, while rejecting the main aspects of Solov′ev's eschatology, Rozanov also assumes the Solov′evian problematic of a Creation followed by a dissociation from God which requires redemption. Rozanov attempts to get round this by a privileging of will over freedom; he focuses on a Fall not of human nature, but of a turning away of human activity from God.

58 V.S. Solov′ev, *Chteniia o Bogochelovechestve* (Minsk: Kharvest, 1999), p. 166.
59 Ibid., pp. 163–70.
60 Ibid., p. 173.

For Rozanov, the Kingdom of God was established at the start of time. The Creation and its link to Eden marks the holiest moment in our history, where matter is in unity with the divine. So Rozanov extols the virtues of sexual difference, as this provides the potential for divinization. God grants us sexual opposition as a gift, as this is the potential to unite with a counterpart and to be reintegrated into the universal. Though appropriating Solov′ev's mode of discourse, Rozanov overcomes his contemporary's separation of God and Creation (which emerges from the falling away of a created Sophia) by presenting divine copulation as taking place within the Godhead; this results in a vision of Earth which is evidently consubstantial with the divine. In contrast to Solov′ev's depiction of an arduous process of reconciliation of matter to God, Rozanov presents a vision of earthly life which is upheld by the concept of an original, terrestrial harmony that emerges from God's sexual act. 'And here is the "unseen copulation", thanks to which exists all "that is seen". It is strange. But it is true. All nature, of course, is the "copulation of things", the "ability of things to copulate"'.[61]

For Rozanov, following a fundamental line in Orthodox teaching, *imitatio Dei* is the key to a religious life. He is interested in the intimate details of the processes and explanations of this divine unity (these come out more in his work on Egypt, though here he pays much more attention to the masculine aspect of God and the activity of the divine Phallus), and his interpretation of sex as an essentially divine act explains his ability to probe into the details of human sexuality without shame. It is Solov′ev's rejection of the sexuality of God and his enormous influence that leads Rozanov to conclude that Solov′ev is the main culprit for promoting eschatological trends in Russian culture.[62]

Both Rozanov and Solov′ev in their own way tackle ancient philosophical concepts over sexual difference, certainly those laid out in Plato's *Symposium*, where the coming together of persons in different contexts demonstrates various types of love. Rozanov's project is a praise of erotic love, but there is an underlying theological necessity for sexual union. For Rozanov, sexual difference should not be seen as problematic, or, as in Plato, as divine punishment for hubris, but as a gift. Remizov

61 V.V. Rozanov, *Poslednie list′ia*, ed. by A.N. Nikoliukin (Moscow: Respublika, 2000), pp. 55–6.

62 V.V. Rozanov, 'Frantsuzskii trud o Vlad. Solov′eve', in *Terror protiv russkogo natsionalizma: Statí i ocherki 1911 g.*, ed. by A.N. Nikoliukin (Moscow: Respublika, 2005), pp. 136–45 (p. 139).

tells us, if we can take his word, that Rozanov believes that during sexual intercourse, every human becomes God.[63] Eroticism is one of the core aspects of Rozanov's concept of love, and is not base or, as it does in Merezhkovskii or Bataille, lead to the dissolution of individuality. Instead, *eros* affirms the person and its movement towards divinity; this distinguishes him from mainstream ancient Greek philosophy and Christian thought. Whereas some thinkers have tended to delineate firmly between different types of love, Rozanov dissolves these boundaries, especially those in the *Symposium* between *eros* and *agape*. For Plato, eroticism is a step towards the foregoing of the body; the Socratic task is ultimately to convert love into a disembodied contemplation of the divine. In contrast, Rozanov aims for a love which is necessarily grounded and affirms God's, and humanity's, links with the Earth. Sexual longing is a natural manifestation of the desire of all living things for reintegration into the universe. Unlike traditional Christian thought, Rozanov does not tend to distinguish between humans and animals, and humans experience this most natural, and holy, desire for unity through sex. And unlike his peers who followed Solov´ev's and Fedorov's division of love from procreation, Rozanov makes a firm connection between love and reproduction. Therefore he argues that the Church is wrong to condemn sex, but should recognize this as a religious duty.

So Rozanov rejects theories of the origins of the world, especially those suggested in the *Timaeus*, that teach that matter is innately evil. Such concepts are present in Christian thinking, and teach that matter exists prior to and separately from the Logos. The physical world is only partly redeemed by the subsequent descent and ordering of divine reason. Such thinking reinforces the idea that the history of the Earth is detached from Christian soteriology, and therefore Rozanov frequently stresses the fact that the physical and ideal came into being simultaneously. Rozanov does not deal at length with the traditions of Manichaeism or Gnosticism that have influenced Christianity, but he does criticize the traditions of Christian scholasticism which have formalized such teaching.

> В средних веках, гораздо ближе к нам и поэтому гораздо ярче для нашего ума, развилась и укрепилась идея искупительной жертвы, идея *зараженности* мира грехом. Эта идея стала чрезвычайно народной [...] Поднялась жгучая и острая идея *вины, греха, страдания*. Мир разделился и противоположился. «Небо» по-прежнему создано Богом; но «земля», земное, неизменное, обыкновенное, если и не прямо, то косвенно, стало

63 Remizov, *Kukkha*, p. 23.

> признаваться тварью дьявола. Люди разделились на святых и грешных, очищаемых и очищающих, прощаемых и прощающих.
>
> In the Middle Ages, much closer to us and therefore much more striking for our mind, the idea of the redemptive sacrifice developed and took hold, the idea of a world *infected* by sin. This idea became exceptionally nationalist [...] The burning and piercing concept of *guilt* took hold, of *sin*, *suffering*. The world was divided and turned on itself. 'Heaven' was as before created by God; but 'Earth', the earthly, the immutable, the ordinary, if not directly, started to be considered a creature of the devil. People were divided into the holy and the sinful, the purifiers and the purified, those who pardon and those who are pardoned.[64]

(The importance of infectedness is also apparent in Tolstoi, as I show later.) Rozanov pushes the identity between the physical and the ideal so far that its leads to heretical conclusions about the relationship of God to Earth. Rozanov insists on God's identity with the Earth. God is in the world, as parents exist in their children. This goes against the usual Christian teaching of a substantial division between Creator and creation. The Orthodox Church insists on the equivalence but difference of divine essence and energies (unlike St Augustine's division of nature and grace as followed in the Western Church). Therefore, Orthodoxy teaches that matter itself cannot be worshipped, as this would imply God was contained within that object. This formal distinction of the essence and the energies of God helps avoid pantheism. However, Rozanov does not make this distinction and revels in labelling himself a 'pantheist'.[65] Therefore we can assume that he does not dissociate the essence from energies, but identifies them. This explains his tendency to examine phenomena in terms of their activity rather than simply their being (as well as having consequences for his vision of narrative which we shall examine later). His position enables Rozanov to accept all aspects of the created world, and not just the areas selected by the Church hierarchy.

Strangely, Rozanov modifies Plato in preserving the identity of the holy and the profane. He writes that the Greek's theory of ideas supports Rozanov's own thinking that all matter is holy. Throughout his career, Rozanov holds on to his early thinking that ideas are bodies in themselves that await incarnation through divine, or human, activity. Rozanov reinterprets Plato as arguing that every single phenomenon, no matter how seemingly insignificant, has its origin in the divine.

---

64 'Nebesnoe i zemnoe', pp. 159–60.

65 V.V. Rozanov, 'Predislovie', in *Okolo tserkovnykh sten*, p. 8.

'"And God created Heaven and Earth", I understand this not only in the planetary sense, but here I see another thought, perhaps even more profound and extremely dear, tender to the human: that God did not only create the heavenly, the angel-like, the pure, the holy, no; but that He created everything that is small, trivial, and pitiful'.[66] This is an unconventional interpretation of Plato, as Rozanov rejects concepts of universal forms, in favour of a belief that all individual phenomena have an aspect within them which is sanctified.

## The elements of religion

The implications of Rozanov's materialism and his vision of contemporary worship are made clearer in the 1902 article 'Ogni sviashchennye'. Here Rozanov brings together seemingly disparate elements of religious thinking and doxology from different periods of human and personal history, in order to demonstrate a relationship with the divine which is essentially unchanging. It also underlines Rozanov's natural theology, in which he shares aspects in common with the approach of thinkers such as Rousseau and Hume.

Rozanov recalls a conversation with his governess over the use of candles during Orthodox Easter services. The interaction of dialogue against recollection is important as it underlines the permanence of religious experience. Rozanov then turns to a description of his own childhood memories from Kostroma and how he watched the worshippers proceed into the town's many churches with their candles.

> «Начинается»... Вот появились два – три – шесть – десять, больше, больше и больше огоньков на высокой колокольне Покровской церкви; оглянулся назад – горит Козьмы и Дамиана церковь; направо – зажигается церковь Алексия Божия человека. И так хорошо станет на душе. А тут на чистой скатерти, под салфетками, благоухают кулич, пасха и красные яички. Поднесешь нос к куличу (ребенком был) – райский запах. «А, как все хорошо! И как хорошо, что есть вера, и как хорошо что она – с куличами, пасхой, яйцами, с горящими на колокольнях плошками, а в конце концов – и с нашей мамашей [...] и с братишками, и с сестренками, и с своим домиком».
>
> 'It begins'... And so there appeared two – three – six – ten, more, more and more little fires in the tall bell tower of the Pokrovskaia Church; I glanced back – the Church of Saints Koz´ma and Damian was ablaze; to the right the Church

66 'Nebesnoe i zemnoe', p. 160.

of Aleksei the Man of God is alight. And it becomes pleasant in the soul. There on the clean tablecloth, under napkins, the Easter cakes and the red-coloured eggs give off their aroma. Bring your nose up to the Easter cake (I was a child) – the smell of Paradise. 'Ah, how good it all is! And how good that there is faith, how good that this faith comes with our Easter cakes, with eggs, with lampions burning in the bell tower, and in the end with our mother [...] and with our little brothers and sisters, and with our little home.'[67]

Rozanov then moves to his experience of religion as an adult, emphasizing the physical aspects of religion.

Да, как хороша религия в звуках, в красках, в движениях, с иконами, с большими непременно иконами, в золотых ризах, а еще лучше – в жемчужных, как в Успенском соборе в Москве, и с огнями. И пусть огни будут в руках, перед образами, на улице, особенно на колокольнях...

Если бы, я думаю, с облака посмотреть в эту ночь на землю – вдруг представилось бы, точно небо упало на землю, но упало и не разбилось, а продолжает пылать звездами. Может быть, бесы и смотрят на землю в Пасхальную ночь, смотрят и злятся, что люди не забыли своего Бога, что они сумели свести на землю небо. Да, огни в религии, лампады и свечи, я думаю, имеют в основании эту идею, эту мечту или философскую догадку: «попробуем устроить на земле, как на небе».

Yes, how beautiful is religion in its sounds, its colours, its movements, with icons, necessarily with large icons, in their golden frames, and even better – in pearls like in the Uspenskii Cathedral in Moscow, and with fires. And let the fires be in people's hands, before the icons, and on the streets, and especially in the bell towers...

If, I think, you looked down this night onto the Earth from a cloud, then you would suddenly think that Heaven had fallen on the Earth, fallen but not shattered, and continued to blaze with stars. Perhaps daemons look down on the Earth on Easter Night, they look and are angered that people have not forgotten their God, that they could bring Heaven down to Earth. Yes, fires in religion, lamps and candles, I think, have their basis in this idea, this dream or philosophical theory: 'Let us try to build on Earth as it is in Heaven'.[68]

For Rozanov, religion is the expression of 'religio', the tie between the human and God. This is essentially unchanging, and the Russian Orthodox Church as an institution does not have exclusive authority over these truths. Rozanov, whose most commonly used pseudonym was

67 V.V. Rozanov, 'Ogni sviashchennye', in *Okolo tserkovnykh sten*, pp. 235–40 (p. 235).

68 Ibid., pp. 235–6.

'Varvarin', criticizes Christianity for its rejection of pagan culture.[69] For Rozanov, the Church is the manner of expressing permanent truths in a national form. This is made particular in the Russian church building, which demonstrates that history for Rozanov is essentially a human construction, like the pyramids. (Rozanov also compares Russian literature to a pyramid.) History should not be seen as the linear progression of time, but as the unity of all moments which enjoy equal significance. As Rozanov said, 'meaning is not in the Eternal; meaning is in Moments'.[70] This focus on the moment rather than the universal grows throughout Rozanov's career, leading to a focus on discontinuity similar to Florenskii's, though Rozanov maintains the significance of each moment by reinterpreting it as giving the opportunity for renewal. (This focus on the construction of history as a project for human activity is also a key part of Fedorov's work.)

Rozanov was often criticized for his subjective approach to religion. For example, Merezhkovskii wrote that the person is a whole, the 'I' and the 'not-I', which are fulfilled through the interaction of the person with the absolute. He accused Rozanov of ignoring the role of the 'not-I', and of focusing on sex instead as a means of fulfilling the self. For Merezhkovskii, sex leads to the dissolution of personality and is therefore similar to death in its function.[71] However, in this article, Rozanov opens up to the universal by positing a link between the individual soul and the elements. This is a definite rejection in Rozanov of the Galilean interpretation of the universe as moving independently from the divine. Instead earlier influences, Aristotelian and Stoic in nature, merge in his thought, in an interpretation of the growth of the universe as an organic whole. Rozanov is also reminiscent of Origen when he insists that stars are alive and have souls.[72]

---

69 This is opened into an aesthetic-moral appreciation of civilization. See especially V.V. Rozanov, 'Zamechatel′naia stat′ia', in *Religiia i kul′tura: Stat′i 1902–1903 gg.*, ed. by A.N. Nikoliukin (Moscow: Respublika, 2008), pp. 618–26 (p. 625).

70 V.V. Rozanov, *Opavshie list′ia: Korob vtoroi*, in *Religiia i kul′tura*, ed. by E.V. Vitkovskii et al. (Moscow: Folio, 2001), pp. 404–632 (p. 631).

71 D.S. Merezhkovskii, 'Rozanov', in *Vasilii Rozanov: Pro et Contra*, I, pp. 408–17 (pp. 415–16).

72 The sun also plays an important place in his thought; heat is associated with holiness, and the bitter cold of his last days at Sergiev Posad with the conquest of Russia by Christ/the Antichrist. He was obsessed with fire from an early age, and this attraction persisted into his adult life (this fascination was shared by Remizov and other Silver Age figures). See Greta N. Slobin, *Remizov's Fictions 1900–1921* (DeKalb: Northern Illinois University Press, 1991), p. 9.

We also note in this article Rozanov's willingness to assume aspects of formal Orthodoxy. Natural light has been a vital component of Christian worship from its origins. Christ described Himself as the light of the world (John 8:12), and early churches were aligned to the movement of the sun, a tradition which still exists today.[73] However, Rozanov provides his own elemental justification for traditional Orthodox truths. He notes that pagans worshipped fire, the very first image of God.[74] 'There is a secret connection between the soul and fire [...] Go into a church in the day, when there is no service, when there are no candles or lamps – and you will see only the architecture and art, you will not pray there, you will not be able to pray.'[75] Rozanov also cites historical examples. He recalls how, on his visit to Rome, he saw on the Arch of Titus depictions of the lamp from Solomon's Temple. Rozanov also refers to one of his favourite historians, Herodotus, and his descriptions of fire in Egyptian worship.[76]

People light fires because these mirror the stars, and this merges the heavenly with the earthly. Stars have their own biology, and are linked to human beings, who also burn with an inner fire.[77] Rozanov states that among Russian writers, only Lermontov fully expressed this reverence for the stars; Lermontov loved them 'not like stones or sand, not mechanically or geometrically', but as living creatures.[78] Rozanov rejects the mechanistic explanation for the universe. He writes: 'Astronomers have divided the sky into constellations, calculated exactly to the second the movement there; they have worked out everything, measured everything; it seems they have rationalized everything, but we do not listen to them, and we say firmly: "God is in Heaven!"'[79] For Rozanov the recollection of the past performs an ontological function; memory is a creative

73 Candles are also essential and it is not uncommon among Russian religious thinkers to find a rejection of artificial light as demonic. Losev insists that sunlight has a 'defined mythology'; conversely, the light of electric lamps is 'dead and mechanic'. A.F. Losev, *Dialektika mifa*, in *Mif, chislo, sushchnost´* (Moscow: Izdatel´stvo 'Mysl', 1994), pp. 5–219 (p. 53). Rozanov also differentiates holy light, lit to glorify God, from 'ordinary light' which just helps us see.

74 'Ogni sviashchennye', p. 238.

75 Ibid., p. 236.

76 Ibid., pp. 238–9.

77 Ibid., p. 237.

78 V.V. Rozanov, 'Iz vostochnykh motivov', in *Vozrozhdaiushchiisia Egipet*, ed. by A.N. Nikoliukin (Moscow: Respublika, 1999), pp. 292–301 (p. 294).

79 'Ogni sviashchennye', p. 237.

act through which the human overcomes the limits of his subjectivity. The investigation of religious behaviour is in itself a religious deed, as Rozanov describes his experience of writing.

> В эту минуту, как я пишу, у меня мир в сердце – и века и народы сдвигаются в него без разделения и вражды. Я думаю о благородном человеке, который никогда не хотел остаться без религии [...] Прекрасна картина всемирная, как человек на разных концах земли, человек-дикий, человек-ребенок что-то думает, склонив голову, усиливается, гадает; а когда поднял голову – глаза его сияют и он уже *верит*.
>
> At this moment, as I write, there is peace in my heart – and the centuries and the peoples shift into it without antagonism or hatred. I think about the noble person who never wanted to be left without religion [...] This is a beautiful picture of the world, like the person at different ends of the Earth, the savage, the child-person, who thinks, bowing his head, strives, wonders; and when he raises his head, his eyes blaze and he *believes*.[80]

One suspects that there is a parallel here Rozanov draws, perhaps unconsciously, between the eyes that are lightened through the restorative or creative act of recollection, and the face that is illuminated in hesychasm. Rozanov owes much to the Christian concept of anamnesis, as does his friend Florenskii, who would later present a similar well-known description of the function of memory as 'the creation of symbols'. Florenskii writes that memory is 'the creativity of thought' through which the 'symbols of Eternity' are revealed within history.[81] The act of anamnesis is made doubly real in this essay by Rozanov's drawing on Herodotus' history of Egypt. In fact, this article relies heavily on the investigation of how past peoples have themselves recaptured and retold historical events, emphasizing recollection as a creative and communal act. Rozanov draws on different events in history, all of which have the same significance.

> Я заговорил о небе, звездах, огнях; приведу самое древнее известие о возжжении священных горящих точек на земле. Оно находится у Геродота и относится к Египту, древней стране, которая ранее всех народов образовала важнейшие религиозные представления: о Боге как Творце и Промыслителе мира.
>
> I started to talk of Heaven, of the stars, of fires; I bring the most ancient news about the lighting of the holiest points on Earth. This can be found in

---

80 Ibid.

81 Pavel Florenskii, *Stolp i utverzhdenie istiny: Opyt pravoslavnoi teoditsei* (Moscow: Izdatel′stvo 'AST', 2002), p. 178.

> Herodotus, and relates to Egypt, the ancient country, which before all other peoples formulated the most important religious concepts: about God as Creator and the Guardian of the world.[82]

Rozanov tries to preserve the sacramental nature of the Church, but this ends up being contingent on the elements and their innate holiness, affirmed during religious acts. Rozanov is intent on reminding the Russians of the true meanings of their relationship with matter. Water is used to cleanse the body at the most important stages in its life, during illness and at death. He especially cherishes the rite of baptism, because of its links with childbirth; but this is given a wider meaning.[83] Rozanov terms baptism a 'physiological-elemental process', which ensures the body becomes a temple to God.[84]

Rozanov demonstrates the manner in which Orthodox doctrine has created a skewed feeling and a type of religious fanaticism. As soul and body should work in tandem, Rozanov considers perverse the Orthodox teaching that physical suffering promotes spiritual wellbeing. Yet the Church's proclamation that the battle against evil cannot be won on this Earth has had massive consequences. The Russians have been told to overcome their bodies. Rozanov cites the case of Avksentii Babenko, a 51-year-old from Ekaterinoslav, who threw himself alive onto a fire in order to seek redemption.[85] He also discusses the story of a young boy who burnt out his eyes with a candle, because he believed this would please Jesus.[86] For Rozanov, these are not individual cases, but symptomatic of the Church's hatred for the world and the body.[87] Whole villages

82 'Ogni sviashchennye', p. 238.

83 V.V. Rozanov, 'Taina stikhii', in *Vo dvore iazychnikov*, ed. by A.N. Nikoliukin (Moscow: Respublika, 1999), pp. 264–7 (p. 265).

84 Ibid.

85 V.V. Rozanov, 'Sluchai v derevne', in *V temnykh religioznykh luchakh*, ed. by A.N. Nikoliukin (Moscow: Respublika, 1994), pp. 143–55 (p. 143). Rozanov wrote this article in 1900, though it is unclear when the incident in question took place.

86 Ibid.

87 During Rozanov's lifetime, cases of religious fundamentalism were widespread across Russia and Europe, involving Orthodox Christians, sectarians and Jews, among others. In such an environment, where it was common for religious activity to result in mutilation, castration, murder and suicide, Rozanov's interpretation of the Beilis Affair is perhaps not so surprising. See Albert S. Lindemann, *The Jew Accused: Three Anti-Semitic Affairs (Dreyfus, Beilis, Frank) 1894–1915* (Cambridge: Cambridge University Press, 1991), p. 185.

have committed mass suicide out of a 'strange Orthodox fanaticism', a false religious feeling. Instead, Rozanov calls on the Church to encourage a 'fruitful' faith and true love between people.[88] In short, this involves putting motherhood at the centre of its worship.

## The social role of the Church

Rozanov redefines what it means to be Christian (in any case, his focus is always on Russian Orthodoxy rather than Christianity in general). The Russian Orthodox Church, which preaches that it alone shows the way to salvation, has entered into theological dialogue with other Christian denominations. However, it retains the position, laid out in its 1903 letter to the Anglicans and Old Catholics, that it considers the Orthodox Church 'the Universal Church' that 'has preserved intact the entire pledge of Christ'; hence it sets its task as 'the combination of a principled dogmatic approach and a fraternal love' towards non-Orthodox Christians, explaining its truths in the hope that they will eventually join it.[89]

Rozanov believes that salvation can lie outside the Russian Church. For this reason, Berdiaev termed him an Orthodox without Christ.[90] Rozanov's soteriology is not contingent on the Orthodox Church and Christ, but on childbirth; we live on in our children. Rozanov even refuses to discuss the immortality of the soul. Like Kant, Rozanov understands the limits of reason in our inability to understand the nature of the afterlife. However, Rozanov does not follow Kant in his *Critique of Practical Reason* (where the German imposes a teleological principle on morality), in positing that the afterlife must by necessity exist; for Rozanov it is simply something that lies beyond the boundaries of knowledge, as well as ethics.

Rozanov argues that no single Church has a monopoly on the eternal truths of religion. He shares much in common with Christian philosophers who were able to present religion as inclusive, existing in the natural order of things, and we are reminded of Clement of Alexandria,

88 V.V. Rozanov, 'Samosozhzhenie', in *V temnykh religioznykh luchakh*, p. 190.

89 See *Eastern Churches Journal*, 7 (2000), p. 146.

90 N.A. Berdiaev, 'O "vechno bab′em" v russkoi dushe', in *Vasilii Rozanov: Pro et Contra*, II, pp. 41–51 (p. 42).

who argued in his *Stromata* that Christians worship the same God as the pagans.[91] Rozanov believes that a church is national, that although it expresses the same truths about God and humanity, its form is shaped nationally, by the biology of the people (here 'narod' with its genetic connotations) of which it is constituted. This approach to religiosity is founded generally on biological difference rather than ethnic supremacy. Rozanov presents a national religiosity and believes that it is no more possible for a plant to be detached from its roots as it is to remove a Russian from his soil.[92] This is why Rozanov cannot see ecumenicalism as a practical project. Rather than the unity of the Churches, humanity should strive towards an end to hostility (characterized by his term 'primirenie') between different denominations.[93] Unlike some of his contemporaries, Rozanov maintained a rather pragmatic approach to other national churches and does not generally identify a messianic role for the Russian Church as such. He does not make the exclusive link between Russianness and divinity which is often found in, say, Dostoevskii, and mainly advocates that other nations should be permitted to base their own churches within their national culture (Rozanov often says that his focus is on 'natsional′nost′' rather than on 'natsionalizm').[94]

---

91 Clement of Alexandria argued that Hellenic philosophy should not be condemned as it provided some evidence of the truth of this world; all Greek thinkers were 'illumined by the dawn of light'. Quoted in Gerald R. McDermott, *God's Rivals: Insights from the Bible and the Early Church* (Downers Grove, Illinois: IVP Academic, 2007), p. 121.

92 V.V. Rozanov, 'Literaturnye zametki', in *Staraia i molodaia Rossiia*, pp. 366–9 (p. 366).

93 Rozanov believes that it is the task of each Church to assist its people in the embodiment of their natural religion; however, the dogma of their leaders forces the Churches further apart. He compares the Western and Eastern Churches, in typically domestic terms, to two neighbours, who previously enjoyed drinking tea together, but between whom now has been erected a barbed-wire fence. V.V. Rozanov, 'O "sobornom" nachale v tserkve i o primirenii tserkvei', in *Okolo tserkovnykh sten*, pp. 366–81 (pp. 367–8).

94 In his later career, though, Rozanov displays a vicious hostility towards other ethnic and religious groups, in particular Jewish Russians. There is also a highly disturbing essay in which Rozanov suggests that 'the Polish question' can only be resolved genetically, by mixing Polish blood with Slavic blood; this is what we would today call ethnic cleansing. See V.V. Rozanov, 'Belorussiia, Litva i Pol′sha v okrainnom voprose Rossii', in *Staraia i molodaia Rossiia*, pp. 291–304 (p. 302).

Rozanov's focus on nationhood leads us to suppose that the Russian Church would exist even without Christ. In his examination of ancient Egypt, he is content to talk of the 'Egyptian church'. Unlike Leont′ev, Rozanov does not accommodate a purpose for the wider Orthodox community, but concentrates on the Russian Church. Russian religiosity should emerge naturally from the Russians and should be composed of the body of the people;[95] this is Pauline discourse used in a particularly physical, Rozanovian manner. It follows that Rozanov opposes a hierarchical priesthood where the clergy are detached from their flock and elevated above the people. Rozanov shows an admiration for the religious organization of pagan societies, particularly ancient Egypt, where the priesthood emerged from and retained its intimate links with the masses.[96]

Rozanov believes that the Russian Church's leadership has become detached from the people, hostile to *byt*, and has imposed an imported ideology. This exposes the tensions between the practice of tradition and modernity in Rozanov and tensions between dogmatic and experiential religious practice. The Church leadership is dominated by the doctrines it adopted from the Byzantines and is more concerned with preserving dogma than establishing a relationship with the people based on love. 'For the current officialdom or officials in the Church demonstrate the encroachment into the Church of an organization which is *alien* to it, and which does not show the development of the Church itself, from its own principles and according to its inner law and spirit, from its own juices'.[97] Rozanov is looking for a particular kind of 'sobornost' which involves an acknowledgment of genetic relatedness.[98] In seeing

95 V.V. Rozanov, 'O veshchakh beskonechnykh i konechnykh (Po povodu nesostoiavshegosia "otlucheniia ot tserkvi" pisatelei)', in *Zagadki russkoi provokatsii: Stat′i i ocherki 1910 g.*, ed. by A.N. Nikoliukin (Moscow: Respublika, 2005), pp. 365–9 (p. 366).

96 Rozanov is close to other Russian thinkers in advocating what he feels should be the communal nature of the Russian Church, where the priests are not accorded a privileged position above the people. This is supposed to be a characteristic of the Russian Orthodox Church; Basil argues that the Orthodox Church officially recognizes 'no mark of rank', with 'no superior place' for the priest. See John D. Basil, 'Konstantin Petrovich Pobedonostsev: An Argument for a Russian State Church', *Church History*, 64 (1995), 44–61 (p. 47).

97 V.V. Rozanov, 'Pravoslavnaia tserkov′ v 1908 g.', in *Staraia i molodaia Rossiia*, pp. 8–9 (p. 9).

98 Ibid.

an opposition between clergy and people, Rozanov elaborates on the opposition between the activities of mind and of the body, and also reveals something about the aesthetic appreciation of dogma which only becomes fully clear with the materialization of his own *Opavshelistika*. There is also a parallel rejection in Rozanov of the priesthood as the representative of Christ on Earth. Rozanov argues that by maintaining a rigid clerical structure in particular, the Church ensures that talented people do not enter the clergy, and even the most skilled priests within the Church are unable to fulfil their potential in administering to the people. The entire makeup of the Church runs against Rozanov's theory of love.

> Все несчастие духовенства заключалось в том, что за целое столетие и даже за два века, с Петра Великого, оно не выдвинуло ни одной великой *нравственной личности* из себя, вот с этими же, как у Толстого, тревогами совести, с мукой души о *грехе своем*, о долге *своем*, – именно своем, а не чужом, ибо о «чужом долге» духовенство до «преизбыточества» говорило: и никто из него не взволновал душу общества, не изъявил сердца человеческого, как Толстой вечным своим «покаянием», самообличением и самобичиванием.
>
> All the clergy's unhappiness emerged from the fact that for the past century, and even for the last two centuries since Peter the Great, it has not produced one great *moral figure* from its ranks, who, like Tolstoi, has suffered anxieties of the conscience, the soul's torment about its sinfulness, about its duty, and specifically about its own, not anybody else's, for the clergy has spoken about 'other people's duties' since time immemorial; and nobody from its ranks has sparked the soul of the people, has expressed the heart of humanity, in the way that Tolstoi did with his eternal 'penance', his self-exposure and his self-flagellation.[99]

The relationship between the Church and the people cannot be healthy, as the relationship between the Church hierarchy and its own priests has broken down. The clergy receive poor training. Seminaries are run harshly, along military lines, and this hardens the trainee priests' characters, making them insensitive to the needs of the people.[100] In seminaries the focus is not on love, but on dogma: no attention is placed

99 V.V. Rozanov, 'Chego nedostaet Tolstomu?', in *Okolo narodnoi dushi: Stat'i 1906–1908 gg.*, ed. by A.N. Nikoliukin (Moscow: Respublika, 2003), pp. 344–55 (p. 354).

100 V.V. Rozanov, 'K pravitel'stvennomu soobshcheniiu', in *Russkaia gosudarstvennost' i obshchestvo: Stat'i 1906–1907 gg.*, ed. by A.N. Nikoliukin (Moscow: Respublika, 2003), pp. 147–8 (p. 148).

on *byt*. There is no development of the trainees' character, whereas priests should be a 'friend of the soul and of life'.[101] Instead, the Church's emphasis on the 'algebra' of Christianity means that individual priests are ill equipped to use their initiative in their parishes and cannot adopt a spontaneous approach to their flock and the world. 'The deep despair of the Russian Earth can be traced to the realization and the obvious fact that there is a "Church", but that "there is no righteousness of God on the Earth"; that there is nowhere to go, nowhere to make a pilgrimage'.[102]

Rozanov sympathizes with the rural clergy, poorly paid and treated badly by Church authorities who are indifference to their living conditions.[103] Bishops, hostile to real Russian life, refuse to leave their offices and visit the villages under their care.[104] The clergy's impoverishment deflects its attention from the people's spiritual needs. As a result, Russian villages are filled with priests who undertake their tasks mechanically. Even the most enthusiastic of priests are hampered by the Church's hostility to their wellbeing, and Rozanov does not foresee any possibility of remedying this situation. 'This current pessimism *is becoming an eternal state of affairs*. This highly pessimistic situation among the clergy, the fact that the clergy has fallen into decline, has become vulgar, has lost its reason and will, lacks anything to say, and only cares about its own material welfare, wishing to live on "bread alone" – all this has become common knowledge'.[105]

Rozanov concedes that there are able priests within the Russian Church, but these tend to be exceptional individuals, deeply loved by the people but shunned by the Church, such as Ioann Kronshtadtskii and Nikon, Exarch of Georgia. Their deaths represent a serious loss for Russian religious life, and their treatment by the Church hierarchy has further damaged relations between the Russians and their Church: 'This loss has therefore particularly stricken our hearts, that the Russians have

---

101 V.V. Rozanov, 'Eshche o stile veshchei', in *Staraia i molodaia Rossiia*, pp. 395–8 (p. 398).

102 V.V. Rozanov, 'Tserkov′ esteticheskaia i tserkov′ sovestlivaia', in *Russkaia gosudarstvennost′ i obshchestvo*, pp. 134–8 (p. 136).

103 V.V. Rozanov, 'Sud′ba sel′skogo sviashchennika', in *Russkaia gosudarstvennost′ i obshchestvo*, pp. 184–8 (p. 188).

104 V.V. Rozanov, 'Nuzhda very i form ee', in *Zagadki russkoi provokatsii*, pp. 15–19 (p. 16).

105 V.V. Rozanov, 'Chrezvychainyi sobor russkoi tserkvi i ee budushchnost′', in *Russkaia gosudarstvennost′ i obshchestvo*, pp. 453–6 (p. 455).

long looked on the organizational skills of the Church with hopelessness, and, not seeing light in the offices of its chancelleries, have concentrated all their love and all their attention on individual righteous figures, on individual righteous deeds'.[106]

Such people are few. Rozanov believes that the Church, instead of being the body through which the Russian expresses his religion, impedes his relationship with the divine. The Church has neglected the Old Testament and elevated its own doctrine; it is in fact trying to replace God and make itself the object of the Russian people's worship. It has established itself as a false idol, which demands their exclusive obedience.[107] The Church has become, in Rozanov's eyes, a self-obsessed organization which will not permit them to accept the simple pleasures of this life. Herein lies a fundamental problem; Rozanov argues that the clergy has taught the Russians to worship the idea of the afterlife and neglect this world. Ironically, however, Rozanov points out that the Church as an institution has pernicious material concerns and is concerned with exercising secular authority over the Russian people.

Rozanov feels that the Church is unable to manage the harmony of Russian religious and secular affairs. His depressing conclusion is that the Russian people need protection from the Church leadership.[108] This can only be achieved by seeing the state as the best expression of the people's will and ensuring that the state has full guardianship over the Church. Only in this way can the divide between the Church and the people be overcome; the state's failure to reign in the Church will only result in further distance between the ecclesiastical body and the body of the people. Rozanov engages with long-running questions over the competing authority of the Tsar and Patriarch in Russia, which had gained increasing importance in the pre-revolutionary period.[109] Whereas

106 'Pravoslavnaia tserkov′ v 1908 g.', p. 9.

107 V.V. Rozanov, 'O rasstroistve trudovogo goda', in *Staraia i molodaia Rossiia*, pp. 125–8 (p. 126).

108 Ibid.

109 The struggles for authority between Tsar and Patriarch form an important part of Russian history. These polemics demonstrate different perceptions on the mutual relationship between ecclesiastical and secular authorities; Billington notes that until around the 1650s patriarchs were often considered 'virtual rulers' of Russia. Billington, especially pp. 130–3. Rozanov tended to idealize the concept of the Old Testament king (which was also the ideal of the first Russian tsars), especially David and Solomon, as the God-chosen ruler of the people who acted in the best interests of the people. He saw the Tsar as the father of the people who could best

in his adolescence he had wished for the restoration of the Patriarchate, Rozanov concludes that the wounds in Russian society can only be healed through the increased power of the Tsar over the Church through the Ober-Procurator and the Synod.[110]

## The Crisis of Creation

Rozanov makes explicit the link between the Creation and childbirth, positing a direct connection between God's work and the human task on Earth. Thereby Rozanov overcomes the speculative efforts of his peers to posit an abstract and theoretical eschaton for human history that takes precedence over the everyday. By founding his religiosity within the Old Testament, Rozanov also forms a nice link between the demands of formal religion and natural theology which had dogged much of nineteenth-century theology and which would only receive satisfactory treatment later in Barth. What marks Rozanov as distinctive, perhaps unique, is his unflinching attention to the intimacies of Creation and its implications for humanity. His likening of the Creation to a sexual act, and his determined probing at the consequences of this, is a highly important development in Russian religious thought, in particular in Russian personalism. Rozanov's interpretation of Creation preserves the unity of thought and being, overcoming the tendency in Hellenic thought, as demonstrated especially in the *Timaeus*, to separate ontology from epistemology (Plato's work is a principle source for the association of philosophy with death). Rozanov also taps into a more general problem of Christian theology, the relative lack of attention given to the Creation. The Creation has simply been ignored by many Christian theologians, despite its place as the very foundation of Christian thought.[111] This

---

embody the people's will (the pronunciation of such views became more desperate from 1917 onwards). Rozanov eventually came to believe that the Patriarch would act only in the interests of the Church against the interests of the people. Rozanov's eventual call for the religious transfiguration of the state rather than the Church is a vital step in his belief that religion must be made social, and puts him close to Dostoevskii.

110 V.V. Rozanov, 'Beznadezhnoe i beznadezhnye', in *Russkaia gosudarstvennost´ i obshchestvo*, pp. 14–18 (p. 14).

111 Diogenes Allen and Eric O. Springsted, *Philosophy for Understanding Theology* (Louisville: Westminster John Knox Press, 2007), p. 3.

neglect has been serious enough for recent studies to speak of a 'crisis in the doctrine of creation'.[112]

It has been argued that the early Christians had little need to investigate in depth the meaning of the Creation, as they accepted Jewish teachings of God as Creator. There was also a certain eschatological fervour among the first Christians and a wide acceptance that Christ would soon return to establish His Kingdom. Paul's theory of Jesus as the new Adam (I Corinthians 15:45) presents the Creation story in a new mode, providing a new way of understanding the reality of an impending future transfiguration. Scholasticism made important contributions to studies into the Creation, and in many ways Aquinas marked the highpoint of philosophical sophistication in this. Departing from Aristotelian ideas of the prime mover, Aquinas argued that Creation is a single act (i.e. there is no continuing Creation) which presupposes the relativity of the created and a radical contingency which requires us to accept the Creation as a theological event through faith rather than reason.[113]

This separation of faith and reason in understanding the Creation was perpetuated throughout the Middle Ages, and the Creation became an object of philosophical, rather than theological, study. This domination of philosophers continued through the Enlightenment, and the relinquishing of authority to the field of philosophy meant that, as philosophy adapted to the new scientific strands that emerged in the nineteenth century, theology was unable to accommodate the growing influence of natural science, particular theories of evolution.[114] This crisis in Creation studies has also involved the separation of creationist theology from natural theology.[115] Despite a more recent effort, especially in Catholicism, to refocus on the Creation, this aspect of Christian teaching is only secondary to schemes of salvation.

Bevans argues that two basic ways to engage with theology are to adopt either a Creation-orientated or a redemption-orientated approach. The former he describes in following terms:

> A creation-centred orientation sees the world, creation, as sacramental: the world is the place where God reveals Godself; revelation does not happen in

112 See *Encyclopedia of Christian Theology*, ed. by Jean-Yves Lacoste, 3 vols (New York/London: Routledge, 2005), I, p. 385.

113 Ibid.

114 Ibid.

115 Ibid.

> set-apart, particularly holy places, in strange, unworldly circumstances, or in words that are spoken in stilted voice; it comes in daily life, in ordinary words, through ordinary people.[116]

Bevans argues that such an approach 'sees a continuity between human existence and divine reality', whereas an approach based on final redemption 'is characterized by the conviction that culture and human experience are either in need of a radical transformation or in need of total replacement'.[117] Bevans also concludes that the latter approach sees the Word of God as being given from *outside* this world, and therefore the circumstances of this world which require theological interpretation 'could never be interpreted *as* Word of God'.[118] This disjuncture between world and Word appears to reinforce what was said above on the difference between Christian epistemology and ontology, a problem which dogged modern Russian religious thought from its inception in Chaadaev.

Rozanov attempts to reconcile these problems through his faith in the Creation as a creative act of God. For Rozanov, the depiction of Genesis is the starting point of his philosophical outlook, but it is also the basis of a religious worldview ultimately upheld by faith. Faith underlies sensual experiences and unites these into an account of being which opens up subjectivity into a universal response to God's love. This is not strictly worship of the Creation itself, but an apologetic as to how the material world is the locus for our encounter with God. (Hamann argues that theological accounts of Creation are not used as purely scholastic investigation, but as evidence of the meaning of existence; doctrines of Creation reintroduce humanity to its relatedness with God and how to act in response.[119]) Despite Kolyshko's contention that Rozanov worships sex in order to revere the image ('obraz') of God,[120] Rozanov understands that sex plays an iconic role in human experience, enabling us to participate in divine activity. Rozanov would probably side with Florenskii's vision that God is love. What this means for Rozanov is

116 Stephen B. Bevans, *Models of Contextual Theology* (New York: Orbis, 2002), p. 21.
117 Ibid.
118 Ibid.
119 A. Hamman, 'L'enseignement sur la création dans l'Antiquité chrétienne', *Revue des sciences religieuses*, 42 (1968), 1–23 (p. 1).
120 Quoted in V.V. Rozanov, 'Polemicheskie materialy', in *V mire neiasnogo i nereshennogo*, pp. 82–139 (p. 82).

that humans must imitate God, that is we must love in order to achieve theosis. This is demonstrated through the practice of love: Rozanov's understanding of eros means that our love for God can be expressed only through sexuality.

However, in his rejection of an eschatology which stands outside human experience, Rozanov leaves one major question unanswered, that is the direct role of God in earthly experience. In his attempt to present a materialism which allows for the organic growth of objects, without subordinating the endpoint of their development to an extra-temporal telos, Rozanov does often steer into Aristotelian waters. The reader is left wondering what, in Rozanov's view, we should understand as God's role in our day-to-day lives. In his closeness to Aristotle, Rozanov sometimes gives the impression that he believes in some kind of unmoved mover, a creator which, having created, is uninvolved in His work. This is a notable difference from, for instance, Solov´ev, where we are given a sophisticated attempt at theandry, God and humanity working together to bring about the final transfiguration of the cosmos (though some thinkers, especially Khoruzhii, question the effectiveness of Solov´ev's effort). For Solov´ev, the theandric task is given ultimate expression in the Godman, the transfiguration of the material body into the spiritual body, the overcoming of the First Adam by the Second. For all his faults, Solov´ev presents a convincing argument of the joint task; perhaps like no other Russian thinker, he is able to reconcile the demands for theosis and kenosis and the need for God's involvement within the processes of divinization.

Rozanov's focus leaves us at times unsatisfied with what God's involvement within human history should be. Rozanov places a greater responsibility on humanity in the religious task than his peers, as the human is obliged to preserve the sanctity of matter by continually working upon it. Certainly Rozanov believes in Providence ('providenie'), expressed as God's love for His creation. This is demonstrated in His provision of the natural order, and the created world's responding movement. Rozanov here is very close to Stoic thought, but he links the patterns of the created world specifically to God's sexuality. Rozanov rules out magic in worship, as this would imply a limitation to God's freedom. There is in Rozanov no investigation of theandric reconciliation as expressed in Solov´ev. The only time that Rozanov hints at God's direct involvement in our affairs is during sexual activity, and Rozanov writes that although man and woman are obliged to have sex, it is God's decision whether this results in conception. This, perhaps, for Rozanov is enough. There is a sense of resignation which is perhaps an inevitable result of a religiosity that lacks a Christology, reminiscent to some degree of aspects of Judaic thought. Rozanov's belief that God participates in our conception does reinforce His paternity of all of us. Despite this, Rozanov becomes increasingly concerned that other principles are at work that undo God's creative work; hence his turn to the activity of Jesus Christ.

## Chapter 2

# The Sweetest Jesus

In some ways, Rozanov's are close to the ideas of the pagan heretics who were the target of Irenaeus' attacks. Irenaeus' opponents held to the Gnostic concept that there are two principles at work in the cosmos, that of the deity who creates matter and that of a second deity who redeems the universe. Irenaeus argued that the Gnostics were wrong to oppose the creator with the redeemer, as he insisted that Jesus Christ is the same as the God the Creator, and added that as God is good then matter must also be good.[1] Christian theologians attempted to resolve any tensions between God as Creator-Father and God as Redeemer-Son through the establishment of a highly complex Trinitarian theology, a prolonged and still ongoing process which also played a major factor in the split between the Western and Eastern Churches. One of the most important components of this was the belief, referred to in the writings of St Paul and St John (see John 1:3), that Jesus participated in the Creation.[2]

In Orthodoxy, Christology has been a particularly contentious area, with a series of schisms and controversies regarding Christ and His relationship to the Godhead. Christology has provided a rich and complex area in Russian religious thought. Perhaps this is not surprising given the tendency among Russian thinkers to examine in detail the practical consequences of their ideas. In Christian thought in general, as well as for Russian religious philosophers, the nature of Christ has a strong influence on how Christianity should be implemented on Earth. The relationship between the First and Second Hypostases of the Trinity

---

1 See *The Scandal of the Incarnation: Irenaeus Against the Heresies*, ed. by Hans Urs von Balthasar, trans. by John Saward (San Francisco: Ignatius, 1990), pp. 19–20. Hamman investigates the theological tension between faith in Christ and reverence for Old Testament accounts of God's creativity: 'The novelty of the New Testament does not reside in the dogma of the creation but in the mediation of Christ concerning the history of salvation'. Hamman, p. 3. Rozanov's apparent and temporary siding with Gnostic elements comes from his reinterpretation of Christ as the Antichrist who undoes the Creator's work. Several commentators, especially Il´in, have characterized Rozanov (as well as Florenskii) as Gnostic. See Robert Slesinski, *Pavel Florensky: A Metaphysics of Love* (New York: St Vladimir's Seminary Press, 1984), p. 46.

2 Ibid.

informs how Christians should understand the nature of physical reality and how the social mission of Christianity should be fulfilled. Therefore an understanding of Christology is vital for Christian thinkers in their investigation of the Church's role.

Although this book does not have the scope to provide a detailed commentary on the development of Trinitarian thought in Orthodoxy, it is worth tracing some key issues. The first Christian theologian, St Paul, presented Christianity as a religion of individual salvation. For Paul, this soteriology was necessarily contingent on Christ's death, without which faith would be pointless (I Corinthians 15:14–17):

> If Christ was not raised, then our gospel is null and void and so too is your faith; and we turn out to have given false evidence about God, because we bore witness that he raised Christ to life, whereas, if the dead are not raised, it follows that Christ was not raised; and if Christ was not raised, your faith has nothing to it and you are still in your old state of sin.

(Rozanov would present almost the exact reverse of this statement in his *Apokalipsis*.) Paul lays out a theory of Jesus who empties Himself into the form of man to bring salvation to a world in need of redemption, having a large influence on the concept of kenosis.

The presentation of Jesus as having a dual nature in one person was the starting point for thinkers such as Justin Martyr, who in the second century attempted a development of Christology which lent much to the Stoic and Platonic traditions. The start of systematic investigation emerged from two distinct arguments, that of the nature of the power which became incarnate in Christ and that of the nature of Jesus' flesh.[3] In many ways, they later became the crucial issues facing Rozanov and his coevals. These two major problems are interrelated, but one of the major problems introduced by Justin Martyr was the concept of Christ as Logos, derived from the Johannine Gospel, which supported the view that Christ worked as a mediator between God and Earth. This in turn led to several fundamental questions concerning the manner and reasons for the initial Creation of the Earth, the relationship of Christ to God the Father and the value of Christ's body. Irenaeus later rejected the concept of the Logos as a separate mediator between divinity and humanity, and also the Gnostic separation of Creator and Christ, in favour of a conceptualization of Christ as both God and man who redeems. Irenaeus

3 See Richard A. Norris, Jr., *The Christological Controversy* (Philadelphia: Fortress Press, 1980), pp. 5–8.

also made explicit a connection between his opponents' inability to comprehend the unity of God and Christ and their inability to accept the unity of the Old and New Testaments.[4]

The increasing fragmentation of the churches and division in their teachings in the first centuries of Christianity led to a movement to establish a unified Christology, which coincided with Byzantium's emergence as the centre of Orthodoxy. Ecumenical Councils formulated doctrine on the nature of Jesus, with Irenaeus' writings being influential. Christ, being both divine and human, through his Incarnation, death and Resurrection, redeems humanity, atoning for the sins committed by Adam, breaking our servitude to evil and preparing humans for our eventual transfiguration. The basis of Orthodox Christology was formulated at the Council of Chalcedon in 451.

> One and the same Son, our Lord Jesus Christ [...] truly God and truly man [...] one and the same Christ, Son, Lord, only-begotten, acknowledged in two natures which undergo no confusion, no change, no division, no separation; at no point was the difference between the natures taken away through the union, but rather the property of both natures is preserved and comes together into a single person and a single subsistent being; he is not parted or divided into two persons, but is one and the same only-begotten Son, God, Word, Lord Jesus Christ.[5]

Chalcedon was intended as a compromise between rival groups, meant to please all, but at the time it was considered a fudge that satisfied few. There were also debates about the activity of God and Christ, and whether God had two wills (divine and human) or one, as the heretical monothelites proclaimed. As centuries progressed, Orthodoxy further distinguished itself from Western Christianity by arguing that the work of Christ alone cannot save man. Whereas in the West, believers tend to formulate a much more personal relationship with Jesus, in Orthodoxy Christ's function is only assured through the Holy Spirit. For instance, Christ was not able to incarnate and resurrect Himself. For

4 Ibid., p. 11.

5 Taken from *The Encyclopedia of Christianity*, ed. by Erwin Fahlbusch et al. (Michigan/Cambridge: Eerdmans, 2001–2008), p. 399. Although the focus is on the Incarnation, rather than death, of Christ, in the Eastern tradition this same Incarnation points to the end of time. 'The West focuses more on the humanity of Christ, on the earthly life and death of Jesus, whereas the East views the mystery of the incarnation as a theophany and hence sees it in the light of the resurrection, which is the basis of salvation'. Ibid., pp. 467–8.

the Orthodox, Christology must be reconciled with Pneumatology.[6] The Second Person alone is not responsible for man's salvation. This wariness of an over-reliance on the activity of Christ has been apparent in some of the most serious polemics in Eastern Christianity.

These debates took on a particular prominence within the nineteenth-century renaissance of Russian religious thought, with the history of controversies in Russian Christology. There had previously been religious uprisings in Russia, for example the heresies of the so-called Judaizers and Skharia's rejection of the divinity of Christ. There was some confusion among Rozanov and his peers about the specific relevance of Christ's activity. Many of Rozanov's contemporaries saw Jesus as an unreliable guarantor of the communion between the divine and human. Berdiaev noted that the God-Seekers had a poor relationship with the Second Person of the Trinity.[7] Florovskii, a critic of many speculative Russian thinkers, insisted that Rozanov was not a true Christian because of his lack of a proper relationship with the divine Jesus. Florovskii also attacked Florenskii for bypassing the Incarnation and omitting Christology from *Stolp i utverzhdenie istiny*.[8] This lack of faith in Christ's work perhaps explains the reliance on Sophiology by some Russian thinkers.

For Solov´ev, Jesus was the highest in a series of theophanies which marked the unity of divine and human work, who also underlined the organic, divine-human nature of church dogma.[9] He perpetuates the idea of the Logos as the mediator between God and Earth. It is hardly surprising, given Solov´ev's creative approach, that traditional Orthodox thinkers have often been reluctant to see compatibility between his thought and their faith. Valliere speaks of a 'relative absence of Biblical theology' in Solov´ev, in particular in *Chteniia o Bogochelovechestve*.[10] Khoruzhii examines Solov´ev in the context of theosis through hesychasm and examines the potential for conflict with a social form of Christianity. Khoruzhii investigates the 'Manichean reduction' of hesychastic Orthodoxy, in which individual and communal forms of worship are mutually exclusive, and queries whether personal

6 Douglas Davis, 'Christianity', in *Worship*, ed. by Jean Holm with John Bowker (London: Pinter, 1994), pp. 35–62 (p. 36).

7 Berdiaev, *Russkaia ideia*, p. 268.

8 Florovskii, pp. 460–1, 493.

9 Valliere examines the relationship between Godmanhood and the development of dogma in *Modern Russian Theology*, pp. 178–86.

10 Ibid., p. 166.

prayer can be merged with a social, active form of Christianity.[11] Khoruzhii suggests that Solov´ev's 'sociocentrism' overwhelms his focus on hesychasm and that Solov´ev was unable to balance his mysticism with his asceticism.[12]

Khoruzhii poses in a modern form one of the major questions which troubled Rozanov, that is the balance between an individual relationship with God with the need for social activity. A religious life involves freely giving oneself up to the divine will and acting in accordance with this. Therefore, freedom plays an important part in Orthodox salvation, which has a different focus from Augustine's. For the Orthodox, Grace and will should be unified in what Clement of Alexandria termed 'synergy'.[13] Lossky writes that this unification is 'a co-operation, a synergy of the two wills, divine and human', which then becomes a unification of theory and praxis, a type of gnosis which is not necessarily intellectual but requires participation in the divine life.[14] This is essentially worship. Schmemann explains this ideal as a synthesis between the ascetical and mystical where divine and human activities are connected, and argues that Jesus Christ is the example of how this should be achieved.[15]

These questions, why God would require something to mediate between Himself and His creation, stand at the centre of Rozanov's project. Rozanov's understanding of the work of Christ has implications for how he believes humans should act. Rozanov examines the nature of the relationship between God and Earth and whether the mediation of the Logos results in the alienation of creation from the divine. Whereas in Solov´ev, we are left with a vision of Creation which can only take place through the mediation of Sophia, Rozanov presents a direct createdness through paternity. This suggests that Rozanov identifies the essence and the energies of the divine, enabling him to resort to a sophisticated pantheism which has little room for Christ. For Rozanov it is not enough to preserve a tradition of Orthodox

---

11 Sergei Khoruzhii, *O starom i novom* (St Petersburg: Aleteiia, 2000), pp. 196–201.

12 Ibid., p. 203.

13 See *Orthodox Spirituality: An Outline of the Orthodox Ascetical and Mystical Tradition*, ed. by the Fellowship of St Alban and St Sergius (London: SPCK, 1945), pp. 23–24.

14 Vladimir Lossky, *The Mystical Theology of the Eastern Church*, trans. by the Fellowship of St Alban and St Sergius (New York: St Vladimir's Seminary Press, 2002), p. 198.

15 Alexander Schmemann, *Introduction to Liturgical Theology*, trans. by Asheleigh E. Moorhouse (New York: Faith Press, 1966), p. 147.

religiosity which maintains a relationship just with God's energies: Rozanov needs to establish a relationship with God Himself.

## Rozanov's Sweetest Jesus

Rozanov presents an opposition between the work of God, which is creative, and that of Christ, which he argues counteracts God's work. For Rozanov, Christ is created by God. There must be some consubstantiality between God and Christ, as God is present in all His creatures (just as parents are present in their children). However, the question of divine substance is left vague, as Rozanov is more concerned with God's and Christ's activities. Rozanov sidesteps potential conflict between the natures of God and Jesus, by presenting a conflict of wills. The will of God is the most important factor in the cosmos and takes priority even over the nature of God. As God and Christ work in opposite manners to one another, Rozanov believes it is impossible to worship both. Humanity should imitate only the Father. This tension becomes more pronounced as Rozanov investigates more closely the practical implications of Christianity in the first decade of the twentieth century.

There is an element in him of the Eastern Christian tradition of subordinationism, and Rozanov was accused by his critics of Arianism.[16] The Arian heresy contended that Jesus was not God, but a created being. There is a further implication in Arian thought that the Incarnation of Christ, as promoted by the opponents of Arius and incorporated into official Orthodox doctrine, implies the rejection of the Earth and places an obligation upon men to suffer. This is demonstrated in Victorinus' treatise *Against Arius*.

> For this is a great mystery: that God 'emptied Himself when he was in the form of God,' then that he suffered, first by being in the flesh and sharing in the lot of human birth and being raised upon the Cross. These things, however, would not be marvellous if he had come only from man or from nothing, or from God by creation. For what would 'he emptied himself' mean if he did not exist before he was in the flesh? And what was he? He said, 'equal to God.' But if he were created from nothing, how is he equal?[17]

---

16 V.V. Rozanov, 'Spor ob apokrifakh', in *Okolo tserkovnykh sten*, pp. 271–84 (p. 284).

17 Quoted in Mary T. Clark, 'The Trinity in Latin Christianity', in *Christian Spirituality: Origins to the Twelfth Century*, ed. by Bernard McGinn and John Meyendorff in collaboration with Jean Leclercq (London: Routledge & Kegan Paul, 1986), pp. 276–90 (p. 281).

Rozanov's view of Christ does vary in its focus throughout his career. He is fairly consistent on directing his attention on the work of God rather than the Second Person, and much of his writing on Jesus is reactive, drawn up in response to publications by contemporaries such as Merezhkovskii and Grigorii Petrov. In his treatment of the historical man, Rozanov argues (relying on Chamberlain) that Jesus was not ethnically Jewish, but suggests that he was in fact a Galilean pagan.[18]

In his investigation of eschatology in particular, it is impossible to ignore Rozanov's treatment of Christ's place in the Godhead. As Berdiaev and others noted, the omission of Christ does make it difficult to come to terms with Rozanov's approach. However, it is a focus on activity which helps disentangle some of the issues. Rozanov sums up the opposition he sees between God and Jesus in a short passage from the end of his career, in *Apokalipsis nashego vremeni*: 'And Christ in fact "ANTI-created the world", and did not "CO-create the world". This is the "war with God".'[19] The question of whether or not Christ loves the world is one of the most important Rozanov poses. Going against formal Orthodoxy, he argues that Christ took no part in the Creation. This opposition is presented as one between Phallus and Logos. Rozanov complains that the Orthodox have replaced a reverence for the divine Phallus with worship of a Logos that descended to organize a pre-created world. For Rozanov, the sanctity of flesh is marked through the penis, as this part of the human body corresponds most closely to the creative powers of God. This is what humanity should worship and imitate. To engage in sex is to align one's activities with those of God. In this way, Rozanov unifies the personal and social aspects of worship, in a much more direct way than Solov′ev managed. In bringing forth offspring, the human opens himself out into the universal and also transfigures the cosmos through his own creativity.

Rozanov underlines the unity of essence and activity by arguing that those who consider sex evil, and especially religious extremists such as the skoptsy who go so far as to practise castration, destroy the image and likeness of God.[20] This is why the role of Christ becomes particu-

---

18 V.V. Rozanov, 'Byl li I. Khristos evreem po plemeni?', in *Okolo narodnoi dushi*, pp. 60–7.

19 V.V. Rozanov, *Apokalipsis nashego vremeni* (Moscow: Respublika, 2000), p. 325.

20 V.V. Rozanov, 'Psikhologiia russkogo raskola', in *Religiia i kul′tura: Stat′i 1902–1903 gg.*, ed. by A.N. Nikoliukin (Moscow: Respublika, 2008), pp. 37–74 (p. 60).

larly problematic for Rozanov: it offers a rival scheme of worship to the worship of God. Christ disrupts the identity between thought and praxis and injects into human religiosity an alternative system of representation to that offered by the Creation. For Rozanov, Christ disrupts the union of divine and earthly, prioritizing His own spirituality over His humanity.

Christ demonstrates the incompatibility Rozanov identifies in formal Orthodox teaching between the Incarnation and the Crucifixion. Rozanov argues that the Church has rejected the former in favour of the latter.[21] Rozanov does note the importance of the birth of the baby Jesus. However, this event holds just as much cosmological significance as any other birth, as all new life renews the bond with Heaven. Jesus' birth is important only when understood as a repetition of the Creation. It is an 'In-carnation' ('Vo-ploshchenie'), but Rozanov describes a typically human birth which follows from the Creation.[22] Rozanov makes explicit the cosmological significance of each birth, dismissing the uniqueness of Christ's Nativity. However, he does carve the Holy Family a special place in terms of the example it sets of family life and of the mysticism of blood and flesh embodied on Earth.[23] Rozanov notes his love for all babies, but his affection for Jesus' birth and the life of the Christ Child, especially in Rozanov's works in the first six years or so of the twentieth century, is striking when compared with the development of his Christology which we see from around 1907.

Rozanov's attraction to childbirth and pregnant women leads him also to consider Jesus' mother, though his engagement with Mariology is controversial. Here once more, he describes the Holy Family as an excellent example of sanctity, rather than carving them an exclusive role. Instead of discussing the Immaculate Conception, he seems to prefer to talk about 'the immaculate family'.[24] He writes that the Madonna's love for her son demonstrates the eternal miracle of motherhood.[25] Of course, Rozanov cannot stop at abstract principles, but probes at all that is fleshy in Christ's birth. He is fascinated by the intimate physical details of the

---

21 V.V. Rozanov, 'Religiia unizheniia i torzhestva', in *Terror protiv russkogo natsionalizma*, pp. 74–9 (p. 76).

22 See Rozanov's discussion in V.V. Rozanov, 'O nariadnost′ i nariadnykh dniakh kalendaria', in *Okolo tserkovnykh sten*, pp. 382–95.

23 V.V. Rozanov, 'Tema nashego vremeni', in *Vo dvore iazychnikov*, p. 171.

24 V.V. Rozanov, 'O neporochnoi sem′e i ee glavnom uslovii', in *Semeinyi vopros v Rossii*, pp. 82–92.

25 V.V. Rozanov, 'Lev III i katolichestvo', in *Okolo tserkovnykh sten*, pp. 345–56 (p. 352).

Nativity, such as the way Jesus was born from Mary's body and then breastfed, like all children. The fact that animals were present is highly important. Unlike in Orthodoxy, Rozanov does not carve a particular role for Mary; in fact, it is important to him to insist on the likeness of Mary's activity with every other woman's. There is a certain amount of pulling here at the tensions between Orthodoxy and Roman Catholicism. Catholic dogma insists that Mary, 'in the first moment of her conception, by a special grace of the omnipotent God and by a special privilege, for the sake of the future merits of Jesus Christ, the Savior of the human race, was preserved free of all stain of original guilt'.[26] In contrast, Orthodoxy teaches that no human being could be free of original sin before Christ. Nevertheless, Orthodoxy maintains that Mary remained a virgin, even after Jesus' birth. Rozanov tackles this with a typically sexual approach. Pushing religious discourse to its limits, Rozanov (although he does not examine whether Mary and Joseph had sex before Jesus' birth), insists that Jesus' parents certainly had a loving sexual relationship with each other afterwards.

As mentioned above, Rozanov's Christology varies in its focus and intensity through his career. His investigations of the Nativity often merge with his studies into ancient Egypt, forming a parallel between the mysticism of Bethlehem with the reverence for childbirth he sees in pre-Christian religions. Through the first decade of the twentieth century, Rozanov's desire to examine the practical implications of Orthodoxy lead him to become more critical of Church doctrine, and then of the New Testament. This culminates in a turn against the person of Jesus Himself; as Rozanov considers in greater detail the work of the Church, he cannot escape the fact that there is not just a baby Jesus, but an adult Jesus, who tells his followers to reject the world, to leave their families, to avoid sex and to worship Him.[27] And no matter how much Rozanov wishes to be close to this person, how much he longs to feel the reality of Christ by placing his fingers into His wounds, there is ultimately no way for Rozanov to reconcile Christ and the Creator. His attacks on contemporary Christianity culminate in a series of highly critical articles

26 Bull of Pope Pius IX of 1854. Quoted in Mark Miravalle, *Mariology: A Guide for Priests, Deacons, Seminarians, and Consecrated Persons* (Goleta: Queenship, 2007), p. 798.

27 As Gippius writes, Rozanov wanted to know Christ as a person and not the abstract Second Person of the Trinity. Gippius, p. 161.

between around 1907–1911. This becomes not so much a critique of the Orthodox Church, but more of an attack on Christ Himself.

Perhaps the best example of this is a lecture made to the Religious-Philosophical Society on 21 November 1907 (O.S.), a work which Fateev called 'the most striking of all anti-Christian declarations'.[28] The Religious-Philosophical Society was in effect a successor to the Religious-Philosophical Meetings of 1901–1903, but instead of trying to find a type of dialogue between Church and intelligentsia, it was dominated more by the desire to find a reformed Christianity. As Ternavtsev said, the Religious-Philosophical Society had to show that the Church was not ruled by 'the ideal of the afterlife', but wanted to show 'the *truth about the Earth*', which he believed was hidden within Christianity. For Ternavtsev, a civil servant, it was time to establish a new Christian state governed by the social dimensions of Christ's mission.[29]

In 'O Sladchaishem Iisuse i gor´kikh plodakh mira', Rozanov starts by taking issue with a recurrent theme in Merezhkovskii, that the Gospels can be reconciled with contemporary civilization. (Rozanov, a notoriously shy public speaker, did not present his talks himself, but asked friends to read them out on his behalf.[30]) The Russian Orthodox Church's position is that Biblical exegesis must be conducted through the prism of its dogmatic truths: the study of the Gospels 'should not lead to conclusions that contradict the Orthodox Church dogma'.[31] Merezhkovskii was intent on developing a new religion which emerged from the cultural synthesis of paganism and Christianity. Both Merezhkovskii and Rozanov force a cultural interpretation onto New Testament hermeneutics, but end up with opposing conclusions. Merezhkovskii generally sides with Ternavtsev's view that a new form of Russian Christianity was required in a modern state. Much of Merezhkovskii's work around 1907 is centred on this theme, and articles such as 'Tserkov´ griadushchego', or 'Mech', look to a third age of Christianity in which death is overcome in a new Church through the Resurrection of Christ. These were received positively by commentators, including Berdiaev, Askol´dov and the *Novoe Vremia* editors, though, as always with Merezhkovskii, questions persisted over the subjectivity of his approach and his efforts to construct

28 Fateev, *S russkoi bezdnoi v dushe*, p. 390.

29 See *Religiozno-filosofskoe obshchestvo v Peterburge 1907–1917. Khronika zasedanii*, ed. by A.A. Ermichev (St Petersburg: Russkii Put´, 2007), p. 4.

30 *Zapiski peterburgskikh Religiozno-filosofskikh sobranii*, p. 518.

31 Negrov, p. 114.

a new religious programme based on personal religious experience (as was the case also for Rozanov).[32]

In this essay, Rozanov takes issue with Merezhkovskii's claim that the Gospel can be interpreted culturally. Both men think that hermeneutics can open a new way to the development of civilization, but here Rozanov insists on placing the Old and New Testaments in juxtaposition. Rozanov believes that Russian society can only be renewed through a return to Old Testament principles and argues that the development of Russian civilization and the Church have diverged. This is reflected in the antagonism between their representatives, clergy and artists. He writes that there is no way that priests and writers could 'sit harmoniously around the same table, conduct pleasant conversations and drink the same, tasty, tea'. Instead, it is impossible to insert a piece of Gogol′ into any of the Gospels or Epistles of the New Testament.[33] Those who engage in culturally creative deeds cannot find a place in the Church, and likewise the clergy refuse to engage with contemporary civilization. Priests refuse to visit the theatre or read works of literature (he also argues that writers do not harbour an affection for the Church).

Having given a pessimistic appraisal of the current situation, Rozanov then turns to the explanation for this. He argues that the inevitable conflict between the modern world and contemporary Christianity comes from the imposition of an abstract spirituality. This is demonstrated by the sudden transformation of Saul of Tarsus into the Apostle Paul. There is no organic, harmonious graduation, but a sudden and violent break. As soon as Saul became Paul, he stopped going to the theatre. Paul never suggested that the Athenians continue to visit the Olympic Games. This is Rozanov's version of the reality of Shestov's choice of either Athens or Jerusalem: Rozanov rejects Merezhkovskii's proposed harmony between Christianity and civilization, as Saul and Paul 'devour each other's "self"'.[34] This antagonism is reflected in the New Testament, which for Rozanov is not an 'earthly book'. The Gospels focus on purely spiritual rewards, joys which exist only at an 'immeasurable height above the Earth and humanity'.[35] Rozanov portrays an irreconcilable difference

32 See *Religiozno-filosofskoe obshchestvo v Peterburge 1907–1917*, pp. 23–4.

33 V.V. Rozanov, 'O Sladchaishem Iisuse i gor′kikh plodakh mira', in *V temnykh religioznykh luchakh*, pp. 417–26 (p. 418).

34 Ibid., pp. 418–19.

35 Ibid.

between the Church and contemporary culture. 'There is no laughter nor [sexual] love in the Gospel, and one drop of either would burn to ashes all the pages of that mysterious book, would "tear asunder" the curtains of Christianity'.[36]

This is also an aesthetic critique of the Gospel. Rozanov believes that aesthetics and religiosity should not be in opposition, but should merge, similar to Solov′ev's aesthetic vision. But Rozanov's appreciation is highly sexual, and this becomes more pronounced when he turns to Christ. Christ is devoid of the joys of this world and never smiled. Rozanov insists that religious activity must be enjoyable in terms of the earthly pleasures it brings.[37] The question of the smiling Christ has occupied generations of theologians, and it is worth comparing Rozanov's arguments to Solov′ev's description of the human as a 'laughing animal'; Kostalevsky argues that Solov′ev associates laughter with man's ability to elevate himself above the world and 'regard it critically'.[38] Rozanov, on the other hand, understands pleasure in physical terms and sees Orthodoxy as having rejected the natural processes of this world and condemning earthly joys as sinful.

Rozanov criticizes the attempts by Merezhkovskii, other philosophers and clerics who have tried to prove that the Gospel is cultural. Former corporate attempts to critique art religiously, such as those offered in the debates of the original Religious-Philosophical Meetings or the Union of the Russian People, have failed.[39] Rozanov suggests that the interpretation of the Bible can only be conducted within the context of a new Tradition, that is within the framework of a human history which itself is the product of human creativity. (It is his rejection of the Church's definition over Tradition and his return to Scripture which led Rozanov,

36 Ibid., p. 419.

37 Nosov comments that, far from realizing a unity of Heaven and Earth within himself, Rozanov's person was disrupted by his over-bearing attraction to the world. See Sergei Nosov, *V. V. Rozanov: Estetika svobody* (St Petersburg: Izdatel′stvo 'Logos', 1993), p. 9.

38 Marina Kostalevsky, *Dostoevsky and Soloviev: The Art of Integral Vision* (New Haven: Yale University Press, 1997), p. 59. In a similar vein, Averintsev sees Bakhtin's use of laughter as an act of liberation from this world. Sergei Averintsev, 'Bakhtin, Laughter and Christian Culture', in *Bakhtin and Religion: A Feeling for Faith*, ed. by Susan M. Felch and Paul J. Contino (Evanston, Illinois: Northwestern University Press, 2001), pp. 79–96 (p. 80).

39 'O Sladchaishem Iisuse', p. 418.

and others, to refer to him as the 'Russian Luther'.[40]) As soon as Saul became Paul, in Rozanov's view, he renounced human artistic endeavours for the sake of what became his only point of reference, a 'monoflower' which makes Earthly existence redundant.

> Да, Павел трудился, ел, обонял, ходил, был в материальных условиях жизни: но он глубоко из них вышел, ибо уже ничего более *не любил* в них, ничем не любовался. Он брал материю только в необходимости и *утилитарном*, он знал и нуждался только в плоти. Христос был единственным цветком в ней; моноцветком, если позвонительно выразиться. «Я хожу, ем, сплю, вкушаю: но наслаждаюсь только Иисусом», – можно сказать о себе всякий подлинный христианин.
>
> Yes, Paul worked, ate, smelled, walked, experienced the material conditions of life: but he went far from these, for he *no longer loved* anything in them, he admired nothing. He accepted matter only as a necessity and in its *utilitarian aspect*, he knew and had needs only in the flesh. Christ was the only flower in this; a monoflower, if I can put it that way. 'I walk, eat, sleep, I consume; but only have joy in Jesus', – this is what any genuine Christian can say about themselves.[41]

Rozanov finds the root cause in Christianity's difficulties in Christ Himself. Rozanov questions why, if God has already created matter, there is a subsequent a need for a Christ. He blames Jesus for causing a disruption between the earthly and the spiritual, leading to a lack of feeling for the divine. If one focuses exclusively on the spiritual side of religion, this results in a denial of the sanctity of physical reality. The teachings of the New Testament, and by consequence of the Church, posit a division between God and matter. Christianity reframes terminology over the sensual approach to religion. Rozanov writes that Christ's 'sweetness' is a sign of His overpowering spiritual beauty, incompatible with this world, which has made the fruits of the Earth bitter by comparison.[42] Rozanov calls upon the Church to re-spiritualize matter by acknowledging the origin of the world in the First Person of the Trinity. 'The word is holy in the flesh, but holy – not in the flesh

40 Rozanov also often compared himself to the great reformer of Western Christianity and praised the German for the manner in which he personalized the individual's relationship with God and revitalized religious consciousness in Europe. See 'Na chem mozhet povernut´sia "religioznoe soznanie"?', in *Okolo narodnoi dushi*, pp. 364–74.

41 'O Sladchaishem Iisuse', pp. 418–19.

42 Ibid., p. 425.

of the Son, but in its procession from the flesh of the Father'.[43] Here Rozanov manipulates theological terminology to present his own ideas. Readers will be familiar with the word 'procession' ('iskhozhdenie') in its pneumatological sense, referring to the 'procession' of the Holy Spirit from the Father. Yet Rozanov uses this term to depict the physical means by which God marks His economy.[44]

Both Christ and the world are children of God, yet cannot be reconciled. Christ rejects the reproductive obligations placed on all creation and has disrupted the horizontal ties between man and God. The Church has exacerbated the situation by lapsing into crude anthropomorphism, depicting God as an old man and further denying His creative potential.[45] Rozanov's conclusion is that Christ has conquered the world, and as Christ represents the next world, His victory marks the victory of death over creation. Like the violent relationship between Saul and Paul, Orthodoxy has made this world and the next incompatible, leaving the Orthodox unable to participate in the dynamics of God. Rozanov presents the post-Christ-ian world as one of a fundamental conflict between the creativity of God and Christ. There is little room for compromise: Rozanov argues that 'from the Orthodox point of view, activity is impossible'.[46] Christ turns people away from earthly joys and destroys the cultural value of literature, as demonstrated by the fact that priests are not allowed to read Gogol′. In addition, Christ disrupts the meaning of the family, by encouraging men to leave their kin and to follow him.

> «Кто не оставит отца своего и мать свою ради меня» – этот глагол, позвавший Никанора и Филарета к их аскетическому обету, «ребеночка» Нехлюдова и Катерины толкнул к судьбе, рассказанной в «Воскресенье». Всякий зов, всякий идеал есть в то же время отталкивание, расторжение, разделение; и зов к детству есть отторжение от семьи, есть расторжение семьи: «в три дня разрушу *храм* сей», «истинно, истинно: *камня на камне не останется* от стен сих».
>
> 'Whoever does not leave their father and mother for my sake' – this phrase, calling Nikanor and Filaret to their vow of chastity, which decided the fate of

43 Ibid., p. 422.

44 Merezhkovskii also complains that Christianity has demolished the pagan significance of motherhood and instead has reinterpreted genesis as the act of an abstract Holy Spirit. See D. Merezhkovskii, *Taina trekh: Egipet i Vavilon* (Moscow: Respublika, 1999), p. 30.

45 'O Sladchaishem Iisuse', p. 423.

46 Ibid., p. 421.

> Nekhliudov's and Katerina's 'baby', narrated in [Tolstoi's] *Resurrection*. Each call, each ideal is at the same time a repulsion, dissolution, division; and the call to our childhood is a rejection of the family, is the dissolution of the family: 'In three days I shall bring down this *temple*', 'verily, verily: there will not be left here *one stone upon another* from these walls'.[47]

This is a reference to Christ's prophecy of the destruction of the Temple in Jerusalem, which Rozanov subverts to interpret as Jesus' destruction of Old Testament Law. Rozanov's completes his subversion of Christ's achievements, as we shall see in the final chapter, by using this reference (from Matthew 24:2) in order to describe how Jesus Himself is to blame for the sudden destruction of Russia in 1917.

Rozanov's conclusion is that humanity is not saved through Christ. The truth to his soteriology is found within God's creativity and the life of the cosmos. Rozanov makes it clear that we should look not to Christ's death and atonement, but to the life of God in our hope for resurrection: 'All nature in the image of its own being follows in the image of its own Creator. Is the day not resurrected in its morning? Is the year not resurrected in its springtime?'[48] Dostoevskii famously confessed to Natal′ia Fonvizina that if Christ was outside the truth, and 'if the truth really did exclude Christ', then he would side with Jesus.[49] Dostoevskii, like Rozanov, searched for a 'Christianity without Golgotha', a 'Christian naturalism'.[50] However, Dostoevskii clings to Christ, and such an approach appears unlikely for Rozanov. For Rozanov, a seedless and asexual Christ disrupts the divine activity. Hence, as Berdiaev concludes, for Rozanov, Christ becomes 'demonic'.[51]

One is reminded of the warnings, which have existed perhaps since the very beginning of Christianity, or longer, of a Pseudo-Christ who will appear and attempt to lead humans away from God. Some scholars believe the Antichrist is mentioned in the Old Testament, though John warns of one who would come in Jesus' name and who would be

---

47 V.V. Rozanov, 'Ob "otrechennykh", ili apokroficheskikh detiakh', in *Semeinyi vopros v Rossii*, pp. 33–52 (p. 48).

48 V.V. Rozanov, 'Smert′ i voskresenie', in *Staraia i molodaia Rossiia*, pp. 109–12 (pp. 109–10).

49 Letter to N.D. Fonvizina from January-February 1854, reprinted in Dostoevskii, XXVIII, p. 176.

50 V.V. Zen′kovskii, *Istoriia russkoi filosofii*, 2 vols (Paris: YMCA Press, 1989), I, pp. 416–17.

51 Berdiaev, 'Khristos i mir', p. 26.

received by Israel (John 5:43).[52] What makes the Antichrist so pernicious is his likeness to Christ and his ability to impersonate the messiah. Hence St Anthony the Great writes that this imposter 'hides his gall under an appearance of sweetness, so as to avoid detection, and he fabricates various illusions, beautiful to look at – which in reality are not at all what they seem – to seduce your hearts by a cunning imitation of truth'.[53] The theme of the Antichrist was pervasive in Rozanov's time, but his is a peculiar vision of Christ. Instead of positing a rival to the Son of God who dons the guise of Jesus, Rozanov does not differentiate Christ from Antichrist; Christ becomes the Antichrist who leads humanity astray through his 'sweetness'. This unique Rozanovian vision is presented not so much in terms of substance, but in activity, giving a peculiar view of evil which is posed not just ontologically, but in terms of praxis.

## Rozanov's body

If Solov´ev was to draw on Plato in his engagement with Orthodoxy, Rozanov relies on Aristotle throughout his career in order to reaffirm the value of earthly existence. (In many ways, Rozanov's revolt against Solov´ev has the same nature as Aristotle's rejection of Plato, and we note in the two Russian thinkers in many ways a repetition of the divisions in the Greeks.) Rozanov uses Aristotle's writing to engage with Orthodox theology, in particular with the division of essence and energies. Rozanov draws on Aristotelian themes of potentiality and activity, and, although this is not stated explicitly, uses these ideas to modify traditional Orthodox teaching on the karygmata. He merges aspects of Greek and Orthodox teaching (made perhaps all the more complex given Orthodox theology's drawing on Aristotle), and we end up with a type of thinking on activity which in many ways is quite different from both, and which is particularly Rozanovian.

52 Arthur W. Pink, *The Antichrist: A Systematic Study of Satan's Counterfeit Christ* (Grand Rapids, Michigan: Kregel, 1988), p. 12.

53 I have taken this passage from the *Philokalia* as quoted in Pamela Davidson, 'Divine Service or Idol Worship? Russian Views of Art as Demonic', in *Russian Literature and its Demons*, ed. by Pamela Davidson (New York: Berghahn, 2000), pp. 125–64 (p. 125). We shall return to Davidson's useful study in the final chapter in our examination of the ambiguity of the sacral nature of Russian literature as seen by Rozanov.

Aristotle views the soul not in substantive terms, but as an attribute of the body.[54] Rozanov also often leans towards this view, arguing that the soul is a property rather than a substance.[55] It is Aristotle's identification of essence and activity that appears to attract Rozanov. For Rozanov, human existence is dependent on the unity of soul and body, which is only preserved through activity.[56] Rozanov is also particularly drawn to Aristotle's use of the term 'entelecheia' as relating to the capacity for deeds and their directedness. However, Rozanov appears to present entelecheia in positive terms as it manifests the potential to create. We can assume that Rozanov appreciates this in terms of sexual longing which for him proves the immanence of the divine. Nevertheless, Rozanov places a highly positive interpretation on the ideal of potentiality, hinting at a privileging of the activity of creativity over the created act itself, a tendency which comes out more as his career develops. It is Rozanov's focus on unfulfilled potential, examined within the Godhead by Rozanov as the interaction of will and reason, which provides the basis for the creative act. For Rozanov, potential is highly important, but it must be realized through a type of stomatization which is understood sexually. Potential must be practised. Here we see Rozanov's alignment with radical thinkers, especially for example Dobroliubov, who saw in Oblomov an expression of the wider Russian inability to realize one's potential and the need for Russians to engage their skills for the social good.[57]

Of course, Rozanov must also contend with the division of spirit and body posited by Christian theology. The flesh is considered the locus where the soul is held in torment until the next life. In seeing this world as the battlefield between the divine and the demonic, Christianity identifies the tension in the human person as a microcosm of that struggle. These

54 Here I concur with what appears to be the dominant view in scholarship on Aristotle. Herbert Granger, *Aristotle's Idea of the Soul* (Dordrecht: Kluwer Academic, 1996), p. 15.

55 V.V. Rozanov, *Opavshie list'ia: Korob pervyi*, in *Religiia i kul'tura*, ed. by E.V. Vitkovskii et al., pp. 249–403 (pp. 351, 374). Aristotle defines the soul in terms of its potential for activity, the first principle that defines the action of the thing. Aristotle, *On the Soul II*, 412b1–25. Here taken from the translation by Thomas Taylor (Frome: Prometheus Trust, 2003).

56 Any divorce of the soul from the body is seen as an illness. Quoted in Fateev, *S russkoi bezdnoi v dushe*, p. 464.

57 See N.A. Dobroliubov, 'Chto takoe oblomovshchina', in *Sobranie sochinenii v trekh tomakh*, 3 vols (Moscow: Khudozhestvennaia literatura, 1987), II, pp. 218–57.

platonic trends in Christianity were developed by St Paul, who sees the affairs of the flesh as inherently sinful and the soul as the medium for human soteriology (Romans 5:7).[58] Paul states that the body is merely a temporary shelter for the soul and that 'when we are at home in the body we are away from the Lord' (II Corinthians 10:1).[59] For Rozanov, life is the preservation of the unity of flesh and spirit. The soul is the life principle of the person, the person's 'transcendent side', or the 'transcendent noumen of the body'.[60] These parts of the person must work in harmony for religious activity to have a wider cosmological implication for the unity of Heaven and Earth.[61] In terms of the Orthodox theology discussed by Zizioulas, Rozanov attempts to reunite the concepts of person and substance and reaffirm the human being as a whole. Lossky points out that the Greek Fathers distinguished between hypostasis and substance in the same way that they distinguished the particular from the universal. 'The genius of the Fathers made use of the two common synonyms to distinguish in God that which is common – ousia, substance or essence – from that which is particular – *ὑπόστασις* or person.'[62] In striving to reunite the person with its nature, Rozanov uses the body to affirm the physical connection between the individual and the absolute.

Contemporary critics have referred to Rozanov's as a 'monist' theory of the person.[63] This is useful, but does not take into full account Rozanov's reference to activity, particularly sexual activity. Although Rozanov does not provide a clear systematic definition of the soul or its role, he does tell us that the relationship with God is built on participation and involvement, rather than pure contemplation, and sex is a vital method to participate in God. Here it becomes clearer how Rozanov uses ancient philosophy to modify Orthodox theology;

---

58 *The Oxford Companion to the Bible*, ed. by Bruce M. Metzger and Michael D. Coogan (New York/Oxford: Oxford University Press, 1993), p. 296.

59 Frank Bottomley, *Attitudes to the Body in Western Christendom* (London: Lepus Books, 1979), p. 36.

60 V.V. Rozanov, 'Po povodu odnogo stikhotvoreniia Lermontova', in *Vo dvore iazychnikov*, pp. 313–21 (p. 320).

61 V.V. Rozanov, 'Nechto iz tumana "obrazov" i "podobii" (Po povodu "Bessmertnykh voprosov" Gatchinskogo Otshel´nika)', in *V mire neiasnogo i nereshennogo*, pp. 287–317 (p. 302).

62 Lossky, *The Mystical Theology of the Eastern Church*, p. 51.

63 See Efim Kurganov, *Vasilii Rozanov, evrei i russkaia religioznaia filosofiia*, in Efim Kurganov and Genrietta Mondri, *Rozanov i evrei* (St Petersburg: Akademicheskii proekt, 2000), pp. 5–143 (p. 56).

Rozanov argues that sex is the soul. This makes the soul highly personal and avoids its presentation in abstract terms. For Rozanov, the soul is tangible and has an aroma.[64] Hence this is a more nuanced and personal depiction of Aristotle's soul, in which the organizing principle also requires embodiment for affirmation and in turn presents the reality of creation. Like the body, Rozanov's soul is given through creation and intimately linked with the divine. Therefore there is no discussion of an afterlife. As each individual is a constituent part of creation, our minds are unable to affect the division of self and object which would permit the consideration of unworldly events or phenomena. Rozanov cannot consider the soul as separable from the body, or even as being immortal. We can concede that there might be life after the grave, but we are unable to contemplate it. Despite some affinity with the neo-Kantians, Rozanov does not find recourse to Kant's assertion in the intellectual necessity of heavenly existence.

Rozanov has to overcome the abstract demands of Greek philosophy and Orthodox theology by enabling a personal and dynamic link between the person and God. This comes out more in the work of this middle period, where we see that his idea of the soul as the living, vital element associated with life and blood, is close to the Hebrew concept of 'nepash'. There is a definite opposition to the abstract Greek notion of the 'psyche', with its reference to souls that have become cold in their fall from the Godhead. Rozanov presents an artistic description of the soul which is poetic and intimately linked with the functions of the body. Feeling is the primary source of religious experience, and therefore one must reject Volzhskii's contention that Rozanov is relying on a mystical 'sixth sense' to experience the divine.[65] Instead, Rozanov uses all the five bodily senses (primarily those usually considered baser senses, touch and smell) to relate to the holiness of the world. He rejects Orthodox teaching which states that man enters into communion with God through the mind and spirit. Dionysius had written that the intellect (υούς) is initially involved in the movement to God; even the act of negating the initial positive assertions about God is cognitive.[66] It is only at the final stage of perfection that the mind goes beyond concepts to

64 'Ogni sviashchennye', p. 238.

65 Volzhskii, 'Misticheskii panteizm V.V. Rozanova', in *Vasilii Rozanov: Pro et Contra*, I, pp. 418–55 (p. 444).

66 Rorem, pp. 239–40.

unite with 'Him who is beyond understanding'.[67] In apophatic theology, the symbols of this world, especially the body, are denied in order to reach a form of religious ecstasy (the word itself derives from the ancient Greek *ekstas*, meaning to stand outside oneself).[68] In contrast, Rozanov believes that man can only know God though physical activity, hence his call for the Church to cultivate a 'cult of the body'.[69]

Rozanov describes himself as a realist, as Dostoevskii had done a generation previously. Rozanov's writings are filled with descriptions of physical relationships between people and animals. Two people in love with each other feel each other's souls.[70] Animals should be stroked and caressed. The beauty of nature and life inspires Rozanov to pray and a worshipper must possess this religious feeling before he can worship.[71] For this reason Rosenthal terms Rozanov a 'biological mystic'.[72] But there is a deeper theological reason for the positive descriptions of God and the world in his writings; the physical aspects of Rozanov's philosophy help draw God to Earth. There are parallels in Orthodox theology; Maxim the Confessor wrote that apophatic theology affirms God as spirit and cataphatic theology affirms God as flesh.

> If you theologize in an affirmative or cataphatic manner, starting from positive statements about God, you make the Word flesh, for you have no other means of

67 Timothey, p. 9.

68 Rozanov was not the only thinker to fear that the apophatic tendency of Orthodoxy could easily lead to atheism. It is only a short step from recognizing the impossibility of knowing God, to the belief that God does not exist at all. Berdiaev warned in his *Vekhi* article that the Russian populace would turn its back on God if the Church did not engage with the world. See N.A. Berdiaev, 'Filosofskaia istina i intelligentskaia pravda,' in N.A. Berdiaev et al., *Vekhi: Sbornik statei o russkoi intelligentsii* (Sverdlovsk: Izdatel´stvo Ural´skogo universiteta, 1991), pp. 6–25 (pp. 12–13). In similar fashion, Epstein saw the origins of Soviet atheism as lying in the Russian apophatic tradition. See Mikhail Epstein, 'Post-Atheism: From Apophatic Theology to "Minimal Religion"', in Mikhail Epstein et al., *Russian Postmodernism: New Perspectives on Post-Soviet Culture*, trans. and ed. by Slobodanka Vladiv-Glover (New York: Berghahn, 1999), pp. 345–93 (p. 351).

69 V.V. Rozanov, 'S.F. Sharapovu, napomnivshemu slova: "Mogii vmestiti – da vmestit", in *V mire neiasnogo i nereshennogo*, pp. 280–3 (p. 282).

70 'Psikhologiia russkogo raskola', p. 52.

71 V.V. Rozanov, 'V chem raznitsa drevnego i novogo mirov', in *Vo dvore iazychnikov*, pp. 231–6 (p. 236).

72 Bernice Glatzer Rosenthal, *Dmitri Sergeevich Merezhkovsky and the Silver Age* (The Hague: Nijhoff, 1975), p. 73.

> knowing God as cause except from what is visible and tangible. If you theologize in a negative or apophatic manner, by the stripping away of positive attributes, you make the Word spirit as being in the beginning God and with God.[73]

This is one of the foundations of Orthodox worship, the unity of the mystical and the ascetic, which enables a connection between the person and the universal. This is where Rozanov rejects the reliance on the monastic approach, as well as the abstract social-mindedness of Solov´ev. Solov´ev was motivated by the Taboric body, the new body of Christ or the Second Adam, quite different from the human body as it is now. Rozanov worships the energies (sex) which point to the immanence of God. This explains his criticism of Solov´ev's celibacy, a mark of his detachment from this world, despite his emphasis on Christianity's social mission. For Rozanov, God can be described in earthly terms, and his work contains many affirmative comments about God. He labels God sometimes a scarab beetle, sometimes a spider. The world is God's home. It is this use of cataphatic theology, often couched in domestic terminology, that enables Rozanov to ensure that the communion between man and God is embodied, and justifiable only though pantheism.

Iconography helps explain the basis of Rozanov's thought, though he subverts the theological base for this and opens the way for a specific type of organic dogmatics. Rozanov believes that every idea is an icon ('obraz') that longs to be born to find its expression in matter.[74] Traditionally, the use of Orthodox icons is based on the Incarnation. Icons, like Christ, are made up of the divine and the material. The term is derived from the Greek for image (εἰκών), and refers to the belief that man is made in the image and likeness of God. Orthodox prayers are directed towards the icon and help us participate in the life of Christ.[75] The veneration of icons has been a major area of theological discord between the Eastern and Western Churches and has occupied the central point of several Ecumenical Councils, heresies and schisms. The Eighth Ecumenical Council of 869–870 confirmed that icons should have the same status as Scripture, that is they should be considered a 'Bible for the unlettered'.[76]

73 Quoted in Andrew Louth, *Maximus the Confessor* (London: Routledge, 1996), p. 53.

74 *O ponimanii*, p. 305.

75 Myroslaw Tataryn, *How to Pray With Icons: An Introduction* (Toronto: Novalis, 1998), pp. 5–6.

76 Leonid Ouspensky, *Theology of the Icon*, trans. by Anthony Gythiel, 2 vols (New York: St Vladimir's Seminary Press, 1992), II, p. 213.

The key justification behind the icon is that the Incarnation shows how humans can worship the human form of God. God's appearance as Jesus on Earth overrides Moses' Second Commandment on worshipping idols. The practice of venerating icons might go back to the lifetime of Christ Himself. (During His passion, Christ was given a cloth to wipe His face, which was marked with the image of His countenance.) Uspenskii and Losskii suggest that icons of Christ could have existed during His own lifetime. The woman with a haemorrhage whom Jesus healed (Matthew 9:20–23) reportedly erected a statue to Him. So Christianity is not only the revelation of the Word of God, but the revelation of His image.[77] This is an important aspect of Rozanov's project, though he sees parity in the word and God as coming from the start of time. Activity and participation stand at the centre of Orthodox worship, and the icon stands at the point where the activities of God and the human are brought together. Hutchings makes the point that, unlike the English word 'image', which implies a static representation, the icon contains the concept of dynamism.[78] Worshipping an icon is not contemplation, but involves deification through participation in divine activity: '*Seeing* (recognition) is inseparable from *action* (becoming)', and this prepares the way 'for the full integration of aesthetics (vision, likeness, image) and ethics (participation)'.[79]

This iconic notion of participation becomes important to Rozanov. This also has an ethical dimension, revealed through his writings on the Eucharist and in particular in his debates with Ivan Romanov (using the pseudonym Gatchinskii Otshel′nik). Romanov argues that the intestine is an empty vessel through which the Eucharist bread passes; the body becomes merely the container to accept the Holy Gifts, and there is no unison of the Eucharist with the body.[80] Rozanov argues that Romanov's theories imply the separateness of man and God. If one sees the way the body holds the Bread in a similar way as to how a purse contains gold, as Romanov does, then Rozanov argues that once the money is removed, one is left with an empty and valueless purse.[81] Rozanov concedes that the Liturgy and the Eucharist perform an important function in shaping

77 Leonid Ouspensky and Vladimir Lossky, *The Meaning of Icons* (Olton: Urs Graf-Verlag, 1952), pp. 27, 49.
78 Hutchings, *Russian Modernism*, p. 29.
79 Ibid., pp. 29–30.
80 'Nechto iz tumana "obrazov" i "podobii"', p. 287.
81 Ibid., pp. 287, 289.

religious feeling.[82] But this has to be physical; Rozanov insists that the intestines act on the Eucharist bread in the same way that sexual organs come into contact with each other.[83] His desire to unite the substance of the human being with his hypostasis means that man's 'ontological principle', to use Zizioulas' term, is located firmly within his nature. The ontological principle is supposed to mirror that of God, which Rozanov believes is the principle to reproduce. God's creative ability is presented in sexual terms, and our ontology is based on our ability to mirror this creative principle through our own sexual production.

In Christianity, the Eucharist is initially presented precisely as bread and wine, which our bodily senses perceive as existing as such in this world. During the liturgical process, however, the offerings are transmuted into the body and blood of Christ. However, we are unable to sense with our body the Eucharist as the body of Christ – the sacrifice becomes Christ's body only on a metaphysical level. In fact, if the sacrifice does literally turn into flesh and blood, we are required to put the Eucharist aside until it reconverts to bread and wine.[84] The way the Orthodox approaches the Eucharist, therefore, exemplifies the division between the physical and the metaphysical. This division corresponds to the gulf between the earthly and the heavenly, underlining the suggestion that the body relates to the Earth and therefore cannot be saved. As theories of the Eucharist were advanced in the third and fourth centuries, theologians encouraged believers to develop their 'spiritual senses', which existed alongside, but which were superior to, their five physical senses. Although we see and touch the bread and wine, our spiritual senses are required by an act of faith to understand the Eucharist as Christ's body. As Frank explains, these theories were first put forward by the heretic Origen, but were developed by Orthodox teachers, such as Cyril of Jerusalem and Bishop Ambrose of Milan.[85] Such teachings further emphasized the privileging of the soul over the body in Orthodox worship. Frank writes that 'true

---

82 'Nechto o prekrasnoi prirode', in *Vo dvore iazychnikov*, pp. 331–5 (p. 334).

83 'Nechto iz tumana "obrazov" i "podobii"', p. 289.

84 Although Sergii Bulgakov is more rightly seen as someone who favoured the development of religious philosophy, he provides an excellent description of 'traditional' Orthodox theology regarding the approach to the Eucharist. Sergius Bulgakov, *The Holy Grail and the Eucharist*, trans. and ed. by Boris Jakim (New York: Lindisfarne, 1997), pp. 65–7.

85 Georgia Frank, '"Taste and See": The Eucharist and the Eyes of Faith in the Fourth Century', *The American Society of Church History*, 70 (2001), 619–43 (636).

contemplation [...] meant shutting down the eyes of the body in order to see with the eyes of the soul'. No wonder, then, that Origen could insist 'we have no need of a body to know God', since the 'mind alone with the spiritual sense would suffice'.[86]

According to Orthodox teaching, the Eucharist liberates the individual from genealogical links with his relatives by drawing a distinction between the concepts of hypostasis and ousia. Orthodox faith holds that when the human is seen in terms of his biology, what Zizioulas terms his 'biological hypostasis', this can only reaffirm his mortality. If man bases his existence purely on the sexual act which led to his own conception and birth, then his ontological nature 'precedes the person and dictates its laws'. Hence Orthodox thinkers link the biological urge with death, as it places the ontological necessity of the person above his ontological freedom.[87] Zizioulas insists that man must be freed from the body. Otherwise, the individual will prioritize his familial relations over his spiritual commitments.

> When a man loves a biological hypostasis, he inevitably excludes others: the family has priority over 'strangers', the husband lays exclusive claim to the love of his wife – facts altogether understandable and 'natural' for the biological hypostasis. For a man to love someone who is not a member of his family *more* than his own relations constitutes a transcendence of the exclusiveness which is present in the biological hypostasis.[88]

Rozanov does not see in the Eucharist the liberation of the person from its nature and, instead of seeing the Eucharist as vital in the establishment of an Orthodox community, reinterprets this as a proof of the physical relationship with God. However, Rozanov's method of achieving this is to focus on the body and its sexual activity. In order to do this, Rozanov must separate the significance of Christianity, or Russian Orthodoxy, from Christ, an issue which brings him into conflict with Berdiaev.

The body appears to have disappeared for long periods from Christian thinking. There is an overriding thought that the body does not matter

86 Ibid., 627.
87 Fedorov also linked the sexual act with death. Fedorov believed that man could only become immortal when he ceased producing future generations of humans. Hence he links the birth of a new generation with death, where Rozanov associates this with immortality. See for example Nikolai Fedorov, *Filosofiia obshchego dela* (Moscow: Eksmo, 2008) pp. 105–6.
88 Zizioulas, p. 57. Italics in original.

in Christian worship, that our relationship with God is purely spiritual and can only be perfected after death. Of course, Christianity in its various forms has adopted certain aspects of platonic thought. The Desert Fathers, whose writings had a great influence on Russian spirituality, based their belief on practically the entire rejection of the physical. This view, of Christianity being hostile to the flesh, is one that dominates Rozanov's often stereotyped appraisal of Christianity.[89] However, modern scholarship has started to scratch the surface of this preconception that the body does not matter to Christians. An increasing amount of work demonstrates that the body has played an important role in periods of Christian worship, from its early days to the intimate writings about Jesus which emerged in the medieval period.[90]

## Rozanov and philosophy's engagement with Orthodoxy

In appraising his place in the canon of established Russian philosophers, Rozanov is often considered in individual terms and hence difficult to categorize, as opposed to perhaps the more important and influential thinkers such as Khomiakov, Solov´ev, or Berdiaev, whose thought scholars have succeeded in presenting in more general, systematic terms. Much of this is Rozanov's own doing, and his deliberately provocative comments do not make it easier to contextualize his work. His antagonistic relationship with Russian philosophy in general is epitomized in his difficult intercourse with Solov´ev. Indeed, Solov´ev's criticism of Rozanov's subjectivity must have shaped the problems subsequent readers have had in drawing out universal themes, especially in presenting a wider vision of the concept of freedom. Solov´ev criticized

89 Despite his profound knowledge of Christian theology, Rozanov is often guilty of exaggerating his arguments; Berdiaev accused him of presenting a caricature of Orthodoxy. Berdiaev, 'Khristos i mir', p. 28. Tareev concurs. Tareev, p. 68. Copleston argues that both Rozanov and Leont´ev exaggerate the importance of monasticism in Orthodoxy, though notes that both thinkers end up with opposing evaluations. Copleston, *Philosophy in Russia*, p. 194.

90 See for example Patricia Cox Miller, 'Visceral Seeing: The Holy Body in Late Ancient Christianity', *Journal of Early Christian Studies*, 12 (2004), 391–411 (p. 393). Another useful modern study on the sensual in Christianity is Susan Ashbrook Harvey, *Scenting Salvation: Ancient Christianity and the Olfactory Imagination* (Berkeley: University of California Press, 2006).

Rozanov for the latter's highly subjective definition of the term and his inability to transfer his intense subjectivism to the level of the objective. For Solov´ev, Rozanov's personalism exists for itself, ignoring the wider communion of the Church. As a result, Solov´ev concludes that Rozanov favours religious tolerance only for his own philosophy and not for that of others.[91]

An important turn in Russian thought around this time had been an investigation of how to make the specific general, which some thinkers had encapsulated in terms of a national philosophy. This is closely tied with the developing theories of opening out the universal mission of the Russian man, and Russian messianism (which Rozanov largely rejected) and the themes expounded by Dostoevskii in his famous Pushkin memorial speech of 1880 (which Rozanov did not attend). There is a reverse trend in Rozanov, a receptiveness to the ideas of different philosophers and theologians which Rozanov absorbs and makes national. This is shown in his admiration for Aleksandr Ivantsov-Platonov, professor of church history at Moscow University, 'a man of European science' who is also able to assimilate elements of European thought into his Russian character. Ivantsov-Platonov embodies a rare combination of Russian geniality for Rozanov, 'a direct relationship to the act' with a European approach to knowledge and a detached interest in the world.[92]

The question of assimilating a foreign type of thinking is important, especially as Rozanov attributes his country's spiritual malaise to its appropriation of a foreign religion. Rozanov's stance towards Western patterns of thought, for an often antagonistic thinker, is surprisingly more positive than that displayed by many of his peers (although in his readiness to adapt foreign patterns of thinking to a Russian environment he takes the lead from Strakhov). Surveying the landscape of Russian philosophy up to the time of Solov´ev, Rozanov perceives a wider despair among his predecessors with the state of Russian thought. He argues that Giliarov-Platonov and Samarin both agree with Ivantsov-Platonov's view that Russian thought 'had gone no further' than presenting borrowed composites of the ideas of Western thinkers. Explaining this, Rozanov

91 Solov´ev, 'Porfirii Golovlev o svobode i vere', pp. 286–8. Merezhkovskii and Filosofov both shared Solov´ev's contention that Rozanov could not synthesize his understanding of the person with that of the wider community. Rosenthal provides a comparison of Merezhkovskii and Rozanov in this context, pp. 72–3.

92 V.V. Rozanov, 'Ob odnoi osobennoi zasluge Vl. S. Solov´eva', in *Okolo tserkovnykh sten*, pp. 432–41 (pp. 432).

quotes Lopatin's assessment of Solov´ev's contribution: 'He (Solov´ev) was the first of us to study the *themes* or the *subjects of philosophy itself*, rather than the opinions of Western philosophers about these themes; and this is how he became the first Russian philosopher'.[93]

Rozanov finds Lopatin's analysis highly useful. He argues that until Solov´ev, the Russian 'philosopher' had displayed no interest in 'subjects', despite his soulless and encyclopaedic knowledge of the 'opinions' of every philosopher from Thales to the present day. Rozanov's criticism is clear: Russian philosophy has occupied itself with simply gathering and learning about the writings of Western thinkers, rather than with formulating a Russian type of thinking about the world. (This desire to get to the substance of things seems to parallel Rozanov's apparent desire to get beyond the energies of God to His essence.) There is a further implication in Rozanov's thought, in that by rejecting Plato, Rozanov is deliberately reacting against a trend in European philosophy which has tried to negate the world itself.

Returning to Ivantsov-Platonov and Giliarov-Platonov (as well as Samarin) and their lament over the inability of philosophers to come down to Earth, Rozanov identifies a parallel trend in Russian theology and literature. There is a tight relationship that Rozanov posits here between the various disciplines, but he believes that all these fields share a common task in examining the truth of physical reality. It is right for the Russians to adopt some of the techniques of Western thinkers, as Russia requires a way of inquiring into the nature of reality, but this must be made native and firmly embedded in reality. This demand is in marked contrast to examples Rozanov cites of theological examinations, especially in the Eastern Christian tradition. Rozanov quotes at length a passage from an article by Boris Turaev in *Pravoslavnaia bogoslovskaia entsiklopediia* on the Abyssinian Church and its polemics over monophysitism. Rozanov is astonished that the Abyssinians could devote three church councils to the exact nature of Christ's divinity, whether He was born three times (once literally from Mary and twice spiritually from God the Father and by the Holy Spirit), and the exact nature of His experience as a human inside Mary's womb. There is a certain amount of posturing here, given Rozanov's own detailed attention to issues of theology, yet he refuses to see any connection between formal Christology and the practical implications of Christian life. Rozanov implies a link between the abstract debates noted above and the

93 Rozanov's quote of Lopatin. Ibid., p. 433.

irrelevance of thinking about Christ. Other examples of Christological worship, such as how to spell 'Iisus' or how many times the Orthodox worshipper should cross themselves, are likewise dismissed as 'banalities' which have no relevance to a 'national character' or 'the interests of everyday life'.[94]

There is a certain parallel in Rozanov's argumentation with Khoruzhii's description of energetic discourse (which examines 'experience', desires and impulses) and essential discourse (which involves discussions of substances and pure facts).[95] Rozanov pushes the debate over what the subject of philosophy should be from pure existence to an examination of life in all its facets. Rozanov appears to suggest that, in opposition to the strict division in formal Orthodoxy, there is in fact a coincidence in essence and energy, that life cannot be stripped of its debt to the work of God or of its obligation to reciprocate. A phenomenon can only be understood in terms of its contribution to perpetuating the divine work on Earth. The implications of this identity of essence and energy might also be appropriate in Rozanov's understanding of the relationship between history and mythology, which appears to have relevance for his Egyptian studies.

This link between God and life, understood by Rozanov in terms of directed activity, is what Rozanov terms 'religio', that is 'the "tie" of human with God'.[96] The failure of Eastern theologians to examine phenomena is for Rozanov one of the causes of Russia's spiritual malaise, as the foundation of the Russian state coincided with the discovery of the West's preoccupation with ideas, especially the artificial notion of sin which impedes a direct relationship with God. 'Our kingdom was born: but it thought nothing about God, but only about these Greek thoughts of god, fearing to copy them inaccurately, and rejoicing when the copy came out exactly.'[97] Here again Rozanov's preoccupation is with how thought is transferred onto the Russian land, but the consequence of this emphasis on ideas about God means that the Russian has been left with no real feeling for God Himself, leading to atheism. Although religion is higher than philosophy and literature, Rozanov writes, theology, which holds the real potential to raise the nation's strength, must assume these other disciplines' focus on '*genuine* Russian reality', on 'the

94 Ibid., p. 434.
95 Khoruzhii, p. 10.
96 'Ob odnoi osobennoi zasluge Vl. S. Solov´eva', p. 434.
97 Ibid., p. 435.

substantial interests of Russia'.[98] This is, Rozanov argues, Solov´ev's true contribution, that alongside Samarin and Khomiakov, he acted as an 'icebreaker' of religious formalism and turned the attention of Russian thinkers to things themselves.[99] Here also Rozanov suggests a certain history of uniquely Russian religious thought, running from Avvakum through Solov´ev to himself, in an attempt to restore 'the old Russian faith' in the face of 'the Greek old faith'. Rozanov resurrects Solov´ev's question, in that if it was acceptable for the Byzantines to ask how they could find a specifically Greek religiosity, it is not enough for the Russian to be simply a Christian, but should be also 'by faith a Russian'.[100]

In trying to reconnect religious faith with nationality, Rozanov places himself in stark opposition to his friend Leont´ev, who rejected an exclusively Russian religion in favour of pan-Orthodoxy.[101] There is a distinct separation which Rozanov picks up on between theology and anthropology. The laws of the Church have been laid down abstractly and do not account for the earthly life of man. This mirrors Rozanov's complaint that Orthodoxy is based on knowledge, rather than on facts. St Paul's claim that 'the law is spiritual, but I am carnal' (Romans 7:14–24) only appears to reinforce the separation of dogma from body. Florenskii also noted the tendency in Orthodoxy to posit two principles in opposition to one another, the dogmatic and the earthly. He speaks of two dogmas, one of God and the other of creation, both of which can be unified only through the triunity of God. For Florenskii, it is the Christological basis of the Trinity that provides the base for theology, philosophy and science. The tension between Orthodox dogma and lived experience as examined by nineteenth- and early twentieth-century thinkers has become a rich field of study and has provided the basis of useful works by scholars such as Meerson and Valliere. One important issue both discuss here is the 'anthropological paradigm shift' which has informed perspectives on how Orthodoxy might be reconciled to modernity. Valliere speaks of a renewed theology that takes as its starting point 'not revelatory tradition alone but the complicated dialogue between tradition and human experience'.[102] Feodor provides a nice anthropological twist to the

98 Ibid.
99 Ibid., p. 436.
100 Ibid., p. 440.
101 Konstantin Leont´ev, 'Vizantizm i slavianstvo', in *Vizantizm i slavianstvo* (Moscow: Izdatel´stvo 'AST', 2007), pp. 145–308.
102 Valliere, *Modern Russian Theology*, p. 3.

question of how doctrine should engage with modern life. For Rozanov, though, there is more to Feodor than just his writings, as attention must be paid to his deeds. One of the reasons for Rozanov's deep admiration for Bukharev was his decision to leave the priesthood and marry. (It is not surprising that Rozanov later engaged Bukharev's widow in an intimate correspondence, as Rozanov was highly interested in the marital lives of his idols, such as the relations between Tolstoi and his wife, and of course between Dostoevskii and Suslova.)

For Rozanov and his peers, it was no longer enough for Russian society to adhere to dogma. Florenskii's 'experiential dogmatics' have been examined by Valliere.[103] Rozanov and Florenskii in fact stand in the tradition initiated by Chaadaev, that is the attempt to reconcile historical consciousness with the permanent tenets of Christianity. As noted in the previous chapter, Chaadaev advocated the assimilation of a historical vision into the patterns of family life. Rozanov takes this further and adopts a literal truth, the need for religious truth to be modified through bodily experience. In addition, Rozanov believes that the method of transmitting religion is the same as the content of that religion itself.

Despite arguments investigated in the previous chapter that the apophatic tradition encouraged a distinction of history from salvation in Russian thought, there is a thread of scholarship that has conversely argued that the Christological experience can bridge the gap between history and redemption. However, as Prishvin noted, Rozanov did not take Communion,[104] and there is no account of him participating in hesychasm (although his eldest daughter Tat′iana loved the *Otkrovennye rasskazy strannika*). These two elements, the Eucharistic and the hesychastic, are probably not in opposition with one another, resting as they do on the theology of Christ's Incarnation. However Khoruzhii makes explicit the body's experience in history through its transfiguration, reversing the stance that hesychasm marks the body's retreat from history.[105]

---

103 See Paul Valliere, 'The Theology of Culture in Late Imperial Russia', in *Sacred Stories: Religion and Spirituality in Modern Russia*, ed. by Mark D. Steinberg and Heather J. Coleman (Bloomington: Indiana University Press, 2007), pp. 377–95.

104 Prishvin recalls that Rozanov only finally agreed to take the Eucharist once he realized that he was dying. M.M. Prishvin, 'O V.V. Rozanove (Iz "Dnevnika")', in *Vasilii Rozanov: Pro et Contra*, I, pp. 103–31 (p. 117).

105 Khoruzhii discusses theosis through hesychasm as 'an experientially achievable reality'. Khoruzhii, p. 25.

It is a peculiar form of faith in which Rozanov attempts to bridge the gap between Orthodox dogma and the need for a contemporary, national religious experience. Biology and dogma can only be reconciled through an understanding that dogma in the formal Orthodox mode is Christological and requires a certain modification.[106] Rozanov was doubtlessly inspired, perhaps even directly, by Samarin's focus on freedom and his belief that this can only be achieved through a rethinking of dogma. Samarin insists that the 'church is not doctrine or an institution, but an organism of the truth [istiny]'.[107] This is similar to Solov´ev's view of dogma as organic, sharing in the nature of Godmanhood, though Rozanov finds a different theological basis for this.

This is the tension between the anthropological and the doctrinal which becomes prominent in the nineteenth century and which Rozanov adapts. Where his peers use the organic as a metaphor for the development of religious thinking, Rozanov uses the body as a literal model for this. Specifically, he uses the Russian body. Although in *O ponimanii* Rozanov made a distinction between the idea and the body, while preserving the link between the two, we do note a burgeoning interest in embodied experience as mediating between thought and life. 'Reason [razum] is potential being, but it cannot cross into real being without joining itself to something to provide it with reality'.

> Процесс образования полного понимании неизменно и вечно слагается из соединения идущего от разума с идущим из природы, т.е. из умозрения и опыта, а самое понимание, как результат этого процесса, возникает через соприкосновение чувственных впечатлений, получаемых в опыте от мира вещей, с абстрактною сущностью самого разума, пробуждающеюся к жизни в умозрении.
>
> The process of the formulation of full understanding is invariably and eternally composed of the union of that which proceeds from reason with that which proceeds from nature, i.e. from speculation and experience; and understanding itself, as a result of this process, arises through the contact of sense

106 In Christianity, and in Orthodoxy especially, dogma is Christological: 'Christology is the sole starting point for a Christian understanding of truth'. Zizioulas, p. 67.

107 Iu.F. Samarin, 'Programma predisloviia ko II tomu sochinenii A.S. Khomiakova', in *Slavianofil´stvo: Pro et Contra. Tvorchestvo i deiatel´nost´ slavianofilov v otsenke russkikh myslitelei i issledovatelei*, ed. by V.A. Fateev (St Petersburg: Izdatel´stvo Russkogo Khristianskogo gumanitarnoi akademii, 2006), pp. 60–5 (p. 63).

> impressions received from the world of phenomena with the abstract essence of reason itself, brought to life through speculation.[108]

Although in his very first work he reserves a special place for the beauty of the ideal as provided by religious dogma,[109] Rozanov leaves a gap for bodily experience, especially its creative work, to build on this. This reaffirms the unity of phenomena by acknowledging a common origin in the Creator. Of course, there is a hint of Kant's antinomial negotiation between faith and reason here, in that this is a considered reliance on God specifically as Creator. However, despite Rozanov's desire to tackle the Church hierarchy's hold over dogma, Rozanov maintains a specifically dogmatic type of approach to Biblical truths. He appreciates the need shown by others to reconcile Church teaching with modern life, while rejecting the basis of their approach and providing his own method of reconciling dogma with modernity.

Rozanov's approach is demonstrated in a 1908 article written for *Russkoe Slovo*, partly as a response to personal attacks on Metropolitan Antonii by the Union of the Russian People which had appeared in various journals; Antonii had been criticized for his introverted character and his stubborn refusal to engage more actively with the realities of modern Russian life. Rozanov was also writing in response to Nikita Griniakin, prominent theologian and a senior member of staff at Vasilii Skvortsov's *Missionerskoe Obozrenie*. In his article 'O deistvennosti tserkovnykh kanonov', which appeared in the December 1906 edition of *Missionerskoe Obozrenie*, Griniakin accused senior clergy of losing sight of Church doctrine and of ignoring the *Kormchaia Kniga*, the book of Church teachings and decrees given to Russia by Byzantium. (Griniakin frequently sparred with Rozanov on theological matters, and aroused widespread criticism for his intellectual pretentions.) Rozanov responded to Griniakin by contending that Church teaching should return to the basics of God's teaching. In his article, Rozanov also demonstrates his knowledge of church officials and their deeds throughout history and discusses in detail the work of Archbishop Antonii of Volynsk, Nikon of Vologod and Iliodor.

Rozanov criticizes the 'conservative' Griniakin for calling in his article for 'a review of church laws which have "ceased to be", but about which the Church has not spoken out'. According to Rozanov, Griniakin accepts

108 *O ponimanii*, p. 63.
109 Ibid., pp. 531–2.

that 'the new life has met with the old practice. *The former demands recognition of its rights, the latter silently points to the anathemas that protect its inviolability*. And both are correct'.[110] Rozanov acknowledges Griniakin's attempts to bring these two aspects together, though at the same time he criticizes Griniakin's searching for a resolution within ecclesiastical history itself, and especially in the Church Councils, when the answer should be found directly in God's commands. Rozanov also reprimands Griniakin for his mocking of Antonii, and responds to irony with irony.

> Для всякого читателя со стороны, для г. Гринякина, для «Миссионерского Обозрения», для всех совершенно ясно, что дело заключается не в живой жизни, которая изменялась и двигалась, понеже Бог велел всему «раститися и множитися»: индивидуумам это повелел, и их сцеплению – жизни, быту, цивилизации, всему.
>
> It is completely clear to every reader from the outside, to Mr Griniakin, to *Missionerskoe Obozrenie*, to everybody, that the issue is not about living life, which changes and progresses, for God ordered everything 'to grow and multiply': He ordered this to individuals, and to their bond to each other – life, *byt*, civilization, everything.[111]

The solution should be found in life itself as a dynamic response to God's creativity. However, for Rozanov is it not enough simply to live. This is not a free, symbol-less type of religiosity as advocated by Tareev or the irrational kind of religious response found in Shestov. Faith for Rozanov must be rooted in the Bible, but specifically in the Old Testament, not Christologically. This is a peculiar type of restorative approach to religion from Rozanov, in that all faith must be founded firmly in the commandments given at the very start of Bible. Immediately after God created the Earth, He ordered man to grow and multiply, and the relationship between divine action and divine command should be the foundation on which we subsequently build our understanding of religion, as well as our obligation to act on Earth. 'The *growth* of all earthly history is determined, foretold, and consecrated by the creativity of the divine blessing: "grow, multiply"'.[112]

This might allow Orthodoxy room in which to develop its teaching. However, once Rozanov has attacked the formal Church's authority over

110 Quoted in V.V. Rozanov, 'Mitropolit Antonii v sovremennoi smute', in *V nashei smute*, pp. 43–52 (p. 48). Emphasis in Rozanov's quotes.

111 Ibid., p. 49.

112 Ibid.

doctrine, he reverts to a pre-Christian way of relating to God. The divine command to reproduce has 'filled everything', man is firmly obliged to make this the core of his belief. Rozanov criticizes Griniakin, as well as centuries of Ecumenical Councils and Church dogma, for ignoring God's own word and replacing this with his own beliefs.[113] This is Rozanov's 'reformation', which is in fact a type of restoration, but which Rozanov describes as 'a return to the word of God'.[114] The acceptance of impractical canon and laws has led to a 'devolution' of the Church and the currency of its teaching, and only the rejection and removal of several of its laws can remedy this.

Hence Rozanov's approach becomes clearer. The reformation of Orthodoxy requires an examination of facts, not just words.[115] Rozanov acknowledges Solov′ev's contribution in tackling the Church hierarchy's monopoly over religious truths and for paving the way for laymen to engage with Church teaching. However, having praised Solov′ev, Rozanov then dismisses Solov′ev's approach and his conclusions and sets very firmly down his own course which is highly intolerant of opposition. Rozanov's frequent repetition of his beliefs and constant self-reference only reinforce the point that this is a thinker who is strictly doctrinaire in many aspects. The focus on the Old Testament and the commandment to reproduce is a means to attack Church rigidity and provide a means for reformation, but also serves as the basis of an often inflexible approach. This is one of the complexities of Rozanov, that he attacks the content of Church dogma, its truths and conclusions, whilst preserving himself the highly dogmatic character of the Russian Orthodox Church's approach. During the Religious-Philosophical Meetings, priests and philosophers lined up to criticize Rozanov, Leporskii calling him 'a dogmatist to the marrow of his bones'.[116] Yet the command to create is both a dogmatic appeal and at the same time the basis on which to build organically on dogma.

For Rozanov, the relationship between thought and praxis can only be established though a restoration of what he sees as the permanent Old Testament exigencies handed to humanity directly from God. This tension between creativity and dogma runs through all his thought, but can only be reconciled through the constant reference to

113 Ibid., p. 50.
114 Ibid.
115 Ibid., p. 52.
116 *Zapiski peterburgskikh Religiozno-filosofskikh sobranii*, p. 392.

production, especially that of children. Although the basis of man's freedom comes through creative work, this can only be achieved by the free subjugation of human will to the divine. For Rozanov there can be no alternative to the obligation to reproduce. Dogma is generally understood to be the truth revealed by God, presented by the Church for belief. While Catholicism has permitted some degree of dogmatic development and poses the concepts of *fides divina* and *fides catholica*, Orthodoxy stresses that the 'dogma of the church is present and closed in the doctrinal decisions of the first seven ecumenical councils'.[117] Rozanov develops the concept of the church to an anthropological theology; the truth rests in the people, and their capacity to give birth.

Rozanov's apologetics for productivity also help explain the relationship between theology and philosophy in his approach. Rozanov places religion as an area of human activity higher than other aspects such as philosophy or literature. Remizov, in his pairing of Russian writers and thinkers, puts Rozanov together with Shestov, over-emphasizing the irrational in Rozanov.[118] However, Rozanov posits a less antagonistic relationship between theology and philosophy than some of his peers, preparing the way for later speculative Orthodox thinkers. He approaches the truth with a rigid approach that often seeks to negate the thought of his opponents (in this way Rozanov shares some of the patterns of Western philosophical discourse). Rozanov, especially in his earlier, more historically orientated work, sees the task of the modern Christian as merging the Western tradition of 'Reason' with the Semitic focus on 'Sex'; for Rozanov, these two concepts are opposed, and it is only the culturalization of philosophy, the overturning of the legacy of Plato, which can resolve this.[119] Reason provides the form through which man makes sense of his physicality. Although the irrational does lean towards overwhelming the universal and philosophical towards the end of his career, Rozanov generally holds the importance of reflective thought where, as in Solov´ev, it focuses on phenomena. He rejects Descartes and Hegel and argues that philosophy must return to things,

---

117 See *Encyclopedia of Religion*, ed. by Lindsay Jones (Detroit/London: Macmillan Reference USA, 2005), IV, p. 2387.

118 Remizov, *Kukkha*, p. 56.

119 See V.V. Rozanov, 'N.I. Barsov. Neskol´ko issledovanii istoricheskikh i rassuzhdenii o voprosakh sovremennykh', in *Iudaizm*, pp. 141–2.

not the idea of the thing.[120] He in fact advocates a dynamic, creative relationship between religion and philosophy, where religious thinking adopts aspects of philosophy, history and even literature to produce a new way of looking at the world which emerges from a faithful acceptance of and living response to the truths of the Old Testament.

So Rozanov sees the relationship between faith and thought as less antagonistic, and more dynamic, than many of his coevals suggest. In many ways, Rozanov anticipates the creative approach of Khoruzhii, dismantling the abstract schemes of nineteenth-century religious thought and laying the way for a theosis through personal experience. Khoruzhii's contribution appears to substantiate Zen′kovskii's claim that Rozanov provides a crucial link from the nineteenth century to the personalism of the twentieth century – Zen′kovskii contends that Russian personalism must absorb the cosmological nature of Rozanov's thought if it is to avoid an excess of 'pure ethicism'.[121] Rozanov's focus on personhood and individual activity is repeated in Khoruzhii's work.

Rozanov argues that religion and philosophy can only be reconciled through culture.[122] The manner of thinking must be rethought into something theological, as with Solov′ev and others from their period. But above all, the relationship between religion and philosophy must be grounded in culture as personal activity. Rozanov's revolt against Orthodoxy is informed by the very same doctrinal traditions of the Church of which he considered himself a proud member; it is Orthodoxy's stress on religion as personal experience which Rozanov adopts and uses to attempt his religious reforms. Therefore, through personal activity Rozanov offers a new way to understand the viability of Orthodoxy in a contemporary context. Just as significant for the purposes of Russian philosophy is Rozanov's attempt to offer a new manner in which to realize some of the abstract theories of Solov′ev regarding religious behaviour.

As I have pointed out, Rozanov's main struggle in securing the viability of his project is the manner in which he tries to force primeval types of worship into a modern-day setting. Cultural activity helps solve this. Rozanov also targets the divide between history and mythology

---

120 V.V. Rozanov, 'Iudaizm', in *Novyi Put′* (November 1903), pp. 155–84 (p. 174).

121 Zen′kovskii, I, p. 468.

122 See his comments on Stanisław Ptaszycki. V.V. Rozanov, 'Poeticheskii material', in *Iudaizm*, pp. 109–11.

which has arisen from the dephallicization of religion. Rozanov must circumvent Christ as the historical and unrepeatable, through a Creation-based mythology in which the link with God (through the penis) is preserved. This explains his fondness for pre-Christian religions and, in particular, Egypt.

## Chapter 3

# Ancient Egypt

Rozanov's fascination with the beginning of the universe leads him to look back to pre-Christian religions which he believes were based on the Creation of the world. He writes positively of various ancient religions, such as those of the Assyrians, Phoenicians and the Hebrews, and their worship, but reserves a special place for the Egyptians. They alone understood the true meaning of the Creation, according to Rozanov, and they were able to construct a proper religious lifestyle which reflected their reverence for God and His work.

Although he does not state so explicitly, Rozanov's syncretism leads the reader to believe, despite hearsay to the contrary, that the Christian God is the same God as the creator Gods worshipped by the Egyptians, and Rozanov seems to associate the Elohim with Osiris and Isis.[1] This tolerance of others' thought is reminiscent of other Christian thinkers such as Clement of Alexandria, and his attempt to syncretize religions and their development is similar to Solov´ev's (though Rozanov disagrees with Solov´ev's vision of the ethical progression of religion).

Rozanov's work on Egypt can be contextualized in the explosion during his period of an interest in the exotic, the occult and Eastern religions and their practices.[2] There is already existing scholarship on the re-examination of ancient religions in this period.[3] However, as yet little

1 V.V. Rozanov, 'Résumé ob Egipte', in *Vozrozhdaiushchiisia Egipet*, pp. 240–4 (p. 241).

2 For a discussion of some of the major recent arguments over defining the term 'Silver Age' and its association with the twilight of Russian culture, see Roger Keys, *The Reluctant Modernist: Andrei Bely and the Development of Russian Fiction 1902–1914* (Oxford: Clarendon, 1996), pp. 3–18. Rozanov became sensitive to the sense of living at the end of time, but saw in this the opportunity for the rebirth of Russian spirituality, and it is worth noting that in many ancient Semitic religions, the moon, a symbol of the Silver Age, was seen as the symbol of rebirth. Theodor Reik, *Pagan Rites in Judaism: From Sex Initiation, Magic, Moon-Cult, Tattooing, Mutilation and Other Primitive Rituals to Family Loyalty and Solidarity* (New York: Farrar, Straus and Company, 1964), p. 92. This point has significance in the context of this chapter and Rozanov's attempt to redefine death as a possibility for rebirth.

3 Bernice Glatzer Rosenthal, 'Introduction', in *The Occult in Russian and Soviet Culture*, ed. by Bernice Glatzer Rosenthal (Ithaca/London: Cornell University Press, 1997), pp. 1–32 (p. 1).

attention has been directed towards Rozanov's contribution. Many of his peers turned their attention towards theosophy, magic, cultish forms of worship and the ancient religions of the orient. There was a growth of interest in mystical writings which lay outside the Orthodox tradition, such as those of Boehme or Swedenborg.[4] To a large extent, this interest in the esoteric was a common theme across Europe. However, the Russian approach was marked by a belief in the practical reality of such ideas and by a conviction that such ideas should be realized for Russia's wellbeing.[5] This interest in foreign religions emerged as a result of the growing dissatisfaction with the established religious institutions and practices.[6] Rosenthal notes that the fascination in the occult stemmed from a loss of confidence in the dominant myths maintained by the establishment.[7] Pyman, among other scholars, has written extensively not only on the fascination with the esoteric, but also on the maximalist approach that thinkers adopted towards such cults, and their desire 'whole-heartedly [to] embrace and act out [their] ideas'.[8] In the Silver Age, this belief in

---

4 Boehme's influence on Solov´ev has been given attention in existing scholarship. See for example, D. Strémooukhoff, *Vladimir Soloviev and his Messianic Work*, trans. by Elizabeth Meyendorff, ed. by Phillip Guilbeau and Heather Elise MacGregor (Belmont: Nordland, 1980), p. 64. In this passage, Strémooukhoff quotes a letter from Solov´ev to S.A. Tolstaia, in which Solov´ev rejects the subjectivism of Gichtel, Arnold and Pordage, but underlines the importance of Paracelsus, Boehme and Swedenborg. The original letter, dated 27 April 1877 (O.S.), is reprinted in V.S. Solov´ev, *Pis´ma Vladimira Sergeevicha Solov´eva*, ed. by E.L. Radlov, 4 vols (St Petersburg: Obshchestvennaia Pol´za, 1903–1923), II (1909), p. 200. Florenskii quotes the same letter in his examination of Sophiology. See Florenskii, *Stolp i utverzhdenie istiny*, p. 131.

5 Mikhail Epstein has characterized Russia as an 'ideocracy', a cultural arena in which ideas can be readily put into practice. He also, however, marks the negative aspect of this and describes Russia as historically imprisoned by the ideas implemented ruthlessly by a thinking elite. He presents the Russian, and especially the Soviet, ideocracy as a tyranny, where Plato's concept of the 'czardom of ideas' has reached its final stage of development. See <http://www.emory.edu/INTELNET/rus_thought_overview.html, last accessed 4 January 2011.

6 Rosenthal, 'Introduction', in *The Occult in Russian and Soviet Culture*, p. 7.

7 Ibid., p. 6.

8 Avril Pyman, *A History of Russian Symbolism* (Cambridge: Cambridge University Press, 1994), p. 240. Lidia Zinov´eva-Annibal once famously, at a party hosted by Minskii, mixed blood taken from the guests in a goblet with wine and passed this round for all to drink. In his Petersburg period,

the reality of ideas, coupled with an interest in the exotic, and often downright bizarre, made for a potent cultural mix. Many of Rozanov's contemporaries drew on the rituals of non-Orthodox religions. For example, Merezhkovskii, Gippius and Filosofov put into practice their belief in the holiness of the number three. They lived together and promoted their triumvirate as the first step to realizing a new religion. Viacheslav Ivanov hosted regular Wednesday evening gatherings in his 'Tower', which soon gained notoriety as a home of 'a dangerous and, on occasion, rather ridiculous mix of mystic eroticism and sociological maximalism'.[9]

One of the major focuses of their investigation was ancient Egypt, though this was part of a broader European phenomenon and the growing opinion that the classical world was not the exclusive basis for European civilization. The tendency for Europeans to accord themselves a privileged position above pagans saw mounting challenges in the Renaissance and beyond; such influential thinkers who challenged the established view included (though by no means exclusively) Michel de Montaigne, Rousseau and Vico.[10] By the start of the twentieth century, scholars had begun seriously to re-evaluate the relevance specifically of Egypt for the origins of their civilization, challenging the view that European civilization emerged from the classical world, in particular Greece.[11]

Towards the end of the nineteenth century, scholars in Europe and Russia were already looking to rediscover a cultural heritage in Egypt.[12]

---

Rozanov would often attend such ceremonies but kept his participation secret from his wife. Rozanov later comments on the Zinov′eva-Annibal incident with curiosity, but cites this as proof of the Jews' unique attraction to human blood. See V.V. Rozanov, *Oboniatel′noe i osiazatel′noe otnoshenie evreev k krovi*, p. 337.

9 Pyman, p. 272.

10 For an investigation of challenges to the view that European history is superior to non-European cultures, see especially Joseph Mali, *The Rehabilitation of Myth: Vico's 'New Science'* (Cambridge: Cambridge University Press, 1992), pp. 82–5. Rozanov has something in common with Montaigne's view that man is no higher than the beasts; in this regard they both reject intellectual achievement as the basis for a culture's success.

11 For example, Hamilton's 1930 classic work *The Greek Way* is a paean to the contribution of Athens to European civilization. Edith Hamilton, *The Greek Way* (New York: Norton, 1964), pp. 13–14.

12 Hare exposes the manner in which classicists such as Hamilton underlined the formative influence of Athens on European civilization. He also discusses the work of modern scholars, such as Bernal, who have challenged

Interest was further aroused by archaeological discoveries in northern Africa by scholars such as William Petrie and Howard Carter. Some writers have hinted at Russia's supremacy in this field, suggesting that Russian pilgrims opened up Egypt during their journeys to the Holy Lands.[13] The Russian diplomat A.N. Murav′ev ensured that two granite sphinxes from the reign of Amenhotep III (Amenhotep the Magnificent, reigned 1390–1353 BCE) were brought to St Petersburg, where they were placed on the Neva's University Embankment in 1834.[14] Many Western scholarly works on Egypt around the turn of the nineteenth and twentieth centuries quickly reached Russia and were translated. Rozanov had access to the Russian versions of works by the leading Egyptologists of his time, including James Henry Breasted, Karl Richard Lepsius and Gaston Maspero. Rozanov often turned to these for the basis of many of his own works on ancient Egyptian religion, and his essays abound in quotes and copies of drawings from their output. He was also knowledgeable of the work of Russian Egyptologists such as Vladimir Golenishchev and Boris Turaev.

---

Hamilton's view, and stresses the role of the Egyptian legacy in European culture. Tom Hare, *ReMembering Osiris: Number, Gender and the Word in Ancient Egyptian Representational Systems* (Stanford: Stanford University Press, 1999), pp. 215–18. Bernal calls for the replacement of the Aryan model of ancient Greece (which he considers anti-Semitic) with the 'Revised Ancient Model', which, while noting the Indo-European origin of the Greek language, highlights the fact that Egyptians settled in the Aegean in the late Bronze Age and wielded a massive influence over the development of Greek culture. Martin Bernal, *Black Athena: The Afroasiatic Roots of Classical Civilization*, 2 vols (London: Free Association Books, 1991), II: *The Archaeological and Documentary Evidence*, p. 78. Rozanov, nearly a century prior to Bernal, argues that the Greeks took all their main religious concepts from the Egyptians (though for Rozanov Greek religion is only a poor and incomplete adaptation of Egyptian worship). See V.V. Rozanov, 'Sem′ia i sozhitie s zhivotnymi', in *Vozrozhdaiushchiisia Egipet*, pp. 128–37 (p. 129). Interestingly, more recent research argues that the ancient Greeks themselves recognized Egypt as the cradle of all civilization; it was apparently well known to the Greeks that Homer, Solon, Thales, Plato, Eudoxus and Pythagoras had all travelled to Egypt to study. See Luc Brisson, *How Philosophers Saved Myths: Allegorical Interpretation and Classical Mythology*, trans. by Catherine Tihanyi (Chicago/London: University of Chicago Press, 2004), p. 141.

13 Viktor Solkin, 'Peterburgskie sfinksy: Istoriia priobreteniia i obshchii analiz pamiatnikov', in *Peterburgskie sfinksy: Solntse Egipta na beregakh Nevy*, ed. by V.V. Solkin (St Petersburg: Neva, 2005), pp. 14–36 (p. 15).

14 Ibid., p. 17.

In Russian culture, particularly from the nineteenth century, Egypt played an important role which scholars are only just starting to examine.[15] Egyptian motifs were very common in Russian romanticism, feeding into the art of Pushkin (who was well aware of his own African heritage). For Dostoevskii's Raskol′nikov, Egypt becomes the setting for an imaginary paradise before the tumult of murder.[16] In the Silver Age, the Egyptian body in particular was re-examined in the light of the burgeoning interest in new religions, theosophy and mysticism.[17] Solov′ev wielded considerable influence on these new trends; he had travelled to Egypt in 1875 to investigate the relationship between Sophia and primeval religions.[18] The interest in the oriental is pronounced in many spheres of artistic creativity among Rozanov's peers, such as in the music of Rimskii-Korsakov and his associates and in the literature of writers as diverse as Bal′mont, Viacheslav Ivanov, Khlebnikov, Mandel′shtam, Nikolai Gumilev and Merezhkovskii. Bakst, who was close to Rozanov (even painting him), journeyed to Egypt to 'touch the marble shoulders and breasts of the Nubian bodies'.[19] This interest was not confined to religious thinkers. Soviet Russian artists continued, at least for some years following the Revolution, to use Egyptian motives in their work. Perhaps the most famous example of this is Aleksei Shchusev's avant-garde pyramid design for Lenin's Mausoleum which still stands today on Moscow's Red Square.[20]

Rozanov is distinguished among his contemporaries in that his exploitation of Egypt is a genuine attempt to look for a way to reform or restore Orthodoxy. At one point he does hint at an elevated religious

---

15 Henrietta Mondry, 'Beyond the Boundary: Vasilii Rozanov and the Animal Body', *Slavic and East European Journal*, 4 (1999), 651–73 (p. 659).

16 Gwen Walker, 'Andrei Bely's Armchair Journey through the Legendary Land of "Ophir": Russia, Africa and the Dream of Distance', *Slavic and East European Journal*, 46 (2002), 47–74 (p. 50).

17 Mondry, 'Beyond the Boundary', p. 659.

18 A.F. Losev, *Vladimir Solov′ev i ego vremia* (Moscow: Molodaia gvardiia, 2000), pp. 45–7.

19 Mondry, 'Beyond the Boundary', p. 659.

20 The mummification of Lenin's body, performed by Boris Zbarskii and Vladimir Vorob′ev, and its location in the antechamber within the Mausoleum, has obvious connotations with Egyptian practices. In addition, in the manner in which the body is displayed for public reverence, it is also reminiscent of the Orthodox belief that the incorruptibility of the corpse is a sign of saintliness and suggests the forgotten links between ancient Egypt and Christianity.

mission for the Russians, in that he argues that their task is to help heal Western civilization by reintroducing it to the religion of the East.[21] Contemporary thinkers such as Solov´ev, Berdiaev and Florenskii see Christianity as the synthesis of all previous religions, standing at the pinnacle of man's religious experience and preparing the world for its eventual transfiguration at the end of time. Egyptian practices do not generally hold a superior position among other pagan systems, and are merely signposts which point to the later wonders of Christ and Christianity. Both Solov´ev and Merezhkovskii consider Egyptian beliefs to be simply one of the many pagan systems surrounding the Hebrews and they assign a superior position to Israel. In a reverse understanding of human history, Rozanov places Egypt at the zenith of religious experience and tends to view the course of history thereafter as a growing detachment of humanity from God.

Although work is emerging on Rozanov's approach to Judaism, hardly any attention has been devoted to his fascination for Egypt and Egyptology. Rozanov had from a young age a profound interest in the pre-Christian world and was well aware of the problems he faced trying to reconcile this with his innate Orthodoxy.[22] His love for the ancient world was developed at university, and once he had moved to the imperial capital with its various museums he was able to indulge his curiosity. However, his interest in Egypt was not just academic, although he did over the years become very familiar with publications by Western archaeologists; it was intensely religious. He focused on examining the physical symbols left behind by ancient civilizations more than on academic studies into Egyptology. This search led Rozanov to become a frequent visitor to Petersburg's museums, including the Hermitage and the Imperial Museum of Egyptology. It also extended into his personal collections. Rozanov was a keen and knowledgeable collector of coins from the ancient world.

Through his investigations, Rozanov concludes that only the Egyptians understood the Creation.[23] He believes that Christianity emerged

21 See Rozanov's comments on Enlightenment Minister Ivan Tolstoi and his colleagues O.P. Gerasimov and Petr Kaufman. V.V. Rozanov, 'O blizhaishei rabote uchebnogo vedomstva' in *V nashie smute*, pp. 41–3.

22 On 23 February 1893 (O.S.) Rozanov wrote to Leont´ev: 'Yes, I love the ancient world, in a manner inappropriate for a Christian, but I have expressed this love, and continue to express it'. *Literaturnye izgnanniki*, p. 295.

23 'Sem´ia i sozhitie s zhivotnymi', p. 129.

naturally from pagan beliefs, specifically from ancient Egyptian religion. Rozanov's project is to explain that religion emerges from Egypt. He frequently identifies aspects of paganism still existent in Orthodoxy, and re-clarifies the original meaning of their practices. Rozanov examines apparently separate themes such as circumcision, pyramids, hieroglyphics, Christmas trees, the Apocalypse and medical scholarship, and he relies on Hebrew, Greek, Latin, Russian and European historical sources.

As in his interpretation of other religions, Rozanov adopts a pick-and-mix attitude towards Egypt, selecting elements of history and religion which can be accommodated within his own utopian vision. Rozanov treats Egyptian religion as unified and unchanging and believes that its success lies in the fact that throughout their history the Egyptians preserved their youthfulness and respect for the Creation. He does not comment that throughout history, religious beliefs in Egypt were subject to much development and often violent change. He does not mention the brutal wars, revolutions and hardships experienced by the Egyptian people, but portrays them as a race which permanently smiled.[24] Nor does he discuss the rich pantheon of Egyptian deities, which changed according to location or period, but concentrates primarily on Osiris and his phallus.[25] However, he does occasionally also discuss other gods, such as Isis and the cow-goddess Hathor.[26] He rejects the scientific approach to Egyptian history, as this does not examine the Egyptians' understanding of the family and the Creation.[27] Rozanov even rejects the phrase 'Egyptology' in his criticism of European scholars in the field. Rozanov adopts facets of Aristotelian thought when he denies a rationalist examination of history detached from the intimacies of life itself. In an essay from 1901 Rozanov lays out the basis for his investigation of Egypt, recollecting the very first time he saw Murav´ev's Sphinxes on the Neva.

> Самая коротенькая река в мире течет мимо их, как три тысячи лет назад текла самая длинная; и город самый новый из европейских шумит

24 Ibid., p. 133.

25 Berdiaev tells us that Rozanov confided him that he prayed not to the Orthodox God, but to Osiris. N.A. Berdiaev, *Samopoznanie (Opty filosofskoi avtobiografii)* (Moscow: Kniga, 1991), p. 149.

26 V.V. Rozanov, 'Istoricheskie kategorii', in *Vozrozhdaiushchiisia Egipet*, pp. 244–52 (p. 246).

27 'Sem´ia i sozhitie s zhivotnymi', p. 130.

около обитателей самого ветхого в истории города. Однако все эти мысли-сопоставления пришли мне на ум гораздо позднее: при первом же разглядывании меня остановило удивительное выражение лица сфинксов. Как это может проверить наблюдением всякий, – это суть *молодые лица с необыкновенно веселым выражением*, которое я не мог бы определить выше и лучше, как известною поговоркою: «Хочется прыснуть со смеху». Я долго, внимательно, пытливо в них всматривался, и так как позднее мне случилось два года ежедневно ездить мимо их, то я не могу думать, чтобы обманулся во впечатлении: это были *самые веселые и живые из встреченных мною в Петербурге* действительно, казалось бы, живых *лиц*!

The smallest river in the world flows past them, just as the longest river did three millennia ago; and the newest city of the Europeans bustles among the occupants of the most ancient city in history. However, all these thoughts and associations came to my mind much later. When I looked at them for the first time, I was captured by the miraculous expression on the sphinxes' faces. Anybody can look and check this for themselves – these are *young faces with an unusually joyful expression*, which I could not describe better than by using the well-known saying: 'They make you want to splutter with laughter'. I looked at them long, carefully, inquisitively, and for the next two years I had to drive past them every day, and so I do not think that I am mistaken in my impression: they were definitely *the most joyful and alive of all the faces I encountered in Petersburg!*[28]

Rozanov's Egyptology is not mere artistic innovation, but a serious endeavour to help effect a renewal of Russian spiritual life. Although Rozanov never visited Egypt, unlike some of his contemporaries, he berated European archaeologists for neglecting the true religious meaning of their discoveries. He opposes the youthful energy of Egypt to the decline of Russian and European civilization. Furthermore, Rozanov is intensely critical of his artistic contemporaries who use Egyptian themes purely for aesthetic purposes, but insists that his own interest in Egypt emerged from a love for the concrete.[29] It is worth comparing Rozanov's passage above on the Neva Sphinxes with Ivanov's poem on the same theme, which depicts the Sphinxes as unmoving and aloof.[30] Ivanov's highly stylized verse

---

28 V.V. Rozanov, 'Egipet', in *Vozrozhdaiushchiisia Egipet*, pp. 301–6 (p. 302).

29 Rozanov writes, '"Artiness" was always the least importance issue for me, and there was never a focus on cold aesthetics in any of my pages. Surely the reader feels this? All my strength [...] is in my love: but in a real love for the real'. V.V. Rozanov, 'Literaturnye i politicheskie aforizmy', in *Zagadki russkoi provokatsii*, pp. 412–43 (p. 423).

30 Viacheslav Ivanov, *Sfinksy nad Nevoi*, in *Sobranie sochinenii*, 4 vols (Brussels: Foyer Oriental Chrétien, 1974), II, p. 323. Like Solov´ev, Ivanov uses humour, an haughty arrogance which looks down on the world, to perpetuate the division between Earth and consciousness.

reveals much about the conflicting ways in which the Egyptian heritage was interpreted in the Silver Age, and it also displays a division between the aesthetic and the religious which Rozanov wishes to overcome. Whereas in Ivanov's poem the Sphinxes have a somewhat arrogant attitude towards the Earth, Rozanov's description concentrates on content, highlighting the reality of their earthly presence and the possibility of renewal. The smile of their Sphinxes is not the arrogant laughter which comes from hidden knowledge and an elevation above the Earth, but emerges from a joy for the beginnings of life (the basis for what Rozanov terms 'style'). Moreover, throughout Rozanov's life it is the Volga, rather than the Neva, which should be the focal point for Russian religiosity.[31] For Rozanov, Egypt was founded on a joy of the new, creativity and childbirth, and he contrasts this with the Church's hostility to the family.

His first major series of essays on the religious philosophy of the family, *V mire neiasnogo i nereshennogo*, draws heavily on Egyptian motifs. At the same time, he started to publish articles devoted specifically to the history of Egyptian religion which appeared in periodicals such as *Novyi Put´*, or *Mir Iskusstva*. His first major notable essay on pre-Christian religions (principally Judaism and Egypt), and their relationship to modern Russian religiosity, was 'Nechto iz sedoi drevnosti', which first appeared in his 1899 book *Religiia i kul´tura*. This was quickly followed by 'Velichaishaia minuta istorii', published the following year in *Novyi zhurnal inostrannoi literatury*. In 1901, he wrote a series of articles for *Mir Iskusstva* under the title 'Zvezdy'. Over the next 16 years he wrote scores of articles on Egypt and Eastern religions, which appeared in various organs such as *Novoe Vremia*, *Mir Iskusstva* and *Vesy*. In November 1916, Rozanov started to consider writing a book devoted specifically to Egyptian religion. He thought about a variety of different titles for this compilation, including *Moi Egipet*, *Vozrozhdaiushchiisia Egipet* (which conveyed the idea of rebirth he was trying to express), before settling on *Iz vostochnykh motivov*; this was also adopted for the title of the thirty-eighth volume of Rozanov's projected complete works, which would contain his Egyptian studies.[32] Several more articles, desig-

31 Rozanov starts his most famous travel writings in following fashion: 'I want to call our Volga "the Russian Nile". What is the Nile, not in its geographical or physical sense, but in a different, more profound sense, for the people that live on its banks? "A great, sacred river", just like we say "Holy Russia" when describing the country and its people'. See 'Russkii Nil', p. 145.

32 For a history of the publication of Rozanov's Egyptian work, see A.N. Nikoliukin, 'Kommentarii', in *Vozrozhdaiushchiisia Egipet*, pp. 500–13.

nated for this compilation, were written but not published in Rozanov's lifetime and remained in archives until the post-Soviet period. For the same reasons as in the previous chapters, these works will be treated here largely synchronically, rather than diachronically.

## Myth, beginnings and ends

One of the most important facets of any religion is the method of its transmission. For Rozanov this is highly important, as religion must realize each human's physical relatedness to God at any point in history. In establishing a parallel between the Creation and childbirth, the act of procreation with the content, Rozanov manages to set up an identity of praxis and ontology. This appears to have a parallel in the coincidence Rozanov seeks between mythos and logos, which as we shall see helps the human preserve the union with God throughout history. In this context, the narration of stories which convey the eternal significance of the Creation within human experience takes on a special role. This is more than an intellectual transmission. Rozanov examines the meaning of ancient Egyptian myths, often repeating them or placing them alongside his own narration of events taken from contemporary Russian life concerning love, marriage and childbirth. Rozanov's own work itself becomes in a sense 'mythological', in that it fulfils the same religious purpose as the original sources he researches. It is not surprising that Rozanov's growing dissatisfaction with systematic philosophy would lead him from his first organized philosophical work to the types of narrative one observes in his later journalistic work and the *Opavshelistika*.[33]

Scholarship in Russia and the West has begun to recognize the special role played by mythology in Russian culture, and many scholars argue that a mythological outlook has been a powerful force in Russian culture.[34]

---

33 It is a trait of pre-modern life, especially in the Near East, that profound ideas can be conveyed through simple narrative forms. See Richard J. Clifford, 'The Roots of Apocalypticism in Near Eastern Myth', in *The Encyclopedia of Apocalypticism*, ed. by Bernard McGinn, John J. Collins, and Stephen J. Stein, 3 vols (New York: Continuum, 1999), I, pp. 3–35 (p. 34).

34 M.Iu. Smirnov, *Mifologiia i religiia v rossiiskom soznanii* (St Petersburg: Letnii Sad, 2000), p. 9. Recent studies have examined the role of mythology specifically in Soviet culture. See Zh.F. Konovalova, 'Sovetskii mif i ritual', in *Ritual i ritual'nyi predmet*, ed. by L.V. Konovalov (St Petersburg: GMIR, 1995), pp. 143–51.

Lotman has investigated the meaning of ancient narratives and the way these structure contemporary cultural forms.[35] Ethnographic studies have underlined the peculiar role of myths in Russian popular culture, which have survived alongside the teachings of the organized Church as 'dvoeverie', partially because of the Church's inability to engage with the people at parish level.[36] Rozanov had good knowledge of the works of contemporary folklorists and ethnographers, such as Pavel Rybnikov, Pavel Shein, and Petr Bessonov. Here one witnesses the predilection in Russian culture for the domestic and intimate (such as in the domovoi, bannik or the vodianoi), rather than the complex mythology of the ancient Greeks. In Russian culture, myth often provides an explanation for a supposed natural relationship between man and the universe, in which consciousness and the world do not stand in opposition to one another, but where the human is a vital component of a unified cosmos.[37] There was already in nineteenth-century Russian writing a tendency to merge the literary with the mythological, the aesthetic with the philosophical. This is apparent in Dostoevskii, perhaps most famously in his 'legend' of the Grand Inquisitor, and in Tolstoi, who especially in his later moral tales such as 'Chem liudi zhivy' or 'Molitva' used myths to convey universal truths as well as deliberately rejecting existing narrative forms.[38] For Shklovskii, myths provide the formal element in the artist's memory through which familiar material is made new; they are not the peaceful domain of

---

35 Lotman's investigation into the anti-modernist nature of mythological writing is particularly useful for our investigation; as Lotman notes, myth is not designed to teach us something new about the world, but predominantly helps organize the world of the reader. See Yuri M. Lotman, *Universe of the Mind: A Semiotic Theory of Culture*, trans. by Ann Shukman (London: Tauris, 1990), p. 154.

36 Geoffrey Hosking, *Russia: People and Empire 1552–1917* (London: HarperCollins, 1997), pp. 211–12. Warner's valuable studies have examined Russian myths 'concerned with the natural world, the family and basic needs of ordinary people', compared to the 'elaborate corpus of myths' belonging to the Greeks and other cultures. Elizabeth Warner, *Russian Myths* (London: British Museum, 2002), pp. 7–8.

37 Smirnov, pp. 14–18. Eliade argues that myths point to a pre-philosophical period, where consciousness and reality emerge simultaneously. Mircea Eliade, *Myth and Reality*, trans. by William R. Trask (London: George Allen & Unwin, 1964), p. 37. Losev describes this unity of thought and reality and argues that mythology reflects a 'primitive-intuitive reaction to a thing'. Losev, *Dialektika mifa*, p. 68.

38 Slobin, pp. 22–5.

containing one's relationship with the ancient world, but are violent places of battle.[39]

There is a peculiar convergence in Rozanov's time of the religious and the mythological, which must have come about in part due to concerns over the nature of Russian religiosity and the desire to portray the eschatological reality of Russian culture. Recent academic work has focused on the importance of myth building in coming to terms with an increasing apocalyptic fervour. Gasparov argues that mythologizing was a vital tool in this time for a 'total eschatological synthesis', as writers and thinkers saw their period as the culmination of all prior cultural achievements which were being re-experienced simultaneously in a final flourish.[40] Gasparov writes that the protagonists of the time did not ignore 'traditional historical and aesthetic problems', but re-examined such issues according to the mythological worldview they established; this mythology was typically eschatological.[41]

This coming together of the religious and the mythological in Rozanov's time was given special impetus by Solov´ev, whose work was a major inspiration in the way his successors merged myths with their aesthetic concerns.[42] In 'Mifologicheskii protsess v drevnem iazychestve' (1873), Solov´ev draws on the theories of Khomiakov and Schelling to explain the development from primeval beliefs to more developed religious systems.[43] Early religions proclaim the unity of being and do not have the ability to distinguish between the abstract-spiritual and the earthly. Nature is the external manifestation of God and is born by the 'material cause of the phenomenon'. This cause is associated in mythology with the mother god, as the ancients did not conceptualize purely spiritual deities.[44] The movement of spirit onto the Earth is

39 Viktor Shklovskii, '"Mif" i "roman-mif"', in *Izbrannoe v dvukh tomakh*, 2 vols (Moscow: Khudozhestvennaia literatura, 1983), II, pp. 246–8 (p. 247).

40 Boris Gasparov, 'Introduction: The "Golden Age" and Its Role in the Cultural Mythology of Russian Modernism', in *Cultural Mythologies of Russian Modernism: From the Golden Age to the Silver Age*, ed. by Boris Gasparov, Robert P. Hughes, and Irina Paperno (Berkeley/Oxford: University of California Press, 1992), pp. 1–16 (p. 3).

41 Ibid., pp. 2–3. Rozanov's work is an attempt to contradict this.

42 For the rediscovery of mythology in this period see Evelies Schmidt, *Ägypten und Ägyptische Mythologie: Bilder der Transition im Werk Andrej Belyjs* (Munich: Otto Sagner, 1986), pp. 1–10.

43 Jonathan Sutton, *The Religious Philosophy of Vladimir Solovyov* (Basingstoke: Macmillan, 1988), p. 104.

44 Solov´ev draws a nice analogy between the words matter and maternal, which we note in modified form in Rozanov. V.S. Solov´ev, 'Mifologicheskii

characterized as the activity of the counterpart male god, the father and creator of all things, and so mythology is the way that the energies of the divine are understood to work through nature. Solov′ev's investigation of mythology would give way to a more sophisticated sophiology which explains the connection between God and humanity. Nor does Solov′ev reserve a special place for the Egyptian god Osiris, but equates him directly with the creator-god in other cultures, such as Shiva, Adonis, Fro and Iarilo.[45] Solov′ev notes the importance of the ithyphallic Osiris in Egypt, but does not accord the penis a specific role in the downwards motion of the energies of the creator-god.[46]

However, it is Solov′ev's attempt to draw an eschatology into religious and artistic narratives (as well as the coincidence one notes in his work of the spiritual and the aesthetic) which inspired the Russian Symbolists. They sought a new narrative to unify previous religions and found in mythology a useful tool; myth offers a pre-logical interpretation of contemporary society, embodying the collective consciousness, one of the aims of the God-Seekers.[47] However, they tended to see such myths not independently, but as signposts to the realization of a future, final form of Christianity.[48] Like Solov′ev, most of these thinkers preserved the distinction between narrative discourse and the essence of God, by consequence perpetuating the separation of God and human with which Rozanov engages. For example, Merezhkovskii, who ascribes a higher role than Solov′ev to pre-Christian myths, argues that pagan myths contain the secrets of Christianity. He believes that all myths contain some degree of truth and even writes that 'all gods are true' (although he does not reserve an elevated position for Osiris).[49] However, Merezhkovskii insists on the inability of the human to commune directly with God and therefore consigns all theology to the sphere of the mythological.[50] Merezhkovskii insists that the eternal truths of religion

---

protsess v drevnem iazychestve', in *Polnoe sobranie sochinenii* (Moscow: Nauka, 2000-), I, pp. 17–37 (pp. 24–5).

45 Ibid., p. 33.

46 In contrast from Rozanov, Solov′ev reserves a unique place for the Jews in his discussion of mythologies. Ibid., p. 24.

47 Schmidt, p. 9.

48 Ibid., p. 19.

49 Merezhkovskii, *Taina trekh*, p. 16.

50 Ibid., p. 205. Rozanov would agree with the correspondence between the theological and the mythological, though his interpretation of myths as conveying an essential truth differs from Merezhkovskii's.

can be unlocked only through the Sacraments of the Church,[51] and his focus concurs largely with Solov′ev's, as he believes that pagan myths point towards the future third age of the Spirit. For both, myths serve in directing our focus to the final transfiguration of the cosmos.

Rozanov must overcome the division between essence and energies in the interpretation of myths' function. Rozanov does not venture a complex theory of mythology, however his approach is illuminated by the work of Losev, one of the most important Russian theoreticians of myth, and in particular by Losev's criticism of Rozanov.[52] For Losev, all myths act as symbols, as they bridge the divine between God and the world. However, Losev preserves a dialectical relationship between the divine and myth, which parallels Orthodox teachings on the essence and energies of God. Therefore, although God and myth are identical, at the same time they are also distinct. In similar fashion, the image of a person (which corresponds to myth in Losev's description) is identical to, but also separate from, that person's essence. Myth is the expression of personhood in words, and all myths are part of the Absolute Myth, forming part of the expression of God and our relationship to Him.[53] Losev carries forward this identification of myth and the divine energies into the way we relate to all symbols, drawing together theology and anthropology. Each living thing has a substance, but also possesses its own myth, its energistic expression. The greatest symbol is the Name of God, the 'unfolding magical name'.[54]

Losev's insistence on the identity of real and ideal and the mythological-symbolic value of life puts him closer to Rozanov than to more abstract thinkers such as Belyi, who valued the symbol for the way it points to the 'new, third world'.[55] Moreover, in identifying myth with the karygmatic expression of all living things, Losev posits an open-ended vision of culture in which life is not shunned, but glorified. However, it is his rejection of Rozanov in which we might discern the innovation in the latter's approach. Losev posits the ontological equality of creature and creation, as does

51 Ibid., pp. 14–15.

52 Losev's work is only now undergoing reappraisal after its prohibition by the Soviet authorities. See Vladimir Marchenkov, 'Aleksei Losev and His Theory of Myth', in *The Dialectics of Myth*, trans. by Vladimir Marchenkov (London/New York: Routledge, 2003), pp. 3–65 (p. 4–15).

53 Losev, *Dialektika mifa*, pp. 99–100.

54 Ibid., p. 196.

55 Belyi suggests that the symbol creates a third, new world, enabling the artist to privilege himself over reality. Losev writes that the symbol signifies itself and nothing exterior to itself. Losev, *Dialektika mifa*, p. 42.

Rozanov, but maintains the distinction of Creator and creation, as do formal Orthodox thinkers, in order to avoid the crude pantheism which Losev detects in Rozanov.[56] Losev seems to support the view that Rozanov identifies essence and energies, a view which would have important implications for his understanding of myths. For a start, Losev's careful distinction delineates mythology from history. So for Rozanov, we can suppose that the historical and mythological converge, enabling Rozanov to treat history in a creative, mythological and often personal manner, which has important consequences (especially for Rozanov's Jewish 'studies').

Rozanov's interpretations of myths are complex and inconsistent. Rozanov uses the word 'mif' in his descriptions of pagan narratives, though he also uses the terms 'saga' or 'legenda'. He denounces certain myths as 'untrue' and fabricated, while simultaneously relying on myths which corroborate his own worldview. Egyptian myths of the family are valid, as they underline the significance of beginnings. At the same time, Rozanov is prepared to reject, for example, myths of ancient Greece which have nothing to do with childbirth, but which are superficial, 'marble-like' and unable to penetrate to the essence of things.[57] True myths express the continuing sanctity of the Creator's work and mitigate against potential involution. They also reject the idea of history as a movement towards the revelation of truth. This is demonstrated in an article from 1911, in which he narrates how desert nomads from Mesopotamia were suddenly filled with a feeling for the divine.

> Сухие, высокие старики пустынь были мудрые люди. Великий жар безмолвной души связался с великим жаром палящего солнца, полнокровных, полносочных звезд; и стало что-то одно, между Землею и Небом, не Земля и не Небо…
>
> Стала молитва. Стало чувство Бога.
>
> Стала религия.
>
> Без догм. Без определений, без границ… Религия бесконечна, как бесконечна пустыня. Религия как торжественность. Религия как святость.
>
> Религия как «мое» у каждого старика.
>
> The dry, tall old men of the hermitages were wise men. The great heat of their silent souls merged with the great heat of the burning sun and the stars, full of blood and juices; and something appeared, something between Earth and Heaven, but that was not Earth or Heaven…
>
> Prayer appeared. The feeling of God appeared.
>
> Religion appeared.

56 Losev, *Dialektika mifa*, pp. 76–9.

57 *Poslednie list´ia*, p. 228.

> Without dogma. Without prescriptions, without limits... Infinite religion, like the infinite desert. Religion as a solemnity. Religion as holiness.
> Religion as 'something personal' for each old man.[58]

Rozanov believes that myths spring naturally and spontaneously from this encounter with God.[59] In describing the unification of souls with the heat of the sun, Rozanov is manipulating the tradition of hesychasm by expressing a physical union of ideal and the real. Humans react instinctively to this possibility of encountering the divine, automatically raising their hands to Heaven in prayer and thanks.[60] This spontaneous response is felt by each new mother.[61] Rozanov uses his own life as the example for the way this encounter, based ultimately on the Creation, forms the basis for future religious experience. As a rebellious schoolboy, Rozanov had turned away from Christianity and like so many Russian religious thinkers had for a time considered himself a nihilist, investigating socialism and avidly reading the works, among others, of Pisarev, Nekrasov, Bentham, J.S. Mill and Malthus. However, Rozanov's moment of revelation came as a student when, sleepless after an unsuccessful Greek examination, he picked up a Bible and started to read it at random. Despite his limited knowledge of Old Church Slavonic, as Rozanov read through the Old Testament he was suddenly taken by an unknown feeling.

> И тут я почувствовал, именно сейчас после смены тех греческих впечатлений, до чего же это могущественнее, *проще*, *нужнее*, святее всего, всего... Первый раз я понял, почему это «боговдохновенно», т.е. почему так решили люди вот об этой единственной книге, а не о других. Это шло куда-то в бездонную глубину души.
> And then I felt the conversion from all those Greek impressions, I felt that this was much more powerful, *simpler, more necessary*, and holier than everything, than everything... For the first time I understood why this was 'divinely inspired', that is to say, why people decided on this book, and not on others. It touched me somewhere in the fathomless depths of my soul.[62]

At the same time, there is a certain admiration in Rozanov of the Renaissance and a sense that this period of reform in Christianity and its

58 V.V. Rozanov, 'Bibleiskaia poeziia', in *Vozrozhdaiushchiisia Egipet*, pp. 441–56 (pp. 441–2).
59 V.V. Rozanov, 'Grekh', in *Okolo narodnoi dushi*, pp. 347–55 (p. 349).
60 'Bibleiskaia poeziia', p. 442.
61 'Sem'ia i sozhitie s zhivotnymi', p. 131.
62 V.V. Rozanov, 'Slovo Bozhie v nashem uchen'i', in *Okolo tserkovnykh sten*, pp. 75–81 (p. 77).

reconciliation with certain pagan truths feeds into his work.[63] Rozanov plays down the supremacy of Biblical myths where he feels that pagan myths express the same truths. The obelisks of ancient Egypt connect the Earth with Heaven and hold the same function as the Temple in Jerusalem.[64] The story of Diana has a similar value as the stories of the Old Testament, those of Abraham and Job. He is happy to neglect New Testament stories which do not correspond to his own worldview. Many of Jesus' parables, such as that of the wealthy youth who wished to enter Heaven, and those which attack family life, are dismissed as 'fairy tales' ('skazki').[65]

## Rozanov, Egypt and the Creation

Rozanov turns to Egypt specifically in order to investigate the meaning of the Creation, which he sees as not understood in Russian culture.

> Более всего я люблю египтян. Не буду отвергать и не буду порицать: в день и год юбилея надлежит быть мирным. Но никогда греки и римляне меня не притягивали, а евреи притягивали лишь временно – и, как я потом догадался, они притягивали меня отсветом, какой у них упал от Египта. Корень всего – Египет. Он дал человечеству первую естественную Религию Отчества, религию Отца миров и Матери миров… научили человечество молитве, – сообщил всем людям тайну «молитвы», тайну псалма…
>
> More than anything I love the Egyptians. I will not deny it or reproach anybody: on a special birthday it is fitting to be peaceful. But I was never drawn to the Greeks or the Romans, and I was only drawn to the Jews for a short

63 For a detailed description of the reinterpretation of ancient myths in the Renaissance, see Brisson, pp. 137–61. Despite frequent references to Rozanov as the Russian Luther, he is also particularly drawn to the Renaissance as a period in Christianity which rejected the asceticism of the Middle Ages. V.V. Rozanov, 'Na chem mozhet povernut′sia "religioznoe soznanie"?', in *Okolo narodnoi dushi*, pp. 364–74 (pp. 365–6). One of Rozanov's stated aims was to bring together Egypt and the Renaissance. V.V. Rozanov, 'Iz sedoi drevnosti', in *Vozrozhdaiushchiisia Egipet*, pp. 22–68 (p. 32). One of Rozanov's favourite painters was Raphael, and Rozanov discusses images of the Madonna in Raphael's work, whilst examining pagan motifs in them. For Rozanov, Raphael was able to express the universal truths of motherhood. Ibid., p. 31.

64 V.V. Rozanov, 'O drevneegipetskikh obeliskakh', in *Vo dvore iazychnikov*, pp. 10–14 (pp. 11–12).

65 Rozanov is often critical of Christ's parables which encourage man to reject the family. See especially V.V. Rozanov, 'Khristos i bogatyi iunosha', in *V temnykh religioznykh luchakh*, pp. 139–42 (p. 142).

> time – and, as I later realized, I was only drawn to them for the glow which was reflected from the light of Egypt. Egypt is the root of everything. Egypt gave humanity the first real Religion of the Fatherland, the religion of the Father of Worlds and of the Mother of Worlds… They taught humanity how to pray, they taught humanity the secret of 'prayer', the secret of the psalm…[66]

The Egyptians laid the basis for all future religions and cultures. However, the link between modern Russia and Egypt has been lost.[67] Therefore Rozanov searches for a reconnection through the family.

> Египтяне *открыли семью* – семейность, семейственность. До них… Хотя кто же был раньше их на земле? – Они предшествовали всяким номадам. Таким образом, вернее сказать, что *около* них, *в соседстве с ними* бродили и жили племена, которые имели случки, работу женщины на мужчину, роды ребенка и кормление его грудью. Ребенок вырастал и также случался, и около него росли дети, которые, выросши, начинали охотиться и тоже случались. Нить эта продолжалась бесконечно и еще могла бы продолжаться бесконечно. И собственно человеку предстояло оставаться дикарем, а человечеству – собранием диких племен, если бы египтяне первые во всемирной истории не задумались: «Что же это значит, что человек рождается? Как он рождается? И отчего?»
>
> The Egyptians *discovered the family* – family life, the importance of being in a family… Before them… But who on Earth came before them? They preceded any nomads. In such a way, I should say, tribes wandered and lived *around* them, *were their neighbours*, the tribes that had mating seasons, the work of a woman on a man, childbirth and breastfeeding. The child grew and also mated, other children grew up around him, children who, when grown, started to hunt and also mated. This thread continued endlessly and could still continue endlessly. And as such, man would have remained wild, and humanity would have remained a gathering of wild tribes, if the Egyptians had not been the first in human history to think: 'What does it mean for a person to be born? How is he born? And from what?'[68]

It was their fascination with childbirth that led the Egyptians to realize the significance of the Creation.[69] Consequently, the Egyptians were the first fully to understand the religious value of the family, the foundation of their civilization.

---

66 Taken from Rozanov's foreword to *Iz vostochnykh motivov*, recollecting his 60th birthday. V.V. Rozanov, 'Predislovie', in *Vozrozhdaiushchiisia Egipet*, p. 7.

67 Ibid.

68 'Sem´ia i sozhitie s zhivotnymi', p. 128.

69 Ibid., p. 129.

А поняв, вернее *создав* семью, они пришли ко всем прочим идеям строительного и религиозного характера: провидения, загробного суда, греха, фараонов, каст, жрецов, воинов. Дело в том, что идея семьи есть бесконечно построящая идея и бесконечно источающая идея. Можно до некоторой степени сказать, что семья есть *лицо человечества к Богу* – к Богу, *в вечность и в будущее*.

And having understood, or rather having *created* the family, they arrived at all other ideas of a constructive or religious character: providence, the judgement of the afterlife, sin, pharaohs, castes, priests, warriors. The thing is, the idea of the family is the infinite idea of construction, the infinitely emanative idea. One could say to a certain extent that the family is *humanity's face to God* – to God, *into eternity and into the future*.[70]

Rozanov believes that the modern Russian must open himself up to family life.[71] This reveals the true 'religio', the tie between man and God. The Church refuses to acknowledge this, and Rozanov wishes to re-establish a natural continuity from what he terms the 'Egyptian church' ('egipetskaia tserkov′') to the body of the Russian people.[72] Each people might have an undeveloped theology, yet they all possess a latent feeling for God. As with other religions, Rozanov accords himself a privileged position as uniquely able to interpret religious truths. Although he relies on the texts of Egyptologists and archaeologists, he is prepared to dismiss their work.

Но «задуматься о плодородии» не было обязательно и Шамполиону, и Бругшу, и Лепсиусу. «Они читали иероглифы». И натолкнувшись на сообщение египетского жреца: «Это – спинная кость Озириса», так как ничего сами не соединяли со «спинной костью», ибо ведь и анатомия, и физиология для них не была обязательна, отбросила его, – *отбросила уже вопреки требованию науки* – дать Египту египетские объяснения, – натворили с ней то же, что «необрезанные» натворили с объяснениями «обрезания».

Вообще, тема объясняется из темы; не нося темы в душе – нельзя понять темы у другого. И если не носить в душе главных тем Египта:

ПРОВИДЕНИЕ.

РОД, РОДОСЛОВИЯ; ПРЕДКИ И ПОТОМКИ.

СЕМЬЯ.

РЕЛИГИЯ. И в основе, и в стержне всего названного как «колыбель» религии, молитвы и рода:

ЖИЗНЬ И ПОЛ.

---

70 Ibid.

71 Ibid.

72 Ibid., p. 131.

> Если всего не иметь *лично* и *самому* задачею жизни, то нельзя ничего понять в Египте.
>
> But Champollion did not find it necessary to 'think about fecundity', nor did Brugsch, nor Lepsius. 'They read hieroglyphics'. And they came up against the message of the Egyptian priest: 'This is the backbone of Osiris', as if they themselves did not connect anything with 'the backbone', for they did not find anatomy or physiology necessary, they discarded it – *discarded it despite the demands of science*. They refused to give Egypt an Egyptian explanation. They concocted something along the lines of what they who are 'uncircumcised' concoct about those who are 'circumcised'. In general, subjects are explained by other subjects; it is impossible to understand other issues without carrying the matter into one's soul. They did not carry into their soul the main themes concerning Egypt:
>
> PROVIDENCE.
>
> BIRTH, GENEALOGY; ANCESTORS AND DESCENDANTS.
>
> FAMILY.
>
> RELIGION. And basically, the core of all that named above as the 'cradle' of religion, prayer and birth:
>
> LIFE AND SEX.
>
> If you do not have this as the *personal* task of your life, you will not understand anything about Egypt.[73]

Rozanov criticizes the Symbolists, who adopt Egyptian themes but miss the true meaning of their religion. Rozanov explains the true reverence of the Egyptians for living creatures.

> Они, и ТОЛЬКО они, ЕДИНСТВЕННО они, были «пантеистами», не «говорунами», а «делом»: ибо если ты, мой друг литератор, воистину «пантеист», то поди и пососи у коровы вымя, «как бы она была мать тебе». А если корова не «сестра тебе», то ты воистину литератор и ничем больше не можешь быть.
>
> They, and ONLY they, they ALONE were 'pantheists', not 'talkers', but 'doers'; for if you, my dear writer, are truly a 'pantheist', then go and suck the udders of a cow 'as if it were your mother'. And if the cow is not a 'sister to you', then verily you are a wordsmith and can amount to nothing more.[74]

All life emanates from God and is open to veneration, whether human or animal. Rozanov frequently refers to the Egyptian adoration of animals, especially the cow, and believes that contact with animals helped them to worship God (this is important in seeing the cosmological implications of his religion within the confines of his own family). Rozanov argues: 'Many

73 'Sem´ia i sozhitie s zhivotnymi', pp. 136–7.
74 Ibid., p. 132.

animals led the Egyptians to the most striking discoveries: and they were not mistaken in considering Osiris and Isis "their own kin", "mythological emperors", as well as the sheep, the pig, among others. All of them. "All animals are in fact our teachers. They taught us about god and prayer."'[75] His obsession with breasts is not limited to human females. Rozanov had a special love for cows, often recalling the cow which his poor family owned when he was a child in Kostroma. It is not surprising that this idealization of the cow is tied to his attention to breasts, suckling and the life-giving properties of milk. In his Egyptian essays he uses the term '*korovotsentrizm*', or 'cowcentricism', to describe his own fascination with the animal. Rozanov associates his own family cow with the entire cosmos, the stars, and the processes of the world which give life.[76] Rozanov treasures his intimate connection with this cow and its heavenly milk (he bizarrely wrote that the cow resembled his own mother).[77] Animals worship God through their natural behaviour; Rozanov's term for this is 'to osirisinize' ('ozirianstvovat´'), and humans should copy this.[78] This does not demean humans to the level of animals but elevates all forms of life to the divine. By breaking the categories between forms of life, Rozanov displays the unity of the world in its multiplicity of manifestations. This is best demonstrated by the Sphinx, a combination of different animals.[79] Rozanov also notes drawings of men with animals' tails, noting the parallels between humans and animals.[80] This was clear at the end of his life.

> Господи, как сладко даже помнить. Увы, теперь «сладки» только поминания и пуста еда. У меня мечта: когда пройдет револ., «назваться» к Вам в гости, и Вашего [...] папу и маму упросить МЕНЯ УГОСТИТЬ. Ну так... пир богов [...] Я хотел бы быть Полифемом и пасти коз и овец, а молоко бы у них высасывал СОБСТВЕННЫМ РТОМ. Кстати, меня давно уже манит собственным ртом напиться у коровы молока, насосаться из вымени это так красиво.
>
> Lord, how sweet it is to remember. Alas, only memories are 'sweet' now, and the food is dull. I have a dream: when the revol. passes, to invite myself to

75 V.V. Rozanov, 'Pered zevom smerti', in *Vozrozhdaiushchiisia Egipet*, pp. 264–70 (p. 270).

76 'Sem´ia i sozhitie s zhivotnymi', p. 129.

77 S. Fediakin, 'Sokrovennyi trud Rozanova', in *Vozrozhdaiushchiisia Egipet*, pp. 492–9 (p. 496).

78 'Pered zevom smerti', p. 267.

79 V.V. Rozanov, 'Deti egipetskie', in *Vozrozhdaiushchiisia Egipet*, pp. 86–8 (p. 87).

80 'Sem´ia i sozhitie s zhivotnymi', p. 135.

> your house, and entreat your father and mother TO TREAT ME. Just like... a feast of the gods [...] I would like to be a Polyphemus and herd goats and sheep, and suck milk from them WITH MY OWN MOUTH. In fact, I have long been enticed by the idea of drinking milk from cows with my own mouth, sucking from their udders. How beautiful that would be.[81]

Rozanov was able to tie together the beginnings and ends of his own life, spending his childhood and his last days in desperate provincial poverty. His final starving reminiscences lend a dream-like quality to his recollections of former Petersburg affluence, destroying the sense of reality of those years.

Rozanov glorifies sexual activity between men and cattle and suggests that such proximity to animals can help man to reach God. Rozanov highlights the physical relationship between man and beast, especially cows. (This is made particularly personal in his conflation of his own mother with the mother-cow.) He describes man's interaction with the world as sucking at the teats of Osiris. In particular, he highlights a case taken from the press of a peasant who engaged in bestiality with his cattle, here merging the mythological with the historical.[82] (Such acts of sexuality are strange given the emphasis in Rozanov on reproduction, but he does often seem to permit erotic deeds where desire is coupled with genuine reverence of the other, and of God. Bestiality helps dismantle the division between humans and animals. This stance also explains his tolerance of male homosexuality, especially in his musings over the public perceptions of Chaikovskii.[83] Rozanov is also very much in favour of the holy prostitution of the ancient temples of Egypt, whereas he was a staunch opponent of street prostitution in contemporary Russia, which involved loveless, irreverent sex.)

Matter is dead unless life acts upon it to make it holy. Rozanov frequently expresses his fear that life on Earth might die out, leaving a planet devoid of all living things. The life of animals – especially their mating rituals – is intimately linked with the life of the Earth, in particular its seasonal cycles, and the movement of the sun.[84] In this

---

81 Letter to Gollerbakh of 29 August 1918, reprinted in *V nashei smute*, p. 370.

82 See *Poslednie list'ia*, p. 221.

83 For a detailed discussion on the positive aspects of homosexual love, as manifested between Plato and Socrates, Harmodius and Aristogeiton, and Achilles and Patroclus, see V.V. Rozanov, 'Nechto iz tumana "obrazov" i "podobii". Sudebnoe nedorazumenie v Berline', in *Staraia i molodaia Rossiia*, pp. 70–5. Rozanov relies here on Krafft-Ebing's research.

84 V.V. Rozanov, 'Muzhestvo i otchestvo', in *Vozrozhdaiushchiisia Egipet*, pp. 237–9 (p. 237).

respect, Rozanov diverges from the view expounded in the mythological investigations of Merezhkovskii and Solov′ev, who both suggest that God is essentially masculine and acts upon a feminine world.

## Rozanov and Osiris

Rozanov posits an embodied God who can reproduce, merging the transcendent and the immanent. The human body is sanctified, made in the divine image and likeness. Although this truth is made clear in the Bible, Rozanov sees it as appropriate and real in Egypt. God has a penis (as well as a vagina, though in his Egyptian work he concentrates more on the male genitalia, a predilection which Rozanov often demonstrates and which appears to reveal a latent traditionalist view of the supremacy of the male), and this guarantees His relationship with man. The unity of real and ideal is affirmed through circumcision, a ritual which Rozanov believes originated in Egypt and which the Hebrews assumed from their neighbours.

He engages with the history of ideas over the physicality and emasculation of divinity, but in particular the disappearance of God's body in the transition from paganism to modern Christianity.[85] Rozanov's project

85 The Hebrew God, especially in early Judaism, was understood as embodied. Eilberg-Schwartz argues that it was the fact that the Jewish priesthood was forced into a homoerotic relationship with its God that encouraged its members to configure Yaweh as a genderless spirit. Eilberg-Schwartz studies the problems inherent in the masculinity of the Jewish deity and the implications for the Hebrews of having to relate intimately to a father figure. Much of the language of (especially early) Judaism describes the relationship between God and the Jews in erotic terms. For example, Eilberg-Schwartz argues that the reason that men were not allowed to gaze upon God was the fact that men were not permitted to see His penis. There are instances in the Old Testament where prophets were allowed to see God, but only from behind; he compares the language of Exodus 33:21–33, where God warns Moses only to view His back, to Genesis 9:20–25, where Shem and Japeth avert their eyes from their own drunken father's nakedness. See Howard Eilberg-Schwartz, *God's Phallus and Other Problems for Men and Monotheism* (Boston: Beacon Press, 1994), especially pp. 60–4, 81–6. Rozanov frequently displays great fondness for the Song of Songs, which he considers justification for the sensual experience in religion, though we can understand this as the sexual relationship between two humans leading to theosis, rather than positing the person's erotic encounter directly with the divine.

involves the 're-membering' of God, the re-insertion into religion of the divine Phallus.[86] Hence the fact that out of all the Egyptian deities Rozanov is drawn most to Osiris.[87] Rozanov draws parallels between Osiris and Isis the Christian God; these in his worldview are the same, and the Osiris myth proves that man may be deified.[88] Osiris becomes tied into a recurrent pattern of rebirth, where there is no such thing as death but only the transition from one form of life to another. Osiris proves the immortality of the person through his children, but also the direct identity of man and God. For Rozanov this differs from the Orthodox variant, as the resurrection of the human does not involve his abstraction from this world but takes place on Earth and within human time.[89]

Rozanov contends that the Osiris myth has greater validity than the New Testament parables, as it expresses God's paternity of the world. Rozanov argues that the Egyptians were the first to understand that the world is produced from God's phallus.[90] The world is understood as the seed of God, and divine semen is the building-block of the world.[91] The sexual organs are images of the divine (Rozanov uses the word 'obraz' with its obvious connotations of the Orthodox icon), through which all mankind is united.[92]

> Египтяне имели гениальную догадку: в сути полового органа человека, именно мужского, его solo – увидеть прообраз, да прямо зерно и суть всей

86 The term 're-membering' is Hare's, taken from his investigation of how the Christian deity has been disembodied through philosophy. See Hare, p. 224.

87 'Résumé ob Egipte', p. 241.

88 V.V. Rozanov, 'Taina chetyrekh lits, shesti kryl i omovenie', in *Vozrozhdaiushchiisia Egipet*, pp. 91–106 (p. 104). For detailed investigations of the Osiris myth, see Hare, pp. 20–34, and also Jan Assmann, *The Search for God in Ancient Egypt*, trans. by David Lorton (Ithaca/London: Cornell University Press, 2001), p. 125.

89 This explains Rozanov's frequent references to myths which narrate a resurrection on Earth, not only concerning Osiris, but also the phoenix. See, for example, V.V. Rozanov, 'Homines novi', in *Kogda nachal´stvo ushlo…*, pp. 16–22 (p. 22).

90 'Résumé ob Egipte', p. 241.

91 V.V. Rozanov, 'Vechnoe afrodizianstvo', in *Vozrozhdaiushchiisia Egipet*, pp. 186–91 (p. 188). Rozanov depicts a cosmos whose principal component is not the atom, but the eternally flowing semen of God. See his letter of 9 March 1918 (O.S.) to Gollerbakh, reprinted in E. Gollerbakh, *V.V. Rozanov: Zhizn´ i tvorchestvo* (Paris: YMCA Press, 1976), p. 43.

92 'Résumé ob Egipte', p. 241.

вообще космогонии, самого сложения мира, как бы сказать главнейшее: половой орган и рождает новое бытие оттого, что будучи и кажась «органом», он на самом деле есть зародыш и зерно мира, parvum in omne, pars pro toto, и еще как там выходит по-латыни или по-гречески. Отчего и проистекает не только сила его, но еще и те другие потрясающие феномены, что «боги и люди» (начало почитания животного у египтян), собаки, фараоны, девушки, царицы, волчицы, «чтут его одинаково» – чтут как египтяне в своих «таинствах».

The Egyptians had an ingenious idea: they saw the essence of the sexual organ of the person – that is the male's organ, his solo – as the prototype, in fact as the core and the essence of all cosmogony, of the very makeup of the world. They realized the most important thing: the sexual organ bears new life because, being and appearing an 'organ', it is in fact the seed and kernel of the world, parvum in omne, pars pro toto, as we would say in Latin or in Greek. This is the source not only of its potency, but also of those astonishing phenomena, the fact that 'gods and men' (the principle of the Egyptians' reverence for animals), dogs, pharaohs, girls, empresses, she-wolfs, 'worship it as one' – worship it like the Egyptians in their 'rites'.[93]

Alongside the Osiris myth, Rozanov also draws heavily throughout his work on the tale of Oedipus.[94] This crops up across many areas of Rozanov's studies, from his investigations of Egypt and the meaning of Christianity to his depictions of real-life incidents from Russia. Oedipus is important as he opens to humanity the secret of perpetuating life, but also hints at a belief in Rozanov that all love should be expressed physically. Every wife can also be a mother to her husband, and vice-versa. Rozanov writes that men cannot help but suck on their wife's breasts like a child.[95] The wife then also becomes the Madonna, the universal

---

93 For the importance of Oedipus see V.V. Rozanov, 'Skuka', in *Vozrozhdaiushchiisia Egipet*, pp. 277–81 (p. 280).

94 This book does not have the scope to delve into the psychoanalytical aspects of Rozanov's thought, though a Freudian examination of his beliefs would undoubtedly provide interesting conclusions. Rozanov often discussed his mother in candid and sexual terms, yet in his work and correspondence there is scant mention of his father. Freud did not consider mythology itself central to his views, but works backwards from psychology – for him, the complex explains the construction of the myth, not vice versa. This point is also examined in Jean-Joseph Goux, *Oedipus, Philosopher*, trans. by Catherine Porter (Stanford: Stanford University Press, 1993), pp. 1–2. Rozanov often reveals his sexual attraction to his own mother as a (fatherless) boy, and understands this urge cosmologically. See Boldyrev, pp. 36–7.

95 V.V. Rozanov, 'Demetra i mif Edipa', in *Vozrozhdaiushchiisia Egipet*, pp. 256–60 (p. 257).

mother.[96] Rozanov called his second wife 'mama', and rumours (almost certainly unfounded) circulated in Petersburg that he had an affair with his step-daughter.[97] Yet Rozanov believes that people are instinctively drawn to their genealogical relatives. He draws parallels between Egypt and incidents from contemporary Russian life, drawn from newspaper articles, which narrate tales of families (ostracized and ridiculed) whose members engage in sexual relations with each other. Rozanov writes that such cases of incest are common, though kept private from mainstream society, and perfectly natural. There is a cosmological model for this; although Rozanov posits the consubstantiality of God and Earth, God enjoys at the same time an erotic relationship with His creation. He also draws examples from the Old Testament to consolidate his position.

> Сеют: и посмотрите, ведь земля не только по виду своему, но и по существу своему – брюхата, посев есть совокупление зерна и планеты, ибо зерно есть старший и первый, есть Адам, а планета – только Ева, вторая и менее тяжеловесная. Зерно, падающее с дерева или с травы на землю, – оплодотворяет ее совершенно, как мужчина женщину. Но в «порядке личного существования» дерево, конечно, «выросло из земли», – это единичное дерево, – и есть сын ее. И что же мы видим? Великую тайну Эдипа: что сын оплодотворяет мать свою. Но смотрите, смотрите, как ноумен пронизывает феномены: если мужу даже 50 лет, а жене только 20, жена обнимает его сверху книзу, совершенно, как мать, баюкает его и психически смотрит на него как на своего ребенка. Всякая любовь – всякий раз, как мужчина и женщина совокупились между собой, жена таинственно усваивается в мать мужу: и «Эдипова тайна» есть вообще в браке.
>
> Seeds are sown: and look, the whole Earth – in its essence, not just in its appearance – is pregnant. Sowing is the copulation of the seeds and the planet, for the seed is the oldest and the first, the seed is Adam, and the planet is only Eve, secondary and lighter. The seed, falling from the tree or grass, fully impregnates the Earth, just as man impregnates a woman. But in terms of its own lifespan, the tree, of course, 'grew from the Earth' – it is a single tree, and is the Earth's son. And what do we see? The eternal secret of Oedipus: the son impregnates his own mother. But look, look, how the noumen penetrates the phenomenon: if the husband is 50 years old, and the wife only 20, the wife embraces him from top to bottom, completely, like a mother. She lulls him and sees him as her own child. Each time, each time the husband and wife copulate, the wife mysteriously becomes a mother to the husband; all in all, the 'secret of Oedipus' is the general secret of marriage.[98]

---

96 Ibid., p. 257.
97 Gippius, p. 166.
98 'Demetra i mif Edipa', pp. 256–7.

This oedipalism ('edipstvo') is thriving in Russia, and people who engage in it lead holy and happy lives.[99] In upholding incest, Rozanov sides with Bataille in rejecting the shift from 'nature' to 'culture' examined by Levi-Strauss. This lost sexuality is for Rozanov part of a lost epistemology. He believes that Oedipus was blessed with knowledge superior to that of contemporary Russians, a revelation that came to him when watching a production of Sophocles' play in Petersburg. 'Watching the tragedy and its concluding act, I felt that the ancients, or at least some portion of the ancients, although they stood below us in their general development – in another sense, in fact, in their "behaviour", their "knowledge", they were much higher than us'.[100]

Oedipus grasps the secrets of eternal life, the fact that each man becomes Osiris when he dies. He realizes that death does not lead to non-being, but is merely a change in status, the reverse side of the same coin as this life. In Egyptian thought, death is an opportunity for a new beginning, a form of renewal where the unity of the person is preserved.[101] In Rozanov's interpretation, the myth of Oedipus merges (Rozanov uses the word 'slivat´sia') with Egyptian thought, and also with the first books of the Bible. Therefore one of the major reasons for Rozanov's use of Egyptian myths is his need to understand death, to overcome the pessimism of Orthodox theology and the unhappiness of his own family life. 'In the general sense, there were no "dead" in Egypt, nobody "died" there. Instead, they took on a new form of life, a new type of being. Without this conviction they would not have built their pyramids, or would not have built castles for their graves'.[102] As distinct from Orthodoxy, the Osiris myth provides a cyclical dimension to life, marking the renewed significance of birth.[103] Rozanov ties together both

99 Ibid., p. 258.

100 V.V. Rozanov, 'Chto skazal Teziiu Edip?', in *Vo dvore iazychnikov*, pp. 287–98 (p. 289).

101 V.V. Rozanov, 'Pervaia kolybel´naia pesnia na zemle', in *Vozrozhdaiushchiisia Egipet*, p. 89.

102 V.V. Rozanov, 'Iz "Knigi Mertvykh..."', in *Vozrozhdaiushchiisia Egipet*, pp. 144–9 (p. 144). Many commentators have remarked that the obsession with death formed the fundamental part of Egyptian culture, a pessimistic contrast to Rozanov's positive interpretation of their thought. For example, see Bertrand Russell, *History of Western Philosophy, and its Connections with Political and Social Circumstances from the Earliest Times to the Present Day* (London: Allen and Unwin, 1946, 1961), p. 26.

103 V.V. Rozanov, 'K risunku: "Anubis prinimaet mumiiu iz ruk plachushchei zheny, chtoby vnesti ee v mogilu"', in *Vozrozhdaiushchiisia Egipet*, p. 144.

ends of man's life, ensuring that his death is seen as a rebirth; the cradle pulls towards the grave as the grave pulls towards the cradle.[104]

In positing continuity from Russia to Egypt, Rozanov resurrects the religious beliefs of the ancients, especially their mythology, the foundation of their religion.[105] Rozanov sees the development of formal philosophy as a separation of epistemology and ontology, or consciousness from matter. This shift, from the Egyptian religious outlook to the Greek philosophical tradition, comes across as a loss of an innocence of vision, crucial to human history. Whereas the Egyptians understand the Creation, Rozanov criticizes the ancient Greeks for the lightness of their prayers.[106] Rozanov describes the Greek worldview as obsessed with the external and superficial, and lacking an internal, and therefore moral, quality. Greeks worship the flesh, but without regard for its essence or its potential. This permitted them to abstract thought from physical categories.

> Египтяне, узнавая греческие мифы (то же – и о милом Зевесе), могли только пожать плечами и сказать: «Это – пошлость». И прибавить: «У вас вообще нет религии, а мифы, сказки, – и о пошлых существах. У вас нет религии, а какие-то имена богов. У вас нет плача Изиды об Озирисе, – и целования Возлюбленного. Уйдите. Уйдите с глаз долой!».
>
> The Egyptians, learning the Greek myths (that is, about kind Zeus) could only shrug their shoulders and say: 'This is vulgarity'. And add: 'You have no religion at all, but only myths, fairytales, and all about vulgar subjects. You have no religion at all, but just some names of gods. You do not have Isis' lament over Osiris, or the kiss of the Beloved. Go! Get out of our sight!'[107]

Ultimately, Greek philosophy fed into Christianity, where the fixation on the spiritual disregards the physical.[108] Christianity consolidates the loss of the Edenic image, but this trend starts in ancient Greece. Rozanov had a great fondness for classical culture, especially the tales from Greek mythology, and frequently called for the Russian education system to pay more attention to classics (on this matter he engaged Men′shikov in a long and bitter argument). However, Rozanov sees the Greeks as

---

104 V.V. Rozanov, 'Tut est′ nekaia taina', in *Vo dvore iazychnikov*, pp. 309–12 (p. 311).

105 'Sem′ia i sozhitie s zhivotnymi', p. 129.

106 V.V. Rozanov, 'Velichaishaia minuta istorii', in *Vozrozhdaiushchiisia Egipet*, pp. 8–19 (p. 19).

107 'Sem′ia i sozhitie s zhivotnymi', p. 129.

108 V.V. Rozanov, 'Ellinizm', in *Vo dvore iazychnikov*, pp. 171–7 (p. 173).

portraying only part of the truth. Whereas Rozanov appreciates the formal aspects of classical art, he consistently warns that this does not express the true content of religion.

There is a long-standing tradition in European thought, most likely emerging from Plato's *Phaedo*, that associates philosophy with death. This is major reason for Rozanov's use of mythology, in that he is searching for a form of discourse which instead has ties with life. The transition from the Egyptian mythological to the Greek philosophical worldview is crucial in Rozanov's religion. Rozanov is in many ways a liminal figure, drawn to ruptures in history; he wishes to examine these breaches in the context of his broader studies of how the historical human maintains their links to the Creation. This helps explain the significance of Oedipus in Rozanov's thought. The Oedipus tale is traditionally understood as marking the transition from myth to philosophy. In particular the Sphinx, providing as she does the bridge between Egypt and ancient Greece, is seen as the symbol of this shift.[109]

Oedipus solves the Sphinx's riddle and focuses our attention not on God or the world, but on man. Yet Rozanov is not content with this and follows with another question: what is man? He is unsure; following the traditions of Orthodoxy, he contends that the essence of man, being made in the image of God, is unknowable. Divine apophaticism leads to anthropological apophaticism. Yet there are aspects in which Rozanov is clear: man is made in the image and likeness of God and Rozanov insists that this connection must be demonstrated physiologically. He wants the Russians to 're-member' God, by re-establishing physical ties with Him through the phallus. This is achieved sexually. More broadly, in all his activity man is called on to foster a sensual relationship with the past and to re-establish a tangible relationship with history, rather than simply studying his past intellectually.[110] Throughout his work, Rozanov

---

109 Goux, *Oedipus, Philosopher*, pp. 143–5. In mythology, the Sphinx has often been seen as the beast which performs rites of initiation on young men. She has been considered the object of man's deepest and darkest sexual urges, a strange feminine creature who tempts young men on the transition into adulthood into a potentially fatal union. One notes on an individual basis Rozanov's fascination in the transition of humans from one state to another, from adolescence to adulthood, and the rites which manage these changes. In mythology, teranthropomorphic beasts typically oversee these 'liminal ritual situations'. Ibid., pp. 37, 47.

110 V.V. Rozanov, 'Zheltyi chelovek v peredelke', in *Okolo tserkovnykh sten*, pp. 48–57 (p. 53). This is a particularly Rozanovian form of anamnesis,

displays a preference for physical contact with the past, rather than its intellectual examination.[111] Perhaps one of the most vivid examples of how Rozanov practises this is in his numismatics; Rozanov does just not study his coins abstractly, but constantly fondles them and uses them to make contact with the ancient world. It is this attempt to restore the physical links between modernity and with ancient, Creation-orientated, religions, to make the significance of the Creation real in everyday Russian life, that leads Rozanov to perhaps the most contentious area of his study, that is to that of the Jews in Russia.

---

the remembrance of God. In general Christian terms, anamnesis is more than a 'straightforward "remembering"', but has 'confessional implications', where the worshipper enters into a relationship with Christ based on future salvation. See Richard J. Ginn, *The Present and the Past: A Study of Anamnesis* (Allison Park: Pickwick Publications, 1989), pp. 25–6. Concepts of anamnesis are contingent on theological interpretations of history. Rozanov's remembrance constitutes entering into a historical link with God, founded on the ongoing chain of human procreation and generation through which man traces his origins to the beginning of time. Christ, who has 'dephallicized' religion, disrupts this link.

111 For example, at the end of March or the beginning of April 1901, on his return to Russia after a trip to Italy, Rozanov wrote to Suvorin of his joy in being able to come into contact with the same objects Pushkin had, displaying Rozanov's love for the tangible aspects of history over the merely cerebral. Rozanov writes: 'It is good to touch history with your hands, but not so good to read about it'. Reprinted in V.V. Rozanov, *Priznaki vremeni: Stat'i i ocherki 1911 g. Pis'ma A.S. Suvorina k V.V. Rozanovu. Pis'ma V.V. Rozanova k A.S. Suvorinu*, ed. by A.N. Nikoliukin (Moscow: Respublika, 2006), pp. 348–9.

Chapter 4

# Creation and *Byt*

Rozanov's concern that the cosmos could fall into disunity at the moment of Creation leads him to look for ways to make the significance of that single moment a continuing reality in everyday life. In searching for ways to imitate the Egyptian reverence for the Creation, Rozanov looks to the Jews, neighbours to the Egyptians, as he suspects that they took from Egypt the secrets of the Creation and preserved them for themselves.[1] One significant example of this, which also shows the correspondence of his Egyptology and his Biblical exegesis, is his belief that the Song of Songs was written by Egyptians as a religious text and that the Jews assumed this for themselves. Rozanov believes that the Russians should imitate this erotic intensity.[2] More specifically, Rozanov examines Jewish ritual practices, the external marks of their religion, and therefore his critiques of Egypt, Christianity and Judaism cannot be understood independently from each other.[3] Rozanov's work on Judaism emerges not from affection, but from a hope that Jewish rituals constitute the best surviving example of ancient Egyptian life. Rozanov is fascinated by the lifestyle of contemporary Russian Jews and demonstrates an often uncomfortable enthralment with the details of Jewish home life and sexuality. Underlying this is an expectation, and also a fear, that the Russians and Jews might share a similar approach in their religiosity, particularly in the physical way in which they accept God.[4]

---

1 V.V. Rozanov, 'Iudaizm', in *Novyi Put´* (July 1903), pp. 145–88 (p. 148).

2 'Pervaia kolybel´naia pesnia na zemle', p. 89.

3 Katsis notes that whenever Rozanov discusses the Jews, he is focused on his project for the Orthodox Church. L.F. Katsis, '"Delo Beilisa" v kontekste "Serebrianogo veka"', in *Delo Beilisa: Tsarskaia Rossiia i delo Beilisa*, ed. by A.S. Tager (Moscow: Gesharim, 1995), pp. 412–34 (p. 414).

4 Rozanov writes that 'the Jewish soul is close to the Russian soul, and the Russian soul to the Jewish'. 'Ogni sviashchennye', p. 238. Despite the fact that Rozanov's, like so many theological and philosophical positions, is built on certainty, perhaps we could mischievously suggest that Rozanov often appears less sure in his convictions than he would care to admit. This is notable in his investigations of Jewish sexuality. This appears to be the conclusion of perhaps one of his biggest contemporary Jewish fans, Saul Bellow, whose characters are filled with the erotic confusion the Canadian author sees in Rozanov's work. In *More Die of Heartbreak*, Bellow opposes

Rozanov grew up in nineteenth-century provincial Russia to a pious Orthodox family and his work is tinged with the suspicion of Jews which often characterized that society. It is possible to contextualize his outlook within the broad framework of Russian conservative thinkers who expressed animosity towards the Jews and who presented them as the other, an alien nation with an independent history.[5] Such ideas are present in the figures that inspired Rozanov, including Dostoevskii and Suvorin.[6] However, Rozanov provides a unique approach to the Jewish question in basing his attitude towards them on their proximity to the Creation and relationship to Egypt. This belief in the Jews' access to a superior knowledge fuels Rozanov's philosemitism, but also paradoxically his negative feelings towards them.

Rozanov insists that the Jews kept the Egyptian secrets of Creation hidden from the rest of humanity. He sets himself a privileged position as the only person (with perhaps the exception of Florenskii) capable of taking these secrets back from the Jews. There is also a more general tension at issue here in the way Rozanov approaches the knowable nature of religious matters. Within Rozanov's project to open up all the secrets of religion and to relocate the lost knowledge of the ancients, there is a fear that the most vital elements of religion, the mysteries of the Creation, might be beyond human knowledge and that it is possibly dangerous to attempt to discover them. Even God does not know the reasons for Creation.[7] There is the latent influence of Orthodox apophaticism here, and Rozanov, like the Symbolists, makes reference

---

bodily knowledge to scientific reasoning, a common tension among Jewish scholars who are torn between their love for learning and their physical roots; in this work Bellow, like Rozanov, opposes the Tree of Life to the Tree of Knowledge, concluding that 'knowledge divorced from life equals sickness'. The inference is that both Rozanov and Bellow suspect that the Jews and the Russians might be more closely related to one another than they are both able to understand.

5 N.P. Giliarov-Platonov, *Evreiskii vopros v Rossii* (St Petersburg, no given publisher, 1906), p. 6. For state policy towards the Jews at the time, and especially Pobedonostsev's influence, see Leo Errera, *The Russian Jews: Extermination or Emancipation?*, trans. by B. Löwy (London: D. Nutt, 1894), pp. 16–18.

6 Dostoevskii, 'Evreiskii vopros', XXV, pp. 74–7. Suvorin admits his hostility towards the Jews in a letter to Rozanov, dated 30 July 1901 (O.S.). *Priznaki vremeni*, p. 303.

7 *Poslednie list'ia*, p. 26.

to Tiutchev's maxim that each thought expressed is a lie.[8] Yet at the end of the day, Rozanov is bold enough to make the revelation (or recovery) of religious truth the core part of his project, hence his aggressive probing at Judaism and his arrogant self-styling. In August 1918, he wrote to Izmailov, 'I do not understand: either the Jews do not understand themselves, or they have forgotten their history, or they have been corrupted by the Russians. Otherwise, they should [...] embrace my feet. I honestly consider myself... not even "a Russian writer", but genuinely the last Jewish prophet'.[9]

It is difficult to prise apart Rozanov's Judophilia and his Judophobia, as these are components of the same approach.[10] Rozanov himself divided his Jewish studies into his works with a positive assessment and those with a negative appraisal.[11] Subsequent scholarship has accordingly often fallen into the trap of categorizing his work as either positive (in particular his earlier career), or negative (in his later career), and scholars have struggled to find the turning point in Rozanov's thought which forces his change of opinion. I argue that it is not possible to separate and categorize Rozanov's work in such a manner. Rather, the motivation behind Rozanov's study of Jewish worship does not change, but remains his determination to unlock the secrets of the Creation. Furthermore, the interpretation of Rozanov's Jewish studies as some kind of turning point, and a return to Christianity, does not fully account for the fact that in the last year of his life Rozanov asked the Jewish people for forgiveness and constructed his most aggressive work against

---

8 Rozanov admired Tiutchev's work, which he considered to have a religious value and which he placed higher than the poetry of Vladimir Solov´ev. 'Literaturnyi rod Solov´evykh', p. 83. One of the most problematic of Rozanov's essays concerns the limits of human understanding and how the holy (in Rozanov's case, the sexual) can be expressed linguistically. See V.V. Rozanov, 'Kak razreshaetsia nedoumenie', in *Russkaia gosudarstvennost´ i obshchestvo*, pp. 457–9 (p. 457).

9 Quoted in A. Nikoliukin, 'K voprosu o mifologeme natsional´nogo v tvorchestve V.V. Rozanova', in *Sakharna*, pp. 414–20 (p. 418).

10 There is often a very fine line between admiration for, and hatred of, Jewish practices. Mondry, 'Is the End of Censorship in the Former Soviet Union a Good Thing?', pp. 115–16.

11 In his draft plan for a proposed complete works, Rozanov divides his work on Jewish worship into essays 'expressing a positive relationship to Judaism' in volume 9, and works 'with a negative relationship to Judaism' in volume 10. 'Plan Polnogo sobraniia sochinenii, sostavlennyi V.V. Rozanovym v 1917 godu'.

Jesus Christ. There is certainly an intensification in the expression of his bitterness towards the Jews, but this stems from his inability to answer the questions he himself poses about religion. Despite the fact that Rozanov in 1903 wrote a series of essays positively comparing aspects of Jewish worship and Orthodoxy, one also finds in Rozanov's earlier (pre-1910) works many critical references to the Jews.[12] He consistently maintains a deep distrust, and often a violent hatred, towards the Jews as a race, and is particularly fearful of their political and literary strength in Russia. Ironically, the strength of the Jewish family and their reproductive qualities – traits which Rozanov admires and which the Russians must replicate in order to survive – are also the characteristics which fuel his concerns over the perceived threat to Russia.

There is still relatively little scholarly work on Rozanov's Jewish studies, although this is growing. His contemporaries had long been aware that the Jews played an important role in his investigation of Christianity. In one of the Religious-Philosophical Meetings from the 1902–1903 season, Minskii criticized Rozanov for his over-enthusiasm for Jewish marriage and his inability to see that any other path outside family life might also lead to the good.[13] As Rozanov's work became more openly hostile towards the Jews, his contemporaries and friends started to become more aggressive in their critique of his output. In autumn 1913, Rozanov released a selection of hagiographical essays

---

12 Throughout his work Rozanov manifests a suspicion of other ethnic groups who might disturb Russian unity. He was also concerned about the influence Jewish groups held over Russian literature (including Russian journalism) and often associated – as did many of his contemporaries – Jews with the revolutionaries, even prior to Stolypin's assassination. See the 1906 essay, V.V. Rozanov, 'Molchashchie sily', in *Russkaia gosudarstvennost´ i obshchestvo*, pp. 99–101 (p. 100).

13 Minskii points out that it is Rozanov's inability to permit a multiplicity of truths which restricts his focus to the 'cult of the family'. In highlighting his monism (an interpretation of Rozanov which Bakhtin repeats a generation later), Minskii compared Rozanov to Tolstoi. In Minskii's view, both 'see only one ideal of the good, and in its name reject any alternatives'. Quoted in *Zapiski peterburgskikh Religiozno-filosofskikh sobranii*, p. 272. Six years later, Minskii wrote an essay opposing Rozanov and Tolstoi, to which Rozanov would retort that the differences between himself and Tolstoi were not so great, but that both in fact agreed that love was the 'only and fully adequate sanction of the physical union of the sexes'. See V.V. Rozanov, 'Voprosy sem´i i vospitaniia (Po povodu dvukh novykh broshiur g-zhi N. Zharintsevoi), in *Okolo narodnoi dushi*, pp. 50–60 (p. 54).

for the murdered youth Andrei Iushchinskii, proclaiming the guilt of Mendel′ Beilis and reviving the Jewish Blood Accusation. The respectable conservative press, including *Novoe Vremia*, refused to publish these articles, and they were only accepted by the notorious *Zemshchina*. This marked Rozanov's ostracism from what might tentatively be labelled the mainstream of Russian religious philosophers (I use this terminology with care, as the Religious-Philosophical Society itself was an esoteric clique, detached from mainstream Russian society). Merezhkovskii and Kartashev especially were outraged by Rozanov's essays, and other senior members of the Society, particularly Filosofov, moved to have Rozanov thrown out of the association. However, Rozanov did not fight attempts to expel him. By 1913 he was unwilling to associate further with Merezhkovskii and Filosofov. He had already stopped attending the Religious-Philosophical Society, before the meeting on 26 January 1914 (O.S.) which formally proclaimed the 'impossibility of cooperation with V.V. Rozanov'.[14] However, not all of Rozanov's colleagues turned against him. Spasovskii, for example, claimed that Rozanov was not anti-Semitic, but had sought the manner in which the Jews' connection to blood was manifested through their rituals.[15]

More recent scholarship has also struggled with the apparent contradictions in Rozanov's Jewish studies. Glouberman has argued that Rozanov's anti-Semitism emerges from his own 'perverted utopianism', the fact that Rozanov simultaneously admires and envies the Jews for their special relationship with God. In Glouberman's interpretation, Rozanov believes that he cannot achieve communion with the divine as

14 It is important to note that the Jewish question was not the only reason for Rozanov's exclusion. Filosofov also condemned at length Rozanov's proclamation that returning political emigrants should not be given amnesties. He also points out Rozanov's contradictoriness. According to Filosofov, Rozanov's words had lost their value, and had even started to destroy each other. '"Sud" nad Rozanovym. Zapiski S.-Peterburgskogo Religiozno-filosofskogo obshchestva', in *Vasilii Rozanov: Pro et Contra*, II, pp. 184–215 (p. 187). Nevertheless, Mondry indicates how the two issues, both of Beilis and political radicals, have become conflated in contemporary Russian scholarship and have been turned into a patriotic issue where the Russians are portrayed as victims of revolutionaries and Jews – essentially the same phenomenon. See Mondry, 'Is the End of Censorship in the Former Soviet Union a Good Thing?', p. 118.

15 M.M. Spasovskii, *V.V. Rozanov v poslednie gody svoei zhizni* (New York: Vseslavianskoe izdatel′stvo, 1968), p. 45.

long as there are still Jews on Earth.[16] Nikoliukin (who did not prioritize the republication of many of Rozanov's important works on Jewish worship) explains Rozanov's apparently contradictory attitude towards the Jews by contextualizing him within the antinomial traditions of Russian anti-rationalism. Nikoliukin also investigates Rozanov's myth-making about the Jews and the manner in which this was misunderstood by his contemporaries.[17] Nikoliukin contends that Stolypin's murder proved the turning point in Rozanov's anti-Jewish stance, after which Rozanov always felt guilty that his anti-Semitic works would be hurtful to Gershenzon.[18] In a similar fashion, Fateev points out Rozanov's antinomies and describes his attitude towards the Jews as vacillating between a 'passionate fascination with their Old Testament life [*byt*] and an extreme rejection of their role in the political life of Russia'.[19] Of the Western scholars, Mondry has worked on Rozanov within the framework of modern cultural studies and has contextualized Rozanov's views within the scientific racial theories of his time, especially those of Jung, Weininger and Sander Gilman.[20] Mondry also echoes Glouberman in pointing to Rozanov's deep envy of the Jews' privileged position in world history. In particular, she criticizes Nikoliukin's apologetics for Rozanov's antinomical thought as clichéd (though at the same time she praises Nikoliukin's efforts in opening up Rozanov's work to contemporary academics). Mondry's major criticism of Nikoliukin is that he discusses the Jews in Rozanov's interpretation as an intellectual construct, or a myth, constructed by Rozanov, but that at the same time Nikoliukin also argues that Rozanov treats the Jews as real people whom Rozanov detests.[21] However, both Mondry and Nikoliukin omit the processes through which Rozanov creates new myths about Jewish life.

16 Emanuel Glouberman, 'Vasilii Rozanov: The Antisemitism of a Russian Judephile', *Jewish Social Studies*, 38 (1976), 117–44 (pp. 138–9).

17 Nikoliukin, 'K voprosu o mifologeme natsional′nogo v tvorchestve V.V. Rozanova', p. 419.

18 Nikoliukin, *Golgofa Vasiliia Rozanova*, p. 409.

19 Fateev, *S russkoi bezdnoi v dushe*, p. 527.

20 Genrietta Mondri, 'Vasilii Rozanov, evrei i russkaia literatura', in *Rozanov i evrei*, pp. 155–267 (p. 159).

21 Mondry does not comment on the fact that some degree of flexibility is central to Rozanov's thought; monolithic truth is located only in the totality of competing ideas. Rozanov even defends Merezhkovskii against Minskii's accusations of inconsistency: 'Nobody who knows Merezhkovskii would ever think that he was ever insincere in his diametrically opposed views [...] We are not gods, we do not know the absolute truth; this is why we

One reason offered for Rozanov's turn against the Jews concerns his wife's illness. There is some degree of truth in this. Rozanov often sees the world in terms of opposites and despite his best efforts finds no way to reconcile Judaism and Christianity. During his most virulent anti-Christ moments, he uses the Jewish proximity to blood as a positive thing, to attack the disembodiment of the Orthodox Church. However, when his wife fell suddenly ill, Rozanov saw this as divine retribution for his campaign against Christ. On 26 August 1910 (O.S.), Rudneva suffered what appears to be a stroke, which left her left side paralysed. According to his daughter Tat′iana, Rozanov saw Rudneva's illness as punishment for his blasphemy. This represents a profound shift from the playful probing of religion which had marked Rozanov's earlier works, to a much more serious and sadder mood in his later period. According to his own recollections and the memoirs of relatives and friends, Rozanov was deeply shaken by Rudneva's illness. He spent nights on his knees before an icon, begging for forgiveness for eleven years of attacks on the Church and on Christ.[22]

Another point lies in Rozanov's response to the 1911 murder of Andrei Iushchinskii, a young Christian boy from Kiev whose body was deliberately mutilated in order to create the impression that he had been the victim of a Jewish ritual killing. Although it became quickly apparent that a criminal gang was responsible for the murder, many individuals in the Russian state selected to pursue a Jewish factory worker, Mendel′ Beilis. Reviving the ancient Blood Accusation, they accused Beilis of involvement in anti-Christian Jewish practices. To the modern mind (as to many observers at the time), the accusations levelled against Beilis are bizarre. Rozanov's response must be contextualized within the intense interest in religious issues of the Silver Age.[23] This was a cultural environment where religious matters were not

---

vacillate, we make contentions and then refute them'. This is a rejection of dry philosophical systems, which Rozanov believes demonstrate a lack of real conviction. V.V. Rozanov, 'Dva obyska v odin den′', in *V nashei smute*, pp. 98–101 (p. 100). However, despite some degree of movement in Rozanov, his approach to any phenomenon remains dogmatic, and he remains rooted to examining the concrete reality of experience in all his work; in this he is highly consistent.

22 Tat′iana Rozanova, pp. 60–1.

23 Tat′iana Rozanova notes that her father, when reading about ancient religious beliefs, never doubted that these were real facts which actually took place. Ibid., p. 43.

restricted to scholarly examination, but were lived out and made real in a climate of intense apocalypticism. Although many Russian statesmen and philosophers spoke out fiercely against the persecution of Beilis, many important cultural figures were convinced in the reality of Jewish sacrificial worship and supported the authorities' actions against him.[24] Many religious thinkers were convinced in the Blood Accusation. Former friends and allies fell out with each other over the affair. Khlebnikov and Mandel′shtam almost duelled with each other.[25] Rozanov can only be fully understood within this highly charged eschatological culture. Moreover, for all his faults, Rozanov, alongside Florenskii, was the only person to attempt an in-depth investigation of Jewish rituals.[26]

Rozanov started to explore Judaism towards the end of the nineteenth century, at the same time that he started seriously to investigate Egypt and to criticize the Russian Orthodox Church's attitude to the family. He devoted scores of articles specifically to the subject of Judaism, and many of his other articles nominally addressed towards other topics also discuss Judaism and the Jews. It is now clear that he had a limited, and often erroneous, knowledge of the formal precepts of Jewish religion.[27] He had access to certain works on Judaism, including Naum Pereferkovich's translation of the Torah.[28] It is highly doubtful, however, that Rozanov read such theological texts systematically – the evidence seems to suggest that he merely browsed through these books and extracted certain choice phrases which appeared to fit with his own ideas.[29] Hence this chapter will not assess the accuracy of Rozanov's assessment of Judaic theology and scholarship, but will critique instead the way in which he compares aspects of Jewish practices against his own religious framework.

---

24 Many Russians, including Vasilii Skvortsov and other senior government officials, as well as large sections of society, believed in Jewish ritual killings and in Beilis' guilt. See Fateev, *S russkoi bezdnoi v dushe*, pp. 517–18.

25 Katsis, '"Delo Beilisa" v kontekste "Serebrianogo veka"', p. 417.

26 Fateev, *S russkoi bezdnoi v dushe*, p. 518.

27 L.F. Katsis, 'Iz kommentariia k iudeiskim motivam V.V. Rozanova', *Nachala*, 3 (Moscow, 1992), 75–8 (p. 78).

28 Naum Pereferkovich, *Talmud, Mishna i Tosefta* (St Petersburg, no given publisher, 1889–1904). See Glouberman, p. 120.

29 Fediakin discusses how Rozanov handles other scholars' writing, to which Fediakin refers not as 'chtenie', but as 'vgliadyvanie'. See Fediakin, 'Sokrovennyi trud Rozanova', p. 493. Rozanov admitted that he did not read books properly, lacking a 'reading angel' ('angel chteniia'). Even Strakhov questioned the undisciplined manner in which Rozanov read: see *Literaturnye izgnanniki*, p. 163.

## Rituals of the family

Rozanov establishes a connection between the Creation and the family. Family life is the holiest form of existence, and provides the framework through which humans realize their relationship with God. The family connects us through history to Eden, and outside the family a relationship with God is impossible; the family is 'the step to God'.[30]

Families are the form through which humanity repeats the Creation on an ongoing basis in the modern world, hence the importance of ritualistic practices for Rozanov.[31] Each ritual act represents a new event and a new opportunity for creativity. Rituals maintain an intricate relationship between tradition and the present, the beginning and repeated time. The complexity of Rozanov's thought lies in his belief that Russia must return to old religious practices by being renewed through the continual presentation of new life.

Recent scholarship, particularly in the West, has tended to emphasize Rozanov's interest in new and original forms of life. Such work, partly influenced by the theories of Bakhtin, rightly underlines Rozanov's attention to the value of creativity and new life. Crone writes of Rozanov's 'impulse towards the dissolution of old and hackneyed literary forms'.[32] Dimbleby concentrates on Rozanov's desire to overcome existing forms of literature and his love for the miracle of new birth.[33] This focus on the new can only be explained in terms of Rozanov's preoccupation with ancient forms of human behaviour. Rozanov was in many ways backward looking and professed a hatred of the new. He loved old and dead languages, despite his own admission that he had no talent for languages.[34] His earliest philosophical examinations are filled with studies of the meanings of Greek terms, especially those used by Aristotle.[35] He used Latin terms in many of his studies, for example his investigation of the manner in which

30 V.V. Rozanov, 'Predislovie ko vtoromu izdaniiu', in *V mire neiasnogo i nereshennogo*, p. 8.

31 Gippius notes Rozanov's fondness for rituals. See Gippius, p. 153.

32 Crone, *Rozanov and the End of Literature*, p. 16.

33 See Liza Dimbleby, 'Rozanov and His Literary Demons', in *Russian Literature and its Demons*, pp. 307–32.

34 Rozanov admits to Strakhov in a letter of 15 February 1888 (O.S.) his struggle to co-produce, along with his fellow teacher Pavel Pervov, a translation of Aristotle's *Metaphysics*. *Literaturnye izgnanniki*, p. 154.

35 See for example the same letter, in which Rozanov re-explores the meaning of understanding and form, reprinted in ibid., p. 155.

blood, sperm and the body should be considered 'in statu agente'.[36] He also used Old Church Slavonic and revived archaic Russian words.[37] He was considered one of the most extreme conservative thinkers of his time and to no small extent won this notoriety through his work for *Novoe Vremia*.[38] However, his worldview is also orientated towards the future. It is only by creating new life, based on repeated and known patterns, that the miracle of the Creation can be continually re-enacted.

Hence the significance of *byt* for Rozanov and his peers. More radical thinkers saw *byt* as stultifying, the repressive tedium which had poisoned Russian history. Maiakovskii famously talked about fighting *byt* by hammering his head into it.[39] The Formalists looked specifically to artistic production as a vital means of overcoming the tedium of the everyday. Shklovskii saw Russian culture as having been killed by the habitual, and looks to the 'device of estrangement', by which the familiar is made new through artistic creativity, avoiding the dull repetition of the recognizable.[40] Rozanov shares these concerns over a cultural revival, though he manages this in a different manner. It is within the comfort of *byt* that Rozanov attempted to revive Russian spirituality and literature. His writings are filled with seemingly trivial descriptions of home life, friends and family. On a stylistic level, Rozanov often repeats himself, and re-quotes his own work, both to reinforce his arguments and to reaffirm the theme of the old as new. Essential to this is the manner in which he deliberately maintains a childlike sense of wonder at the world, a constant enchantment with the everyday as if it were new to him.[41]

---

36 See the Introduction, n. 47.

37 For example, in *Okolo tserkovnykh sten*, Rozanov includes essays such as 'Nashi vozliublennye usopshie', relying on archaic Russian terms; or alternatively 'O sobornom nachale v tserkvi i o primirenii tserkvei', in which the word 'sobor' is throughout printed in an Old Slavonic typeface.

38 Fateev, *S russkoi bezdnoi v dushe*, p. 142.

39 From Vladimir Maiakovskii, *Pro eto*, in *Polnoe sobranie sochinenii v trinadtsati tomakh*, 13 vols (Moscow: Gosudarstvennoe izdatel′stvo khudozhestvennoi literatury, 1961), IV, pp. 135–85 (p. 165). Hutchings, who also quotes this Maiakovskii passage, discusses in depth the manner in which Formalists struggled with the opposition of art and everyday life. See Hutchings, *Russian Modernism*, pp. 46–8.

40 Viktor Shklovskii, 'Iskusstvo kak priem', in *Gamburgskii schet* (Moscow: Sovetskii pisatel′, 1990), pp. 58–72 (especially pp. 68–70).

41 *Opavshie list′ia I*, p. 341. Rozanov deliberately cultivated a childlike naivety in his behaviour, which others misinterpreted as immaturity or even debauchedness.

Rozanov was a deeply habitual person who loved the comfort of the home and the security of the known.[42] There he is able to order his sense of self and structure his relationship with his family. In her memoirs, Tat´iana Rozanova depicts a cosy family life run on routine. The family rise and eat, the father drinks coffee and reads the same newspapers before leaving for the *Novoe Vremia* offices at the same time.[43] Tat´iana recollected the relationship with her father as being structured around repeated references to the same passages of Russian literature.[44] Rozanov crossed himself after meals and on seeing church buildings. Ideal home life is built around these simple, daily pleasures. Rozanov takes revolutionary terminology and subverts it, making it domestic. 'A cigarette after bathing, raspberry with milk, lightly-salted cucumber at the end of June with a sliver of dill clinging to the side (but leave it there) – this is my "17th October". In this sense I am an "Octobrist".'[45] Rozanov was addicted to smoking (in Russia traditionally considered a demonic vice), although this unrestrained love for tobacco was never something he was able to explain rationally. He was pleased when his mother died, as this meant that he would be able to smoke at will. In a strange way, this seems to fit in with Rozanov's mechanism for coping with death; death is reinterpreted as the opportunity for new life which is then mitigated by cycles of pleasurable activity.

Rozanov privileges the spontaneous acts of men which pay reverence to God. The Sacraments of the Church should not be a priori constructs,

42 Contemporary work notes that certain aspects of Rozanov's behaviour exhibit possible autistic and schizophrenic symptoms. Zhelobov points out that the love of the familiar and personal, as displayed frequently in Rozanov's work – most notably his frequent references to 'my God' and 'my religion' – is commonly observed in autistic patients, and he also suggests that Rozanov's love of suffering might be a sign of masochism. A.P. Zhelobov, 'K voprosu psikhopatologii tvorchestva V.V. Rozanova', *Entelekhiia* (2000), 100–6 (pp. 100–3). During his own lifetime, Rozanov was often accused of insanity by many critics, including Pobedonostsev. Rozanov himself admitted: 'I always had a trace of madness about me'. *Literaturnye izgnanniki*, p. 211. Rozanov's background as a provincial schoolmaster added to accusations that he suffered from a peculiarly Russian and literary illness of the time, Peredonovism, as well as a pathological obsession with sex.

43 Tat´iana Rozanova, pp. 29–30.

44 *Opavshie list´ia I*, pp. 342–5.

45 Ibid., p. 356. Rozanov refers here to the October Manifesto, signed 17 October 1905 (O.S.) after a period of revolutionary turmoil in Russia, in which Tsar Nicholas II ceded some of his powers to a Council of Ministers.

but must be tied to the lifecycles of human and nature. Church rituals should acknowledge the Creation, especially its manifestation through childbirth.[46] In this aspect, Rozanov is close to Jewish traditions which view embodied rituals as 'the producers and sustainers of life-generating religious values and traditions', providing a crucial link between the individual and society.[47] Rozanov also refers in particular to marriage. Marriage allows man to be reborn,[48] leave the New Testament and 'return to the Prophets'.[49]

In his series of essays 'Iudaizm', Rozanov investigates how Judaism has incorporated natural human activity into its ceremonies. He compares the family-orientated aspects of Jewish worship to abstract Orthodox ceremonies. Rozanov writes that Orthodox rituals are repeated acts, but are performed out of a mechanical sense of duty, not out of real love for God. In this negative sense, Rozanov uses the word 'ritual' to describe such meaningless acts which lack the capacity for creativity.[50] Priority is given to form over content, and the believer devotes his attention to ensuring that the ritual is performed in exactly the correct manner.[51] Rozanov rejects as irrelevant debates over how many times to sing 'alleluia' or how many fingers should be used to cross oneself: what is important for him is the potential of rituals to bring forth new life.[52]

In contrast to Orthodoxy, Rozanov insists that Jewish worship is dominated not by meaningless rituals, but by rites ('obriady'). These rites are full of joy and each time are filled with new content. Rozanov idealizes Jewish ceremonial behaviour, as it cleanses man of the sin he has accrued during his life on Earth and recreates his primeval innocence. He rejects Christian sacraments as they require only the passive involvement of the worshipper. In Orthodox sacraments, such as baptism and Christian marriage, the Church is the active participant and demands the

---

46 V.V. Rozanov, 'Predislovie ko vtoromu izdaniiu', in *Semeinyi vopros v Rossii*, pp. 19–22 (p. 19).

47 Colleen M. Griffith, 'Spirituality and the Body', in *Bodies of Worship: Explorations in Theory and Practice*, ed. by Bruce T. Morrill (Collegeville: Liturgical Press, 1999), pp. 67–83 (p. 78).

48 *Sakharna*, p. 118.

49 *Priznaki vremeni*, p. 354.

50 'Iudaizm' (November 1903), p. 159.

51 Rozanov touches on ancient arguments over the formal value of ritual behaviour in Orthodoxy, where there has been a tendency to understand the forms of rituals as in themselves containing the truths of God. Billington, pp. 135–7.

52 'Ob odnoi osobennoi zasluge Vl. S. Solov´eva', p. 435.

loyalty of the passive worshipper.[53] However, the Jews have a different psychology of prayer and a real passion for God.[54] They pray not out of a sense of compulsion, but out of a genuine religious feeling. Although the form of their worship has remained constant, Rozanov admires the fact that in each performance the rite is filled with new content and a renewed love for the divine. This is the strength of Jews – they are able to configure time religiously, around the creative activities of God. The failure to do so means that human experience becomes meaningless monotony.[55] Fedorov, in a similar vein, complains that the Russians have lost a sense of the inner content of religion and have turned the Liturgy into a mere rite, whose formal aspects alone they observe. Fedorov also calls for the re-establishment of a link between ecclesiastical and lay life for the resurrection project to succeed.[56]

Most important in the Jewish ability to recreate Paradise here is their real understanding of the Sabbath, through which they merge the principles of time and place. Their success is built on a strong generational focus, and Rozanov admires the Jewish family for its strength, opposing its sexual powers and reproductive strength to the weakness of the Russian family. Rozanov sees the only course for Russian salvation in adopting the type of attitude towards the family by which the Jews have survived through the millennia.[57]

Rozanov believes that the union of man and wife is a natural and holy act which has existed since the beginning of time, predating the Christian Church.[58] The Church places its emphasis on the ceremony of marriage,

53 V.V. Rozanov, 'Iz sovremmennykh gazetnykh tolkov o khristianskom brake', in *Semeinyi vopros v Rossii*, pp. 138–55 (p. 148).

54 'Iudaizm' (November 1903), p. 159.

55 'Résumé ob Egipte', p. 242.

56 See Fedorov, p. 169.

57 Scholarship supports Rozanov's view that the family plays a strong role in Jewish society. Freeze writes that the family is, at least for Eastern European Jews, 'a basic institution, the critical unit for social bonding and cultural transmission'. ChaeRan Y. Freeze, *Jewish Marriage and Divorce in Imperial Russia* (Hanover, NH/London: Brandeis University Press, 2002), p. 11. Engelstein discusses the contradictions inherent in Russian anti-Semitic discourse and the manner in which anti-Jewish discourse was often portrayed in sexual terms. See Laura Engelstein, *The Keys to Happiness: Sex and the Search for Modernity in Fin-de-Siècle Russia* (Ithaca/London: Cornell University Press, 1992), pp. 302–5.

58 V.V. Rozanov, 'Brak – kak religiia i zhizn′', in *Semeinyi vopros v Rossii*, pp. 82–103 (p. 88).

rather than the loving relationship between the couple. Rozanov wants the Church to return to the pre-Christian idea of marriage as a rite.[59] Marriage, like all such acts, cleanses the individual and the human race, and childbirth redeems our sins.[60] In marriage, the spouses should worship God, not Christ. Rozanov opposes the Orthodox teaching that marriage is a sacrament which starts from the teachings of Jesus and which therefore can only be sanctioned by the Church. Rozanov uses the example of Abraham to demonstrate the tender love which should exist between couples and in particular the manner in which parents should prioritize procreation as their religious duty. He cites the manner in which Sarah gave up her servant Hagar for Abraham to have a child with (Genesis 16:1–5) as the ideal of sexual love, outside formal ceremonies.[61] Rozanov believes that the Church, regardless of its teachings which might permit wedlock, in practice views all conjugal relationships as sinful. He thinks that marriage is condoned only with extreme reluctance; in any case, following St Paul's example (I Corinthians 7:8), the Church will always prefer celibacy.

In privileging nature over doctrine, Rozanov insists that Russians should be allowed to abandon failed marriages and remarry. Rozanov believes that it is natural for the initial frenzy of love to fade away and for spouses to find new love with different partners. Indeed, he states that people usually fall in love twice or three times in their life and only very rarely once.[62] However, the Church's strict rules on divorce mean that people are trapped in loveless marriages. This also harms the children, who would be happier if their parents could remarry and provide a more loving home. The ability to divorce is a factor in the success of the Jewish family.[63] Divorce on the other hand ritually cleanses and strengthens the family.[64] On the contrary, Rozanov believes that the Orthodox

59 'It appears to me that marriage should involve *ritual behaviour*; rituals should be involved (somewhat) in marriage, in motherhood, in fatherhood'. See V.V. Rozanov, 'Neskol′ko raz′′iasnitel′nykh slov', in *Semeinyi vopros v Rossii*, pp. 370–2 (p. 372).

60 V.V. Rozanov, 'Elementy braka', in *Semeinyi vopros v Rossii*, pp. 119–22 (p. 120).

61 V.V. Rozanov, 'Deti solntsa... Kak oni byli prekrasny!...', in *Semeinyi vopros v Rossii*, pp. 659–80 (p. 673).

62 V.V. Rozanov, 'Smeshannye braki', in *V nashei smute*, pp. 229–32 (p. 229).

63 V.V. Rozanov, 'Sredi obmanutykh i obmanuvshikhsia', in *Semeinyi vopros v Rossii*, pp. 718–92 (p. 776).

64 V.V. Rozanov, 'O neporochnoi sem′e i ee glavnom uslovii', in *Semeinyi vopros v Rossii*, pp. 82–92 (p. 91). In the late imperial period, Jews, just

Church's imposition of regulations upon marriage proves its desire for secular power and control over the Russian people and a neglect of their spiritual requirements.[65]

Circumcision is also an important ritual for Rozanov.[66] The phallus provides the most intimate link between human and divine activity, and through circumcision man enters into a relationship with God, a state of permanent prayer.[67] Again, circumcision is not Jewish but has sources in ancient Egypt, where Abraham formulated his covenant with God and then took the rite with him into Israel.[68] Rozanov makes explicit the link between circumcision and fertility, in particular in references to Abraham.[69] When Abraham was circumcised, he entered into an intimate covenant with God and was promised numerous offspring.[70] Rozanov also insists on the biological ties which unite the Jewish race – all Israel was 'created from one circumcision'.[71] Rozanov notes the Talmud quotation that God created the world specifically so that man would be circumcised.[72] He also establishes a very clear link between Paradise and the penis.

> Глубина обрезания (у евреев) и заключалась главным образом в том, что им снимался *упрек* и *осуждение* (возможные) с genital'ий, а следовательно, и снимался стыд с точки всемирной стыдливости. Обрезание снимает «кожаное препоясание» с Адама, – а снова вводит его в Эдем. Этот Эдем – семья: через нее открывается, что все и течет в бытии своем и в благе своем из genital'ий.
>
> The profundity of circumcision (for the Jews) arises principally from the fact that it removed the concepts of (possible) *reproach* and *condemnation*

like all non-Orthodox groups, were accorded greater legal freedoms in marriage and divorce. Their unions were performed outside the established Church, and therefore considered invalid by the state, meaning they were far easier to dissolve. Freeze, pp. 137–48.

65 V.V. Rozanov, 'Kakov razvod, takov i brak', in *V nashei smute*, pp. 70–3 (p. 71).

66 'Iudaizm' (July 1903), p. 151.

67 In circumcision, the Angel of Jehova descends on the boy and remains with him until his death. 'Iudaizm' (November 1903), p. 155.

68 Ibid., p. 149.

69 V.V. Rozanov, 'Angel Iegovy u evreev', in *Vozrozhdaiushchiisia Egipet*, pp. 465–74 (p. 466). For circumcision as a fertility rite, see Hoffman, p. 39.

70 'Iudaizm' (July 1903), p. 150.

71 V.V. Rozanov, 'Po kanve egipetskikh risunok', in *Vozrozhdaiushchiisia Egipet*, pp. 127–8 (p. 128).

72 'Angel Iegovy u evreev', p. 467.

> from matters of the genitalia, and consequently removed guilt from the point of universal shame. Circumcision removes the 'leather girdle' from Adam – and leads him once more into Eden. This Eden is the family: through it we discover that everything flows in its being and its goodness from the genitalia.[73]

Rozanov criticizes St Paul for abolishing the rite of circumcision and replacing this with New Testament law.[74] As well as circumcision, Rozanov also examines other Jewish ceremonies which link the body to God. He examines Nazaritehood.[75] Through procreation the Jewish worshipper dedicates himself to God. The Nazarite fulfils God's command to be fruitful and multiply, whereas the Christian monk falsely believes that he can enter Paradise through castration.[76]

The complexity of transferring foreign forms of worship to modern-day Russia is demonstrated in the investigation of the mikvah, the core section of *Uedinennoe*. As Clowes notes, Rozanov takes this aspect of Jewish worship, subverts its meaning and makes it his own.[77] The mikvah is used to achieve ritual purity after bodily functions associated with childbirth, such as menstruation, labour or circumcision (for males). The mikvah is also used by the Jewish bride and groom to cleanse themselves before marriage. The word 'mikvah' derives from the Hebrew word for a gathering of waters and is used in the Creation narrative when God creates the seas on the third day ('God said, "Let the water under the heavens be gathered into one place, so that dry land might appear", and so it was. God called the dry land Earth, and the gathering of the water he called sea; and God saw that it was good'; Genesis 1:9–10). Even today, the connection is preserved between the mikvah and the primordial waters. There are strict conditions governing how the water for the mikvah is gathered. Living water must be used which has never been stagnant, and which has been collected naturally from an underground source, from rainwater or even melted snow.[78]

73 'Deti solntsa... Kak oni byli prekrasny!...', p. 679.

74 Kurganov, 'Vasilii Rozanov, evrei i russkaia religioznaia filosofiia', pp. 121–3.

75 *Liudi lunnogo sveta*, pp. 39–41.

76 Ibid., p. 45.

77 Clowes, p. 172.

78 Rozanov insists that the subject of the mikvah is taboo and argues that in Jewish culture the indecent and the holy can coincide; this seems to contradict his criticism of the strict Jewish division between the sanctified and profane. In *Uedinennoe*, Rozanov contrasts the unspoken, esoteric nature of Jewish rituals, against Christian rituals, which he claims are open

Rozanov writes on the exact depth of the water, the length of time the worshipper should be immersed and the processes involved. He is aware of the primeval origins of the water, and he narrates how this is used to cleanse and refresh the various parts of the body. Candles are lit, and the room is filled with aroma. God *is* the mikvah, who cleans the soul of Israel.[79] Rozanov explains how contemporary Jews perform the ritual cleansing, following Moses and Abraham, but having done so provides a contemporary, Russian and subverted version.

> Но оставим старика и перекинемся к нам, в нашу обстановку, в наш быт, – чтобы объяснить это древнее установление евреев и дать почувствовать его душу. Представим себе наш бал. Движение, разговоры, «новости», и «политика». Роскошь всего и туалеты дам... Анфилада зала с белыми колоннами и стенами. И вот кто-нибудь из гостей, из танцевавших кавалеров, утомленный танцами, отходит совсем в боковую комнату: и, увидя на столе миску с прохладною водою, кем-то забытую и ненужную, осторожно оглядывается кругом, притворяет дверь и, вынув несколько возбужденную и волнующуюся часть, – погрузил в холодную воду... «пока – остынет».
>
> Он делает то, что иудеи в микве и мусульмане в омовениях («намаз»).
>
> И ушел. Вся разгоревшаяся впорхнула сюда же женщина... Она разгорелась, потому что ей жали руку, потому что она назначила свидание, – и назначила сейчас после бала, в эту же ночь. Увидев ту же миску, она берет ее, ставит на пол, – и, так же осторожно оглянувшись кругом и положив крючок на дверь, повторяет то, что ранее сделал мужчина.
>
> Это – то, что делают иудеянки в микве.
>
> But let us leave the old man and come back to us, to our world, to our *byt*, in order to explain this ancient Jewish institution, and to feel its soul. Let us imagine our ball. Movement, conversations, 'news' and 'politics'. The finery of it all, the ladies' toilettes... The suite of rooms with white columns and walls. And then one of the guests, one of the dancing knights exhausted from the dances, leaves them all and comes into a sideroom. Seeing on the table a bowl with chilled water, forgotten by someone who did not need it, he carefully looks around, and locks the door. Taking out his somewhat aroused and agitated part, he immerses it in the cold water, 'until it is cooled'.
>
> He does what the Jews did in the mikvah, and Muslims in their cleansing (the 'namaz').

---

and easily understandable. Eventually, this frustration at his own inability to get to the core of Jewish rites develops into a deep bitterness at the Jews' supposed refusal to share their secrets. In any case, Rozanov is mistaken about the mikvah; there is no evidence to suggest that it is forbidden to pronounce the word 'mikvah', and there is ample writing which discusses the matter in depth.

79 V.V. Rozanov, *Uedinennoe*, in *Religiia i kul'tura*, ed. by E.V. Vitkovskii, pp. 161–248 (pp. 190–1).

> And he goes out. And then a woman bursts in, all inflamed… She has become inflamed because somebody pressed her hand, because she had arranged to meet somebody, and arranged to meet him now after the ball, this very night. Seeing the same bowl, she takes it, places it on the floor, and – looking around carefully and putting the hook on the door – does exactly what the man did earlier.
> This is what Jewish women do in the mikvah.[80]

The above passage is an excellent example of the way Rozanov engages with Judaism. It is also obliquely demonstrative of his dissatisfaction with systematic philosophy and formal theology, and indicates the transition he makes from around 1911 onwards to his own genre, which is more suitable to his creativity.[81]

Rozanov is particularly critical of the Jewish distinction between the holy and the profane. He dismantles boundaries between categories, drawing religious activity into the mainstream. He merges the categories of the temple and home, where the most sacred activity can be performed.[82] One example of this is his frequent suggestion that newly married couples should live in the church after their wedding until their first child is conceived. Rozanov also identifies specific places and objects which make the transcendent immanent on Earth. The body is the model for this; the body is a temple to God on Earth.[83] The phallus is the guarantor of this creative activity. Both temple and home are places where man feels the divine.[84] In many religions, particularly in ancient Egypt, the temple is seen as the locus where Heaven is recreated on Earth. For Rozanov this is sexual and he stresses rituals where sexual processes are performed, in the home or the temple.

Rituals allow Rozanov to recreate a sense of self through the reformulation of memories. Memory for Rozanov is not simply a mental

80 Ibid., pp. 191–2. For Rozanov the ball is the quintessential immersion in the concrete.

81 Clowes discusses the incompatibility between 'Rozanov the philosopher' and 'Rozanov the social commentator', arguing that the former creates problems which the latter is unable to deal with. See Clowes, p. 181. I argue in the subsequent chapter that Rozanov's focus on creativity holds together this fractious relationship.

82 'Iz sedoi drevnosti', pp. 27–9.

83 Rozanov creates a correspondence between body and temple. This point is also made in Mondri, 'Vasilii Rozanov, evrei i russkaia literatura', p. 159. In this regard, Rozanov is close to St Paul's quote that the body should be a temple to God (I Corinthians 6:19).

84 'Iz sedoi drevnosti', pp. 27–9.

recollection of the past, but has an ontological quality. Here he is close to Heidegger in associating *Unheimlichkeit* with the anxiety over the disruption of the relationship with the home. Rozanov's religion is grounded in his own home, and through his relationship with Rudneva.[85] As Hutchings argues, the unity of the self for Rozanov is 'intrinsically linked with the home'.[86] Rozanov stands in opposition to Leont′ev, who associates the home and comfort with 'a lack of vitality and creativity'.[87] Relatively little of Rozanov's writing relates contact with strangers, but tends to describe friends and relatives and seemingly trivial domestic incidents. Although the inspiration for many of his thoughts takes place outside, he cannot wait to get back to his home where he can properly feel God: 'It is better to eat a crust of bread at home than someone else's pie'.[88] This is an example of Rozanov's 'domestic prophesying'. Like Gershenzon in *Vekhi*, Rozanov juxtaposes the idea of staying at home to put oneself in order with the chaos and de-personalization brought about by revolution.[89]

This use of the body in Hebrew worship, and the corresponding unity of spiritual and the earthly, is one reason for Rozanov's fascination with Jewish corporeality.[90] The Hebrew word for human being, 'nepesh', was initially understood as flesh and spirit as 'inseparable components of an individual'.[91] The Jewish worshipper sees the body 'almost as a sacrament – its use and relations (particularly sexual ones) symbolize a

---

85 This is close to the idea in Orthodox religious thought that breathing is equated with existence and matches ontological truth. Florenskii, p. 41.

86 Stephen C. Hutchings, 'Breaking the Circle of Self: Domestication, Alienation and the Question of Discourse Type in Rozanov's Late Writings', *Slavic Review*, 52 (1993), 67–86 (p. 72).

87 Kline, p. 41.

88 *Opavshie list′ia I*, p. 303.

89 This point is made in Gary Saul Morson, 'Prosaic Bakhtin: *Landmarks*, Anti-Intelligentsialism and the Russian Countertradition', in *Bakhtin in Contexts*, ed. by A. Mandelker (Evanston: Northwestern University Press, 1995), pp. 33–78 (p. 39). Rozanov stated that he was an observer and not an actor. It is impossible to imagine him participating in revolution. It is significant to highlight Gershenzon's *Vekhi* satire on the radicals, also cited by Morson: 'A handful of revolutionaries has been going from house to house and knocking on every door: "Everyone onto the street. It's shameful to stay at home!"' One can imagine Rozanov's horror at this idea.

90 Jewish worship traditionally emphasizes the use of the body. Bottomley, pp. 16, 22.

91 *The Oxford Companion to the Bible*, p. 295.

relationship to God and the right order of creation'.[92] Rozanov writes that Jewish thought has resisted the tendency in Western philosophy, perpetuated by Plato, Descartes and Hegel, to revere the idea of the thing over the thing itself.[93] Here he resists the delineation of essence from energies. Consequently, Rozanov contends that eschatology is absent from Jewish thought. In the Old Testament there is no 'idea of the end' and no reference to an 'existence beyond the grave'.[94] Jewish worship is physical, whereas Orthodox prayer is abstract and verbal.

> Почему религия должна быть *понятием*, а не фактом? Книга *«Бытия»*, а не книга *«рассуждения»* – так началось ветхое богословие. «Вначале бе *Слово*» – так началось богословие новое. *Слово* и разошлось с *бытием*, «слово» – у духовенства, а *бытие* – у общества; и «слово» это бескровно, а бытие это не божественно. Но, повторяем, где же корень этого расхождения?
>
> Why should religion be a *concept*, and not a fact? The Book of *Genesis*, and not the book of *Reasoning* – this is the principle of the old theology. 'In the beginning was the *Word*' – this is the principle of the new theology. *The Word* was divorced from *being*, 'the word' was taken up by the clergy, and *being* by society; and 'the word' was bloodless, and being was not divine. But, we repeat, what is at the root of this divorce?[95]

Rozanov decides at this point (1905) that the decision in Christianity to abandon Old Testament rituals, especially sacrifice, has resulted in a disembodied religion. He believes that a return to rituals can help reunite word and flesh. However, his fascination with this point leads him to investigate Judaism more closely, where he suspects the secrets of blood are still hidden. Abandoning the ancient practice of sacrifice has led to a detachment from the vital secrets of life. He is astonished by John Chrysostom's dislike of the smell from the blood of sacrificed animals; he insists that 'blood is not a smell, blood is *mysticism* and a *fact*'.[96] Rozanov convinces himself that blood brings man back to God, but this fixation with the body leads him down a path from which it becomes impossible to extricate himself. 'I repeat and set forth in the following way: blood is *life*, blood is a *growing fact*, blood is the source of *strength*

92 Bottomley, p. 30.
93 'Iudaizm' (November 1903), p. 174.
94 'Iz starykh pisem', p. 456.
95 V.V. Rozanov, 'O sviashchenstve i "blagodati" sviashchenstva. – Ob osnovnom ideale Tserkvi. – O drevnikh i novykh zhertvakh', in *Okolo tserkovnykh sten*, pp. 470–9 (p. 476).
96 Ibid.

and *the powerful*. Religion, blood taken as a union with God, is alive, growing and real'.[97] Rozanov shifts from the body to blood, which he comes to see as the dominant symbol in Judaism. In shunning religious abstraction, Rozanov cannot see the Blood Accusation as anything other than a reality.

## The body of evidence: Rozanov and Iushchinskii

On 19 March 1911 (O.S.), the body of a young Christian boy was found in a cave near a brick factory outside Kiev. Thirteen-year-old Andrei Iushchinskii had been brutally murdered just over a week earlier. He had been beaten and stabbed to death, and of the forty-seven knife marks to Iushchinskii, thirteen wounds had supposedly been caused to deliberately draw blood from the body. Traces of semen were found close to the body.[98] Iushchinskii's funeral became an opportunity for nationalist groups to revive anti-Jewish sentiment, where brochures were distributed claiming that Jews ritually sacrificed Christian children and consumed their blood at their Passover meal.[99]

Factory manager Mendel′ Beilis, a non-practising Ukrainian Jew, was charged with ritual murder. There was political motivation, unlike the Dreyfus affair, and Russian Minister of Justice Ivan Shcheglovitov pursued the case believing that he could win favour from the Tsar. However, like the Dreyfus Affair, the Beilis Affair quickly became an issue of immense national and international importance.[100] Many leading Russian writers and thinkers of the time signed a manifesto claiming Beilis' innocence, including Merezhkovskii, Gippius, Aleksei Tolstoi, Viacheslav Ivanov, Sologub and Remizov. Prominent liberal politicians, including Rozanov's bugbear Vladimir Dmitrievich Nabokov, supported Beilis' innocence. Across Europe some of the most important figures of the time signed the petition, including the Archbishops of Canterbury and Westminster, Ramsey MacDonald, George Bernard Shaw, Thomas Hardy, H.G. Wells, Conan Doyle, Thomas Mann, Ernst Mach and de

97 Ibid., p. 477.

98 The best English account of the Beilis Affair is in Lindemann, especially pp. 129–93.

99 Ibid., p. 177.

100 The journalist Vladimir Korolenko claimed that a trial had never before attracted 'the attention of the broad masses' to so great a degree. Quoted in ibid., p. 183.

Régnier.[101] As Katsis notes, the Beilis Affair was not just an intellectual or religious debate, but had real significance in the embittered social conflict between Jews and Christians.[102]

Beilis was acquitted after a farcical trial which offered no hard evidence, in which the prosecution case rested on a claim that ritual sacrifice was widespread among the Jewish population. The notorious Professor Emeritus of Kiev University, Ivan Sikorskii, alleged that the Blood Accusation was a common event.[103] However, the jury concluded that Iushchinskii had indeed been the victim of a ritual murder. Beilis, understandably unsettled, emigrated to Palestine and then America. Rozanov was bitterly disappointed by his acquittal. He was deeply traumatized by Iushchinskii's murder, and dedicated much work at this time to the boy. In this way, Rozanov's writing on Iushchinskii became a kind of prayer for the young boy's soul. Rozanov even insisted that the Russians should educate the Jews on the importance of Christological and pneumatological aspects of worship. Rozanov was initially convinced that Beilis had killed Iushchinskii for his blood, but after the verdict altered his stance slightly, insisting that it was not important who actually killed the boy. The issue for Rozanov was that the thirst for blood was an integral part of Judaism, even if Beilis himself was innocent.

At this time, Rozanov was deeply influenced by Evgeniia Apostolupolo, a conservative landowner whom he befriended at the Religious-Philosophical Meetings. In the summer of 1913, accompanied by his wife and his daughter Vera, Rozanov visited Sakharna, Apostolopulo's estate in Bessarabia which would lend its name to Rozanov's most tendentious work. In this book, Rozanov exposes his fear over the potency of Jewish blood ties. The Jewish body and its ties with God threaten Russian culture. The Jews are joined as a community through their communal

101 *The Kieff Ritual Murder Accusation and the Beilis Case: Protests from Leading Christians in Europe* (London: Jewish Chronicle and Jewish World, 1913). Rozanov's name is absent from the petition.

102 Katsis, '"Delo Beilisa" v kontekste "Serebrianogo veka"', p. 414.

103 The most likely perpetrators were local criminal Vera Cheberiak and her gang, who wanted to silence Iushchinskii after he became aware of their activities. Cheberiak might have also intended to incite a riot against the Jewish community, as her crew had previously profited from looting during pogroms. Lindemann, pp. 182–3.

blood ('edinokrovnost′') and constitute one body with 14 million arms and legs.[104] The Russians lack this physical communality.[105]

Rozanov claims that the Jews are intent on destroying the Russian fatherland and uprooting the Russians from their own soil. This is very close to the clichéd conservative view, as propagated by people such as Dostoevskii and later by Shul′gin, that the Jews are responsible for socialism and want to dismantle traditional forms of the Russian state such as the Church and the Tsar.[106] Rozanov also accuses the Jews of wishing to destroy Russian literature, one of the most important expressions of national spirituality, and counters that the threat can be combated by establishing a correspondence of the Russian book and the Russian body.[107] Rozanov targets literature, as much as the body. As well as noting their overbearing fecundity, in *Sakharna* he frequently expresses his fear of Jewish publishing houses and writes that Russian literary culture requires protection from the Jews. He argues that, when he started writing in the 1880s, there was no such thing as the 'Jew in literature', other than the translator Petr Veinberg. However by 1911, he continues, the Jews had taken over all aspects of Russian literature, not just its creation.[108] The Jews are trying to disrupt the holy element of literature, preventing Russian works from being used as a form of cultural transmission; the Russians are no longer at home in their own books.

*Sakharna* does not only function as a treatise on Jewish worship, but also as an act of worship in its own right, a prayer created for Russia and her people and also Iushchinskii's soul. Rozanov writes that he wants to take Iushchinskii's corpse into his arms and carry it around the country so that the Russians can weep over it.[109] Rozanov draws comparisons between Iushchinskii's dead body and the corpse of Russia, which he claims he alone understands (this prefigures his final appraisal of the Russian Apocalypse). He also stresses the importance of spiritual matters in religion, for which he uses the word 'spiritualisticheskii', rather than the more Russian variant 'dukhovnyi'.[110] In *Sakharna* Rozanov attaches great significance to prayers

104 *Sakharna*, p. 202.
105 Ibid., p. 180.
106 Ibid., p. 68.
107 Mondry notes that Rozanov sees a coincidence of the book and the body. Mondri, 'Vasilii Rozanov, evrei i russkaia literatura', pp. 222, 224.
108 *Sakharna*, p. 65.
109 Ibid., p. 197. Compare this with Rozanov's narration of him carrying his own child around Nikolaevskii train station, to which I turn in the final chapter.
110 Ibid., p. 192.

for the dead: he feels an extra responsibility towards Iushchinskii, because the Church neglected its obligations to the dead boy. Not one metropolitan attended Iushchinskii's funeral, but despite this, Rozanov insists that the boy did go to Heaven and is now with Christ.[111]

Rozanov examines the body of Iushchinskii more closely in *Oboniatel′noe i osiazatel′noe otnoshenie evreev k krovi.*[112] Rozanov turns in the first article to the secrets he believes are deliberately hidden in the Hebrew alphabet ('Iudeiskaia tainopis′'). Noting that the Hebrew language does not contain vowels, he argues that the Jews have deliberately mistranslated the Bible in order to conceal its true meaning from Christians. He compares various translations of Scripture, including Bishop Antonin's, the Jewish text itself, the Greek translation from AD 70, and the Russian version of the Greek text. Rozanov writes that as soon as the Jews realized that other peoples had taken an interest in their Scriptures, they deliberately kept sections concealed to hide the true nature of their religion.[113] Whereas Rozanov had earlier expressed respect for Judaic esotericism, here he displays a deep animosity to the exclusivity of their religion. Here Rozanov sides with a general Christian belief as a religion of Revelation ('Otkrovenie'), arguing that Judaism instead relies on secrecy ('sokrovenie').[114]

---

111 Ibid., p. 202. In Orthodox theology, prayers for the dead are extremely important, as there is no concept of purgatory, and the dead enter a state of limbo to pay penance for their sins on Earth. Rozanov is close here to traditional Orthodox thinking.

112 Recent scholarship has demonstrated that two parts of the book were in fact written by Florenskii, who persuaded Rozanov to publish the work under his own name (though enigmatically signed 'Ω' with its own oblique eschatological connotation). Letters from Florenskii to Rozanov show that the priest was certainly fearful of the public's reaction to the passages he composed. There is much debate as to why Rozanov agreed to Florenskii's request. In Rozanov's later years he spent much time with the priest, who became a close family friend. The two men discussed their ideas on Jewish worship, and there can be little doubt that Rozanov was influenced by Florenskii's ideas. The fact that Rozanov included Florenskii's letters as his own does suggest that Rozanov did not disagree with their content, though Rozanov was suspicious of the Jews and had a very close interest in their worship before he met Florenskii. See Clowes, pp. 176–81.

113 *Oboniatel′noe i osiazatel′noe otnoshenie evreev k krovi*, p. 291.

114 Ibid., p. 278. Davidson makes very interesting points in this context over a deep-seated historical fear among Russian clergy that writing is a tool by which people can 'distort the meaning of sacred texts' and subvert the authority of Scripture. Rozanov appears to extend this concern here to the

Rozanov turns to blood and its ties with the Jewish god. He stresses the ontological meaning of Jewish blood rituals. Here Rozanov insists that the Jews do not worship the Christian god, but instead worship Moloch. Using the work of the writer Viacheslav Sokolov on Jewish rituals, Rozanov writes that circumcision is a ceremony which affirms Moloch's links with blood. During its performance, the rabbi sucks blood from the child's penis, which is then mixed with wine and used ritually to cleanse the child's face.[115] Although Rozanov had started his explorations of Jewish worship in order to find a way of injecting some degree of physicality into Orthodoxy, he is startled, and to some degree confounded, by his conclusions, and finds it impossible to reconcile Christianity and Judaism.[116] Rozanov is aware that his conclusions could have far-reaching consequences. In searching for meaning in the Old Testament, he has to consider that the Jews misuse ancient rituals. These rituals have become formalized among the Jews, who have neglected the content of their rites, their capacity for creativity, and consider only their physical dimension. Consequently, Rozanov's criticism of Jewish worship becomes similar to his rejection of the over-formal and ritualized nature of Orthodox practices. He writes: 'The Jews do not have a proper *religion* as a spiritual condition, as an ideal condition, but they do have an immeasurable *daily rite*: how to wash, how to eat, how to trade. *Material rites* occupy *the place of their religion, material ceremonies, material traditions* ('*the sanctity of things*').[117]

Siding with Florenskii, Rozanov states that it is the duty of the Russians to educate the Jews into the spiritual side of religion.[118] Instead of perceiving the unity of phenomenon and idea, he now states that the Jews have completely neglected the noumenal. Rozanov reverts to aspects of Gnostic thought, which suppose that the Old Testament Jews worshipped the evil demiurge, who was only overcome by the arrival of the true God's Son.[119]

---

Jews and also displays his fear that they became the author of their own texts, deliberately turning people from God. See Davidson, 'Russian Views of Art as Demonic', p. 140. Such fears emerge more clearly in Rozanov's ambivalence towards literature, as we see in Chapter 6.

115 Ibid., p. 297. Rozanov takes his information from Viacheslav Sokolov, *Obrezanie u evreev. Istoriko-bogoslovskoe issledovanie* (Kazan, no given publisher, 1892).

116 *Sakharna*, p. 18.

117 Ibid., p. 318.

118 Ibid., p. 308.

119 Katsis remarks that the Russian religious renaissance of Rozanov's period saw a revival of interest in Gnostic beliefs. Katsis, '"Delo Beilisa" v kontekste "Serebrianogo veka"', p. 414.

Rozanov goes so far as to praise Christ's rejection of Jewish sacrifice and His introduction of spiritual forms of worship. By donating His own blood and flesh, Jesus stopped the Jewish need for sacrifice and the desire for human blood.[120] But Rozanov insists that not only did the Jews practise sacrifice in their pre-history, but they also continue to do so in modern times; blood was, and remains, a Jewish fetish.[121] Rozanov locates this Jewish preoccupation with the bodily and the physical in the ceremony of circumcision, and the fact that, unlike the Christians, the Jews ignored Christ's teachings.[122]

Rozanov concludes that the Jews have no spiritual means to cleanse their soul, and therefore have to rely on physical means. Like their rituals, the Jewish body has become detached from its spiritual side; hence their use of Christian blood to wash themselves. As Moloch is intrinsically attracted to human blood, his worshippers are obliged to shed Christian blood for him. However, Rozanov, in an innovative take on the Blood Accusation, insists that the Jews do not drink the blood or use it in food. Instead, they use it as means of washing the sins from their bodies.[123] Although Rozanov had in the past exalted the example of Abraham, he now uses the Agedah as demonstration of the Jewish love of blood.[124]

Rozanov then turns his attention specifically to the body of Iushchinskii. He investigates the mystical concordance between the wounds inflicted on Iushchinskii's body, the body of God as described in the Kabala, and the Hebrew script. He examines specifically the stab wounds exacted on the boy's right temple, relying on the medical and psychological evidence presented during the trial (despite the fact that this was discredited by scholars). He reproduces several drawings of Iushchinskii's body, as well as diagrams from the Kabala and other studies of Jewish texts. Rozanov even notes that it is irrelevant whether Beilis was guilty: the purpose of his tract is to prove that such ritual killings are commonplace.[125]

Rozanov examines the evidence supplied in court by medical expert Professor Dmitrii Kosorotov, who testifies to the 'defined and systematic manner' in which Iushchinskii was killed. Rozanov argues that this

120 Ibid., p. 311.
121 Ibid., p. 309.
122 Ibid., p. 318.
123 Ibid., p. 305.
124 Ibid., p. 316.
125 Ibid., p. 325.

individual case demonstrates that ritual murders are carried out systematically among the Jews.[126] Rozanov also quotes the Roman Catholic priest Iustin Pranaitis, a self-proclaimed expert in the interpretation of Jewish texts who gave evidence at the trial (and whose 'expertise' was proved as extensively flawed by Beilis' lawyers). Pranaitis links the positioning of the thirteen stab-marks with the text of the Zohar. Rozanov concludes that there cannot be any doubt as to the correspondence of Iushchinskii's wounds with Hebrew script.[127] Echoing his earlier attacks on Orthodox culture, Rozanov insists that Jewish religion posits the discord between word and flesh. In Judaism, the word has become too visceral and has been turned into a weapon with which physical wounds can be inflected.[128]

Rozanov turns to the Hebrew letter 'shin' (ש), which he claims is analogous with a group of five marks on Iushchinskii's forehead which mark out the 'secret' character on the youth's body. Rozanov writes that 'shin' corresponds to the lower portion of the ten sephirot described in the Jewish Kabala.[129] He cites Old Testament teachings (Genesis 9:4), which state that the blood is where the person's life-force is to be found, and insists that the magic letters were inscribed onto Iushchinskii as they form a mystical link with the Jewish god.[130] He sees these five wounds

126 Ibid., p. 368.

127 Ibid., p. 368.

128 The boundary which exists between verbal and physical activity in Russian culture is often perceived as fluid, as Murav has noted. For example, she discusses the manner in which words were used as weapons to cause physical injury against Siniavskii. Harriet Murav, 'The Case against Andrei Siniavskii: The Letter and the Law', *Russian Review*, 53 (1994), 549–60. Murav also discusses the tensions during the Beilis Affair between the discourse of the philosophers and the formal language of the inchoate legal environment. Harriet Murav, 'The Beilis Ritual Murder Trial and the Culture of Apocalypse', *Cardozo Studies in Law and Literature*, 12 (2000), 243–63. Katsis also notes the wider context of 'Imiaslavie' and Rozanov's contemporaries, including Sergii Bulgakov, Florenskii and Ern, who saw ontological value in the Name of God. Katsis, '"Delo Beilisa" v kontekste "Serebrianogo veka"', p. 428.

129 *Oboniatel'noe i osiazatel'noe otnoshenie evreev k krovi*, pp. 371–3. Rozanov takes his information from *De philosophia Occulta* (Leyden, no given publisher, 1531).

130 Kornblatt notes that Rozanov starts to understand Jewish sacrifice as a form of black magic. Judith Deutsch Kornblatt, 'Russian Religious Thought and the Jewish Kabbala', in *The Occult in Russian and Soviet Culture*, pp. 75–95 (p. 91).

in particular as a magical invocation, which must be marked onto virgin flesh to have effect.[131] The Hebrew alphabet has magical powers, and particular letters enjoy a correspondence with a specific sephirot, he argues. Reading the shape of the wounds on Iushchinskii's temple, Rozanov concludes that they read in Hebrew: 'The human was killed with blows to the head and chest, like a sacrificed calf to Jehova'.[132]

The systematic and ritual method by which the wounds were inflicted onto Iushchinskii's temple demonstrates the religious motives for his murder. But Rozanov has more to say: he notes that the positioning of the wounds marks a downward-pointing triangle, which signifies the effort made by the sacrificer to draw God's power down to Earth and to tap the life-powers contained in the victim's blood. As in all his work, Rozanov is concerned over the movement of divine energy to Earth. He once more points to the literal and physical properties in particular of the letter 'shin'. In the Kabala, 'shin' also points symbolically to Christianity. Such power was initially invoked by the early Jews and expresses the unity of the material and spiritual basis of being which they are striving to capture. This is, Rozanov believes, an eternal mission of the Jewish religion, the need to maintain a physical relationship with the divine.[133]

Rozanov concludes that the Jews use their sexual potency to produce more Jews, in order to gain economic, religious and literary supremacy over the Russians. He argues that the Jews have failed to understand the consequences of their unique inheritance, and instead of the Creation, concentrate their efforts on Zionism and commerce.[134] Rozanov's Jewish

---

131 *Oboniatel′noe i osiazatel′noe otnoshenie evreev k krovi*, p. 376.

132 Ibid., p. 380.

133 Ibid., p. 390.

134 V.V. Rozanov, 'Po kanve egipetskikh risunkov', in *Vozrozhdaiushchiisia Egipet* pp. 127–8 (p. 128). Here Rozanov provides a unique distortion to existing stereotypes over the love of money and Jewish reproduction. Whereas Rozanov appears to argue that the Jews' greed arises from their procreative forces, Sander Gilman argued that stereotypes of the Jews' sexual perversions arose from stereotypes of their avarice: 'The taking of interest, according to Thomas Aquinas, was impossible, for money, not being alive, could not reproduce. Jews, in taking money, treated money as if it were alive, as if it were a sexualized object. The Jew takes money as does the prostitute, as a substitute for higher values, for love and beauty. And thus the Jew becomes the representative of the deviant genitalia, the genitalia not under the control of the moral, rational conscience'. Quoted in Allison Pease, *Modernism, Mass Culture, and the Aesthetics of Obscenity* (Cambridge: Cambridge University Press, 2000), p. 86.

studies reveal his certainty in the connection between thought and reality, and a conviction that human activity can bring about the Kingdom of Heaven. Rozanov and his peers felt that they played a central role in this task, being played out right now on Russian soil. It is the conflation of this belief, merged with Rozanov's fondness for rituals and a profound Russian tradition of viewing literature as a sacred act, which informs the way Rozanov puts his own belief into practice, in the construction of his own literature.

Around the same time that Rozanov began to discard the possibility of exploring the Creation through the Jews, Rozanov became more confident in his abilities to locate these secrets himself. This growing detachment from more general schemes of belief also marks his isolation from mainstream Russian philosophy. Rozanov never appeared concerned by this ostracism, but was assured of his own relationship with the divine. In an age of religious indifference, Rozanov is confident that his body has a superior feeling for God. Rozanov equates the religious indifference threatening Russian society with the fact that the Russians have forgotten the true name of God. He suspects that the Jews know this name, but refuse to divulge it.[135] In a 1903 speech to the Religious Philosophic Meeting, Rozanov had explained that, although we often use the word 'God' to describe the concept of the divine, we have lost in the course of human history the true name of the Person of God. We cannot know God, or call upon Him, directly. In 1911, however, Rozanov proclaimed his own personal success in opening up this divine mystery.

> Я разгадал тетраграмму, Боже, я разгадал ее. Это не было *имя*, как «Павел», «Иоанн», а был *зов*; и произносился он даже *тем же самым*

135 The divine name has deep significance. However, in ancient Jewish thought, this name does not relate to the essence of God, but rather refers to His activity. To know God's name is to be aware of His work and divine plan. Recent scholarship suggests that in ancient Hebrew beliefs, the name of God, Yahweh, originally stems from the activity of the sun god on earth. See Tryggve N.D. Mettinger, *The Dethronement of Sabaoth: Studies in the Shem and Kabod Theologies*, trans. by Frederick H. Cryer (Lund: Gleerup, 1982), pp. 15–16. Eilberg-Schwartz argues that the Name of God is intrinsically linked to procreation: God's placing His Name in the Temple is akin to affirming His fathership of the tribes of Israel, and is expressly connected with the obligation on humans to perpetuate their name, or their lineage. See Eilberg-Schwartz, *God's Phallus*, p. 127. In addition, in Egyptian thought the name of the individual had definite powers over that person: the person's identity rested in the vocalization of their name. Hare, p. 27.

> *индивидуумом* не всегда совершенно (абсолютно) одинаково, а чуть-чуть изменяясь в тенях, в гортанных придыханиях… И не *абсолютно одинаково* – разными первосвященниками. От этой нетвердости произношения в конце концов «тайна произнесения его» и затерялась в веках. Но, поистине, благочестивые евреи и до сих пор иногда произносят его, *но только не знают* – когда… Но все это заключено в зове-вздохе… Он состоял из одних гласных с придыханиями.
>
> I divined the Tetragrammaton, oh God, I divined it. It was not a *name*, like 'Paul', 'John', but it was a *call*; and it was pronounced by the very same individual in not completely (absolutely) the same way, but changed slightly in the shadows, a guttural aspirate… And the various high priests did not pronounce it in *absolutely the same way*. This lack of rigidity over its pronunciation eventually led to 'the secret of its pronunciation', which was lost through the ages. But truly, devout Jews still sometimes pronounce it to this day, but *just do not know* when… But all this was held within the sighing call… It was made up only of vowels and aspirates.[136]

It is this mysterious link between the essence of God and language which Rozanov brazenly claims to unlock, and which he seeks to expose in his own vision of literature. This attempt to demystify the divine, paralleled in his attempts to demystify sex, forms the basis of the subsequent chapters.

---

136 *Uedinennoe*, p. 208.

## CHAPTER 5

# THE AESTHETICS OF CREATION

In spite of his confidence when posing questions over the compatibility of ancient religious practices and modern-day society, Rozanov does concede that he is not always sure about how to put aspects of ancient worship into practice.[1] The reader is likewise left sometimes unconvinced as to whether Rozanov's writings should be understood literally or metaphorically. This is where Rozanov is particularly close to Nietzsche, in a merging of the literal and poetic which is often hard to disentangle; however, Rozanov's stance differs from German Idealism in that his merging of essential and energetic discourse helps bridge the division between the literal and the allegorical. Rozanov is able to draw parallels between different areas of religious activity, in particular between literature and religious rituals. Here we note also a similarity with the long-standing view, studied among others by Goethe, that literature is a substitute for sacrifice.

However, Rozanov adopts a personal approach to the Russian tradition of seeing a religious function in literature, posing a correspondence between the Creation and the act of writing. The *Opavshelistika* enabled him to put his own theology into practice and is presented as an example of how the Russians could work to re-establish the Kingdom of God on Earth. Rozanov's literary output then marks the culmination of his previous philosophical probing.

Rozanov operated in a sphere where many saw the function of literature as eschatological. Texts were understood by many as pointing to the end of time and able to transfigure society by helping bring about this endpoint. Such views were prominent in the Silver Age. Many of Rozanov's peers believed that art, especially literature, assumes a higher ethical value as time progresses. Such a view is widespread in diverse thinkers such as Solov´ev and Tolstoi, and also in radicals such as Plekhanov and Lenin. Understanding literature's religious function, Rozanov subverts the eschatological trends in Russian writing. The Creation has significant implications for Rozanov's interpretation of the

1 Rozanov himself confesses the difficulties of introducing circumcision among contemporary Russians, suggesting that some spiritual acts, if understood physically, can replace bodily acts of worship. V.V. Rozanov, 'Kul´turno-religioznye voprosy', in *Okolo narodnoi dushi*, pp. 74–8 (p. 77).

manner in which texts should operate within the framework of Russian religious life. He does not assume that literature should bear testimony to increasingly higher levels of piety, but must reconcile the Creation with a cultural environment which is increasingly detached from Paradise. In this, Rozanov places special emphasis on creativity and the production of texts.

Rozanov, like Fedorov and Solov′ev before him, made a connection between divine and artistic creativity. Rozanov also points to the importance of the erotic in art, which can only be united with the aesthetic through the introduction of the procreative. Art for Rozanov only has meaning through its reference to divine creativity and its imitation in human sexuality. The association of artistic creation and the creation of life at this time is well known,[2] but Rozanov makes explicit the connection between the artistic and childbirth. Rozanov relies on the unity of sexuality and procreation, where many of his peers strived to disassociate the creative from the procreative. In this way, Rozanov reconciles eros and agape, and the corresponding division between nature and grace which emerges in Solov′ev and his successors.

Some of the complexities of Rozanov's approach to art are shown in his engagement with Solov′ev, whose thought Rozanov typically appropriates and simultaneously rejects. In his 1889 essay 'Krasota v prirode', Solov′ev attempts to reject the idea of beauty as mere appearance (Hartman's 'Schein'), but still cannot resist presenting an irreconcilable tension between the ideal and the real.[3] Solov′ev starts this work by insisting that beauty must be embodied and initially understood in terms of its concrete manifestation. Beauty is the 'content of the ideal', the idea made incarnate.[4] Solov′ev draws Christology into his epistemology (as well as into his ethics, as cognition for him is essentially a moral act), and this permits his rejection of a direct link between the Creator and the aesthetics of the natural world. Solov′ev presents (invoking with caveats Darwin's evolutionism) the ethical and aesthetic development of

---

2 Irina Paperno's introduction to *Creating Life: The Aesthetic Utopia of Russian Modernism*, ed. by Irina Paperno and Joan Delaney Grossman (Stanford: Stanford University Press, 1994), pp. 1–12.

3 The question of consistency in Solov′ev's aesthetics is tackled in Zen′kovskii, II, p. 67.

4 V.S. Solov′ev, 'Krasota v prirode', in *Filosofiia iskusstva i literaturnaia kritika* (Moscow: Iskusstvo, 1991), pp. 30–73 (p. 41).

the natural world, which leads painfully to the final transfiguration of nature.[5]

Solov´ev attempts an objective view of beauty through the gradual abandoning of the created world's primeval, chaotic state and its otherness to the mind of God. This results in an aesthetics from Solov´ev which is fundamentally eschatological. There is also a direct attack on the primacy of the initial Creation in this work, as Solov´ev insists that history, the aesthetic and moral improvement of nature, involves the correction of former imperfections in nature, the extinction of unsatisfactory, antediluvian beings such as the ichthyosauri and pterodactyls.[6] The presentation of a mediator between the divine and creation comes out in Solov´ev's aesthetics. It is this objectification of the Earth by God to which Rozanov objects in his reply to Solov´ev's article.[7] Rozanov rejects Solov´ev's presentation of beauty as an abstract category which is external to each organism, and which is guaranteed ultimately by the promise of transfiguration through the spiritual. Instead of Solov´ev's essentially Platonic vision, Rozanov explicitly links beauty with the individual organism's 'vital energy', an internal and specific category. Rozanov confirms this correspondence between aesthetics and potentiality, activity and deed, by his frequent comment that the most beautiful thing is a pregnant woman. Rozanov draws on the strong contemporary sense that artistic creativity should draw on the erotic. However, shunning his peers' tendency to draw on Solov´evian themes of the sublimation of sex (comparable to Plato's elevation of erotic love to the contemplation of the divine), Rozanov identifies the artist's work with that of God's. Hence he demonstrates that it is not art's role to assist in the transcendence of everyday reality; rather art should prove the underlying and permanent sanctity of matter. Rozanov does not see a need for erotic energy to be internalized or converted into some mystical force which helps transform society or nature. Rather the restoration of sexuality at the heart of everyday life will restore humanity's natural relations with one another, returning it to its ideal state. This is a subtle difference confirmed by Rozanov's unique emphasis on the

5 Ibid., p. 57.
6 Ibid., pp. 54–5.
7 V.V. Rozanov, 'Krasota v prirode i ee smysl', in *Priroda i istoriia: Stat´i i ocherki 1904–1905 gg.* (Moscow: Respublika, 2008), pp. 43–103 (p. 48).

artistic and the procreative.[8] It is in Rozanov's rejection of what later would be known as Darwin's evolutionism that he notes the merging of the scientific and mythological, essential and energetic discourse, and his descriptions of natural beauty as a proof of universal love.[9] Rozanov also foreshadows the philosophy and the aesthetics of Vladimir Nabokov, particularly in their common reliance on the life of the butterfly to demonstrate this unity.

Accordingly, Rozanov carves a specific role for Russia's writers as the co-custodians of the nation's spiritual health. But this becomes quite an exoteric vision; rather than an elitist group of intellectuals detached from Russian society, Rozanov extends the task of creativity to all Russians. Hence he calls on his readers to write their own Fallen Leaves. In this way, Rozanov is close to the tradition of the Formalists, which seeks to circumvent the stultification of culture by making the old new through artistic creativity. At the same time, he believes that art can make the modern ancient, by reaffirming the connection between the present and early civilization.

Rozanov's theories on artistic creativity apply to a wide range of forms. Throughout his career, he critiqued not only literary works, but also painting, music and architecture. He prefigures Formalist thinking by asserting that the same rules can be applied to different forms of artistic expression.[10] He believes that all art has a special role in Russian spiritual life; nevertheless, he directs the majority of his critical attention to literature, and therefore this chapter will examine predominantly his interpretation of written texts and their religious function (though Rozanov often discusses other art forms, such as painting, music,

---

8 There is much scholarly work on the convergence of the erotic and the aesthetic in this period, for example Olga Matich, *Erotic Utopia: The Decadent Imagination in Russia's Fin de Siècle* (Wisconsin: University of Wisconsin Press, 2005), especially pp. 59–61.

9 'Zheltyi chelovek v peredelke', pp. 48–57.

10 The Formalists dismantled boundaries separating different art forms. 'We can refer to the possibility of transferring *Wuthering Heights* into a motion picture, medieval legends into frescoes and miniatures, or *L'Après-midi d'un faune* into music, ballet, and graphic art [...] The question of whether W.B. Yeats was right in affirming that William Blake was "the one perfectly fit illustrator for the *Inferno* and the *Purgatorio*" is a proof that different arts are comparable'. Roman Jakobson, 'Linguistics and Poetics', in *Language in Literature*, ed. by Krystyna Pomorska and Stephen Rudy (Cambridge: Belknap Press, 1987), pp. 62–94 (p. 63).

architecture and dance, interpreting these through the same aesthetic framework).

An important area of twentieth-century literary criticism has been the examination of the manner by which literature is shaped by theology. In particular, scholars have paid attention to the close dialogue between Christian eschatology and literature. Christianity and the Bible focus on the Apocalypse as the redeeming factor at end of time. This in turn has informed the traditions of Western narrative literature, typically orientated around plot and its conclusion.[11] In the field of Russian studies, scholarship has also started to examine the relationship between literature and theology. Prominent academics such as Gustafson, Hutchings and Coates have provided sophisticated studies into how the writings of Tolstoi, Chekhov, Bakhtin and Rozanov among others have been shaped by the traditions of Russian Orthodoxy.[12] Nevertheless, there is work still to be done on investigating the way the eschatology of Russian Orthodoxy, and of Russian culture more broadly, has influenced Russian literature.[13] Dostoevskii understood that literature could transform society by ushering in the Apocalypse it was investigating. Berdiaev considered Dostoevskii's prose essentially eschatological, in that it heralded the revelation of humanity in its final condition in unity with God.[14] Hence Rozanov engages with a literary environment that typically privileges the eschaton over the present moment, and he achieves this through making an explicit link in his literary criticism between the artistic and the sexual.

## Aesthetics and sex

The suggestion that art might elicit a sensual response in its audience was made in the *Republic*. Plato was concerned that art could corrupt its

11 Paul S. Fiddes, *The Promised End: Eschatology in Theology and Literature* (Oxford: Blackwell, 2000), p. 6. We return to this point in the following chapter.

12 See Richard Gustafson, *Leo Tolstoy: Resident and Stranger* (Princeton: Princeton University Press, 1986); Hutchings, *Russian Modernism*; Ruth Coates, *Christianity in Bakhtin: God and the Exiled Author* (Cambridge: Cambridge University Press, 1998).

13 See David M. Bethea, *The Shape of Apocalypse in Modern Russian Fiction* (Princeton: Princeton University Press, 1989).

14 N.A. Berdiaev, 'Otkrovenie o cheloveke v tvorchestve Dostoevskogo', *Russkaia mysl′* (March-April 1918), 39–61.

audience by instilling in them the feelings it represents and encouraging them to lose mental supervision of their emotions.

> Our better nature, being with adequate intellectual or moral training, relaxes control over these feelings, on the grounds that it is someone else's sufferings it is watching and that there's nothing to be ashamed of in praising and pitying another man with claims to goodness who shows excessive grief [...] For very few people are capable of realizing that what we must feel for other people must infect what we feel for ourselves, and that if we let our pity for the misfortunes of others grow too strong it will be difficult to restrain our feelings in our own.[15]

This division between mind and body is reflected in his opposition of philosophy to poetry. The sensual response to art is to be avoided. Plato likens this physical reaction to that of a lover's passions, a view which re-emerges in Rozanov's view of art's erotic function. Plato frowns upon all artistic representation, as the physical world art seeks to show is itself just an appearance. All art stands famously 'at third remove from reality'.[16] His conclusion is that poets should be banned from the Republic.

The idea that artists cause their audience to experience the same sensations they themselves have had is crucial to Tolstoi. Tolstoi's interpretation of artistic activity is complex and has clearly been influenced by platonic ideas, despite his rejection of ancient Greek aesthetics. Tolstoi, who engages directly with the *Republic*, bemoans the fact that the Greeks did not distinguish between the good and the beautiful, unlike the Jews or the early Christians. And yet, Tolstoi notes, their flawed aesthetics have formed the basis for European theories of art. For Tolstoi, art should have an expressly religious function, founded on the relationship between author and audience. In his treatise on art, Tolstoi sides with Plato in that art can infect its audience with the experiences of the artist. Nevertheless, Tolstoi does not accept that this necessarily means that all art should be banned (though its potential to infect means that it must be used with extreme caution). Tolstoi posits a distinction between truth ('istina') and beauty. The good in art has nothing to do with formal aesthetics, but in the way the artist explicitly 'infects' his audience with his own feelings. He writes: 'Art begins when a person, with the aim of communicating to other people a feeling he has

15 Plato, *Republic*, X, 606a-c. Here taken from Plato, *The Republic*, trans. by Desmond Lee (Harmondsworth: Penguin, 1987).

16 Ibid., X, 597e.

experienced, once more evokes this in himself and expresses it through certain external signs'.[17]

In defining good art, Tolstoi attempts to overcome Plato's mind-body division, by arguing that the whole person should be infected. However, Tolstoi stresses that art should affect the audience's 'spiritual feelings' and not merely provide physical pleasure. He directly challenges existing schemes of aesthetics which reduce the role of the senses to a minimum.[18] Tolstoi challenges elitist notions of art, insisting that art should be accessible to all.

> Вызвать с себе раз испытанное чувство и, вызвав его в себе, посредством движений, линий, красок, звуков, образов, выраженных словами, передать это чувство так, чтобы другие испытали то же чувство, – в этом состоит деятельность искусства. Искусство есть деятельность человеческая, состоящая в том, что один человек сознательно известными внешними знаками передает другим испытываемые им чувства, а другие люди заражаются этими чувствами и переживают их.
>
> To evoke in oneself a feeling one has experienced, and, having evoked this in oneself, to communicate this by means of movements, lines, colours, sounds, images expressed in words, so that others experience this same feeling – this is the function of art. Art is a human activity which consists in one person consciously communicating to others, through certain external signs, the feelings they have already experienced, and other people are infected by these feelings and experience them.[19]

Tolstoi believes that art can overcome divisions between the intelligentsia and the masses and can unify the people under God. He challenges high literature's claim for cultural dominance and insists that a wide variety of aspects of human creativity can be considered artistic, including lullabies, jokes, clothing and household effects.[20] Art should convey 'the higher feelings which emerge from religious consciousness'. However, in contemporary society, he writes, the ruling elite have

---

17 L.N. Tolstoi, *Chto takoe iskusstvo?*, in *Polnoe sobranie sochinenii*, 90 vols (Moscow: Gosudarstvennoe izdatel′stvo khudozhestvennoi literatury, 1964), XXX, pp. 27–203 (p. 64).

18 Pease writes that in Kantian aesthetics, the body is construed by the bourgeoisie as other and is associated with the uncivilized working classes, who are guided only by their senses. See Pease, *Modernism*, p. 77. It is this distinction between high and low culture which Tolstoi seeks to overcome.

19 Tolstoi, *Chto takoe iskusstvo?*, p. 65.

20 In this way, Tolstoi is also part of the movement of this time which dismantles formal boundaries between art forms. Ibid., p. 82.

imposed their own rules on art, ensuring that it gives pleasure to a select few.[21]

Tolstoi does not explain satisfactorily how he differentiates bad feelings from 'higher and better feelings'. There is also an apparent dualism in his insistence that art, an external expression, is able to convey feelings which are internal to the artist.[22] Yet for all the ambiguity, it is clear that Tolstoi believes that art should not evoke a sexual response in the audience. Very much the opposite: especially in his later period, Tolstoi uses his art to discourage all kinds of sexual activity, for example in his 1903 short story 'Sestry', in which through mistaken identity a sailor accidentally engages his long-lost sister as a prostitute. In this story, Tolstoi puts forward a point of view clearly in opposition to the celebration of biological ties found in Rozanov, especially in his Oedipal writings. In many ways, Tolstoi's work is reminiscent of the *Philokalia*, whose authors called on readers to renounce 'prelest´' and seek spiritual enlightenment instead.

Despite the flaws in Tolstoi's theories, the examination of his ideas permits a broader understanding of the manner in which his contemporaries interpreted the religious role of literature. It is perhaps a commonly held view that Rozanov and Tolstoi stand at opposite ends of the philosophical spectrum given, their different views on the importance of sexual love, and this was certainly the view advanced by Minskii and Archimandrite Mikhail (Semenov). (Rozanov was quick however to reject both men's arguments that there was a chasm between his own and Tolstoi's views on marriage, arguing instead that both he and Tolstoi

21 Ibid., p. 85.

22 In artistic production, there is surely a role for the intellectual faculties, in the conscious recollection of previously experienced emotions and the construction of external signs by which these are conveyed; the artist must know what he feels. The problem over the division between feelings and their external expression has been dismissed by Vincent Tomas as a 'pseudo-question': we are meant to assume that there is no division between thoughts and feelings, nor between the artist and his work. See T.J. Diffey, *Tolstoy's "What is Art?"* (London: Croom Helm, 1985), p. 17. Both Diffey and Tomas take a somewhat Cartesian approach to Tolstoi and they separate the art itself from its means of communication. However, it is fair to say that Tolstoi never adequately resolves the nature or extent of emotional involvement in artistic processes, a fact which is probably demonstrative of his own uncertainty over the role of the physical in his own life and thought.

insist that love is the prerequisite for sexual union.[23]) Despite their dissimilarities, Rozanov shares the same views as Tolstoi concerning the infectiousness of art and its religious function. Rozanov believes in the special place writers enjoyed in Russian society, expressing concern that this was neglected in the pervading atmosphere of religious indifference. This view was supported by Strakhov in a 1890 letter to Rozanov: 'Our writers have had the role of teachers, educators – from time immemorial, since the dawn of time – so this is nothing new. But now this meaning is beginning to be lost'.[24] Rozanov fully agrees with his mentor's views, and it would appear that he took these on in his own writing. That writers have an elevated role in Russia is not new, but what is interesting is how Rozanov attempts to reverse the loss of their authority and ability to enlighten the population.

The question of education was very important to Rozanov, and a sizeable proportion of his work is devoted to this, in particular the issue of schooling in Russia. Rozanov believes that the school should be seen as an extension of the family. It should not be a place where children are merely forced to recite facts or multiplication tables by rote, but where they should be encouraged to develop loving human relations on a natural, not mechanical, basis. The school is the starting point for the Russians' task to become closer to one another. (Although Rozanov was critical of many aspects of Russian education, he thought highly of many university tutors, including Vladimir Ger´e, Matvei Troitskii, Nikolai Storozhenko and Fedor Buslaev.[25])

Rozanov modifies strands of Orthodox thought, especially that of the starets' authority. The Orthodox worshipper was expected to open all his thoughts entirely to his religious counsellor, a practice known as 'exagoreusis' or the manifestation of thoughts.[26] Consequently, he was required to accept the starets' advice without question. Inevitably, this led to tensions between the starets' duty to administer to his flock, and his desire to seclude himself in order to pray.[27] Feofan Zatvornik, for

---

23 See V.V. Rozanov, 'Voprosy sem´i i vospitaniia (Po povodu dvukh novykh broshiur g-zhi N. Zharintsevoi)', in *Okolo narodnoi dushi*, pp. 50–60 (p. 54).

24 *Literaturnye izgnanniki*, p. 67.

25 V.V. Rozanov, 'Avtobiografiia V.V. Rozanova (Pis´mo V.V. Rozanova k Ia.N. Kolubovskomu)' in *Iudaizm*, pp. 273–9 (p. 277).

26 Donald Corcoran, 'Spiritual Guidance', in *Christian Spirituality: Origins to the Twelfth Century*, pp. 444–52 (p. 448).

27 Sergei Chetverikov, *Pravda khristianstva* (Moscow: Krutitskoe Patriarshee Podvor´e: Obshchestvo liubitelei tserkovnoi istorii, 1998), p. 90.

example, saw only two or three people after he retired to Optina, and in the last two decades of his life had no real contact with the world at all.[28] Elders did not rely on doctrine or formula in their work (although they did later begin to compile spiritual teachings and prayers), but responded to each individual case on its own merits. The ideal for this was 'fatherhood in the spirit', the transmission of the Holy Spirit to bring others into the spiritual life of the Church.[29] In return for the disciple's exagoreusis, the teacher was expected to respond with 'diakrisis', or discernment, the ability to ascertain the spiritual state of others and respond accordingly.[30]

Rozanov takes this idea and develops it along familial lines. He believes that priests should act as fathers to their parishioners. This transcends spiritual relationships and requires biological ties; Rozanov is close to the Jewish form of spiritual teaching which is akin to reproduction.[31] Rozanov criticizes Orthodox priests who do not attempt to comprehend the needs of their parishioners, but who only highlight others' sins in order to express their own egoism.[32] Such is the example of Matvei Rzhevskii, who persuaded Gogol′ to renounce his love for earthly affairs, such as ancient Greek, Pushkin and his own writing.[33] Matvei preached that humans could achieve salvation exclusively through the Church, but in doing so expressed himself as the sole source of God's grace, replacing God as the object of worship.[34]

In this way, Rozanov underlines the didactic function of literature. Rozanov insists that literature should not merely portray 'external forms', but should aim also to provide a deeper understanding of the human soul as the 'hidden protagonist and creator of all visible facts'.[35] According to Strakhov, Rozanov 'slavophilizes' ('slavianofil′stvuet') liter-

28 Hackel, p. 459.
29 Corcoran, pp. 446–7.
30 Ibid., p. 448.
31 Howard Eilberg-Schwartz, 'The Problem of the Body for the People of the Book', in *People of the Body: Jews and Judaism from an Embodied Perspective*, ed. by Howard Eilberg-Schwartz (New York: State University of New York Press, 1992), pp. 17–46 (p. 19).
32 V.V. Rozanov, 'Optina pustyn′', in *Okolo tserkovnykh sten*, pp. 285–302 (p. 285).
33 'Nebesnoe i zemnoe', p. 167.
34 V.V. Rozanov, 'Liudi i knigi okolo steny tserkovnoi', in *Okolo tserkovnykh sten*, pp. 128–55 (p. 152).
35 V.V. Rozanov, *Legenda o velikom inkvizitore F.M. Dostoevskogo*, ed. by A.N. Nikoliukin (Moscow: Respublika, 1996), p. 18.

ature, drawing in religious themes and providing a unique interpretation from a native perspective.[36] There is, however, more to it than this. The key to Rozanov's approach is that he insists that Russian literature can bring the Kingdom of Heaven down to Earth, making the Ideal manifest here.[37]

Therefore, the production of literature is a religious duty, and the writer should make the central tenets of religion relevant to everyday life. Literature should have what Rozanov would consider an aesthetic function, but at the same time this is wholly ethical. Unlike Tolstoi, Rozanov relies on a form of aesthetic infection which is much more explicit in its physicality and which encourages and justifies all aspects of family life, including sexual intercourse.[38] This is more than an attempt to arouse the reader's sexuality. Rozanov is careful to combine a physical approach with a reasoning for sexuality, thereby involving both body and mind.

In often highly explicit personal letters to his friends, in particular Gollerbakh, Rozanov frequently describes his own sexual arousal from artistic encounters, especially with phallic drawings and artefacts from the ancient world.[39] This contrasts with the overwhelming sense of shame Rozanov perceives in the Church and in Russian society over questions of sexual activity. This was reflected in Russian literature and its handling of the tension between language and body. Take, for example, the key scene in Tolstoi's *Voskresenie*:

> Он схватил ее, как она была, в жесткой суровой рубашке с обнаженными руками, поднял ее и понес.
>
> – Ах! Что вы? – шептала она.
>
> Но он не обращал внимания на ее слова, неся ее к себе.

---

36 N.N. Strakhov, 'Retsenziia na kn.: V.V. Rozanov, "Legenda o Velikom Inkvizitore F.M. Dostoevskogo. Opyt kriticheskogo kommentariia", SPb., 1894', in *Vasilii Rozanov: Pro et Contra*, I, pp. 263–9 (p. 267).

37 V.V. Rozanov, 'Voprosy russkogo truda (Opyt otveta preosviashchennomu Nikonu)', in *Staraia i molodaia Rossiia*, pp. 100–8 (p. 104).

38 The word aesthetics derives from the ancient Greek term 'aisthesis', relating to sensual pleasure. Rozanov appreciates art predominantly in terms of its aesthetic activity and the sensual pleasure evoked in both writer and reader. Rozanov redefines aesthetics, rejecting a Kantian appreciation for form and instead focusing on visceral experience. This is made explicit in his numismatics.

39 See for example his letter to Gollerbakh dated 8 August 1918, reproduced in *V nashei smute*, p. 359.

> – Ах, не надо, пустите, – говорила она, а сама прижималась к нему.
>
> **
>
> Когда она, дрожащая и молчаливая, ничего не отвечая на его слова, ушла от него, он вышел на крыльцо и остановился, стараясь сообразить значение всего того, что произошло.
>
> He grabbed her, just as she was, in a stiff unbleached shirt with bared arms, lifted her and carried her off.
>
> 'Oh! What are you doing?' she whispered.
>
> But he paid no attention to her words, and carried her into his room.
>
> 'Oh, you mustn't, let me go,' she said, but clung closer to him.
>
> **
>
> When she left him, trembling and silent, not answering his words, he went out onto his porch and stopped, trying to understand the significance of what had happened.[40]

Although Nekhliudov does not yet fully understand the implications of his act, and Tolstoi refuses to depict it, the reader is fully aware of what had happened (and the significance of that deed) in the literary silence between these two paragraphs. (Rozanov would later make a direct link between censorship, the absence of text, with celibacy, comparing Benkendorf and his control over Pushkin to monks who impose an ascetic ideal on Orthodox worshippers.) The most important event in the novel is omitted. Tolstoi problematizes, through its very absence, an act which for him is already riddled with complexity. He underlines this tension between carnality and its verbal expression through the interaction between the two protagonists. Katiusha appeals to her master's reason by warning him that what they are about to do is wrong. Yet she also reveals the breakdown between intellectual and sensual communication, and the inability of literature to provide a remedy. Despite her spoken rejection of Nekhliudov, through her body she reluctantly communicates to him her unsuppressed desire. Likewise, he is unreceptive to what she says, but is only able to read the message reluctantly conveyed by her body. Eventually, language itself assumes a purely somatic function as both succumb: 'I am all yours'.

In not narrating the sexual act itself, omitting a device which is practically obligatory in today's writing, Tolstoi deliberately exploits the literary culture of his own time, which did not permit the artistic expression of intimate activity. The resurrection of this novel is a gradual liberation, as displayed in the development of the relationship between Nekhliudov and Katiusha, from a discourse of the body to one of reason;

---

40 L.N. Tolstoi, *Voskresenie*, in *Polnoe sobranie sochinenii*, XXXII, p. 63.

their final exchanges are disembodied as they both learn to read the Scriptures.[41] Tolstoi relies on written text, which appeals primarily to the mind. However, Tolstoi's work remains problematic, as seen above, because he encodes the reader's desired response in physical terminology.

Rozanov tries to overcome these tensions through his identification of the book and the body, as he attempts to bypass mental oversight over the physical. The manner in which Rozanov transfers sexual themes to the literary plane works as a broader example for the manner in which the ideal is transferred to the real. Rozanov takes the inadequacies of Russian literature, its abstractions, its silences, and tries to fill these with his own sexual content. It is also worth noting as an aside that both Tolstoi and Rozanov note the effects of observing the other's body. Orthodox worship relies heavily on the demonstration of religious behaviour and its observation by others, and Rozanov is full of descriptions he makes of watching other people worship, often unnoticed, demonstrating his emphasis on correct religious activity.

## Overcoming the Apocalypse through literature

Rozanov as literary critic is quick to condemn the writers and books he considers harmful to the Russian religious renewal. He identifies two major problems in Russian literature, which both essentially emerge from the same issue. Firstly, he attacks what he interprets as anti-religious themes. Under this category he interprets people who extolled revolutionary or anti-family ideas in their works, such as Saltykov-Shchedrin, Gogol′ or Tolstoi. The second type of writing is that of the God-Seekers, who use their works to explore the construction of a new religion in Russia. However, both these types of literature are consequences of the same cause, the lack of attachment to man's beginnings.

In insisting on literature's ability to restore pre-Christian values, Rozanov looks back to the example of Pushkin. In his views on Pushkin, Rozanov was influenced by his friend and one-time *Novoe Vremia*

41 However at their parting, once more, Tolstoi ensures their relationship is problematic. Katiusha's attempts to describe logically her reasons not to go with Nekhliudov are interrupted by her emotions, her words become quieter and she is unable to enunciate her final plea for forgiveness; this is only communicated by a smile. She presses his hand as she leaves. Yet this fleeting physical exchange only emphasizes Tolstoi's conclusion, that the two can only be saved through a final renunciation of corporeal relations.

colleague Fedor Shperk. A large part of Shperk's short philosophical career was dedicated to producing universal, speculative schemes of ontology and history, where he investigated the organic development of the cosmos and its seed-like growth.[42] Shperk also developed theories, following in the example of such Slavophile philosophers as Danilevskii, Grigor′ev and Leont′ev, on the organic and historical development of nations, placing the Slavs highest and noting their distinct historical mission.

As well as his production of grand systems of history, Shperk also developed ideas on how these laws affected the individual. He believed that sex provided a link between the universal and the person. Shperk agreed with Rozanov that literature also had a sexual element, as this too reconciled the individual self to the wider growth of the cosmos. He insisted that Russian literature lay in the sphere of spiritual life. Here Shperk reserved a special place for Russian literature which he considered, in Savina's words, to have a 'mystical-artistic' quality. The author imitates God by bringing the object of his writing into life and by loving his work as God loves His children. This was best demonstrated in Russian authors, unlike the Germans, whom Shperk criticized for their abstract and indifferent attitude towards their characters.[43] Shperk believed that the desire to find spatial and temporal harmony with the universe was a profound moral and religious obligation. By entering into a harmonious relationship with the outside world through creative activity, the human is able to return to a state of primeval, divine purity; this type of harmony assumes, in Savina's words, a 'moral character' and becomes a distinctly 'ethical category'.[44] Literature is one of the best means of achieving this, in its production, dissemination and consumption.[45]

---

42 Fedor Shperk, *Dialektika bytiia: Argumenty i vyvody moei filosofii* (St Petersburg, no given publisher, 1897), pp. 5–7.

43 T.V. Savina, 'Pamiati Elizavety Gustavovnoi Shperk', in Fedor Eduardovich Shperk, *Literaturnaia kritika*, ed. by T.V. Savina (Novosobirsk: PITs GNU, 1998), pp. 3–15 (p. 8).

44 Ibid., p. 10.

45 The idea that man could overcome through the medium of literature the religious problems presented by history became common in Rozanov's time. For example, Christensen argues that for Merezhkovskii, literature was the quintessential manner in which the individual became reconciled to history. See Peter G. Christensen, '*Christ and Antichrist* as Historical Novel', *Modern Language Studies*, 20 (1990), 67–77 (p. 72).

Despite their short friendship (Shperk joined *Novoe Vremia* in 1895 and died two years later at the age of 25), Shperk had a large influence on Rozanov. The two writers enjoyed a close personal relationship and spent much time together discussing philosophy, literature and their intimate (often sexual) experiences. Shperk's ideas on the use of literature to restore harmony between individual and the cosmos, are demonstrated in his work on Pushkin. For Shperk, Pushkin was the greatest Russian writer, as (once he had mastered his art, that is from 1822 and the completion of *Boris Godunov* onwards) he was able to express the harmony of his soul and his emotions with the world.[46] Contrary to a dominant trend in literary criticism, Shperk does not oppose Pushkin with Lermontov, but states that both poets were possessed of the same aim, to find a metaphysical and religious harmony with the world through literature. However, according to Shperk, Pushkin was the more successful, as he was better able to synthesize word with deed; Lermontov's word remained less effective, as it was not combined with the harmonious activity of the poet as in Pushkin. Rozanov admired Shperk's critique of Pushkin, and believed that Shperk's biographical insights into Pushkin could not be detached from Shperk's genius as a literary critic. Here Rozanov demonstrates his conviction that a writer's output is an essential component of his existence.

Rozanov examines Pushkin as the central figure in Russian culture, in whom literature is fundamental to the search for religious harmony.[47] Between 1899 and 1900, Rozanov wrote a series of articles in which he assessed the role of Pushkin and his poetry in Russian religious life, and he would return to this question at various points throughout his life. (The fact that Rozanov wrote articles to mark the anniversary of important events in the life of his favourite writers, such as the hundredth anniversary of Pushkin's birth in 1899, or his 1912 article on the seventy-fifth anniversary of Pushkin's death, demonstrates that their lives provided a significant marker of time in his worldview and in the production of his own work.) For Rozanov, Pushkin is a pagan writer,

46 Savina, pp. 10–11.

47 The relationship between Rozanov and Pushkin has been neglected so far in Russian and Western scholarship, though an influential group of scholars in Moscow is working to remedy this and establish Rozanov's place in the Pushkin canon. Nikoliukin is spearheading efforts in this field. For a discussion of Pushkin's influence on Rozanov as a writer, and for Nikoliukin's comparison of Pushkin and Rozanov's understanding of the Russian writer's role, see Nikoliukin, *Rozanov*, pp. 181–90.

who understands the original, Edenic beauty of God's world. More than this, Pushkin is able to bring these eternal, original values and make them real in contemporary life. 'He believed that God was in *everything*, that is this ideal shook him, in every leaf of God's creation, in every human face; searching, he was able, or at least was ready, to find this. All his life was the culmination of these ideals – walking in the Garden of God, he could say to humanity: "And what could you love more that this?"'[48] For Rozanov, Pushkin understood the etymology of the word 'cosmos', deriving from the Greek word 'to make beautiful'. Here Rozanov underlines his view that the artist's task is cosmological and refers to God's creativity. This is a pre-Christian undertaking; Pushkin is the Russian Homer, who comprehends and synthesizes in his self the history of humanity, and then presents this to us anew in his own poetry. In fact, Christ is bypassed. No other Russian poet has the ability to make the ideas of God flesh on Earth. Comprehending the original beauty of the world, and then expressing this through literature, is one of the best forms of *imitatio Dei*. 'He was serious, thoughtful; walking through the Garden of God he did not give out one sigh, but [...] he revelled in it, repeating the work of God's hands'.[49]

Rozanov sees in Pushkin more than an ability to convey the eternal truths found in paganism: on each occasion that Pushkin speaks, he gives these truths a new meaning. This is more than the repetition of archaic motifs. Each time these eternal ideas are brought forth, they hold new significance, and so Pushkin avoids monotony.[50] Pushkin has the ability to insert archaic significance into each moment of contemporary life, but to give this fresh meaning each time. Pushkin's gift is his 'strength for the new', and his 'gift of the eternally new'.[51] Though Pushkin stands above all others, Dostoevskii and Lermontov stand in his tradition by bringing back into contemporary life our pagan roots. 'All these, all three writers, visited Delphi, and brought us the essence of the paganism of the prophets, that is ancient but yet eternally new, but which each generation requires'.[52]

Rozanov is writing in a context where the value of Pushkin was undergoing a profound cultural re-evaluation. Rozanov was one of the many

48 V.V. Rozanov, 'O Pushkinskoi Akademii', in *Mysli o literature* (Moscow: Sovremennik, 1989), pp. 232–9 (pp. 232–3).

49 Ibid., p. 233.

50 Ibid., p. 234.

51 'O Pushkinskoi Akademii', p. 237.

52 V.V. Rozanov, 'Zametka o Pushkine', in *Mysli o literature*, pp. 240–6 (p. 244).

figures who were intent on restoring Pushkin's place in Russia's cultural and literary canon, and who opposed the naturalist interpretations of the 1860s and 1870s, such as those of Pisarev or Dobroliubov.[53] Rozanov was not the only Silver Age writer who revisited the Pushkin myth. These themes occupy a central role in the works of Merezhkovskii, Blok and Briusov, to name a few. Silver Age figures intended to draw parallels between their time and that of the Golden Age and to evade history by promoting the idea of mythological time.[54] Rozanov distinguishes himself by contesting that ultimate cultural significance is conferred by man's past. For Rozanov, the present moment only has renewed value when it is brought into contact with man's past. Literature helps achieve this. Words have an ancient value, which man is obliged to revive. In this regard, Rozanov's understanding of the symbol is close to that of Lotman. For Lotman, the symbol is more than a sign. Every symbol emerges from our prehistory and contains archaic and immutable value.[55] However, the symbol is given new meaning each time it is used, providing for a new relationship between the permanent and the repeated.[56] (This relationship is managed in Rozanov through an emphasis on creativity.) The symbol can operate as an agent of cultural renewal, and for Rozanov, Pushkin masters this, as his poetry has a revitalizing quality and the ability to renew culture.[57] Furthermore, Pushkin upholds the individuality of each character he creates, avoiding typification. Rozanov considers the use of literary types a distortion of reality, which merges the unique significance of each person into a meaningless mass.

> Пушкин есть как бы символ жизни: он – весь в движении, и от этого-то так разнообразно его творчество. Все, что живет, – влечет его, и, подходя

53 Gasparov, 'Introduction', in *Cultural Mythologies of Russian Modernism*, p. 6.

54 Paperno discusses how the heritage of Pushkin was handled among Rozanov's contemporaries. She argues that the mythologization of Pushkin in the Silver Age was an essential means by which writers were able to synthesize historical differences between the two periods, as well as enabling them to overcome the contradictions in Pushkin's life and to present their idol as the quintessential 'life-creating' poet. Irina Paperno, 'Pushkin v zhizni cheloveka Serebrianogo veka', in *Cultural Mythologies of Russian Modernism*, pp. 19–51 (pp. 22–3).

55 See Iu.M. Lotman, 'Simvol v sisteme kul′tury', in *Izbrannye stat′i v trekh tomakh*, 3 vols (Tallinn: Aleksandra, 1992), I, pp. 191–9 (p. 192).

56 Ibid., pp. 192–3.

57 V.V. Rozanov, 'Pushkin i Gogol′', in *Legenda o Velikom Inkvizitore*, pp. 136–42 (p. 137).

ко всему, – он любит его и воплощает. Слова его никогда не остаются без отношения к действительности, они покрывают ее и чрез нее становятся образами, очертаниями. Это он есть истинный основатель *натуральной школы*, всегда верный природе человека, верный и судьбе его. Ничего напряженного в нем нет, никакого болезненного воображения или неправильного чувства.

Pushkin is like a symbol of life: he is all movement, and this is the reason for the variety of his work. He is involved in everything that lives, and in his approach to everything, he loves and embodies it. His words never remain unrelated to reality, they enclose it and through it become images, outlines. He is the true founder of the *natural school*, always faithful to the nature of the human and his fate. There is nothing forced in him, no morbid imagination or wrong feeling.[58]

Rozanov later writes to mark the seventy-fifth anniversary of Pushkin's death that the true spiritual significance of Pushkin's work should be restored not only to the Russian reading elite, but to the Russian home and to every Russian child as part of their spiritual education.[59] Rozanov associates reverence for Pushkin with his utopian vision: 'We should love him [Pushkin], just like the people of "Paradise Lost" love and imagine "Paradise Regained".'[60] One aspect of Pushkin studies which Rozanov found distasteful was the pedantic nature in which 'bibliophiles' poured over every line of his poetry, correcting the text where they felt he had been misprinted and arguing about superficial details, which for Rozanov had nothing to do with the meaning of the texts. Such scholarly squabbles only obscured the true meaning of Pushkin's work and dissuaded ordinary Russian families from taking Pushkin into their homes, making him particularly inaccessible to the young.[61]

As he understands the family as the basic means of cultural transmission, Rozanov demands that literature expresses the importance of genetic links and sees the convergence of literary and biological relations. He married his first wife out of a desire to achieve physical proximity to Dostoevskii. There has been little scholarly work on Rozanov's interpretation of Dostoevskii outside the field of Dostoevskii studies, which

58 Ibid.

59 V.V. Rozanov, 'Vozvrat k Pushkinu (K 75-letiiu dnia ego konchiny)', in *Mysli o literature*, pp. 326–30 (p. 326).

60 Ibid., pp. 329–30.

61 Ibid., p. 327. Rozanov's comments on the pedantic squabbling over spelling in publications of Pushkin's works mirror his complaints over religious arguments in Russian history, particularly in his discussions over the seventeenth-century religious reforms.

have typically focused on the *Legenda o Velikom Inkvizatore*. However, Rozanov's most important thoughts on Dostoevskii are not to be found in this book, but in later works, especially in *V temnykh religioznykh luchakh*. Despite a common view that Rozanov preferred Dostoevskii above all others (along with the Bible, Rozanov kept a copy of *Dnevnik pisatelia* by his bed), this view must be qualified. Rozanov realizes that Dostoevskii does not enjoy the same harmonious relationship with the world as Pushkin does. He frequently criticizes Dostoevskii's intolerance to people and his unrelenting obedience to Christ.[62] It is also important to point out that in many investigations of Dostoevskii's characters as expressing the pagan ideal, Rozanov realizes that Dostoevskii himself does not fully understand the significance of his own characters' beliefs and actions. Nevertheless, the way they are brought to life demonstrates the correct reverence for the created world.

Banerjee writes that, unlike others who try to extract a philosophical system from Dostoevskii, Rozanov investigates him to shed light on his own psychology.[63] However, one must take issue with this point and argue that this is a religious-philosophical investigation. Rozanov sees in Dostoevskii a sensitivity to the processes which connect this world to the divine. The basis for Rozanov's attraction to Dostoevskii is a quote to which he returns again and again, where Father Zosima narrates how God took seeds from other worlds and planted them into this Earth. All religion emerges from the desire to touch these other worlds.[64] Rozanov sees Zosima as close to the ideal Christian. But this is not a version of Orthodoxy that rests on Christ, but an original form of religious behaviour based on the tie with nature.

---

62 Rozanov's appraisal of Dostoevskii is complex and requires much more scholarship. There is no sense in Rozanov's works that Dostoevskii is the religious thinker or writer whom he admires the most. There are fundamental differences in their views. As Jackson notes, Dostoevskii sees man's duty as transcending the world to strive for an ideal which lies outside his nature. Harmony can only be achieved through a 'lofty spirituality in a quest for form and faith'. Robert Louis Jackson, *Dialogues with Dostoevsky: The Overwhelming Questions* (Stanford: Stanford University Press, 1993), p. 179. In contrast, Rozanov locates man's ideal within his nature and his relationship with the world.

63 Maria Banerjee, 'Rozanov on Dostoevskiy', *Slavic and East European Journal*, 15 (1971), 411–24 (p. 411).

64 V.V. Rozanov, 'Russkie mogily', in *V temnykh religioznykh luchakh*, pp. 192–252 (p. 202).

Он выражает до-христианский, первоначальный *натурализм*, то «поклонение *природе*», «поклонение *всему*» (пантеизм), с проклятия чего начало христианство, что́ «срубить до *корня*» уже пришел Иоанн Креститель. Нет строя души, более *противоположного христианству*, чем душевный покой и душевная святость Зосимы, исключающие нужду во Христе.

He expresses a pre-Christian, primordial *naturalism*, the 'worship of *nature*', the 'worship of *everything*' (pantheism), with the damning of which Christianity began, which John the Baptist came to 'cut at the roots'. There is no fabric of the soul more *opposed to Christianity* than the peace and holiness of Zosima's soul, which exclude any need of Christ.[65]

Rozanov argues that Zosima loves all life, without relying on New Testament commandments to express this. Zosima relates to other Christians not in the unforgiving manner of the Russian Orthodox Church, but with warmth and devotion. Rozanov contrasts him with Ferapont and considers Zosima's relationship with Alesha Karamazov the ideal manner in which a monk should relate to people.[66] Rozanov writes that Zosima's and Alesha's love is based on a real attachment to Russia, and not on the fleshless, bloodless religion demanded in Orthodoxy. In their religious outlook, Rozanov writes, Christ plays no role.[67] This literary expression of ideal human life, and Dostoevskii's effect on the reader, has implications for Rozanov's interpretation of the writer. Rozanov does not consider Dostoevskii a writer, journalist or philosopher in the traditional understanding. Dostoevskii is a prophet, whose insight emerges from his attachment not to ideas, but from his striving for unity and a restoration of the primeval relationship with the world. For Rozanov, Dostoevskii's work re-expresses the myths of Egypt, not in an abstract manner, but in a way that has real meaning for the Russian experience. Rozanov understands that Dostoevskii can express the eternal truths of religion and their relevance for the Russians: 'Dostoevskii's "prophetic" character emerges principally from the depth of his love for the "deed", the essence of Russian life, the fate of its history as seen from the perspective of eternity'.[68] Dostoevskii exposes for the Russian people the way in which they should resurrect

65 V.V. Rozanov, 'Predislovie', in *V temnykh religioznykh luchakh*, pp. 95–100 (p. 98).
66 'Russkie mogily', p. 202.
67 Ibid.
68 V.V. Rozanov, 'Pamiati F.M. Dostoevskogo', in *Russkaia mysl´* (Moscow: Algoritm, 2006), pp. 129–38 (p. 130).

ancient religious truths, and it is through his characters that Dostoevskii embodies his prophetic insight.[69]

## Literature, *byt* and revolution

Rozanov shows a particular affection for literature that emerges from, and expresses the ideal of, *byt*. He believes (similar to Merezhkovskii's declaration in *O prichinakh upadka i novykh techeniiakh v sovremennoi russkoi literature*) that there is a close link between a nation's spiritual health and its literature, and the decline of one leads to the decline of the other.[70] Rozanov stands in the traditions of his literary heroes, especially those who supported traditional Russian ways of life and posited the family as the basis of Russian society. It is worth citing the example of Giliarov-Platonov, and the response to his death by his peers, in order to examine the cultural context in which Rozanov was operating. When Giliarov-Platonov, one of Rozanov's favourite writers, was buried in 1887, alongside Sergei Solov´ev and Pogodin in Moscow's Novodevichii Monastery, Sergei Sharapov mourned more than the passing of a friend, but was concerned about the broader consequences for Russia of Giliarov-Platonov's death: 'The dusk sets ever more thickly over Russian society, over Russian literature [...] The lights of Russian thought are extinguished, and looking at their heirs who ask yourself in horror: "Who can replace them?"'[71] This suggests the influence Russian thinkers had on their nation's wellbeing. The death of a writer is posited almost as an apocalyptic event. There is also a wider point to be made about Russian conservatism, in that in certain contexts it contains within itself a dimension of the apocalyptic. In a philosophical scheme where the preservation of culture lies at the centre of man's religious obligations, any deviation from tradition, including even seemingly insignificant changes, can be seen as having calamitous consequences.

---

69 Rozanov lauds Dostoevskii for the manner in which he expresses the love of what Rozanov calls the 'pochva', or 'the people [narod], the tribe, one's blood and traditions'. Dostoevskii circumvents for Rozanov the rootless, bloodless religion brought by Christ. 'Pamiati F.M. Dostoevskogo', p. 133.

70 'Mater´ialy k resheniiu voprosa', p. 225.

71 *Neopoznannyi genii: Sbornik statei i materialov, posviashchennykh pamiati N.P. Giliarova-Platonova*, ed. by S. Sharapov (no publication information), p. 5.

Giliarov-Platonov and Sharapov belong to a distinct branch of Russian thought which handled these problems by returning to the family hearth and *byt*. They set themselves apart from formal Slavophilism by eschewing formal schemes, but by attaching themselves predominantly to the Russian people as an organic body and not necessarily to the established Church. They share many similarities with the *pochvennichestvo* movement. They believed in the natural development of Russian society and rejected the programme of Slavophilism, viewing their a priori theories as over-schematic and abstract.[72] They were by no means ultra-conservative and were pragmatic enough to accept that, while human nature remained unchanged since the beginning of time, society would develop. They adopted a pragmatic stance towards technological advancements, welcoming them where they improved social welfare without damaging Russian traditions. Hence their main concern in their work was the difficult task of reconciling the permanent needs of the person with history and a developing society. Rozanov felt a deep attachment to thinkers who stood within this tradition, among whom could be counted Grigor′ev, Strakhov, Giliarov-Platonov, Sharapov, Rtsy, Pobedonostsev and Filippov. In Rozanov we witness perhaps one of the last flourishes of Russian organic criticism, assumed from thinkers such as Grigor′ev and Strakhov and in particular Leont′ev. Rozanov frequently takes issue with the systematic approach of theoretical Slavophilism, in favour of the organic, creative view taken by the *pochvenniki*, based on the growth of the 'people' ('narod').[73] However, in Rozanov, the organic nature of literature assumes a particular ethical-dogmatic category, rooted in the belief of the body as the locus of the person's encounter with the divine.

Of these, the work and personality of Rtsy had a particularly deep and lasting influence on Rozanov. The fact that Rtsy lived in St

72 Dowler discusses at length the differences between the *pochvenniki* and the Slavophiles. He examines how the former school were critical of Slavophile theories, attending instead to the natural development of Russian society and the priority of experience: 'the obvious eclecticism of *pochvennichestvo* permitted it considerable flexibility in the formulation of a program. The whole concept of an integrated culture presupposed an amalgam of widely diverse components [...] The vagueness of *Vremia* was by no means mitigated by the editors' insistence that only life could determine the course of Russian development. The principles guiding the evolution of a nation could not be known in advance of their revelation in life itself.' Wayne Dowler, *Dostoevsky, Grigor′ev and Native Soil Conservatism* (Toronto/London: University of Toronto Press, 1982), p. 92.

73 See especially 'Perstye temy', p. 132.

Petersburg was one of the factors in Rozanov's decision to move to the capital (although, as Rozanov got to know him better, he developed a more ambivalent relationship towards the elder writer). However, he deeply admired Rtsy's writing, which he considered misunderstood and undervalued. Rtsy's most famous work, *Listopad*, contains a mix of philosophical musings, childhood reminiscences, political comments, recollections of amusing events from his home and society gatherings. It was an influence for Rozanov's *Opavshie list'ia* in more than title. One aspect which runs through *Listopad* is the author's love for the home, his affection for his childhood and his desire to find eternal meaning in family life. 'At home, everything remained untroubled. Not one black spot on the political horizon, not one sharp question, no rage or daily anger. Everything remains untroubled. We eat, drink, marry, endeavour – as it was in the days of Noah, it is now'.[74] However, Rtsy believes that man should not preserve all traditions purely out of dogmatic conservatism. Society should protect only that which is good. He argues that society is not yet at its perfect state, and that there is room for improvement. Therefore he criticizes conservatives who demand adherence to tradition, simply out of tradition's sake. Rtsy is also critical of political liberalism, which teaches that the present is not a basis for social life.[75] Hence Rtsy steers a careful course between conservatism and liberalism. In *Listopad* he extols the value of the present moment, whilst at the same time searching to imbue it with eternal meaning. This desire to find harmony between eternity and the present was a common concern of Rozanov's favourite writers, but such figures were dying out and their work was being forgotten. 'They chimed their hand bells, while the rest of the country banged their gongs. Nobody heard then, nobody paid them attention'.[76]

The end of their contribution to Russian culture only exacerbated the apocalyptic fervour sweeping across the nation, making the need for a new literature all the more pressing in Rozanov's mind. He insisted that there should be nothing artificial, stylized or indulgent in literature and he quite often rejected the greats of Russian literature in favour of

74 Rtsy, *Listopad* (Moscow, no given publisher, 1895), p. 2. Remizov evokes a similar scene of the eternal bliss of home life; *Kukkha*, p. 57.

75 Rtsy, *Listopad*, pp. 7–8.

76 V.V. Rozanov, 'S vershiny tysiacheletnei piramidy (Razmyshlenie o khode russkoi literatury)', in *Sochineniia* (Moscow: Sovetskaia Rossiia, 1990), pp. 448–64 (p. 461).

the simple and the homely. For example, one of the writers he admired most was the provincial diarist from Kostroma, Elizaveta D′iakonova (1874–1902), with whom Rozanov corresponded.[77] Rozanov bemoans the fact that unpretentious, domestic literature like this is being forgotten and that Russia has succumbed to the artificiality and atheism of writers who do not understand the true meaning of religion.

The most harmful figure in Russian literature is Gogol′, though Rozanov's critique of the Ukrainian is lengthy and complex. Rozanov condemns Gogol′ for his atheism and for his un-Russianness and the way this is manifested through his characters. Rozanov opposes Gogol′ to Pushkin in order to demonstrate the way authors should understand the life-creating potential of literature. In contrast to Pushkin, Gogol′'s work is full of dead souls, grotesque caricatures who walk like zombies through Russian culture. Referring to this novel, Rozanov remarks that Gogol′'s language is closed to the possibility of new life.

> Всмотримся в течение этой речи – и мы увидим, что оно безжизненно. Это восковой язык, в котором ничего не шевелится, ни одно слово не выдвигается вперед и не хочет сказать больше, чем сказано во всех других. И где бы мы ни открыли книгу, на какую бы смешную сцену ни попали, мы увидим всюду эту же мертвую ткань языка, в которую обернуты все выведенные фигуры, как в свой общий саван. Уже отсюда, как обусловленное и вторичное, вытекает то, что у всех этих фигур мысли не продолжаются, впечатления не связываются, но все они стоят неподвижно, с чертами, докуда довел их автор, и не растут далее ни внутри себя, ни в душе читателя [...] Это – мертвая ткань, которая каковою введена была в душу читателя, таковою в ней и останется навсегда.
>
> If we examine the flow of this speech, we see that it is lifeless. It is waxen language in which nothing moves, words do not move forward and refuse to say anything other than what is said in other words. And wherever we open the book, whichever amusing scene we come across, we still see the same dead fabric of language, wrapped around the same derivative characters like some communal shroud. As a by-product of this, the thoughts of these characters are not extended, impressions are not joined together; everything remains motionless, with properties bestowed by the author that do not grow from within him or in the soul of the reader [...] It is a dead fabric, drawn into the soul of the reader and which will remain there forever.[78]

---

77 Rozanov calls D′iakonova's diary one of the greatest books of Russian nineteenth-century literature, writing that no other student could write 'so simply, so complexly, so innocently and cleanly'. See his letter to Gollerbakh of February 1916, published in *V nashei smute*, p. 342.

78 'Pushkin i Gogol′', p. 139.

Where Pushkin reflects the true relationship of outer form to inner content, Gogol′ only depicts externalities. Gogol′ has no ability to depict the essence of the human being, but fills his books with fleshless ghosts who despise this world and only look upwards to Heaven. The celibate Gogol′ never married, never had children and therefore cannot write properly. He creates distorted characters which lack real flesh. This flawed method of creating literary characters is reminiscent of Rozanov's critique of the theories of Incarnation propounded by his opponents within the Orthodox Church.

> Они все, как и Плюшкин, произошли каким-то особым способом, ничего не имеющим с естественным рождением: они сделаны из какой-то восковой массы слов, и тайну этого художественного делания знал один Гоголь. Мы над ними смеемся: но замечательно, что это не есть живой смех, которым мы отвечаем на то, чтó, встретив в жизни, – отрицаем, с чем боремся. Мир Гоголя – чудно отошедший от нас вдаль мир.
>
> They all [Gogol′s characters], like Pliushkin, appeared in a manner which has nothing to do with real birth: they are made from some waxen mass of words, and the secret of this artistic work was known only to Gogol′. We laugh at them: but it is notable that it is not the living laughter we use to respond to things which, when encountered in life, we reject and fight against. The world of Gogol′ is a world which strangely has gone far from us.[79]

Gogol′ did not give birth to his characters, but created abstract, lifeless puppets. Gogol′ devoted his entire life to portraying people but could only reflect their fixed, lifeless forms and outer appearance. He never understood, and could not describe, the human soul. Consequently, Gogol′ 'told us that this soul does not exist and, drawing dead figures, made them with such artistry that we actually believed for decades that there was a whole generation of walking corpses'.[80]

This examination of Gogol′ demonstrates the complex relationship between the production and reception of literature within a cultural environment which, for Rozanov, often struggles to reconcile the aesthetic and didactic functions of texts. The religious function of literature puts extra responsibility on writers, as their influence on society is far-reaching. The revolutionary characters which inhabit the works of Saltykov-Shchedrin and Chernyshevskii encourage radicals like Azef to

79 Ibid., p. 140.
80 *Legenda o Velikom Inkvizitore*, p. 21.

imitate their atheist activities.[81] Writers are directly responsible for the revolutionary movement in Russia. Rozanov criticizes Tolstoi for introducing into Russian culture figures opposed to the ideal of the happy family. Lavretskii, Karenin and Pozdnyshev are all 'half-alive', people who, like their creator, live according to the idea of discord and unhappiness within the family.[82]

Rozanov insists that writers should emphasize the importance of family life. However, the influence that literature has on the Russian people is highly problematic, because it is open to abuse by those, such as aesthetes, revolutionaries or Decadents, who exploit the sacral nature of literature in order to spread atheism, celibacy or radicalism. Rozanov is highly aware that the Russian readership tends to receive texts not as fanciful constructions or trivial inventions. I shall examine this view in the context of how Rozanov himself writes in the next chapter, but it is worth noting here the similarity of his approach to that of Trithemius, who like Rozanov upheld the importance of hand-written texts, and who also noted that there is often little difference between texts which have a sacred nature and those which have an evil function. (This emerges in the pervasive Christian fear, also discussed in Chapter 6, that the satanic is extremely close to the holy, and parallels Rozanov's attempts to remove the boundaries between the sacred and the profane in sexual matters, as well as his approximation of Christ to the Antichrist.) Rozanov knows that literary works, even when intended as fantasy, are understood as bearing a truth which has an undeniable religious quality. Such ideas emerge in Rozanov's treatment of Gogol′.[83] Rozanov understands the extreme sensitivity of the Russian readership. Gogol′'s stories cannot be seen as trivial fantasies; instead, Russians interpret them as reality. Gogol′, who according to Rozanov had no real love for the family, persuades the Russians to likewise shun such relations. In his last days, Rozanov was to decide that Gogol′, more than anyone else, is responsible for atheism in Russia: he concludes that the 'terrible Ukrainian' is responsible for the Russian Revolution.[84]

81 V.V. Rozanov, 'Mezhdu Azefom i "Vekhami"', in *Staraia i molodaia Rossiia*, pp. 263–72 (p. 267).

82 V.V. Rozanov, 'K novomu zakonoproekty o razvode', in *Staraia i molodaia Rossiia*, pp. 140–3 (p. 141).

83 Rozanov appears to believe that he alone understood Gogol′ correctly and read his works properly, a view mirrored in his opinion that only he 'read' the imposter Azef correctly and understood his true intentions.

84 *Poslednie list′ia*, p. 24.

Interestingly, Rozanov's views on the problem of realism are repeated by his younger contemporary Ivan Bunin in his discussion of Goncharov (a writer whom Rozanov sometimes did not enjoy). Bunin complains that Russia has been spoilt by an over-complicated approach to life and by the incursion of the 'crowd' and the 'street' into the security of domestic life.[85] Bunin argues that the 'literary approach to life has simply poisoned us'.[86] This is because writers have brought forth destructive literary characters, such Pechorin and Bazarov, who have become for Russians hyper-realistic, the referential of the ideal life which they should emulate. Consequently, the Russians have destroyed their natural approach to the world and now define themselves according to artificial constructs; they are left unable to distinguish between reality and the literary.[87]

Insisting that the artist must create new life, Rozanov is also critical of the artificiality and abstraction of Symbolist art. In the Silver Age, rival trends competed for authority over the definition and use of art. Writers such as Bal′mont or Briusov assimilated religious motifs and appropriated these for artistic means.[88] Some of Rozanov's contemporaries were inspired by the English art-for-art's-sake movement, and in particular by the formal beauty of Oscar Wilde. The *Mir Iskusstva* group emphasized the formal aspects of art (though never disregarding completely the value of its content) and particularly valued individual creativity. An important point which Diagilev made, opposing the dominant trend in religious thought, was that art should be evaluated in detachment from its historical setting. He rejected the view, especially prominent in Solov′ev and Tolstoi, that the ethical dimension of art improved throughout history.

Competing ideas over aesthetics and artistic function battled over the way in which ideas were transferred to the artistic level. Some

85 Ivan Bunin, *Okaiannye dni*, here taken from *Polnoe sobranie sochinenii v XIII tomakh* (Moscow: Voskresen′e, 2005-), VI, pp. 275–382 (p. 320).

86 Ibid., p. 329.

87 Ibid., p. 330.

88 For the aestheticization of the religious for stylistic purposes, see Aage A. Hansen-Love, 'Iskusstvo kak religiia: Poeziia rannego simvolizma', in *Christianity and the Eastern Slavs*, ed. by Boris Gasparov, Robert P. Hughes, Irina Paperno, and Olga Raevsky-Hughes, 3 vols (Berkeley/London: University of California Press, 1995), III, *Russian Literature in Modern Times*, pp. 57–111 (pp. 57–8). The exploitation of religious tropes for aesthetic means is also a broader characteristic of literary modernism, witnessed in many European and American writers from Mann to Joyce.

writers focused on the spiritual function of literature and its use in the construction of a new religion. Others emphasized the aestheticization of religious ideas predominantly for stylistic purposes. However, in practice, similar themes were exploited, and corresponding themes and ideas overlapped. These trends ran concurrently, and it is often difficult to delineate competing tendencies as the ideologies of seemingly rival groups were not rigid. In addition, although groups defined their project in opposition to their rivals, in reality opponents emerged from the same cultural traditions and shared the same artistic theories. Rozanov's own approach highlights this interrelationship of mutual influence and rebellion. He often defined his own work in opposition to these movements, while at the same time drawing heavily on their themes and ideas and giving inspiration to new currents.

Although Rozanov associated with Russia's Symbolists and Decadents (for him, as for Merezhkovskii, the two terms are synonymous) after his move to Petersburg, he was never a central member of their movement. He sees Symbolism as a distinctly foreign, specifically French, movement, which has found fertile soil in Russia and spread rapidly. For Rozanov it is not surprising that the homeland of the Marquis de Sade should bring forth poetry which only has an erotic, and unloving, attitude towards its object.[89] Rozanov regards Symbolist poetry as superficial, with no regard for the essence of its subject. Moreover, Symbolism does not encourage the reader to be creative himself.

Rozanov writes that Symbolism's erotic superficiality has engulfed most areas of Russian art. In an 1896 essay, Rozanov discusses Briusov's one-line poem from 1894, *O, zakroi svoi blednye nogi!*.[90] This for Rozanov exemplifies the problems with Symbolism. Where art should involve the unified person, the poet only refers to the object's legs, omitting her head. There is no regard for the essence of the heroine of the poem. All that is left is an unloving, purely sexual attitude between author and poet. This eroticism is also reflected in the fine arts. Visiting the 1892 French exhibition in Moscow, Rozanov was confronted not

89 V.V. Rozanov, 'O simvolistakh i dekadentakh', in *Religiia, filosofiia, kul'tura*, pp. 125–35 (p. 127).

90 Valerii Briusov, *Sobranie sochinenii v semi tomakh* (Moscow: Khudozhestvennaia literatura, 1973), I, p. 36. It is amusing to note the (apparently unfounded) rumours circulating in particular among the Futurists, that Briusov originally had the 'pedestrian' first name 'Vasilii', but altered this to the more stylized 'Valerii'. Vladimir Markov, *Russian Futurism: A History* (London: MacGibbon & Kee, 1969), p. 169.

with scenes of the home, but with erotic images of women, with no real love for the object.[91] This type of art excludes family life and the possibility of real closeness between people.[92] 'Decadence is the ultra without the object to which this refers; it is the exaggeration without the exaggerated; pretentious forms with a content which has already vanished; without rhythm, without a beat, and still without the sense of "poetry" – this is Decadence'.[93]

In his work on the Symbolists, Rozanov demonstrates further the interrelationship of what it means to be an artist and to have children. Good art can only come from those who properly understand family life. Merezhkovskii, whose writing Rozanov never regarded highly, is compared to a woman 'who is eternally pregnant but cannot give birth'.[94] Belyi is incapable of giving birth to good art: he was never properly born himself.[95] Moreover, Rozanov reveals much in these investigations over differing interpretations of cultural history and over others' attempts to renew Russian society. One of his major criticisms of the Symbolists is that they are misguided in their search for a cultural basis for their inspiration. His contemporaries define their period as a type of Renaissance, but Rozanov believes that they did not understand the true meaning of this time in European history. He argues that the Renaissance should be interpreted as a reconnection of humanity with the Earth, after the strict asceticism of the Middle Ages.[96] The Symbolists try to found their work simply on the artistic forms developed in the Renaissance, without understanding the true creative implications of the content of the art of that period. Rozanov explains that their art is 'too disinterested', and consequently the audience could also feel disinterested in the true meaning of life. Increasingly, the audience forgets how to pray and becomes self-absorbed.[97] Rozanov is also aware of the relationship between Symbolist writings and Church texts, and the fact that his peers have assumed the style of religious texts without infecting the reader with a love of life. Russian literature has assumed religious forms but

---

91 'O simvolistakh i dekadentakh', pp. 127–8.

92 Ibid., pp. 129–30.

93 Ibid., p. 131.

94 V.V. Rozanov, 'Predstaviteli "novogo religioznogo soznaniia"', in *Okolo narodnoi dushi*, pp. 355–60 (p. 359).

95 *Uedinennoe*, p. 194.

96 'O simvolistakh i dekadentakh', p. 131.

97 Ibid., p. 132.

neglected the content. Hence Rozanov spots a crisis in the stylization of religious themes.

> Вот еще грех духовной литературы – нашей и не только нашей, – новой, но и также древней. Она есть вся – стилизация, стилизациею исчерпывается, кроме стилизации, ничего в себе не содержит.
>
> Когда появилась стилизация по мотивам эстетическим, все ужаснулись; восхитились сперва и потом ужаснулись: каким образам Валерий Брюсов или Андрей Белый могут так волшебно и изумительно «стилизовать» в своих новеллах и рассказах и хронику XIII века, и рыцарский роман, и напр., хлыстов. Но не заметили, что это – старое явление в Европе. Именно все проповеди, поучения, апологетика «стилизуют» инде пророка Моисея (Влад. Соловьев), инде Иоанна Златоуста, и т.д., и т.д. Самое воспроизведение в себе «подвигов аскетизма» есть уже стилизация.
>
> There is another sin of spiritual literature – this concerns Russian literature, but not just Russian – modern and ancient, it is worn out by stylization, and has no content but stylization.
>
> When stylization was first used for aesthetic motives, everyone was horrified; at first they were amazed, and then horrified: how could Valerii Briusov or Andrei Belyi in such magical and amazing fashion 'stylize' their novellas and tales and chronicles of the XIII century, and their epic tales, and their tales of the khlysty? But they did not realize that this is an old phenomenon in Europe. For all sermons, all lectures, all apologetics, 'stylize' the Prophet Moses (Vlad. Solov′ev), John Chrysostom etc. Even when they reproduce 'the trials of asceticism', it is still stylization.[98]

The relationship between form and content is revealed in Rozanov's re-definition of style. In contrast to the artificiality of his opponents, Rozanov argues that good literature should express true 'style', that is an attachment to each entity's original nature, its eternal principle or 'causa formalis'. Rozanov adheres to an internal, rather than external, principle: 'Style is the soul of all things, it is the ideal in each separate thing, not dictated from outside, but emerging from its makeup, from its own nature'.[99] When discussing an object stylistically, for example the Tsar or the clergy, the artist should respect tradition and this object's connection to history and to God. As Rozanov writes in an aphorism from *Opavshie list′ia*, 'style is where God has kissed a thing'.[100] Rozanov's reliance on the ethical goes further. It is vital that only holy, decent people become

98 *Poslednie list′ia*, p. 128.

99 V.V. Rozanov, 'Stil′ veshchei', in *Staraia i molodaia Rossiia*, pp. 392–5 (p. 392).

100 *Opavshie list′ia II*, p. 629.

writers. A bad person can only write bad literature.[101] Hence Rozanov's ambivalence to the book is grounded in the fact that literary discourse has become the violent battleground between those who express a true religious feeling and those who have wrongly exploited this medium in order to wage war on Russia and the Russian family. Rozanov insists on reclaiming literature and restoring its original, religious purpose. He demands a rebirth of Russian literature, but this involves bringing the literary environment as it exists to an end.

> Мысль моя и была и есть и *останется* взломать литературу. Подрубить те подмостки, на которых она пялится и выпячивает брюхо. Явно они также должны давать мне оплеухи.
>
> Верочка Мордвинова, невинная и прелестная девушка, написала же в частом письме ко мне – «ненавижу Тургенева», а о Толстом я даже испугался: «Лучше бы он повесился». Отчего же мне в свой черед не ненавидеть литературу?
>
> О, я делаю исключения:
> Державин
> Жуковский
> Карамзин
> Батюшков
> Крылов
> Пушкин
> Лермонтов
> Кольцов
> Грановский
> С.Т. Аксаков «с сыновьями»
> Никита Гиляров-Платонов
> Катков? Нет – нужно *мне*
> Рцы
> Шперк
> Розанов
> Мордвинова (письма, не напечатаны)
> Дьяконова
> Л. Толстой (первая ½)
> Гончаров
> Ал. Толстой
> Лесков
> Тургенев
> Печерский («В лесах»)
> ........................................
> ........................................
> ........................................

101 'Perstye temy', p. 136.

Майков
Полонский
Фет
Страхов
К. Леонтьев
Н.Я. Данилевский

My thought was, and is, and *will remain*, to blow literature apart. To pull down the scaffolding from which it stares and puffs out its belly. Clearly somebody should give my ears a good boxing.

Verochka Mordvinova, an innocent and delightful girl, wrote in the same letter to me, 'I too hate Turgenev', and I was even frightened by what she wrote about Tolstoi: 'He should have hanged himself.' Why should I too not hate literature in my turn?

Oh, I make exceptions:
Derzhavin
Zhukovskii
Karamzin
Batiushkov
Krylov
Pushkin
Lermontov
Kol´tsov
Granovskii
S.T. Aksakov 'and his sons'
Nikita Giliarov-Platonov
Katkov? No – *I* need him
Rtsy
Shperk
Rozanov
Mordvinova (unpublished letters)
D´iakonova
L. Tolstoi (first ½)
Goncharov
Al. Tolstoi
Leskov
Turgenev
Pecherskii (*In the Woods*)
......................................
......................................
......................................
Maikov
Polonskii
Fet
Strakhov
K. Leont´ev
N.Ia. Danilevskii[102]

102 V.V. Rozanov, *Mimoletnoe* (Moscow: Respublika, 1994), pp. 294–5.

The complex nature of Rozanov's rejection of Russian writers is revealed by the fact that his 'exceptions' form a fairly comprehensive list of what some might consider the authors behind the Russian classics. However, Rozanov does continue to reiterate that he could never accept Kantemir, Fonvizin, Griboedov, Gogol′, the second half of Tolstoi or the reformist writers of the 1860s because of their rejection of Russia.[103] Rozanov wishes to reassert the religious authority and patriotic nature of Russian literature. Furthermore, he wishes to show that the means of producing writing must be restored to its intimate, pre-mechanical level. Only family-orientated people should write, and it is the very act of writing itself which underlines the importance of bringing forth new life. In advancing his own definition of aesthetics, Rozanov rejects the disinterested separation of artist and art noted in traditional Kantian theories of art, and hence places a specific emphasis on the creative act itself.

Before we turn to a closer investigation of how Rozanov realizes these principles in his own 'literary' works, it is worth now drawing on the broader social problems which help to contextualize his efforts and give an extra dimension to Rozanov's fear of endings. There is long-standing position in European thought that associates the concept of the *deus ex machina* with periods of spiritual crisis and social malaise. The use of external devices to provide an artificial conclusion to seemingly desperate situations, the breakdown of internal logic within literary plot to provide the consolation of denouement regardless of circumstance, has been seen as a symptom of people's desire to look for subjective conclusions to situations which deny the true processes of this world.[104] Nietzsche injected a slightly different direction to the concept in his discussion of tragedy, but adopts a similar position to Rozanov when he laments the giving way of the Dionysian spirit of mythology which formerly provided 'metaphysical consolation', to a Socratic type of rationalism which seeks to overcome nature. For Nietzsche, the *deus ex machina* reflects a dissatisfaction with the Earth, 'it believes in correcting the world

103 Ibid., p, 295.

104 Ratzinger writes that the *deus ex machina* of Greek tragedy gave 'dramatic form to a contestation or denial of the actual world'. Joseph Ratzinger, *Eschatology: Death and Eternal Life*, trans. by Michael Waldstein (Washington: Catholic University of America Press, 1988), p. 77. Weiner discusses the concept of *deus ex machina* in the context of the cultural turbulence of this time, through the prism of Belyi's engagement with Gogol′. See Adam Weiner, *By Authors Possessed: The Demonic Novel in Russia* (Illinois: Northwestern University Press, 1998), p. 145.

through knowledge, a life led by scientific knowledge'.[105] (Nietzsche, like Rozanov, looks to Oedipus at this liminal period in cultural history in investigating the transition from mythology to abstract knowledge.) It is only through writing as a creative act, the imitation of the Creation, in which these tensions can be overcome.

105 Friedrich Nietzsche, *The Birth of Tragedy*, trans. by Douglas Smith (Oxford: Oxford University Press, 2000), p. 96.

## Chapter 6

# The *Opavshelistika*

I argue that Russian philosophy is distinguished by its emphasis on praxis. Rozanov is an exponent of this tendency in his interpretation of how literature should help recreate the Kingdom of Heaven. Eschewing the artificial and external, Rozanov believes that literature should emerge naturally from the writer's own life and reaffirm the link between writing and family life. Such a position also helps ensure that writer and reader share the same (highly physical) experience. Therefore Rozanov also emphasizes the processes of literary creation. In underlining the manner in which his work was written, he intensifies the effect his books have on his audience and encourages the reader to be fruitful. This commandment is mirrored by Rozanov's insistence that the reader should write his own fallen leaves; imitation becomes a form of ontological likeness. The fact that the *Opavshelistika* is the fulfilment of the ideas discussed in Rozanov's earlier career suggests a similar relationship between activity and product as that in Rozanov's vision of Genesis, presenting his final works almost as a literary Eden.

Rozanov published *Uedinennoe* in 1912, a work which had a profound effect on the Russian philosophical and literary environment. In response, Berdiaev called Rozanov the 'foremost Russian stylist, a writer with real sparks of genius'.[1] Marina Tsvetaeva gushed with praise after reading *Uedinennoe*.[2] Gor´kii, Rozanov's frequent sparring partner, but someone who shared a deep mutual respect with the philosopher, admitted that on reading *Uedinennoe* he burst into tears with 'the deepest yearning and pain for the Russian person'.[3] *Uedinennoe*, like the other books and fragments in archives which we might informally label the *Opavshelistika*, is presented as a series of passages which discuss home life, his finances, religion and political affairs, as well as philosophy

1 Berdiaev, 'O "vechno bab´em" v russkoi dushe', p. 41.

2 Tsvetaeva wrote in a letter to Rozanov dated 7 March 1914 (O.S.) that so far she had only read *Uedinennoe*, but that she considered him a genius. Marina Tsvetaeva, *Sobranie sochinenii v semi tomakh*, 7 vols (Moscow: Ellis Lak, 1995), VI, p. 119.

3 Quoted in Aleksandr Nikoliukin, 'Miniatiury Vasiliia Rozanova', in Vasilii Rozanov, *Miniatiury*, ed. by A.N. Nikoliukin (Moscow: Progress-Pleiada, 2004), pp. 5–34 (p. 22).

and literature and the personal lives of prominent Russian figures. Some are aphoristic, others are longer narrative sections. Stylistically they differ from Rozanov's journalistic essayistic work, as the *Opavshelistika* is the fulfilment of Rozanov's demands that religiosity must be expressed as a concrete reality. The *Opavshelistika* must be seen in this broader context, but crucially emphasizes the processes of creation rather than the theoretical reasoning for this. Paradoxically, it is this stress on praxis rather than theory which threatens the whole viability of the Rozanov project.

After *Uedinennoe*, Rozanov went on to compose several more works of this genre, among them the two bundles of *Opavshie list'ia*, *Sakharna*, *Mimoletnoe* and *Apokalipsis nashego vremeni*. There are also many more sections written in this style which were not released in Rozanov's time, but which have subsequently appeared in Moscow. The bold style of these works, and Rozanov's fierce criticism of Christ and Christianity, drew inevitable comparisons with Nietzsche – although this appears to have been a stock insult among Russian religious thinkers. There is no evidence to suggest that Rozanov was directly influenced by the German.[4] In addition, the style of these works has also been compared to St Augustine and Rousseau (though as Nikoliukin indicates, Rozanov has no intention of using these books as a personal confession), as well as Pascal and Freud.[5] Rozanov received greater inspiration from the 'plotless' writings of Giliarov-Platonov and Rtsy, texts where the subject matter emerges from within rather than from fanciful plotlines. The term *Opavshie list'ia* itself is deliberately taken from Rtsy's *Listopad*. There can be also little doubt that Shperk's *Mysli i refleksy* played a significant role in Rozanov's thought; this 1895 collection of aphorisms discusses the philosophy of ethics, personality, history and sex.[6] More broadly in Russian philosophy, there were previous examples of its protagonists eschewing systematic theorizing in favour of more informal passages, for example Kireevskii's *Otryvki*.[7]

The groundbreaking style of the *Opavshelistika* evoked a new form of criticism of Rozanov's work. The first major in-depth study into the

4 Rozanov denied that he was influenced by Nietzsche. See *Opavshie list'ia II*, p. 449.

5 See Nikoliukin's commentary to *Mimoletnoe*, p. 473.

6 See Shperk, *Mysli i refleksy*, in *Literaturnaia kritika*, pp. 149–64.

7 I.V. Kireevskii, *Otryvki*, in *Polnoe sobranie sochinenii*, 2 vols (Ann Arbor: Ardis, 1983) (facsimile reprint, originally published Moscow: Tipografiia P. Bakhmeteva), I, pp. 326–43.

formal aspect of Rozanov's style was Shklovskii's seminal pamphlet, first printed in 1921 and later as a section in the 1925 book *O teorii prozy*. Shklovskii intentionally ignores any philosophical-religious intentions which might lie behind Rozanov's works and concentrates instead on their structure, seeing in *Uedinennoe* and *Opavshie list'ia* a new type of novel. Shklovskii, who contends that the driving force in literary development is the rebellion against existing literary forms, presents a vision of art as in part destructive; art relies on revolt, the breaking down of old forms. In Shklovskii's work, the 'soul' of the author, which Rozanov appears to identify as the immanent organizing principle of the integrated person, becomes the organizing principle of the novel, its 'structure' or the 'geometric relationship' between its various devices.[8] In his examination of how Rozanov's work affected his own writing (in a work heavily peppered with deliberate Rozanovian motifs), Shklovskii explains that in Formalism, so-called content is simply 'one of the manifestations of form'.[9] However, in this chapter I argue that a focus on the rebellion of form in Rozanov is not enough to explain the aesthetics of the *Opavshelistika*. I argue that there is a complex and fragile relationship between form and content in Rozanov, which is a result of his focus on the Creation and its counterpart in childbirth.

Rozanov's adoption of an intensely personal style of writing reveals the way in which the production and reception of literature converge. Rozanov hopes for the ability of writing to help bring about spiritual salvation for Russia. Nevertheless, there was certainly an attempt by Rozanov to secure some kind of immortality by ensuring that he would remain read after his death. He considered his work some kind of mausoleum, a monument to his own life (a view which reflects his appreciation of construction as means of mitigating against history, as discussed in Chapter 1).[10] The similarity between writing and bearing children shows that this new writing was part of Rozanov's 'immortality programme'.[11] Just as parents live on in their children, Rozanov hoped to overcome death through the products of his literary activity.

---

8 Viktor Shklovskii, *O teorii prozy* (Ann Arbor: Ardis, 1985), p. 228.

9 V. Shklovskii, *Sentimental'noe puteshestvie* (Moscow: Novosti, 1990), p. 235.

10 *Apokalipsis nashego vremeni*, p. 66.

11 This term is taken from Irene Masing-Delic, *Abolishing Death: A Salvation Myth of Russian Twentieth-Century Literature* (Stanford: Stanford University Press, 1992).

In examining the religious function of literature in Russia, scholars have looked at the tradition, following the Johaninne Gospel, of identifying the word with the Word of God and consequently any type of writing with sacredness.[12] This has permitted the sacralization of written texts which stand outside the domain of the official Church; Davidson suggests that Russian literary culture left scarce room for secular texts, and her seminal study of the ambiguity of the sacred and the demonic in Russian literature, especially in Rozanov's time, is extremely useful for our current purposes. Before we turn in greater depth to Rozanov's modification of the themes which Davidson investigates, and in particular his reliance on the Old Testament, it is worth touching briefly on Siniavskii, who places Rozanov in the tradition of Avvakum.[13] Rozanov displays genuine fondness for Avvakum and a regret that the Russian Church was split over the superficial issue, as Rozanov sees it, of Nikon's reforms. Both Rozanov and Avvakum share a focus on what they consider to be native religious values, and both use an innovative, informal style of writing to oppose the leadership of the Church and emphasize domestic life. Avvakum's *Zhitie* has a definite religious function, although it is not part of the official ecclesiastical canon. It subverts formal Church ceremonies by merging prayer with autobiography and trivia, sexual issues with theological and political commentary. It fuses complex religious themes with apparently insignificant and intimate aspects of domestic life, often bypassing formal ecclesiastical issues which Avvakum considered devoid of the true meaning of Russian religious experience. Avvakum understands that, where there is a danger that the Church might become distanced from its people, literature has the potential to help reconcile dogma and everyday life.[14]

---

12 Recent scholarship has investigated the importance of the word for Rozanov. Dimbleby pays attention to Rozanov's love for archaic hand-written texts (shared with Remizov) and his apprehension of printed works, apparently substantiating the argument that for Rozanov the process of writing is as important as its content. See Liza Dimbleby, 'Rozanov and His Literary Demons'. Crone has written on the importance of Rozanov's theories of the word for Mandel´shtam. See Anna Lisa Crone, 'Mandelstam's Rozanov', in *Stoletie Mandel´shtama: materialy simpoziuma*, ed. by Robin Aizlewood and Diana Myers (Tenafly: Hermitage, 1994), pp. 56–71.

13 Andrei Siniavskii, "*Opavshie list´ia*" *V.V. Rozanova* (Paris: Sintaxis, 1982), p. 198.

14 For an examination of how Avvakum transformed Russian literature and challenged Church dogma through his focus on 'the living instinct of life', see N.K. Gudzii, 'Protopop Avvakum kak pisatel´ i kul´turnoe iavlenie', in *Zhitie*

Avvakum uses his writing to express the fleshy aspects of religion, challenging a religious elite which considers discourse of earthly affairs heretical. He uses an innovative form of literature which is based on the realities of Russian life, in order to overcome the detachment of an alien church (both he and Rozanov challenge the authority of Greek theology over Russian experience). Avvakum offers frequent descriptions of the physical, for instance his startling admission of his own arousal during a young woman's confession (giving another example of the strained transference of sexual aesthetics) or his physical torment while imprisoned at Dauria. Both Avvakum and Rozanov refer to the Volga as the locus for a possible domestic utopia. So Avvakum suggests an organic alternative to ecclesiastical dogma. The subject of his investigations is not Avvakum himself, despite their intimacy and frankness. He takes the example of his and his family's life and exposes this for the sake of wider spiritual enlightenment. Avvakum stands at the head of a tradition which includes works such as Rtsy's *Listopad* and his *Chervotochina istorii*, Dostoevskii's *Dnevnik pisatelia* and the writings of Pobedonostsev, which break down the boundaries between the high-religious and the quotidian. Rozanov's own work was heavily influenced by such writers, and he saw in their writing a means to combine the aesthetic with a more realistic version of love. He particularly valued the manner in which these books express the sanctity of *byt*.

As we shall see, Rozanov also tapped into this strong sense of literature as a vehicle for rebellion. There were already examples of Russian writers who had rejected conventional notions of plot, from the very beginnings of modern Russian prose. By the early twentieth century, there was a growing feeling that literature in its current state had ran its course and was badly in need of renewal.[15] This literary revolution was in part fuelled by a search for new literary forms, as Shklovskii suggests. Rozanov played a major part in this rebellion, but his approach is unique. His is not so much a prioritization of form or content. In the *Opavshelistika* Rozanov sees the development of both as emerging simultaneously from his desire to reform Orthodoxy. For Rozanov, who sees the creation and reception of literature in predominantly religious terms, it is not surprising that literary and religious revolution should

*Protopopa Avvakuma, im samym napisannoe, i drugie ego sochineniia*, ed. by N.K. Gudzii (Moscow: Academia, 1934), pp. 7–59 (p. 27).

15 Slobin talks of the malaise surrounding the 'stagnation' of Russian literature and the efforts among Rozanov's contemporaries at 'revitalizing the worn out word'. Slobin, pp. 24–5.

come hand in hand, and in his *Opavshelistika* we note a unique fusion of style and content, aesthetics and ethics.

## The Bible as literary ideal

As Davidson has noted, there is some ambiguity between the sacred and the demonic in Russian literature. She explains that pre-Christian peoples often understood language as holy, as it was used by God to create the universe (Genesis 1:3). Language was also God's gift to man.[16] One aspect which makes Davidson's study important for our investigation of Rozanov is her explanation of the possibility of misusing this divine gift for purposes contrary to the divine will. Davidson notes the delicate balance between the visions of the artist who takes his message directly from God (like Moses and the prophets) and the artist who creates autonomously, losing sight of the ultimate Creator and in fact falling into idolatry. She remarks that the latter type of artist can confer sanctity on the world through his work, but only if he recalls in the process the original holiness of God's initial Creation. In this context she notes the pivotal image of the expulsion from Eden as 'loss of intimate contact with the divine source of creativity'.[17]

Such views appear to have informed Rozanov's attitude towards literary works.[18] Rozanov frequently highlights his dislike of literature and his intention to bring about its end. In this regard he was a major inspiration for the Futurists. Yet Rozanov must also contend with the eschatological nature of literature, as it emerges from the eschatology of the Bible.[19] The act of writing itself is vital to him. Although the content of his writings highlights the importance of the Creation, the manner in which they are constructed demonstrates the identity of the artist's

16 Davidson, 'Russian Views of Art as Demonic', pp. 129–31.

17 Ibid., p. 130. In comparison, the Roman Catholic Church provides for a more cooperative encounter between God and humans in the authorship of Biblical texts. See Denis Farkasfalvy, 'Inspiration and Interpretation', in *Vatican II: Renewal Within Tradition*, ed. by Matthew L. Lamb (Oxford: Oxford University Press, 2008), pp. 77–100.

18 Dimbleby's contribution is important in this context.

19 A study of how Biblical eschatology shapes European literature is made in Gerald Gillespie, 'Bible Lessons: The Gospel According to Frye, Girard, Kermode, and Voegelin', *Comparative Literature*, 38 (1986), 289–97 (pp. 291–2).

and God's creativity. The complex relationship between creativity and reception, author and reader, is based upon Rozanov's understanding of religion. Writing a book involves the same processes God used in creating the world. Books are not written, but are 'born into the world'.[20]

This appears to be the key thought in Rozanov's vision of how literature should be constructed. Rozanov underlines the importance of the sincere and the natural in literature, and the author should do his best to imitate the creative processes of God. Rozanov has a keen eye for the artificial, hence his apparent preference for writers who present not invented stories (he forbid his children from reading Sherlock Holmes, with all the problems associated with Russia's assimilation at that time of the Western detective story), but who retell stories from their own family life. He even underlines the unique fusion of the categories of literature and life in Russian culture, for which he is grateful to the 'family concerns of the Aksakovs' and to the 'home life of the Kireevskiis and the Tiutchevs'.[21] This is close to the division drawn by Davidson between the 'mediator' and the 'originator' in artistic composition, that is the (holy) art which is created by God and passed on through a prophet-figure, and the idolatrous creations of those who make in their own image.[22] This view is substantiated by Rozanov's interpretation of the difference in the composition of the Old and New Testaments. Rozanov believes that writers should imitate the manner in which the Old Testament was written, as this is the best example of the way in which the ideas of God are expressed in words. Rozanov argues that the Old Testament was dictated directly by God to Moses,[23] unlike the New Testament which was concocted by men who upheld the ascetic ideal.

Interestingly, this concern over false writing is apparent in Bunin, who like Rozanov suggests that bad literature is responsible for encouraging the revolutionary spirit among the Russians. However, despite their similarities, it is the distinct ahistorical nature of the *Opavshelistika* that distinguishes the two. Bunin's diaries are by their nature linked to specific dates, and historical events. In contrast, the passages in Rozanov's

20 *Poslednie list′ia*, p. 73. Rozanov also makes a comparison of sexual desire and the urge to write, which in turn corresponds to God's (sexual) desire to create. *Sakharna*, p. 12.

21 V.V. Rozanov, 'Kul′turnaia khronika russkogo obshchestva', in *Religiia, filosofiia, kul′tura*, p. 73.

22 Davidson, p. 128.

23 V.V. Rozanov, 'Mater′ialy k resheniiu voprosa', in *Semeinyi vopros v Rossii*, pp. 195–270 (p. 225).

'leaves' are not labelled with dates, but with the routine events of the Rozanov household (Florovskii dismisses Rozanov's work as simply a diary, neglecting the transition Rozanov attempts from the subjective to the universal.[24]) This is part of Rozanov's attempt to give his work a significance that extends beyond the merely historical. So we have moved here, in his later stages, a long way from the concerns of Rozanov's early career, which predominantly looked at theories of history and the historical contextualization of events, to an anti-Hegelian position which divorces occurrences from a unifying theory of time.

Correspondingly, Rozanov shuns endings and conclusions in works. There is a connection between Christian eschatology and literature, investigated in recent studies of plot. Redemption comes only at the conclusion of the novel, which corresponds to the Apocalypse of the Bible, and all moments in the literary work only have value in so far as they direct our consciousness to the denouement. Meaning is only conferred in the manner in which the conclusion organizes the whole, and the end of the book confers a sense of hopefulness that corresponds to Christian salvation. Fiddes argues that all texts are intrinsically eschatological, 'both in being open to the new meaning which is to come to them in the future, and also in being "seriously" open to the horizon which death gives to life'.[25] There is a sense that Rozanov's fear of endings, and his focus on beginnings, is reflected more broadly in his rejection of plot, especially in his *Opavshelistika*. However, within the apocalyptic tradition of Russian literature in which Rozanov operated, there was also a counter-tradition, where Russian writers such as Pushkin or Lermontov, or later Nabokov, deliberately rejected conventional notions of plot or storyline.[26] Rozanov rejects traditional ideas

---

24 Florovskii, pp. 461–2.

25 Fiddes, pp. 6, 49. Other scholars also argue that plot in literature is connected with the idea of a final redemption of the physical realm at the end of time, necessary as this world has been separated from God. See for example Lotman, *Universe of the Mind*, pp. 158–9.

26 There has been no academic work on the relationship of Rozanov and Nabokov, though this would be an important area of study. Like Rozanov, Nabokov considered the idea of a Russian utopia within human time. Nabokov deliberately subverted denouements in his work. Rozanov knew personally – and frequently criticized – Nabokov's father. Nabokov himself went to school with Rozanov's son. Although Nabokov was not Orthodox, his deep attachment for the Russian way of life and his artistic manipulation of *byt* to represent the lost paradise of childhood are close to Rozanov's project. For one, the Russian Revolution destroyed an idealized

of plot, but seeks to reorganize literature around the family hearth. His work is born from *byt* and depicts it, but also preserves the temporal and spatial organization through which family life is framed.

For Rozanov, the Bible is the prime example of how ideas should be expressed in writing, the ideal literary expression of religious life. Rozanov calls the Bible 'the Book of Books', 'the canon of literature'.[27] The Bible should be the model for all literature and is the marker by which Rozanov appraises other writers. It is this fusion of ideal life and literature which Rozanov strives for in his own work. The Old Testament is based, for Rozanov, principally on the Creation, family and the holy seed. Rozanov neglects the violence and suffering of the Old Testament, and refuses to acknowledge the Old Testament God as vengeful and punitive. The Bible is devoid of dirtiness and sinfulness, but is inextricably linked with nature.[28] There is nothing forced or artificial, everything emerges from the idea of the family. Rozanov argues that the only relations of importance in the Old Testament are those of kin.[29]

The importance of the Bible lies in how it conveys the meanings of humanity's original relationship with God, the point where the aesthetic and the ethical merge. For Rozanov, the organic is beautiful, even in the simplest biological acts.[30] However, Rozanov's aesthetic vision occurs not in terms of external attributes but in terms of activity; the beautiful for Rozanov is that which has potentiality to create and the ability to encourage some kind of mimesis in the audience (the influence of Aristotle). It is the pregnant woman, the human with the obvious potential to bring forth new life, in which Rozanov finds his aesthetic ideal.[31] This is where the noumen of the family is realized as the phenomenon of the family, demonstrating the 'family as Eden'.[32] This focus on praxis rather than being is the only way of unlocking the

---

childhood, for the other an idealized old age. Both shun conclusions in favour of earthly utopias grounded in cyclical time. In 'Krug', Nabokov expresses this by tying the beginning and ends of the short story together. Nabokov also plays with the relationship between sex as build-up and climax and literature in *Dar* (*The Gift*), where he ends the novel prematurely, leaving the expected denouement between Fedor and Zina outside the end of the book and ensuring that sex cannot be seen as a conclusion.

27 'Bibleiskaia poeziia', p. 449.

28 Ibid, p. 446.

29 'Zamechatel′naia stat′ia', p. 623.

30 Ibid., p. 622.

31 Ibid., p. 623,

32 Ibid., p. 624.

meaning of holiness as an aesthetic category; 'one must return to Eden in order to understand this'.[33]

The reader is brought to mind of Balthasar's Biblical aesthetics, his return to an Ignatian theology which is focused on the practical, not theoretical aspects of Christianity; for Balthasar, as for Rozanov, all aesthetics must have a Biblical foundation. But what Rozanov appears to be suggesting is a lost way of relating to the Creation which can only be restored by a return to an Edenic consciousness and way of behaving. Praxis is based on repetition and imitation, a sense which comes out in Rozanov's finding a new feeling for God with each reading of the Bible.

> Чтение Библии никогда не раздражает, не гневит, не досаждает. Оно омывает душу, и никакой занозы в ней не оставляет. Прочитавший страницу никогда не остается неудовлетворенным. Такие чувства, как «недоумение», никогда не сопутствуют чтению. Вообще, дух от чтения ее не сдавливается, не искажается, не стесняется. «Прочитал, и стало лучше.» [...].
>
> В точном смысле, научно, этого и нельзя отвергнуть: где Бог и где человек, где кончилось божеское и началось человеческое, или наоборот? Невозможность здесь разграничения Библии указывает в первых же строках, рассказывая о сотворении человека: «и вдунул Бог (в форму из земли) душу бессмертную, душу разумную».
>
> Reading the Bible never vexes, never angers, never torments. It cleanses the soul, and leaves behind no splinters. After reading a page we are never left dissatisfied. Such feelings as 'bewilderment' never accompany its reading. And the spirit after reading is never weighed down, never distorted, never restricted. 'I read it, and felt better' [...].
>
> In an exact sense, intellectually, it cannot be denied: where is God and where is the person, where does the divine end and the human start, or vice versa? The impossibility of delineating the Bible is shown even in its first lines, which narrate the Creation of man: 'And God breathed (into the form from the Earth) an immortal soul, the rational soul'.[34]

In his Biblical hermeneutics, unsurprisingly, Rozanov is motivated to get to what he understands as the truth-content of the text itself. It is the 'first lines' that matter most. In Rozanov, as we have seen, there is an aesthetic approach that goes far beyond what might be considered traditionally Biblical. Rozanov demands that reading evokes not a purely spiritual or mental response, but a physical reaction, the desire to have a family or even engage in sex. All writers should aspire to have this effect on their readers. There is of course a manipulation by Rozanov

33 Ibid., p. 623.

34 'Bibleiskaia poeziia', pp. 449–50.

of what we might cautiously term Biblical aesthetics. Scholars cite a certain ambiguity between the externally aesthetic and the ethical in the Old Testament description of God's opinion of His creation, when He looked upon and saw that it was good (Genesis 1:26; the translators of the Septuagint use the Greek word 'kalos' which implies an intellectually moral quality). However, for the Hebrews there was also a sense that a purely external appreciation of beauty led to vanity and was therefore sinful, which certainly comes out in Scripture over the fear of the demonic beauty of the Tree of Knowledge; instead they believed that appearances should be judged symbolically as a manifestation of internal moral qualities.[35]

Rozanov also draws on Johannine theories on the word made flesh. However, he rejects Christology as the explanation behind this and instead inserts an ideological foundation based on the Creation. Debates on the nature of the word became particularly intense among Rozanov's contemporaries, ranging from Sergii Bulgakov, to Mandel′shtam and Bakhtin. The dominant paradigm for these thinkers and writers (even non-religious thinkers adapted aspects of these ideas) was that the potency of the word was guaranteed by Johannine theories on incarnation. Discourse repeats the Incarnation of God as Christ.[36] Rozanov is typical of Russian religious thinkers in his affection for the Johannine Gospel, and the processes by which the word becomes flesh. But, as noted, he worries over the potential for division between the word and the flesh in Russian culture. This is made clear more broadly in Rozanov's interpretation of the relationship between the word and the Creation, and correspondingly in the relationship between the word and matter. For Rozanov, it is essential to insist that word and matter are not prior to one another, but come into being at the same moment. Any suggestion that matter existed before the word would leave the way open for suggestions that the physical world might be essentially unholy and in need of a later transfiguration through the eventual Incarnation of the Logos. Rozanov believes that words came into being with all things at the Creation, guaranteeing equivalence between word and thing.[37] In emphasizing the closeness of word and creation, Rozanov is very close

35 See Wladyslaw Tatarkiewicz, *History of Aesthetics*, trans. by Adam and Ann Czerniawski, 3 vols (The Hague/Paris: PWN, 1970, 2005), II, pp. 6–7.

36 Alexandar Mihailovic, *Corporeal Words: Mikhail Bakhtin's Theology of Discourse* (Evanston: Northwestern University Press, 1997), pp. 10, 25.

37 'Ob odnoi osobennoi zasluge Vl.S. Solov′eva', p. 438.

to the Acmeists and literary trends which focused on the original, Edenic nature of the word. He also shares some similarities with the Futurists and their emphasis on the value of the word in itself, without reference to an independent, higher reality.[38]

Scholars have argued that the structure of a text itself forms a utopia which rebels against the reality of everyday existence. Many writers, including Blake, have seen the Bible as the 'Great Code of Art', the ultimate text which 'expresses human desire for the Kingdom of God'.[39] This longing is only redeemed at the end of the Bible, the narrative of the final revelation of God. This vision of the manner of texts' role within a given religious or cultural framework also comes out in Lotman and Piatigorskii's examination of the function of texts. They make the point that, certainly in medieval Russia, writing was identified with sacredness. They also argue that all texts are by definition true, as a false piece of writing cannot be admitted as a text. This leads them to conclude that there are two types of culture as regards the function of texts, which emerge from opposing interpretations of history.

> 'Culture of the closed type' sees itself as continuing according to tradition, from the time [...] when there existed 'fullness of truth', i.e., a 'full text'; while 'history' is the gradual loss of this fullness which lies at the sources of the culture. 'Culture of the nonclosed type' sees itself as arising from zero, 'from nothing', and as gradually accumulating elements of 'truth' whose fullness is believed to lie in the future.[40]

They conclude that in the former scenario, texts are holy precisely because they are texts, whereas in the second case emphasis is placed on the texts' function within that culture. Rozanov's understanding of culture should be placed in the former category, opposed to the dominant tradition in contemporary Russian thought. Despite an initial attraction to Hegel (which is apparent in his first work and criticism therefore), Rozanov comes to reject the concept, highly influential among his peers, of knowledge as historical and contingent on an eschaton.

However, Rozanov must reconcile the Bible with his own worldview, especially its final book, the Revelation of St John (the linking of

38 For Rozanov's influence on Maiakovskii, see L.F. Katsis, *Vladimir Maiakovskii: Poet v intellektual'nom kontekste epokhi* (Moscow: Rossiiskii gosudarstvennyi gumanitarnyi universitet, 2004), pp. 47–60.

39 Fiddes, p. 16. There are interesting parallels between Rozanov and Blake which warrant consideration in future scholarship.

40 Yu.M. Lotman and A.M. Piatigorsky, 'Text and Function', trans. by Ann Shukman, *New Literary History*, 9 (1978), 233–44 (pp. 234–6).

'revelation' with the end of the world reveals Christianity's position that knowledge is historically-orientated). Rozanov only achieves this through a modified hermeneutics. Gippius informs us that the Revelation was the only New Testament Book which Rozanov would accept (with the occasional concession to St John's Gospel).[41] However, Rozanov understands the Revelation by reinterpreting its message not as an end, but as a rebirth, the book of Genesis providing the hermeneutical basis for this. In Rozanov's description of his own Bible (which reveals his focus not just on content, but also the physical presence of books, their covers, the quality of the paper), Rozanov explains that the Apocalypse is found buried at the very bottom all the 'Biblical-Evangelical text', which in turn is topped off by the key book of the Bible for Rozanov, Genesis.[42] But it is the beginning that frames the end.[43] Rozanov only accepts the Revelation as offering the possibility that we can return to Paradise. For Rozanov, the Apocalypse of the Bible is intimately linked with the Creation. The scenes portrayed in John's Revelation repeat the Biblical descriptions of the Garden of Eden. This does not describe the end of time, where his world is done away with and replaced by something supernatural, but rather demonstrates the restoration of the sanctity of Creation. This is somewhat an expression of an eternal return in Rozanov; beginnings and ends are tied together. Salvation takes place within historical time, not outside human experience.

The Book of Revelation does not herald the end of the world, but instead brings us back to its beginnings, the pre-historical period where the heavenly was equal to the earthly.[44] The depiction of the four creatures sat round the throne of Heaven (Revelation 4:6–8) mirrors the narration of the wild animals and the birds of the air in Eden (Genesis 2:19). There is also a definite likeness between these beasts and the mythical creatures Rozanov describes in his discussions of the Egyptians. The intimate proximity of the creatures to each other in a state of peace repeats the idyllic harmony of Eden. For this reason, the number of the beast in the Apocalypse should be read not 'six hundred and sixty-six', but 'six, six, six', as it refers specifically to the sixth day of Creation, where God creates man. Rozanov's ideal rests on the most intense form of love, which

41 Gippius, p. 174.
42 V.V. Rozanov, 'Zverinoe chislo', in *Vo dvore iazychnikov*, pp. 237–42 (p. 238).
43 Ibid.
44 Ibid., p. 241.

necessarily emerges from a biological closeness; hence his idealization of the mythical hybrid creatures of the Egyptians or Revelation and his insistence that humans should become familiar to each other. At the end of the Bible, humanity is redeemed through a rebirth that retains its connections to the Earth and the physical aspects of God.[45] This rejection of eschatology has implications for Rozanov's interpretation of literature and also informs the way he himself writes and works.

## Towards a theology of labour[46]

Rozanov worked in a time where European philosophy was turning to the importance of activity rather than pure thought. One of the most important sources for this was the contribution of Marx, who challenged the crisis of subjectivity in his time by arguing that genuine knowledge could only come about through the coupling of reason with activity. Marxist thought has had a far-reaching impact on Christian theology, especially in twentieth-century liberation theology which challenged the formal authority of the Roman Catholic Church. Scholars argue that the Marxist focus on praxis helped Christian theology develop in such a way that it 'becomes a way of articulating one's faith that comes out of a Christian commitment to a particular way of acting and sets the agenda for an even more thoughtful and committed plan of action in the future'; Bevans writes that such theologians talk less of 'ortho-doxy', and more of 'ortho-praxis'.[47]

The activity turn occupied many philosophers in the early twentieth century, and Rozanov anticipates many of the problems in subjective thinking tackled by thinkers such as Heidegger, Husserl and Merleau-Ponty. Marx insisted that the human can only overcome their alienation though a proper relationship with nature, a relationship that emerges through the correct application of labour. Such ideas play an important role in Rozanov. (There is also a pre-empting in Rozanov of Arendt's examination of action and natality as providing an opportunity for new ways of being and doing.) Rozanov insists that the natural world

45 Ibid., p. 239.

46 Material for this section is taken from Adam Ure, 'Rozanov and the Coin', *Slavonica*, 16 (April 2010), 15–28. Used with kind permission from the *Slavonica* editors.

47 Bevans, p. 72.

needs humans to work upon it to maintain its sanctity. For this reason, Rozanov often cites agriculture as the highest form of work: farming reunites God and the Earth. However, Rozanov saw writing itself as a sanctified form of work, a religious act that parallels childbirth, and this theme is a major driving factor in the *Opavshelistika*. In providing a positive assessment of labour, Rozanov attacks what he perceives to be two critical and related issues in Russian society: Russian idleness and the Orthodox idealization of poverty.

Questions of the relation of the economy to Russian thought and literature played an important role in pre- and post-revolutionary debates. Many religious thinkers turned to interpretations of the economy as the environment where human activity mediates between God and Earth. These themes play an important role in the work of Sergei Sharapov and in those influenced by Rozanov. Berdiaev writes that property is intrinsically linked with the person's metaphysical aspect, as it regulates his relationship with nature and enables him to act religiously on earth.[48] Sergii Bulgakov defines economy as man's 'humanization of nature', the transfiguration of the world through creative activity.[49]

Rozanov attaches a religious significance to work and places extra religious demands on literature by extending the definition of labour to writing. In Rozanov, the categories of the religious and the literary converge principally through the mediation of writing as a creative act. This has its basis in the Old Testament and its narration of the Creation. As noted, Rozanov sees the working week as holy, modelled on the six days of God's creative activity and the one day of rest. The Bible tells us that we are obliged to imitate this. In addition, parents who work have the means to support their families.[50] Rozanov is highly critical of what he perceives to be an innate Russian laziness.

48 N.A. Berdiaev, 'Filosofiia neravenstva: pis´ma k nedrugam po sotsial´noi filosofii. Pis´mo dvenadtsatoe', in *Russkaia filosofiia sobstvennosti*, ed. by K. Isupov and I. Savkin (St Petersburg: SP Ganza, 1993), pp. 290–305 (pp. 303–4).

49 Bulgakov draws attention to the cognates 'khoziaistvo' and 'khoziainin', where we are called upon to master the world and make it divine. S.N. Bulgakov, 'Filosofiia khoziaistva', in *Sochinenie v dvukh tomakh*, 2 vols (Moscow: Nauka, 1993), I, pp. 49–297 (pp. 84–5). This point is also made by Valliere, who argues that Bulgakov sees economics, like art, as a form of human creativity. Valliere, *Modern Russian Theology*, pp. 256–7.

50 'Voprosy russkogo truda', p. 100.

> Болен ли труд русский? Об этом нечего и спрашивать. Девять десятых русского упадка объясняются именно этою болезнью – исключительно. Невозможно представить себе того поистине «преображения», поистине «воскресения», какое наступило бы в каждом маленьком кусочке русской действительности и, наконец, в картине всей страны, если бы вдруг в русском человеке пробудилась жадность к работе, жажда работы, скука без работы, тоска по работе.
>
> Is Russian labour sick? There is no question of this. Nine tenths of the Russian decline can be explained precisely by this illness – exclusively. It is impossible to imagine the genuine 'transfiguration', the genuine 'resurrection' which would take place in every small piece of real life in Russia, and eventually across the whole country, if the Russian suddenly found a thirst for work, a desire to work, boredom from not working, a longing for work.[51]

The human has divine energies embedded in him, and the correct use of these would lead to Russia's material and spiritual revival.[52] However, the Russian Orthodox Church has done nothing to help the people and failed to propagate the ideal of industriousness. Labour is alien to Orthodoxy, unlike Protestantism (Rozanov also insists that Catholicism is imbued with laziness). In attributing different evaluations of the value of labour of the different denominations, Rozanov anticipates the work of Max Weber (whom, to our knowledge, Rozanov had not read), especially his theories in *The Protestant Ethic and the Spirit of Capitalism*.

Consequently, Rozanov looks to labour, and its financial reward, as one of the greatest forms of prayer. Industriousness in itself is holy. Rozanov writes that 'for a healthy person, work is the norm and the ideal, "a prayer" and "a commandment"'.[53] He believes that time follows holy patterns, as it emerges from the six days of God's creative activity and His day of rest. All days belong to God, the 'Great Gardener', and earthly life follows the cyclical patterns of nature to which man should also adhere, particularly the working week.[54] Rituals emerge naturally from these patterns. Likewise, the work of the Church should revolve around the movement of nature. In this way, Rozanov provides his answer to the most accursed of all questions in Russian philosophy, posed by thinkers as diverse as Chernyshevskii, Turgenev, Lenin and

51 Ibid., p. 101.
52 Ibid., p. 107.
53 Ibid. For Rozanov on Weber, see Aleksandr Medvedev, 'Kind and Quiet: Vasilii Rozanov's Reading of Chekhov', in *Anton Chekhov Through the Eyes of Russian Thinkers*, ed. Olga Tabachnikova (Anthem: London, 2010), pp. 13–35, p. 15.
54 'O rasstroistve trudovogo goda', p. 125.

Nazhivin: '"What is to be done?": if it is summer, clean your berries and make jam; and if it is winter, take this jam and drink tea with it.'[55]

His leaning towards a theology of labour leads Rozanov to encounter another issue in Russian culture, the ideal of poverty. He believes that money and the accumulation of wealth assume a religious quality when used to support the family. Rozanov frequently attacks the Orthodox Church for glorifying suffering and imposing the ideal of poverty on the people. Rozanov, with his love for ancient civilizations, appears to return to the original meaning of the word 'economy'; he sees economics principally in terms of how religious relationships are structured around the home.[56] In Christian terminology, economy refers to the work of the Persons of God upon Earth, which seems to go hand in hand with Rozanov's fixation with religious activity in a physical setting.

Rozanov's main critique of the Russian Church is that it has no proper theology of the family; however, he also says that the Russians have 'no philosophy of money'.[57] There are plenty of examples in Scripture which underline the sinfulness of wealth (see for instance Matthew 20:1–17). Instead, Rozanov points as an example back to the hard work of Old Testament figures, such as Job, which was rewarded by God with wealth.

55 V.V. Rozanov, 'Embriony', in *Religiia, filosofiia, kul'tura*, pp. 225–32 (p. 225). All activity for Rozanov should be configured around nature. Rozanov frequently noted that the Old Testament command to observe the Sabbath is immediately followed by the order to honour our parents. The best way of fulfilling this obligation is to repeat the activity by which they brought you into the world and bear them a child.

56 The word 'economy' derives from the Greek 'oikonomia', referring to the management of a household. Economy does not refer exclusively to the financial transactions of the home, but has wider consequences in the way in which religious activity is structured and passed on from generation to generation. John Jones, *On Aristotle and Greek Tragedy* (Stanford: Stanford University Press, 1962), pp. 83–4. Quoted in Clare Cavanagh, *Osip Mandelstam and the Modernist Creation of Tradition* (Princeton: Princeton University Press, 1995), p. 335.

57 *Sakharna*, p. 95. Rozanov, especially in his works concerned with his stay at Sakharna in Bessarabia, opposes the Russians' flawed attitude towards the family and money, with harsh criticism of the Jews' apparent supremacy in both these fields. Again, Rozanov ties these two themes to that of the production of literature, by frequent complaints that Jews control the major publishing houses in Russia and therefore the nation's literary output. Ibid., p. 91. In the traditions of Christian thought, there has long been a link between criticism of the Jews' apparent love for money and stereotypes over their sexual practices. See Pease, p. 86.

He even notes that in Russian, the words 'Bog' and 'bogatstvo' share an etymological root.[58]

For Rozanov, creative activity is closely linked to the themes of labour and possessions. A large factor in the Church's rejection of society was its idealization of poverty and its condemnation of wealth.[59] Instead, Rozanov argues that the Church has made poverty an ideal and considers financial success a sin.[60] Therefore he contends that Russians shun honest work. There is a parallel here in Rozanov's arguments between laziness and celibacy. Russians should seek work with the same fervour that a groom seeks his bride. Labour and childbirth work in similar ways, affirming the meaningfulness of matter and man's activity upon it. Family life and work life go hand in hand for Rozanov.

Lauding the Protestant work ethic, Rozanov criticizes the Orthodox Church for idealizing laziness. Just as he frequently complains that the Church does not have prayers for women in childbirth, he also criticizes the Russian clergy for not propagating labour as a virtue, or for failing to write religious tracts extolling the religious benefits of hard work; he claims that the concept of labour has been 'cast out from the registry of religious-Orthodox contemplation'.[61] Despite the fact that Rozanov appears to suggest that laziness is an innate national trait among the Russians, he attributes the underlying cause to the Russian Church.[62]

Rozanov concludes that, because of the Church, Russian labour is 'sick' and in need of healing. As the Church is wholly inadequate to the task, Rozanov presents his work as an alternative religious message. However, it is not just the content of Rozanov's work which is designed to have a religious effect on his countrymen; the very manner in which Rozanov writes also has a religious quality. This is an intended attack

---

58 'Voprosy russkogo truda', p. 100.

59 Many scholars have examined the ideal of poverty in Russian culture. The idealization of destitution is seen in many religious writers. For example, Ioann Kronshtadtskii writes: 'Wealth makes one proud, and hardens the heart of the man who uses it without consideration or gratitude. He loathes others, who share the same nature as himself, who are the same as him; he does not recognize them as his brothers, but sees them as worse than the animals, for he strokes and feeds the animals, but scorns the poor and does not even give them his crumbs'. Quoted in Mitropolit Veniamin, *Otets Ioann Kronshtadtskii* (St Petersburg/Kronshtadt: Voskresenie, 2000), p. 644.

60 'Voprosy russkogo truda', p. 100.

61 Ibid., p. 105.

62 Ibid.

on a tendency for Russian writers, such as Nekrasov and Dostoevskii, to idealize the concept of virtuous indolence, teaching that there is an invisible kingdom like Kitezh, filled with 'philosophizing drunks, pure-hearted prostitutes and landowners without estates'.[63] Rozanov writes that Russian literature has played an important role in damaging society. Rozanov points out the dangers in reading Dostoevskii's apology for Orthodoxy, as expressed in the humility of characters such as Sonia Marmeladova. Russian literature fails in its obligation to underline the importance of labour.

> Нет, вы мне покажите в литературе: 1) трезвого, 2) трудолюбца, 3) здорового и нормального человека, который был бы опоэтизирован, и я зачеркну свои строки. Но от Обломова до нигилистов тургеневской «Нови» – все это инвалидный дом калек, убогих, нищих… «Блаженны нищие… Им Царство небесное». Русская литература широко разработала это «царство», сведя его с неба на землю, перенеся его из Галилеи в Великороссию.
>
> No, show me in literature: 1) a sober, 2) hardworking, 3) healthy or normal person who has become poetized, and I shall cross out these lines. But from Oblomov to the nihilists in Turgenev's *Nov´* [*Virgin Soil*] – it is all a house of invalids, wretched, the poor… 'Blessed are the poor… for theirs is the Kingdom of Heaven'. Russian literature has prepared the way for this 'Kingdom', bringing it down from Heaven to Earth, spreading it from Galilee to Russia.[64]

Despite frequent insistences that he is lazy, that he came to Earth to observe and not to participate, and despite his expressed desire to return to the womb, Rozanov did work very hard. His output during his career as a professional writer was impressive. Over a sustained period Rozanov wrote three articles a week for *Novoe Vremia* alone, not counting his contributions to other periodicals. It must be said that Rozanov saw the truth as multifaceted and open-ended; the world must be examined from a multitude of different perspectives in order to understand being. This explains many of the *Opavshelistika* aphorisms which deliberately present different, but each time new, appraisals of phenomena. Rozanov was driven by a religious need to examine the world each time from various perspectives to provide as complete a version of the truth as possible.[65] This is an important aspect of Rozanov's intention that each encounter with the world should be approached each time as if this were the first, with the care that Adam showed for the newly created world.

63 Ibid., p. 104.
64 Ibid.
65 *Opavshie list´ia II*, p. 469.

But our love for the world is also multifaceted and demands that we consider each phenomenon carefully, from every possible perspective. This fusion of the philosophical and artistic vision anticipates many of the demands of Cubism.[66]

However, there is a further reason for Rozanov's desire to publish as much as he could with sometimes scant regard to what he wrote: one must accept his desire to earn as much as possible, however the content of his work is designed to convey a religious and didactic message, as the very process of writing is a religious obligation in itself. In writing, Rozanov opens up a relationship between the content of his writing and the manner in which it is produced. For Rozanov, the religious function of literature is not only revealed in its subject matter. Perhaps the most potent way this is demonstrated appears at the beginning of *Uedinennoe*, where he writes: 'Ten people sit around my table, including the servant. All are fed by my work. Through my work all these people *found their place in the world*'.[67]

This passage encapsulates the variety of purposes behind his work. His texts provide religious instruction and assist the reader in structuring his own religious activity. On a more personal level, Rozanov writes, and receives payment for his articles (at *Novoe Vremia* he was paid per line), which he then uses to support his household, fulfilling the most intimate of religious obligations and providing the framework in which he and his family can operate religiously within the world. The content of his literature is designed to influence Russian society. The depiction of happy, loving families encourages the reader to enter into family life. Rozanov's books operate as an organizing principle for the religious behaviour of his own family and as spiritual education for families all over Russia. His works help the reader to find his place on Earth, by teaching him to enter into a harmonious relationship with matter. In addition, by interpreting writing as a form of labour, Rozanov fulfils his religious duties as head of his household, earning money for his works and providing for his family.

So there is a metaphysical aspect in his attitude towards money. The acquisition of money to support one's wife and children is not greed, but a religious obligation. The construction of literature, providing that its content is religious, is in itself holy, but the reward for such labour

---

66 Rozanov also labels 'Cubists' philosophers who are able to examine their subjects from multiple angles, such as Aristotle, Plato. 'Perstye temy', p. 159.

67 *Uedinennoe*, p. 164.

is also sacrosanct. Critics accused Rozanov of a mercenary attitude towards literature, for the fact that he expressed a myriad of opposing ideas in rival journals, often simultaneously. Many of his *Novoe Vremia* colleagues criticized Rozanov for writing so many articles purely for the money. This was especially the case with his rival Men´shikov, who greatly envied Rozanov's higher salary (even though this appeared to be balanced out somewhat by the fact that Rozanov, who did not have his own working space at *Novoe Vremia*, was jealous of Men´shikov's office). Even Suvorin warned Rozanov about selling his soul, but reluctantly refused to forbid Rozanov from writing for rival periodicals.[68] Perhaps one of the most notorious critiques of Rozanov's apparent lack of principles was levelled by Trotskii, who cites several instances of Rozanov's shameless vacillating opinion and venality (criticizing especially Rozanov's approach to the Russian Jews and the Beilis Affair):

> Даже и парадоксальнейшие преувеличения Фрейда куда более значительны и плодотворны, чем размашистые догадки Розанова, который сплошь сбивается на умышленное юродство и прямую болтовню, твердит зады и врет за двух [...] Червеобразный человек и писатель: избивающийся, скользкий, липкий, укорачивается и растягивается по мере нужды – и как червь, противен.
>
> Even the most paradoxical exaggerations of Freud are more significant and fruitful than the broad suppositions of Rozanov, who constantly flounders in intentional foolishness and straightforward babbling, who harps on about the same things and lies for two [...] A wormlike person and writer: wriggly, slippery, sticky, contracting and stretching according to need – and like a worm, repellent.[69]

Trotskii goes on to criticize the manner in which Rozanov 'sold himself for a coin', subverting Rozanov's own views on prostitution. However, much of the explanation for Rozanov's apparent disloyalty to Suvorin lay in the fact that Rozanov was motivated to earn as much money as possible for his family.

Hence Rozanov's positive assessment of money is revealed in his interest in numismatics, which sheds more light on his love of ancient civilizations and also by extension on the way in which writing for Rozanov helps restore a connection to the ancient world. In the content and the production of his work, Rozanov establishes a close link between

68 These problems are discussed in a 1903 letter from Suvorin to Rozanov, reprinted in *Priznaki vremeni*, pp. 308–9.

69 Trotskii, pp. 34–5.

literature and ancient coins. Numismatics was one of Rozanov's great loves, and out of the many subjects discussed in his works, was one of the areas where he possessed profound scholarly knowledge. It is no coincidence that Rozanov's interest in ancient coins developed alongside his fascination with ancient Egypt. As a student, Rozanov was unable fully to pursue his interest in either of these topics, and it was only once he had moved permanently to St Petersburg that he had the resources and finances to pursue these interests. Once established as a publicist, Rozanov devoted much of his earnings to building up a significant coin collection. This contained predominantly coins from the ancient Middle East, and by 1911 comprised around 4500 coins from the ancient Greek world, and around 1300 from the Roman Empire. In Rozanov's collection they were ordered according to their image.[70] Rozanov corresponded with the most prominent collectors in Russia, including A.V. Oreshnikov, Kh.Kh. Gil′, A.K. Markov, O.F. Retovskii and I.I. Tolstoi. He also knew and admired Ivan Tsvetaev (as well as establishing a close relationship with his daughters) and encouraged the head of the Museum of Fine Arts to make annual purchases of coins to exhibit there.[71]

Although space does not permit a detailed study of the history of numismatics, it is worth pointing out that coins have historically been used more than simply as a means of exchange and have enjoyed wider cultural and religious significance. In ancient communities, and in ancient Russian settlements, coins were often used in religious rituals; they were sometimes placed in sacred locations as a gift to the gods, such as under the foundations of a new house or in a dead person's mouth. Later, coins were specifically offered in churches, regardless of their value; it appears that the ritual act of donating a coin took precedence over its worth. Coins were also placed as gifts alongside icons, in churches and around soldiers' necks.[72] From a slightly different perspective, in religious thought there has long been a tradition of assigning to material objects a variety of different values, ranging from the demonic to the heavenly. For example, the desert hermit Evagrius in the *Philokalia*

---

70 A.N. Benua, 'Religiozno-filosofskoe obshchestvo. Kruzhok Merezhkovskikh. Vasilii Rozanov', in *Vasilii Rozanov: Pro et Contra*, I, pp. 132–42 (p. 141).

71 See <http://www.museum.ru/gmii/exh.asp?last=26apr-1june2006>, last accessed 4 January 2011.

72 For a history of Russian numismatics and of the use of coins in ancient religious practices, see *Medals and Coins of the Age of Peter the Great*, ed. by I. Spassky and E. Shchukina (Leningrad: Aurora Art Publishers, 1974), pp. 9–15.

wrote that a mere lump of gold could be understood in several different ways.

> [The thoughts] of the angels seek to discover the nature of things and their spiritual meaning: for instance, for what purpose gold is created [...] The thought of the demons does not know or understand this, but shamelessly suggests only the acquisition of physical gold, predicting the pleasure and glory to be had from it. And human thought neither seeks to possess it nor is curious about what gold symbolises; it merely introduces into the human mind a bare image of gold.[73]

We are also reminded of the work of mystical thinkers such as Paracelsus and Boehme, who sought multiple layers of meaning in base metals. It is this tradition of religious thought, the possibility of perceiving in physical objects a higher significance which gives meaning to the material world, which Rozanov develops. However, whereas his more mystical predecessors look to how the material points to higher spiritual values, Rozanov looks to how these eternal values give meaning to the immanent. His interest in numismatics was not limited to a scientific examination. In his collection, Rozanov was certainly keen to know the historical facts behind his coins, such as their dates, and under whose rule they were made. Alongside this, Rozanov maintained a tactile relationship with his collection. He enjoyed fondling them and carried around in his pocket his three favourite gold coins. Through the coins, it has been suggested that Rozanov constructed a direct and personal connection to ancient peoples.

> И кто из нумизматов когда-либо ставил перед собой и решал вопрос – «Как и почему пришло на ум собирать древние монеты»? А вот Розанову пришло на ум задать себе этот вопрос – по той простой причине, что в древних монетах он ВИДЕЛ историю народа, – видел во всем объеме внутреннее содержание этой истории со всей ее мистикой. И монета в руках Розанова превращалась в ключ, открывавший ему «вход» – через века и тысячелетия в мир ЖИВЫХ теней, с которыми он любил и умел беседовать, вглядываться в них и рассказывать о них.
>
> Who among the numismaticians ever asked themselves – 'How and why did people decide to collect ancient coins?' And so Rozanov decided to ask the same question – for the simple reason that he SAW a people's history in their

73 Quoted in *Early Fathers from the Philokalia, together with some writings of St. Abba Dorotheus, St. Isaac of Syria and St. Gregory Palamas*, trans. and ed. by E. Kadloubovsky and G.E.H. Palmer (London: Faber, 1954), p. 119.

> ancient coins, he saw the inner content of their history in its full scope and its full mystery. And in Rozanov's hands a coin became the key which unlocked the 'entrance' through the centuries and millennia into the world of LIVING shadows, which he loved and could converse with, which he loved to look into and tell us about.[74]

This description encourages comparisons with the manner in which the Orthodox approach their icons. It is possible to argue that the way Rozanov seeks communion with ancient peoples through the coin has parallels with the way Orthodox worshippers seek through icons participation in the life of the saints. Rozanov insists on the ability of coins to link us to the ancient world. He describes the coin as '"a metallic mirror which opened up the ancient world"; *now* it reflects, before the eye of the numismatician, how this world lived, was stirred, but never died!'[75] His fascination with immortality stretches to the collectors of coins, and he writes that numismaticians' work and heritage keeps them immortal.[76]

Rozanov was not just interested in numismatics as a science. Through a tangible engagement with his collection he felt communion with ancient civilizations. Coins for Rozanov held a mystical quality. He writes: 'My collecting ancient coins has, it is not strange to say, a definite historical principle and an almost mythical birth'.[77] He also underlines the privileged relationship of numismatics to the ancient world: 'Nobody has such a tactile relationship with ancient world as numismaticians'.[78] This is supported by those who knew Rozanov. Benua noted: 'He collected ancient coins and found boundless joy in examining them, finding in their profiles of all the monarchs and emperors and the symbolic figures which decorated the reverse, new and newer evidence for the ideas and aspirations which held sway at that time'.[79]

This study of ancient coins forms an essential component of Rozanov's daily routine, enabling him to re-vitalize the present moment by introducing into it the validity of ancient beliefs. This repeated contact with his coin collection was a major inspiration for his new books. Whilst

---

74 Spasovskii, p. 90. The words in upper case letters are the author's own.

75 V.V. Rozanov, 'Ob antichnykh monetakh', in *V chadu voiny: Stat'i i ocherki 1916–1918 gg.* (Moscow: Respublika, 2008), pp. 450–61 (p. 457).

76 V.V. Rozanov, 'Eshche uchenaia utrata', in *Okolo narodnoi dushi*, pp. 382–4 (p. 382).

77 'Ob antichnykh monetakh', p. 451.

78 Ibid., p. 457.

79 A.N. Benua, 'Religiozno-filosofskoe obshchestvo. Kruzhok Merezhkovskikh. Vasilii Rozanov', p. 141.

examining and fondling his coins, he was inspired to label many of the passages in the *Opavshelistika* 'za numizmatikoi'. Rozanov appropriates for the coin and the word similar functions. He uses ancient coins as inspiration for his philosophical writings, which are then exchanged for contemporary money. At *Novoe Vremia* Rozanov is paid by the line and so he establishes a direct link between the word and the coin. He uses his earnings to fulfil his familial obligations, and also to purchase more ancient coins. Thus the cycle is repeated.

Rozanov adapts the relationship of money and aesthetics in his ruminations of Alekseev's painting *Christ and the Wealthy Man*, which Rozanov saw in the Academy of Arts presumably in 1904. Rozanov confesses not to like the painting, though he appreciates the portrayal of the people that surround Christ, who are shown in a contemporary realistic style, far from the techniques used in icon painting. However, there is a lifelessness about the stylization of the characters, who come out not as 'people', but as 'figures'.[80] There is no connection between the characters and no words to join them together. Here Rozanov gives more complexity to the differences between coins and icons. He uses as an example Grand Prince Vladimir of Kiev, who on coins is depicted as an individual, with lifelike detail, but who on icons is portrayed in a general style. Rozanov complains that the sanctification of historical figures, their iconographication, leads to 'abstraction' and 'schematization'.[81] Here Rozanov, though relying heavily on iconographic techniques, opposes coins to icons – the shift from one to the other reveals in Orthodoxy 'a hatred for *realism*, for the concrete'.[82] Rozanov complains that Alekseev has privileged the poverty idealized by Christ over the justification of wealth shown in Job. Rozanov cites the description of Eden as a land of gold (Genesis 2:12), revealing the tensions between the Old Testament emphasis on family and its sacred ties with money. Rozanov contrasts this with Christ's admonishment of the wealthy young man and His rejection of family ties.[83] Favouring the specific and the concrete, Rozanov also points to the practical implications of giving away all one's wealth, which would in the long term not solve any issues among Russia's deprived population (here he gives the example of the

80 V.V. Rozanov, 'Khristos i "bogatyi iunosha"', in *V temnykh religioznykh luchakh*, pp. 139–42 (p. 141).

81 Ibid., p. 140.

82 Ibid.

83 Ibid., p. 142.

typhus epidemics ravaging the country, which would not be prevented if everyone gave away everything).[84] So the coin can be seen a vital tool for regulating human activity, ensuring that our religious behaviour is firmly grounded.

Rozanov's love for the coin demonstrates his desire for personal contact with pre-Christian cultures, and his interest in their social organizations. It is possible to contextualize Rozanov's view within a more general concern in Europe that an increasing abstraction in financial relations was leading to instability in social relations. In European culture, the coin was considered the guarantor of social relations, and its replacement by banknotes brought about 'vanishing frames of reference and floating signifiers'.[85] Likewise, Shell, following Aristotle, demonstrates that a coin has two values: the 'natural (as stamped art) and unnatural (as monetary tokens)'.[86]

Although Rozanov does not engage directly with the themes discussed by Shell, standing behind his work is a consistent concern over the detachment of the word from physical reality. Searching to find the means to reconcile word and flesh, he sees in old coins a way to achieve this. For Rozanov, the connection between language and the coin is not merely understood linguistically or politically, but also religiously. The coin manages the relationship between thing and its representation, and this underpins Rozanov's understanding of the function of literature. Literature can demonstrate the equality of the ideal with the real, and the permanent relevance of pre-Christian lifestyles. Rozanov's love for the Edenic word, as it first appeared to man, with its original meanings, is paralleled in his fascination for ancient coins.[87] Rozanov probes at the

84 Ibid.

85 Jean-Joseph Goux, *The Coiners of Language*, trans. by Jennifer Curtiss Gage (Norman/London: University of Oklahoma Press, 1994), p. 3.

86 Marc Shell, *The Economy of Literature* (Baltimore/London: The John Hopkins University Press,, 1978), p. 82.

87 In the pre-modern societies to which Rozanov often refers, the coin was melted from a metal whose value was equal to its face value and therefore guaranteed the permanent equality of thing and its symbol. In European thought, the word and the coin, both deriving from the Greek sēmē, have long held corresponding functions in systems of intellectual and economic discourse. The coin has traditionally been used to demonstrate the relationship between ideas and the material world. In similar fashion, in Byzantium, the Eucharist was stamped with Christ's name on it, proving the reality of Christ's incarnation. See Marc Shell, *Money, Language and Thought: Literature and Philosophic Economies from the Medieval*

way in which language has become abstract in Russian religious writing in his criticism of Nikon's pedantic and unnecessary reforms. Rozanov contends that there is no real currency standing behind Nikon's purely verbal changes to Russian religious discourse.

> Вся эта область – вербальная (verbum = слово), словесная, а – не *эссенцальная*, не существенная, до вещи, до «religio» относящаяся. Только в пространстве пустом, где вовсе не было «вещи» религии, rei religionis, или, что то же, при явно покинувшем нас Боге, мог возникнуть наш спор о словах. Ну, вещей нет, тогда будем заниматься словами, нет золота, довольствуемся «кредитными знаками». Но страшно, что «кредитные-то знаки» (в поле нашего религиозного сознания) не обеспечивались никаким позади лежащим фондом золота.
>
> All this field is verbal (verbum = the word), oral, and not *essential*, not substantive, does not relate to the thing, to the 'religio'. Our controversy about words could only arise in an empty space, where there were no 'things' of religion, rei religionis, or even where God had abandoned us. Well, there are no things, so let us engage with words, there is no gold, let us be satisfied with 'credit notes'. But it is terrifying that 'credit notes' (in the field of our religious consciousness) were not guaranteed by an underlying fund of gold.[88]

Rozanov's arguments over the meaninglessness of merely verbal reforms in Russian religious texts are reminiscent of his criticism of the pedantry of arguments over misspellings in publications of Pushkin.

Rozanov is part of a wider movement which viewed with suspicion developments in Russian literature where attention was diverted from the reality of this world, especially in its original form, to a supposed higher plane. Rozanov is not alone in seeing the battle over language in terms of the struggle over this Earth. Such arguments were at the centre of debates over Russian Symbolism. Rozanov was never a fully-fledged member of the Symbolist movement, although he was close personally to many members of the first wave of Russian Symbolists (though generally disliked by the second wave). He was never a member of the Acmeist group, but his views can be contextualized partially within their

---

*through to the Modern Era* (Berkeley/London: University of California Press, 1982), p. 2. Such relationships feed into linguistic theory: Goux argues that there is a 'structural homology' between money and language and that the crisis of realist literature which swept through Europe towards the end of the nineteenth century was caused by a crisis in banking and the replacement of coins by notes that held their value in name only. Goux, *The Coiners of Language*, p. 3.

88 'Ob odnoi osobennoi zasluge Vl.S. Solov´eva', p. 438.

movement to renew literature by examining the world through fresh eyes. A major treatise for the Acmeists was Gorodetskii's 1913 manifesto 'Neskol′ko techenii v sovremennoi russkoi kul′ture', where he attacked Symbolist abstraction. Gorodetskii portrayed Acmeism as 'a battle for this world', where 'a rose became better in itself' through its physical beauty, without reference to the mystical.[89] Gorodetskii sees the poet's task as that of a new Adam, who bestows on all things their own name again. In this way, the Acmeists see language as mediating between the present moment and eternity. The true poet, Gorodetskii contests, should bring into art the moment which can then be made eternal; this is a subtle difference from the Symbolists' desire to use each moment to see into the eternal.[90] Therefore for Gorodetskii, each moment is given its own permanent meaning. Rozanov takes up a similar position, but insists on language's ability to renew society by reinforcing lost values.

Rozanov engages with these problems in his consideration of the word's value. In crude terms, the difference between the two traditions rests in the fact that in the Symbolists, the unity of the physical world is preserved only through a correspondence, forged in the poet's mind, with a higher reality, where the ideal plane bestows ultimate meaning.[91] Rozanov has some similarities with both the Acmeist and Symbolist movements, but yet he is different in that he sees ultimate value in this world, but only because this world is Heaven, a parity guaranteed, lost and potentially restored through human creativity. His belief that Russian literature should reinforce man's pre-Fall innocence, leads him, like some of the Acmeists and Adamists, to look back to our Edenic state. However, Rozanov is also drawn specifically to the act of Creation, and the methods he uses to write suggest that literary endeavour is in itself a form of *imitatio Dei*.[92] Rozanov often privileges the act of writing over the meaning of his work: he characterized this spontaneous type of

89 Sergei Gorodetskii, 'Neskol′ko techenii v sovremennoi russkoi kul′ture', *Apollon*, 13 (1913), pp. 46–50 (p. 48).

90 Ibid., p. 50.

91 Justin Doherty, *The Acmeist Movement in Russian Poetry: Culture and the Word* (Oxford: Clarendon Press, 1995), p. 133.

92 Here, Rozanov shares similarities with some of his peers. Doherty discusses how, for Gorodetskii, the creation of poetry is explicitly likened to the Creation. Doherty also discusses the tactile relationship the Acmeists tried to develop with the world, by comparing the naming of each object to caressing it. Ibid., p. 132.

writing as his 'Otsebiatina'.[93] He is compelled to put his feelings immediately into words (this need to voice the word is another hint of the Stoic in him). Sometimes this happens at his desk, though such impulses occur at other times as well, in the bath or even the lavatory. All movements of the soul must be uttered out loud.[94] Here too Rozanov anticipates the focus of the Formalists on the 'poetic function' of language, rather than on its 'referential function'.[95] However, Rozanov takes this further, and stresses the symbiotic relationship between these roles. For Rozanov, the process of writing is its own message, designed to encourage creativity in his readership.

## The art of writing

We have already examined the importance of repeated behaviour in Rozanov's life. The repeated plays an important role in the *Opavshelistika*, not only in its content but also in its construction. Commentators have paid attention to the fact that writers adopt habitual patterns of behaviour in order to create an environment where they can produce new material. Pushkin felt most comfortable writing sat back on his bed with his notepad on his thighs.[96] Dostoevskii maintained a strict writing regime, drinking a set amount of tea each evening before working, shutting himself away to write through the night. The Russophile Anthony Burgess devotes much of his work to themes of habit, thought and inspiration for literature, and in particular the relationship between sexual and literary activity. Rozanov himself had his own habits when writing. He would sit in his study, re-examining and fondling his coins while he sought inspiration for new work. When he wrote, he would do so with his left hand holding his groin, confirming the association of his reproductive organs with the

93 See his letter to Suvorin dated 8 February 1908 (O.S.), reprinted in *Priznaki vremeni*, p. 365. In return, Suvorin appreciated Rozanov for writing not what he knew, but what he felt, although even Suvorin himself often did not understand his employee's articles. Ibid., p. 332.

94 *Uedinennoe*, p. 197. Slobin argues that for Remizov the word cannot remain unspoken, but must always be uttered. Slobin, p. 30.

95 Jakobson, 'Linguistics and Poetics', p. 85.

96 Binyon describes the routine Pushkin adopted to assist his writing. T.J. Binyon, *Pushkin: A Biography* (London: HarperCollins, 2002), p. 200.

production of new work, and possibly also his sexual relationship with his readership.

However, within the framework of the habitual, Rozanov appears motivated by a need continually to create more material as a response to God's work. In his *Opavshelistika*, each passage is constructed independently, as a new beginning, elevating Rozanov's fetishism of trivial things to a religious and literary principle. The presentation of each new passage reflects Rozanov's emphasis on new beginnings. The *Opavshelistika* passages have a definite resemblance to the Creation, in that each one is created naturally, spontaneously, without prior consideration or contemplation.[97] They emerge independently and have their own unique significance. In style and in manner of their construction, they acknowledge the sanctity of this world. This obviously has links with the ritualistic, and for Rozanov this must be creative. There is a reinvention in Rozanov of the concept of sacrifice, as a link between mystical experience as a continual event and the discontinuity involved in our engagement with individual phenomena; in this way Rozanov adopts a similar position to Bataille in the latter's reinterpretation of sacrifice (though Rozanov is more interested in the links between sex and procreation than in tying childbirth to death). This growing interest in discontinuity comes out more in his later periods, under the influence most probably of Florenskii. Hence Rozanov also insisted that each new passage in the *Opavshelistika* was printed on a fresh page, highlighting the meaning of the new. Rozanov makes explicit the link between the body and book, by drawing a direct parallel between the Bible, the 'written Book of God' and the human being, the 'unwritten, created, physical book of God'.[98] The implication is that man should write books in the same way that God created man. The correspondence between the book and the person is reinforced in Rozanov's emphasis on the appearance of each new life on Earth.

> Есть *одна книга*, которую человек обязан внимательно прочитать, – это книга его собственной жизни. И, собственно, есть одна книга, которая для него по-настоящему поучителньа, – это книга его личной жизни.
>
> Она ему открыта вполне, и – *ему одному*. Собственно, это и есть то *новое, совершенно новое в мире*, ни на что чужое *не похожее*, чтó он может прочитать, узнать. *Его личная жизнь* – единственный новый факт, который он с собой приносит на землю.

97 *Poslednie list'ia*, p. 24.
98 'Psikhologiia russkogo raskola', p. 47.

> There is *one book* that the human is obliged to read carefully – this is the book of his own life. And there is certainly one book which he can learn from, and that is the book of his personal life.
>
> It is open fully to him, and *to him alone*. In fact, this is something *new, completely new in the world*, which is unlike anything else he could read or learn. His *personal life* is the single new fact which he brings onto the Earth.[99]

There are precedents in European thought for the comparison of philosophical teaching and insemination. In the *Republic*, Socrates plants ideas in his listeners' heads where they grow like children; Socrates also draws parallels between genetic harmony and the ability to see the truth, insisting that illegitimate children can never become philosophers.[100] (This is somewhat reminiscent of Rozanov's demand that bachelors cannot become writers.) Rozanov's identification of literature and the body has long been established by contemporary and later critics.[101] Berdiaev was sensitive to this fact and wrote that Rozanov's words are not mere symbols, but living flesh. According to Berdiaev, Rozanov's genius lies in the fact that he imbues his words with a life of their own: 'His words are not abstract, dead, or bookish. All his words are alive, biological, full of blood'.[102] Nevertheless, this approach must take into account Rozanov's belief that the creation of literature is not merely an end in itself. The product of literary endeavour should also have further creative potential and produce an environment in which the continuing somatization of divinity can take place. Such an approach focuses on the activity of literature.

Throughout Rozanov's work, there is a deep suspicion of silence which matches his suspicion of ascetic isolation and celibacy. Contrary to the careful guarding of the heart by the body advocated by the hesychasts, Rozanov places great importance on the uttered word. For Rozanov, to speak is to engage with the world and the word must always be reproductive.[103] The activity of speech often becomes more important than the content, explaining Crone's humorous reference to Rozanov's 'verbal diarrhoea'.[104] Rozanov frequently criticizes Benkendorf for his

---

99 *Sakharna*, p. 25.

100 Plato, *Republic*, VII, 538a.

101 The comparison of literature and the body was a common paradigm among early twentieth-century Russian writers. See Doherty, p. 100.

102 Berdiaev, 'O "vechno bab′em" v russkoi dushe', p. 41.

103 'Nechto iz tumana "obrazov" i "podobii"', p. 287.

104 Crone, 'Remizov's "Kukkha"', pp. 210–11.

censorship, and he compares the damage done by the restrictions on Pushkin's works to a monk who advocates celibacy and endangers family life.[105] In presenting the correspondence between literary and sexual activity, silence provokes considerable frustration for Rozanov. It is worth comparing the above quote from Tolstoi's *Voskresenie* with the following passage from Rozanov's *Poslednie list'ia*.

> Самое совокупление – кто поверит и даже как возможно? – Но иногда оно было у меня сквозь слезы. Никогда без задумчивости. И никогда, никогда с сытым самоудовольствием.
>
> ЭТОГО (ужаса) – никогда.
>
> Всегда это было выражением любви, любования, нежности, чуть-чуть грациозной игры. Всегда и непременно – уважения.
>
> Как бык и собака – никогда.
>
> Впрочем, у них – серьезно, но человек, «ходячая пошлость», воображает, будто повторяет их, когда у него «сыто».
>
> Фу.
>
> Copulation – who would believe it, and how is it even possible? – But sometimes I did it through tears. Never without meditation. And never, never, with self-gratification.
>
> THIS (horror) – never.
>
> It was always an expression of love, of loving, tenderness, a graceful game. Always and without fail – an expression of respect.
>
> Never like a bull or a dog.
>
> In fact, for them it is serious, but for a human, 'baseness personified', he copies them, even repeats them, when he 'has had his fill'.
>
> Fie.[106]

Rozanov fills the silences in Russian literature with sex. However, this is more complex than a narration of the sexual act or Briusov's aestheticization of sexual attraction. When Rozanov describes his attitude towards sexuality, he is trying to encourage a physical response in his reader, but he also provides a reasoned justification for engaging in sexual acts. This is meant to overcome the reticence and shame common in contemporary Russian literature when it comes to such matters. Rozanov writes that he wants to see the whole world pregnant.[107] However, in writing this aphorism, it is not just the content which has a spiritual effect on the reader. The fact that Rozanov has made his ideas flesh is intended

---

105 V.V. Rozanov, 'V mire liubvi, zastenchivosti i strakha', in *Staraia i molodaia Rossiia*, pp. 203–10 (p. 205).

106 *Poslednie list'ia*, p. 29.

107 *Opavshie list'ia I*, p. 336.

to encourage the reader to do likewise. Writing is a sexual act which perpetuates sexuality in the reader. The creative act of exposing his ideas for Rozanov comes in fits and bursts of activity which is explicitly likened to sex, conception and birth. 'With a special feeling, almost through my skin, I sense that "sweat left me", and I grew tired – I glow and grow tired – because "it was born", "I gave birth,", because "semen left me", and after this I shall sleep until the next accumulation of semen'.[108]

Rozanov seeks to make reading and writing identical experiences, bringing together reader and writer.[109] Writing is not a substitute for sex, as Crone suggests, but instead an accompaniment. (Merezhkovskii also suggests that the book is replacement for the child,[110] which seems contrary to Rozanov's position.) Rozanov's output is designed to encourage others to make their ideas fleshy – his books are mixed not with water or ink, but with sperm. In investigating parallels between money and literature in Rozanov,[111] it is interesting to note that he deliberately set the price of his books high, precisely because they were reproductive words, immersed in his seed.[112] Reader and writer are joined through the transmission of writing, in a unity which is intensely physical and domestic.

Contrary to this, Rozanov sees the Russian Orthodox Church as presenting a stark choice between the body or the book. He raises serious questions about the compatibility of scriptural study and family life. Scholars isolated in theological research cannot interact with the world. Instead, Rozanov expects our response to his work to be not just cerebral, but intensely visceral. The reader is meant to share the same physical experiences, the smells, the sounds and the feelings, as Rozanov himself.[113] His work anticipates, and in some cases directly inspired, the type of literature which emerged in the twentieth century, where the reader is called upon to cultivate a physical, anti-intellectual response, for example in writers like D.H. Lawrence or Anaïs Nin (the latter's

---

108 *Poslednie list'ia*, p. 87. Rozanov's account of how he writes.

109 This is a common feature of the Russian Silver Age. See Doherty, p. 134.

110 Merezhkovskii, *Taina trekh*, p. 6.

111 Anna Lisa Crone, *Eros and Creativity in Russian Religious Renewal: The Philosopher and the Freudians* (Leiden: Brill, 2010), p. 80.

112 *Opavshie list'ia I*, p. 350.

113 This in part explains Rozanov's attraction to Dostoevskii: as Boldyrev notes, Rozanov is drawn to Dostoevskii because he believes that Dostoevskii enjoys a unique ability to dismantle the boundaries between writer and reader. See Boldyrev, p. 462.

works contain many Russian elements that are strongly reminiscent of Rozanov).[114] The reader is called upon not to consider Rozanov's work in a detached manner, but to participate in it. As Siniavskii points out, Rozanov's literature is not only read, but becomes 'a part of our life'.[115]

Critics differ in their appreciation of how the tensions between the subjective and the objective in Rozanov can be reconciled. Hutchings argues that this can be achieved through the 'domestication of public discourse'.[116] He argues that iconography provides the key to understanding these tensions, as the icon mediates between the particular and the universal, and 'accommodates' concepts of the divine into everyday life.[117] Hutchings contends that the role of the other is crucial in Rozanov's construction of self and he qualifies Rozanov's work as 'the circular process of self's alienation from, domestication of, surrender to and re-alienation from the other'.[118] However, Clowes rejects the theory that there can be harmony between the private and the public in Rozanov's later works and instead writes that in *Uedinennoe* and *Oboniatel′noe i osiazatel′noe otnoshenie evreev k krovi*, 'the gap between religious and secular, and between elite, philosophical discourse and middlebrow, journalistic discourse has never been greater. Indeed, the authenticity of the one breaks down in the face of the other'.[119]

These tensions can only reconciled by the concept of childbirth as continuing activity. Rozanov attempts to make his own subjective and creative experience a universal category. This was not appreciated by many of his readers, who perhaps did not understand the universal meaning in the expression of a personal religious framework. Tsvetaeva, although having appreciated the genius behind *Uedinennoe*, was critical of the apparently over-subjective nature of the *Opavshie list′ia*.[120]

114 Pease explores the tensions between the intellectual and physical response to modernist literature, and the ways that writers, especially Lawrence, experiment with these issues. She writes that one of the characteristics of modernist art was the replacement of the content of objects whose form was preserved, so that 'the aesthetic object becomes for its viewer or reader a substitute body', whose objectification means that the physical and irrational [can] be safely transubstantiated into the reflective reason of the aesthetic moment'. Pease, p. 67.

115 Siniavskii, p. 113.

116 Hutchings, 'Breaking the Circle of Self', p. 79.

117 Hutchings, *Russian Modernism*, p. 37.

118 Ibid., p. 191.

119 Clowes, p. 180.

120 Tsvetaeva, *Sobranie sochinenii*, V, pp. 301–2.

Nevertheless, Rozanov's desire to overcome ascetic silence leads him to privilege the act of writing over its content. This is the paradox of the Rozanovian focus on activity. Rozanov insists on demonstrating the validity of his views in his own literature, proving the underlying necessity of creating the new. Yet in demonstrating the processes by which the individual engages with society, Rozanov is often in danger of privileging personal activity, placing pressure on the wider value of his work. This often means that he is willing to write anything, despite the fact that it might offend. Criticism along the line of Tsvetaeva's appears a result of a neglect of the importance for Rozanov of activity. For Rozanov, the act of writing is the message. Although Rozanov involves himself in his work, his interest is not in his own ontology, but in the example of his sexual work. The unity in Rozanov's work between physical and mental appreciation, form and content, can only be upheld through creative activity, the demand for a new child.

Rozanov saw his mission as fighting against the stultification of Russian culture caused by positivism, socialism, atheism and mostly by an indifference to God. Rozanov entered the literary sphere with a new genre deliberately orientated to reform the reader's relationship to literature. Engelstein goes further than Clowes and presents Rozanov's attempt as deliberately subversive; she characterizes his technique as 'literary terrorism designed to disorganize public discourse'.[121] However, Rozanov's work rests in his attempts to take specific events from his life and human history, and his efforts to find laws of religion from these. He complicates the relationship between personal and communal religion by sometimes appearing to privileging the former. He writes that God is always 'only my God, and nobody else's'.[122] Here again Rozanov uses familial terminology to describe how this relationship works in practice. God is father to us all, in a biological sense, and there is a part of God in each one of us. Likewise, he insists on enjoying intimacy with his audience. It is only through the activity of childbirth that Rozanov can bring together these issues. This is made clear in one of the essays from his early period.

> В течение всей своей жизни одиноко растущая или прихотливо движущаяся особь является уединенною от всех других, свободною от их влияния и с ними не связанною; но в один миг своего существования, первый и самый важный

121 Engelstein, p. 314.
122 *Uedinennoe*, p. 200.

– когда рождается, она примыкает непосредственно к морю органической жизни, разлитой по земле и уже продолжающейся тысячелетия; и в краткие же мговения своего последующего существования – когда рождает, она соединяется с тою жизнью, которая останется на земле.

Throughout the course of its life, an individual which grows alone or acts capriciously is isolated from all others, is free from their influence, and is not connected to them. But in one moment of its existence, the first and most important – when it is born – it is linked directly to the sea of organic life, diffused throughout the Earth and spread across the millennia. And in the short moments of its future existence, when it gives birth, it is joined to the life which will remain on Earth.[123]

Through childbirth, parents and offspring enter into a relationship with the entire cosmos. And the book, if written correctly, can also be the locus where humans do this. Rozanov has no shame about involving the reader into an intensely close relationship, at work, at home, in his family and in his sex life with his wife. 'The book, in essence, means to be *together*. To be "as one". As long as the reader reads my book, he will be "as one" with me, and may the reader believe, I shall be "with him" in his deeds, in his home, in his children and surely in his sweet, gentle wife. "At his house for tea".'[124]

Rozanov sees writing as a type of sacrifice, the offering of his own self as it is immersed into the cosmos. Here he redefines the relationship between sex, sacrifice and literature, pretty much as Bataille would a generation later. Without childbirth, the personal and the universal would collapse on one another. This is clarified by the significance of each passage in his *Opavshelistika*. Each aphorism has its own religious and literary significance which is permanent, and yet this value is only affirmed by its presence within the book as a whole. Each aphorism is grounded on Rozanov's concept of the child as ultimate symbol of the Creation.

In 1899, Rozanov recollected the fear he had when he had moved from the town of Belyi to the Russian capital six years previously. This was a movement from a paradise of sorts, from the Russian provinces he loved so dearly, to the most un-Russian of all the Empire's cities. Rozanov explains he moved with the hope of 'prolonging or maintaining' the ideas of those he deeply loved – Aksakov, Khomiakov,

---

123 V.V. Rozanov, 'Krasota v prirode i ee smysl', in *Russkaia mysl´*, pp. 47–120 (p. 56).

124 *Sakharna*, p. 12.

Leont´ev and Giliarov-Platonov,[125] though financial motives lay behind his self-imposed expulsion from Eden. Nevertheless, Rozanov was terrified of Petersburg as the home of revolutionaries. Despite his admiration for Peter the Great's reforms, Rozanov never showed any love for the Russian capital, the centre of Russian atheism and terrorism. (He apparently gathered his convictions that Petersburg was full of revolutionaries from Dostoevskii's *Besy.*) Petersburg was alien to Russian life, built upon 'abstract lines, without a soul, without art, without prayer or memories'.[126] The young men who conspired to bring about the Russian Apocalypse were not only godless, but also childless. For Rozanov it was impossible for a family man to be a revolutionary. It was essential for Russia's salvation that this disenfranchised generation was encouraged to settle into family life, and Rozanov took it upon himself to demonstrate most vividly to the socialists the answer to their problems. Rozanov arrived at the Nikolaevskii train station in Petersburg as a kind of anti-Myshkin, not alone but with his young family, and his recollection of the event is remarkable even by his own standards.

> Мы, русские, все мечтатели, и вот я приехал в Петербург с мучительною мечтою, что тут – чиновники и нигилисты, с которыми «я буду бороться», и мне хотелось чем-нибудь сейчас же выразить свое *неуважение* к ним; прямо – неуважение к столице Российской Империи. Мечтая, мы бываем как мальчики; и вот я взял пятимесячную дочку на руки и понес, а затем я стал носить по зале I класса, перед носом «кушающей» публики; и твердо помню свой внутренний и радостный и неугодующий голос: «Я вас научу».
>
> We Russians are all dreamers, and so I arrived in Petersburg with a tormenting dream, that here were bureaucrats and nihilists with whom 'I would fight'. I wanted somehow to express my *disrespect* for them; in short, my disrespect for the capital of the Russian Empire. We become like children when we dream, and I took my five-month-old daughter in my arms and carried her around the first class hall, before the noses of the 'haughty' classes; and I clearly remember my joyful, inner voice: 'I'll teach you'.[127]

The two types of production coincide. Rozanov lays out before the Russian people the results of his domestic endeavours. Where in 1893 he exhibited his own daughter to the unmarried, he would devote the next

---

125 V.V. Rozanov, 'Sredi liudi "chisto russkogo napravleniia"', in *Russkaia gosudarstvennost´ i obshchestvo,* pp. 195–202 (p. 196).

126 Ibid., pp. 196–7.

127 V.V. Rozanov, 'Granitsy nashei ery', in *Semeinyi vopros v Rossii*, pp. 53–66 (p. 60).

quarter of a century of his family life in bringing forth more children and articles, in which he would exploit the example of Rozanov family life for the nation's enlightenment. Rozanov presents a new form of writing, where his words are flesh and the symbol is full of new content. Abstract thought must be replaced by the family. He explains: 'Our "path" is not philosophy and not science, but the *child*. A new book for study is simply the *reading* of the child, i.e. discourse with it, immersion in its element. It becomes our *symbol*'.[128]

Rozanov rejects the eschatological symbol of his contemporaries, and replaces this with his own, pointing back to the Creation. To a degree, creative freedom becomes a religious duty; man is obliged to have children. There is a certain tension between freedom and necessity here which is mirrored in a similar tension in the Godhead Itself. For Rozanov, only childbirth can hold together the balance between person and cosmos, thought and praxis, history and innovation, philosophy and literature, the mythological and the ritual. This explains Rozanov's decision to use his own person as the subject matter for the *Opavshelistika*. Contrary to the commonly accepted view, the centre of Rozanov's thought is not occupied by Rozanov. He presents his own life as an example to the Russian nation on how to overcome death, through a renewed feeling for God, and through the Creation.

128 Ibid., p. 66.

CHAPTER 7

# Paradise Lost

By way of conclusion, let us return to the beginning. Presumably during the Hermitage's 1905 exhibition, Rozanov saw Franz von Stuck's painting *The Sin* (1893), which depicts in Rozanov's words 'a dark-haired woman with burning eyes, a beautiful chiselled neck, with voluptuous forms', staring directly out of the painting at her admirers.[1] Despite the painting's popularity, Rozanov describes it as base, and although he could excuse 'an inexperienced youth' for its creation, he is unwilling to forgive a 'mature man' for such an image.

Both Stuck and Rozanov have their minds set on the problem of Eve in Eden. Rozanov does not take issue with the sexual depiction of a woman (though at times he does reveal some Victorian prudishness over sexual imagery in art). Rozanov attacks the belief that a semi-naked, beautiful woman, able to lure men with the beauty of her body, could be described as sinful. Rozanov notes the girl's long hair as it falls around her shoulders, and the way Stuck uses this as allegory for the Serpent. He accuses Stuck of a distorted depiction of sin and writes ironically: 'This is what calls man, the descendants of Adam, to sinful thoughts and lustfulness. Here is sin in its origin, at its root.' He remarks sarcastically that any Christian, having viewed the painting, would believe that he would be consequently excluded from entering the Kingdom of God.[2]

Rozanov argues that Stuck presents a false view of what it means to sin. Rozanov develops the 'amusing thought' of Stuck's painting *ad absurdum*, of depicting sin through a painting of a woman in a state of undress, breathing with 'charm, seduction, in a state of arousal'.[3] Here Rozanov returns to the idea of the ball; Stuck presents a picture no worse than Tolstoi's Natasha Rostova at her first dance in an open dress. Natasha's dance has become somewhat of an archetype of the tensions between the collision of native and Western cultures in Russia, but here Rozanov uses it to probe at the tensions between the eternal and the specific. Rozanov confesses, 'I am not for balls, and am not for open dresses: but who would not laugh if Stuck had painted such a ball, and

1 'Grekh', p. 347.
2 Ibid.
3 Ibid., p. 348.

couples dancing around in the light, and had signed this: "This is sin and sinful"?'[4]

Rozanov questions the manner in which Biblical facts (for him they are historical facts) are understood in a modern setting. As in his depiction of the mikvah, he struggles to reconcile the meaning of ancient rituals with the demands of modernity. While Rozanov reserves the intimate for the home, he does accept that in modern life people do participate in dances and reveal parts of their body. This does not mean that dancers should be excluded from Heaven. (Dancing was an essential part of worship for Rozanov, underlining the religious significance of the body, which helps explain his deep admiration for his friend Isadora Duncan.)

In pantheism, an ontological understanding of sin is impossible. This is also apparent in Rozanov.[5] 'Let the people dance a little, and they will pray themselves'.[6] Heaven is ours to experience here. Therefore sin, for Rozanov, can only be manifest in terms of activity. Rozanov sees humanity's fall in terms of our deliberate rejection of God's commandments. 'The direction of God's will remains indisputable for humanity', Rozanov writes.[7] However, humanity has consciously decided to obey its own laws, rather than respect God's will: 'God "commanded", Adam "did not obey God" and "fell". This is a description, this is a fact'.[8] Rozanov sees the 'Fall' of man as 'disobedience', a perspective which arises from Rozanov's association of the will of God with the human's inner nature. The individual can decide not to obey God's laws if they are selfish enough to place their own desires above God's will. Hence rather than seeing sin as an ontological necessity, inherited in our physiognomy from Adam, Rozanov sees sin as the conscious decision to prioritize one's own activities over God's intentions. This happened

4 Ibid.

5 Florenskii (whom it would be more difficult to label a pantheist) also denies that sin is ontological; he associates sin with destructivity, the undoing of God's work. Florenskii, p. 153. Rozanov's pantheism depends on his understanding of the relationship between God and the Earth as one of creative activity, a fact which does not come out in Zen′kovskii's rejection of the pantheistic in Rozanov. Rozanov's rejection of corporeal sin is apparent in his frequent criticism of Jesus Christ's command that 'if your hand or foot causes your downfall, cut it off' (Matthew 18:8).

6 V.V. Rozanov, 'K piatomu izdaniiu "Vekh"', in *Vekhi: Pro et Contra: Antologiia*, ed. by V.V. Sapov (St Petersburg: Izdatel′stvo Russkogo Khristianskogo gumanitarnogo instituta, 1998), pp. 496–504 (p. 502).

7 'Grekh', p. 348.

8 Ibid., p. 350.

for the first time when Adam chose the Tree of Knowledge over the Tree of Life and developed a consciousness of shame for his body. Rozanov goes against mainstream Christianity by refusing to see all humanity as inherently doomed through Adam. Rozanov's Fall is more epistemological than ontological. In this he shares something in common with Pelagius, rejecting Augustine's version of original sin (Rozanov insists that Eve, rather than damning humanity, in fact saves us through her motherhood). However, he does agree that since Eden we also have been confronted with the same choice, of reason or life, and have chosen knowledge. Eden was where Adam and Eve stood face to face with God, innocent and in physical contact with the divine. Rozanov frequently insists that it was God's plan for Adam and Eve to have sexual relations with each other in Eden.[9] It is this naked purity, where the idea of sin had not entered men's, or women's minds, that provides the underlying vision for all Rozanov's thought.

Rozanov goes deeper into the meaning of Eden in a critique of an article by Rtsy, 'Nagota Raia – esteticheskaia teorema', which appeared in issues 3 and 4 of *Mir Iskusstva* in 1903. Rozanov notes that Rtsy in his article does not find any antagonism between Christianity and paganism, and also remarks that Rtsy associates the naive innocence of paganism with the elemental purity of Adam and Eve in Eden. Rozanov agrees with these points, and repeats Rtsy's quote from Genesis 2:25: 'Both were naked, Adam and Eve, *but they had no feeling of shame*'.[10] Rozanov also agrees with Rtsy that there was a fundamental shift in human thinking that came about after the Fall, especially in terms of pleasure and reproduction. Rozanov sides with Rtsy in arguing that the fact that Adam and Eve ate and reproduced in the Garden of Eden proves the absolute holiness of these deeds. However, humans have lost the ability to consider the sacramental nature especially of reproduction; Rozanov argues that this is an intellectual deficiency in present-day thinking about religious rituals. Moreover, as Rtsy writes, and Rozanov agrees, these acts, especially childbirth, have lost their aesthetic character.

Rozanov agrees with some of Rtsy's points, but picks up on a dissociation of beauty and sex which is essential to Rozanov's entire viewpoint. Rtsy posits God as the 'Creator-Artist', and this connection between God's Creation and human reproduction, a tie which has an aesthetic basis, appears to have influenced Rozanov's thinking. However,

9 'Neskol′ko raz′′iasnitel′nykh slov', p. 371.
10 'Zamechatel′naia stat′ia', p. 619.

Rozanov's Edenic aesthetics diverge from Rtsy's, in the former's insistence that reproduction and copulation are inseparable. This disagreement reaffirms Rozanov's aestheticization of sex. In Rtsy there is an opposition between pre- and post-lapsarian physiognomy. He argues that human reproduction in Eden, according to God's initial plan, was analogous to that of flowers, 'without pregnancy or the present form of conception'.[11] Rtsy goes down a Solov´evian and Fedorovian route, sublimating sex and shunning pregnancy; he argues that Adam and Eve originally had superior bodies, which were somehow corrupted after their expulsion. For Rozanov, this marks too great a division between the aesthetic and the divine. Rozanov insists that modern humans are physiologically no different to Adam and Eve. Rozanov cites the description of Adam and Eve's sudden shame in Eden as proof that they had sexual organs. From that, Rozanov insists that they had sex. This is crucial to Rozanov's thinking about Eden: the commandment 'be fruitful and multiply' was given by God to humanity before the Fall. For Rozanov, God's original plan for humanity involves sex, and therefore the sexual act is blessed and is not a sign of our damnation.[12] Adam and Eve had sex in Eden, before their expulsion, and this is at the centre of Rozanov's vision of Paradise.

The idea that sexual reproduction came about as a result of our Fall is common in Christian theology. Adherents of this view insist that God had originally intended for humans in Paradise to reproduce asexually; however, once humans had sinned and were expelled from Eden, one of their punishments was to endure sex. Rozanov rejects the attempt to assign sex to the sphere of sinfulness. In asserting his view that God always wanted humans to have sexual intercourse, Rozanov had to endure frequent attacks from clergy and laymen alike, especially his great conservative rival Meshcherskii (although some clergymen, such as Rozanov's friend the priest Aleksandr Ust´inskii, went out of their way to defend Rozanov and consequently expose themselves to public criticism). The important point is that Rozanov insists that human nature did not change at the Fall, and is the same in the present day as it was when God originally planned it. This opportunity for physiological renewal overcomes a progressive view of history, argues that that the ideal can be recovered, and ensures that through sexual reproduction Paradise can be recreated here. Family life is essential for this, and must

11 Ibid., p. 620.
12 Ibid.

be constituted along the lines set out in the Old Testament. As Rozanov says, 'it is impossible to live in a family unless it is like Eden'.[13] This hope that Paradise can be restored in modern Russia is the most remarkable aspect of Rozanov's thought, and pervades his view of the world until the 1917 Revolution.

Rozanov's ability to draw the sexual into aesthetics ensures his confidence that artists can play a large part in the restoration of ethics. Rozanov draws heavily on Orthodox concepts of the icon and the rejection of art as mere representation. Artistic creation has the ability to recreate other locations and times. This is still an important aspect of contemporary Orthodox worship; for example, the newly restored Novoierusalimskii Monastery at Istra is not designed to serve as a simple replication of Jerusalem, but is meant to recreate the sacred space of the River Jordan and the holy sites of Israel. For Rozanov, the aesthetic is intrinsically linked to holiness. When Rtsy says that reproduction has lost its aesthetic character, he means that humans have lost the ability to be kind to one another. Rozanov interprets this slightly differently. Contrasting pagan aesthetics with classical art, Rozanov notes that the ancient Greeks were able to provide tales of reproduction, but these, according to Rozanov, were essentially asexual.[14] Unlike for Solov′ev, who in his epitaph privileges faith above love, love becomes a necessity for Rozanov's thought, as love and its physical expression is crucial in his vision of theosis (God is love). Rozanov believes that the omission of tenderness from aesthetics is a major cause of the present human malaise.

> Мы категорию *красивого* должны осложнить категориею *милого*, и даже припомнить ветхую поговорку народа нашего: «Не по хорошему мил, а по милу хорош». Вот, я думаю, начало *эстетической перемены*, происшедшей с грехопадением, заключается в том, что целая категория явлений перестала с грехопадением быть *милою* человеку, – и *даже в этом именно и заключалось грехопадение*.
>
> We should refine the category of the *beautiful* through the category of the *kind*, and even bring to mind the ancient saying of our people: 'He is not kind through his goodness, but good through his kindness'. ['Beauty is in the eye of the beholder.'] Here, I think, the principle of the *aesthetic shift* which happened at the Fall emerged from the fact that, since the Fall, the whole category of phenomena stopped being *kind* to humanity – *in fact this is the entire meaning of the Fall*.[15]

13 Ibid., p. 624. Here Rozanov also underlines the importance of divorce as a ritual that can recreate Eden.

14 Ibid., p. 620.

15 Ibid., p. 622.

Matter cannot be divorced from the divine. The turn from a physical, loving, relationship with creation to an intellectual consideration of phenomena is the principle aspect of the Fall. Humanity has lost the ability to treat the world with kindness (this focus on the tender and its aesthetic representation also comes out in D.H. Lawrence). This aversion in Christianity to the material is shown in St Paul's statement that 'the law is spiritual – but I am carnal, sold under sin' (Romans 7:14–24). Rozanov believes that our religious and aesthetic vision has been compromised, and complains that 'our view of bodies has fallen'.[16] However, Rozanov expresses hope that artists can revert to a familial relationship with their subjects.[17] This desire to remove the outer garments and get closer to his subject is widely different from Stuck's discomfort with nudity and his identification of sex and sin. Religion and art converge in Rozanov's belief that the aim of humanity is to restore the kind of physical closeness experienced at the beginning of time. Sex is generally problematic for utopian mentalities,[18] but Rozanov overcomes this through his focus on the possibility of renewal: he continually argues that humanity should rediscover the Tree of Life.

The Tree of Life is an image to which Rozanov frequently returns, and its opposition with the Tree of Knowledge reveals the extent of his apocalyptic fears. Rozanov believes that humanity's decision to foster knowledge instead of life has had serious consequences. Rational thought as an abstract category detracts from our relationship with this world; Rozanov links our Fall with our turn to philosophy (paralleled in the Greeks' rejection of Egyptian mythology). In associating abstract thought with death, Rozanov shares the opinions of other twentieth-century thinkers. Magee argues that European thought has an intrinsic link with death.[19] Other thinkers share Rozanov's view that philosophy is opposed to a Creation-orientated religiosity. For his part, Voegelin describes the advent of philosophy as the entrance of humanity into an ordered history, which in itself is apocalyptic as it creates the 'catastrophe of an old world and its *metastasis* into a new one'.[20] Strauss suggests that philosophy arises from the rejection of Creation accounts hitherto

16 Ibid., p. 623.
17 Ibid.
18 Naiman, p. 15.
19 Bryan Magee, *The Great Philosophers* (London: BBC Books, 1987), p. 240.
20 Eric Voegelin, *Anamnesis*, trans. and ed. by Gerhart Niemeyer (Notre Dame: University of Notre Dame Press, 1978), p. 166.

presented by religion, and argues that the abandonment of religion is the 'primary impulse' for philosophy.[21] Perhaps the most striking twentieth-century interpretation in context of Rozanov's concerns was made by Bloch in his epigraph to *Atheism in Christianity*.

> Religion is re-ligio, binding back. It binds its adherents back, first and foremost, to a mythical God of the Beginning, a Creator-God. So, rightly understood, adherence to the Exodus-figure called 'I will be what I will be,' and to the Christianity of the Son of Man and of the Eschaton, is no longer religion.

Rozanov associates the loss of mythology and the distortion of history explicitly with the de-phallicization of religion.

Rozanov does not reject rational thought outright. It is a crucial part of making sense of experience. From the outset, Rozanov had highlighted his belief that experience and intellect should not stand in opposition, but should be synthesized into an integrated means of understanding the world and behaving in it. Sex is the means of achieving this. Here Rozanov stands in the traditions of integral knowledge which characterize many of his peers. Florenskii, who argued that truth is antinomial, stated that rationality must gather 'all of life into itself, with all of life's diversity and all of its present and future contradictions'.[22] For Rozanov, a reasoned approach to religion is important as this frames humanity's engagement with the world. When Rozanov attacks knowledge, philosophy and theology, it is the abstract forms of these disciplines which he criticizes, the privileging of knowledge over this world; understanding cannot be divorced from life.

Like many thinkers, Rozanov's cognition of the world has a religious basis. Solov′ev posits a theory of knowledge which has a foundation on the Incarnation. Rozanov also appears to present a type of knowledge which is based on his religious view, and it is hardly surprising that, as opposed to Solov′ev, Rozanov bases his epistemology on a pre-Christian way of engaging with phenomena. This emerges essentially from the Creation. Each encounter with a phenomenon should be a creative act in the sense that this relationship with the subject of cognition should

21 Leo Strauss, 'The Mutual Influence of Theology and Philosophy', in *Faith and Political Philosophy: The Correspondence between Leo Strauss and Eric Voegelin, 1934–1964*, trans. and ed. by Peter Emberley and Barry Cooper (Columbia/London: University of Missouri Press, 2004), pp. 217–33 (p. 219).

22 Florenskii, p. 137.

be established afresh each time, as if we had just brought it into being. These ideas emerge in Rozanov's writings on the cult, which initially appear relatively early in his career and are expanded in his later works. In an essay from 1893 on education in Russia, drawing deliberately on the derivation of the word 'kul′tura' from 'kul′t', Rozanov contends that culture should emerge organically from our most basic, pre-philosophical attitude towards the world. The cultish vision is explained as a primeval and elementary understanding where the world is looked upon as a unified entity, but each time with 'new eyes' and with wonder.[23] Rozanov, unlike for instance Spengler, emphasizes that culture depends on a continued renewal of humanity's encounter with the world, that all civilizations must retain a link with their cultural origins. Each event should be understood as being experienced for the first time. This again underlines Rozanov's closeness to the Shklovskian desire to make the old new through creative activity. But for Rozanov this also involves making the new ancient, by understanding the modern world as new, but in terms of its permanent values.

> В понятии *культа* содержится внутренний, духовный смысл культуры; в понятии «сложности» содержится ее внешнее определение. Культурен тот, кто не только носит в себе какой-нибудь культ, но кто и сложен, т.е. не прост, не однообразен в идеях своих, в чувствах, в стремлениях, – наконец, в навыках и всем складе жизни.
>
> The concept of *cult* contains the internal, spiritual sense of culture; the concept of 'complexity' contains its external definition. The cultured person does not only carry within himself some kind of cult, but must be complex, that is, not simple, not one-dimensional in his ideas, his feelings, in his tendencies and finally in his practices and the entire makeup of his life.[24]

The cultish attitude is manifested in the establishment of an exclusive relationship with individual objects. The individual enters into an 'internal and particular' relationship with an object, which is then preferred above all other things.[25] For Rozanov, culture emerges from the external expression of this internal relationship in its contemporary context: 'Culture begins where love begins, where attraction is aroused; where a person's gaze, wondering freely, stops on something and cannot

23 V.V. Rozanov, 'Sumerki prosveshcheniia', in *Sumerki prosveshcheniia: Sbornik statei po voprosam obrazovaniia* (Moscow: Pedagogika, 1990), pp. 1–82 (p. 24).

24 Ibid.

25 Ibid., p. 25.

leave it. That moment is the external expression of culture, refinement: new and particular feelings stand out from the former, usual ones'.[26] Clearly this way of understanding the world is founded on love.

The cultish vision, close to Florenskii's, unlocks the way in which the ancient should be used to create the new. Epstein contends that in Russia there has been, at least since Danilevskii, a tradition of viewing culture as 'a complementary aspect of cult, that is, as a free creative response of man to God's act of creation'.[27] Rozanov calls upon the Church to revert to 'cultural', rather than dogmatic, forms of organization; the Church should bring the cult back into life.[28] Therefore culture opens up and reconciles the tensions between dogma and contemporary existence. Only through culture, in Rozanov's understanding, can the meaning of the Creation be made relevant in each everyday moment. This is revealed in the *Opavshelistika*, where Rozanov gives us proof of the obligation to create as experienced in modern Russia. Moreover, Rozanov believes that we should engage with each thing on an innovative and independent manner each time – a relationship which has permanent potentiality for renewal. This has parallels with the contemporary concerns of the European Phenomenonolgists (interestingly, Husserl often described himself as a 'permanent beginnner'). This is also noted in the 'Cubist' aspect of the *Opavshelistika* shown in the previous chapter, where the relationship with a thing is sanctified on a continuing basis.

It is the manner in which Rozanov 'thinks' and the way in which this leads to the creation of new thought which fills the very content of Rozanov's philosophy. It is not important for Rozanov whether his own ideas are original or derivative. The vital aspect for him is that his thought is presented each time as something entirely new. Izmailov notes that in over 800 pages, *O ponimanii* does not contain a single reference to other people's works.[29] Furthermore, Izmailov recalls that he once questioned an unnamed contact, a 'specialist in philosophy, an academic and friend of Solov′ev', as to the real value of *O ponimanii*. The contact replied that Rozanov arrived at the same conclusions as Hegel despite the fact that he had never read Hegel in his life. The academic concluded

26 Ibid.

27 Epstein, 'From Culturology to Transculture'.

28 V.V. Rozanov, 'Novaia kniga o khristianstve', in *Staraia i molodaia Rossiia*, pp. 9–17 (p. 16).

29 A.A. Izmailov, 'Vifleem ili Golgofa? (V.V. Rozanov i "neudavsheesia khristianstvo")', in *Vasilii Rozanov: Pro et Contra*, II, pp. 81–90 (p. 83).

that it would have been of more benefit if Rozanov had simply learned to read German instead.[30] Yet, as Fediakin astutely notes, the question of prior investigation is irrelevant for Rozanov – what is more important is that his work is presented each time as new.

> Если попытаться проследить путь Розанова к «Уединенному», то он, собственно, начинается с первой же его книги «О понимании», где он выступает как своего рода «робинсон» в философии, все перпетии сложнейших проблем проходит заново, минуя опыт большинства философов прошлого и настоящего (потому-что так бросается в глаза отсутствие ссылок на авторитеты, выводы которых могли бы помочь философу в разрешении того или иного вопроса, Розанов все время старается «изобрести велосипед», т.е. *сам* пройти путь, уже пройденный мировой философией). Он как бы берет то или иное понятие – и начинает мысленно «разглядывать» его (как и вообще любил разглядывать монеты, письма, мелочи жизни).
>
> If we try to follow Rozanov's path to *Uedinennoe*, it starts with his very first book *O ponimanii*, where he acts like some philosophical Robinson Crusoe. He tackles the most complex problems anew, bypassing the experience of the majority of past and present philosophers (this explains the glaring omission of references to authorities whose conclusions could help the philosopher resolve his questions, Rozanov consistently tries to 'reinvent the wheel', i.e. *himself* go down those paths already trodden by world philosophy). It is as if he takes this or that concept and begins to examine it with his thoughts (like he loved to examine his coins, letters, the trivia of life).[31]

Rozanov's desire to view repeatedly the world as new is informed by his desire to understand, and love, the world in its original, pre-Fall form, and this means that Rozanov is constantly seeking to present existing ideas and entities as new beginnings. This leads him to reject other thinkers: Rozanov even admits that he is filled with a longing to 'kill' other people's ideas.[32] Of course, every philosopher is in his own way apocalyptic, as he or she wishes to replace prior schemes of thought with

30 Ibid., p. 85. Critics have noted the closeness of Rozanov's ideas in *O ponimanii* to those of Hegel. See for example Florovskii, p. 460. Also note George Ivask, 'Rozanov', *Slavic and East European Journal*, 5 (1961), 110–22 (p. 112). Strakhov pointed out to the young Rozanov that his ideas on potential already existed in the German Idealists and accordingly advised his young protégé to learn German; see his letter dated 18 March 1888 (O.S.), reprinted in *Literaturnye izgnanniki*, p. 11.

31 S.R. Fediakin, 'Zhanr, otkrytyi V.V. Rozanovym', in V.V. Rozanov, *Kogda nachal′stvo ushlo...*, pp. 597–602 (p. 598).

32 *Literaturnye izgnanniki*, p. 159.

new truths.[33] Here, rather than a constructive, organic way to presenting philosophy, Rozanov maintains some degree of the traditions of Western, counteractive thought. However, Rozanov is motivated by his desire to reinterpret each event as a new beginning.

## The Apocalypse of Rozanov's time

Throughout the majority of his career, Rozanov is hopeful that humanity can abandon the Tree of Knowledge and return to the Tree of Life. However, the Revolution of 1917 marks the brutal intrusion of history into his philosophy. It is perhaps startling that his literary masterpiece should be his final work, *Apokalipsis nashego vremeni*, and it is worth examining the apocalyptic nature of this haunting piece in light of the arguments of this present study. This book was written between 1917 and 1919, after the events which brought down the tsarist regime and eventually led to the Bolshevik Revolution. Therefore one difference here is that this book marks Rozanov's attempt not to change the world, but to explain and to come to terms with Russia's demise.

In his introduction to the *Apokalipsis*, addressed to the reader, Rozanov announces the ritualistic frequency in which he intends to issue these final leaves, and then goes on to explain the reason for their composition:

> Заглавие, не требующее объяснений, ввиду событий, носящих не мимо апокалипсический характер, но действительно апокалипсический характер. Нет сомнения, что глубокий фундамент всего теперь происходящего заключается в том, что в европейском (всем, – и в том числе русском) человечестве образовались колоссальные пустоты от былого христианства; и в это пустóты проваливается все: троны, классы, сословия, труд, богатства. Все потрясены. Все гибнут, все гибнет. Но все это проваливается в пустоту души, которая лишилась древнего содержания.
>
> The title does not require any explanation in light of events which do not just have a passing apocalyptic nature, but have a decidedly apocalyptic nature. There is no doubt that everything that has happened has its foundations in the fact that the European population (including the Russians) has suffered in the void left by Christianity. Everything is collapsing in this emptiness: thrones, classes, estates, labour, wealth. Everybody is shocked. Everybody is perishing,

33 Gerald L. Burns, *Tragic Thoughts at the End of Philosophy: Language, Literature, and Ethical Theory* (Evanston: Northwestern University Press, 1999), p. 15.

everything is perishing. But everything is collapsing in the emptiness of the soul, which has been deprived of its ancient content.[34]

Rozanov then goes on to present several facets of Russian and European culture which are brought together and discussed simultaneously. The fact that in the same passage Rozanov investigates the significance for Russian culture of Peter the Great, Metropolitan Filaret (Vasilii Drozdov), Gogol′, Zhukovskii, Lomonosov, or Aleksandr Malinin, as well as a host of historical and Biblical figures, demonstrates Rozanov's rejection of the progressive view of history.

Что же, в сущности, произошло? Мы все шалили. Мы шалили под солнцем и на земле, не думая, что солнце видит и земля слушает. Серьезен никто не был, и, в сущности, цари было серьезнее всех, так как даже Павел, при его способностях, еще «трудился» и был рыцарь. И, как это нередко случается, – «жертвой пал невинный». Вечная история, и все сводится к Израилю и его тайнам. Но оставим Израиля, сегодня дело до России.

What in fact happened? We all fooled around. We all fooled around, under the sun and on the Earth, not thinking that the sun was watching and the Earth was listening. Nobody was serious, so in fact the Tsars were the most serious of all, as even Paul, for all his abilities, still 'laboured' and was a knight. And, as often happens, 'the innocent were sacrificed'. History is eternal, and everything leads us back to Israel and its secrets. But let us leave Israel, for now our business is with Russia.[35]

Rozanov must deal with the failure of the Russians to restore ancient values on their own soil. He confronts, as is to be expected, the Russian Orthodox Church and its hierarchs (in particular Metropolitan Filaret) for forcing the people to accord them personal reverence, as well as the person of Tsar Nicholas I for turning Russia into an imitation of the German Empire. But here Rozanov also takes to task many of the protagonists of Russian literature for their stylization and inability to depict true love. All we are left with, writes Rozanov, is the superficial narrations of the 'love' between Vronskii and Anna, Litvinov and Irina or Oblomov and Ol′ga. The literary and ethical ideal which Rozanov seeks is buried within the Biblical passage where God makes woman from man's body (Genesis 2:23). This is the Edenic unity, the physical oneness, to which every couple longs to return, and which, according to Rozanov, Katia and Nekhliudov realize (even though Tolstoi himself

34 *Apokalipsis nashego vremeni*, p. 5.
35 Ibid., p. 7.

does not).[36] 'But even in the family,' Rozanov writes, 'we did not love particularly well'.[37] Of course, one of the major literary culprits identified by Rozanov is Gogol′; eventually, Rozanov would squarely blame Gogol′ for the Russian Revolution: 'This is your victory, you dreadful Ukrainian'.[38]

Russian literature has failed to help its people recreate Eden. Here again Rozanov focuses very much on practices. The nihilists whom he attacks in this book, Rozanov writes, have fooled their onlookers by only pretending to pray.[39] Here Rozanov conflates the meaning of the loss of Paradise with contemporary affairs. This marks the failure of his project, the subjugation of religion to history. The lack of true interpersonal love Rozanov sees among his countrymen, which has given cause to the Revolution, parallels the hatred shown by Cain for Abel. Rozanov also complains of a disdain humans have shown towards God's Earth, which Cain stained in murdering his brother (Genesis 4:11–13). In rejecting his nation and his Tsar, and in particular refusing to fight for his people, the contemporary Russian re-enacts humanity's first fratricide.

И солдат бросает ружье. Рабочий уходит от станка.

«Земля – она должна сама родить.»

И уходит от земли.

«Известно – земля Божия. Она всем поровну.»

Да, но не Божий ты человек. И земля, на которую ты надеешься, ничего тебе не даст. И за то, что она не даст тебе, ты обагришь ее кровью.

Земля есть Каинова, и земля есть Авелева. И твоя, русский, земля есть Каинова. Ты проклял свою землю, и земля прокляла тебя. Вот нигилизм и его формула.

And the soldier throws down his gun. The worker leaves his post.

'The Earth will give birth Herself.'

And he leaves the Earth.

---

36 V.V. Rozanov, 'Poputnye zametki. "L.N. Tolstoi. Voskresenie"', in *Iudaizm*, pp. 167–9 (p. 167).

37 *Apokalipsis nashego vremeni*, p. 5.

38 *Poslednie list′ia*, p. 25. There appears to be some obsession in Gogol′ with the 'finis', which perhaps stems from an impatience with the present moment. Bukharev picked up on Gogol′'s apparent desire to rush the reader to the conclusion of his works. See Arkhimandrit Feodor, *Tri pis′ma k N.V. Gogoliu*, p. 75. Bukharev contrasts Gogol′'s literary impatience with the message of the true religious life, which he believes was to 'extend our stay in Eden'. Ibid., p. 182.

39 *Apokalipsis nashego vremeni*, p. 8.

> 'It is known that the Earth belongs to God. She belongs to everybody equally.'
>
> Yes, but you are not a man of God. And the Earth on which you lay your hopes will give you nothing. And because she gives you nothing, you will stain her with blood.
>
> There is the land of Cain, and there is the land of Abel. And yours, oh Russian, is the land of Cain.
>
> You have desecrated your Earth, and the Earth has damned you. This is nihilism and its formula.[40]

Here we shift from the cosmological to the specific. The Biblical motifs become apparent in the hint at the Israelites' expulsion from the Promised Land. The Russians have failed to recreate Paradise, but have led themselves into a false utopia. But what makes this book more disturbing is Rozanov's deliberate merging of the Biblical and the historical. The contemporary crisis is portrayed in terms of Biblical catastrophes, which both underline Rozanov's conviction in the reality of the events portrayed in the Old Testament and provide explanation for Russia's collapse. Throughout this work, Rozanov repeats his belief that the Russian Apocalypse is attributable to the rejection of the Old Testament. This leads Rozanov frequently to turn directly to Jesus Christ and to criticize the writings in the New Testament.[41] He admonishes Jesus for his rejection of the Law and what 'the ancients say'.[42] God's Law, for Rozanov, is laid into the very fabric of the Earth, and Christ has rejected this in favour of a sophisticated yet superficial sentimentality (which seems close to Rozanov's rejection of the over-stylization of emotions portrayed in Russian literature). Rozanov notes specifically Jesus' rejection of the command 'an eye for an eye' (Exodus 21:24).[43] Rozanov also stresses that St Paul echoes Christ's message in his desire to be saved from this body of death. But Rozanov sees Paul's cry as straight from the lips of Cain: 'This is just the shriek of Cain, and relates to the guilt of abandoning sacrifice, i.e. to its destruction, and, it is fully clear,

40 Ibid., p. 9.

41 In Elshina's interpretation of *Apokalipsis nashego vremeni*, Rozanov states that Jesus could not have been God, as he came to Earth. Rozanov finally concludes that God and Christ must remain separate categories. As Jesus was not God, he must have been the Antichrist, who by his appearance brought about Russia's downfall. See T.A. Elshina, 'Dva razgovora ob Akopalipsise (Vl. Solov′ev i Vas. Rozanov)', *Entelekhiia* (2000), 76–82 (p. 78).

42 *Apokalipsis nashego vremeni*, p. 9. Grammar in the original.

43 Ibid.

to the abandonment of all the Old Testament and to the complete lack of understanding of this Testament'.[44]

Rozanov does not blame Adam for leading humanity into sinfulness, but suggests that Paradise could have been obtained if it was not for the appearance of Jesus Christ. Whereas St Paul writes that Christ came to redeem the fallen body (Christ as the 'second Adam'), Rozanov's corporeal focus is firmly on the humanity of the first man. Rozanov hints that there would still be the possibility of human redemption through circumcision, the link between the divine Phallus and the human penis. Instead, Rozanov blames Jesus directly for 'unbearably burdening human life'.[45] He continues: 'This is something clear, simple and eternal that characterizes the "fullness" of the father and our eternal foundations in him; the father, to put a long story short, has been replaced by tears, hysterics and sentimentality. This is the start of Christ's torment'.[46]

For Christians, including the Orthodox, Christ's teachings are not supposed to replace, but fulfil the meanings given in the Old Testament. Yet this approach is firmly rejected in Rozanov. Rozanov's attack on Jesus Christ culminates in a scathing criticism of the entire meaning of Christianity and Christian civilization. In a passage entitled 'Khristos mezhdu dvukh razboinikov', Rozanov notes the futility of the Passion, the impotency of atonement. The despair of all humanity is demonstrated in the cries of the two men crucified either side of Jesus. Rozanov concludes that there is no room for humanity in this humiliation. 'There is no seed, but two shudders.' Rozanov curses Christ Himself: 'Oh, there is no need for Christianity. No need, no need... Horrors, horrors. Lord Jesus. Why did You come to torment the Earth? To torment and lead us into despair?'[47] As Jesus failed in reconciling the Old Testament with contemporary life, Rozanov takes on this task and disturbingly puts himself in Jesus' place. Rozanov not only rejects the meaning of Jesus' sayings, but subsequently assimilates His words, giving his own writing a deliberate and striking Biblical tone. His final call is a cry to God, taking Jesus' own last cry: 'Why have you forsaken me?'[48]

What marks the *Apokalipsis* from Rozanov's other works, and many works of politically and socially-orientated philosophy, is that it is a

44 Ibid.
45 Ibid.
46 Ibid.
47 Ibid., p. 59.
48 Rozanov argues that for Jesus to be necessary would preclude some 'deficiency' in the Father, which he is not prepared to accept. *Apokalipsis nashego vremeni*, p. 26.

realized Apocalypse. Rozanov is reconciled to the final and irreversible downfall of Holy Russia. Hence the title for this book, and this is the reason for its despair. The *Apokalipsis* is written as a final response to events that Rozanov was unable to prevent. It proves founded the fears Rozanov previously voiced over the possible consequences of Russia's rejection of the family, but also acknowledges Rozanov's failure in preventing the Revolution. Therefore in a strange way, this final work is both a justification of the whole Rozanov project, and evidence for its failure. Rozanov, like Solov´ev, and very much unlike Mr Z., had an acute sense of his own demise, and managed to find correspondence between his personal and his literary Apocalypses. What is different for Rozanov is his understanding that he was experiencing a kind of Apocalypse *within* time, a revelation of his own truth discerned within the growing indifference of the Russians to God.

In the Introduction, I argued that Rozanov's project is an attempt to overcome history, to mark the eternal principles of humanity's relationship with God which are not subject to change. However, the tragedy of Rozanov's conclusion is that history has finally overcome religion. Rozanov's was not an Apocalypse as the end of human time, but an entry into a new kind of time, the victory of history as progression over Rozanov's cyclical vision. This was an event made worse by the fact that Russians would be trapped in an earthly hell of their own making. Hence Rozanov's final work is a remarkable achievement, in its literary style and philosophical innovation. It is his proof that all the arguments he had presented throughout his career were in fact correct, and at the same time is an admission that his own project failed. Rozanov concludes, assuming Christ's words (Mark 14:58), that it was no wonder, given the state of formal Orthodoxy, that Russia collapsed in three days; it took even longer than that to close down *Novoe Vremia*.[49]

## The return to the Creation

Apocalypticism has been a potent force in human history, particularly in civilizations influenced by Christianity. One dimension of this was the tendency to perceive progress itself as eschatological, as Altizer writes: 'the very advent of modernity can be understood to be an apocalyptic event, an advent ushering in a new world as a consequence of the ending

49 Ibid., p. 6.

of an old world'.[50] Altizer argues that apocalypticism in Western thought was initially made possible by St Paul's division of body and flesh.[51] He develops his argument by suggesting that Hegel has had most influence here, by defining historical progress in terms of a dialectic that only takes place through the complete negation of the subject.

> Until the advent of modernity, virtually all thinking was closed to the possibility of the truly and the actually new; the future as such then could only finally be a realization of the past, for history itself is ultimately a movement of eternal return, and even revelation or a divine or ultimate order is a movement of eternal return.[52]

The significance of Hegelian thought for Russia has been made by Zimdars-Swartz, who note the importance of the German for Bakunin.[53] They discuss the scholarship of Edward Hyams and Georges Sorel, but also identify the importance of Ernst Bloch for twentieth-century understandings of how utopian visions inform political movements.[54] Bloch posits an opposition between the Creation and the Apocalypse, the former being characterized by God's declaration 'It *was* good', and humanity's desire to remake everything for itself anew.[55] Bloch picks up on the malaise of a humanity that rejects its origins, but also rejects linear progress in favour of a series of knowledge-inspired, apocalyptic bursts in which humanity continually transforms the world. It is the

---

50 Thomas J. Altizer, 'Modern Thought and Apocalypticism', in *The Encyclopedia of Apocalypticism*, III, pp. 325–59 (p. 325).

51 Ibid., 326.

52 Ibid., p. 335.

53 Sandra L. Zimdars-Swartz and Paul F. Zimdars-Swartz, 'Apocalypticism in Modern Western Europe', in *The Encyclopedia of Apocalypticism*, III, pp. 265–92 (p. 287). In turn, Motrenko argues that this attention to Hegel in the Russian religious renaissance stems from Solov´ev's influence, not just in terms of his philosophy, but also in terms of his interpretation of other philosophers. T.V. Motrenko, *Gegelevskie idei v mirovozzrensko-religioznoi paradigme rossiiskoi filosofii XIX – nachala XX vekov* (Kiev: Slovo, 2005), p. 305.

54 Zimdars-Swartz, p. 288.

55 Bloch, *Atheism in Christianity*, p. 22. My emphasis. Bloch connects his ideas of progression with the biology of humans and suggests that man 'broke through, exceeded the genus fixed for so long among the animals'. Ernst Bloch, *The Spirit of Utopia*, trans. by Anthony A. Nassar (Stanford: Stanford University Press, 2000), p. 234. For him, attaining utopia involves overcoming one's own humanity. Rozanov would disagree.

apocalyptic vision, a knowledge of the future state of the world, that inspires these leaps.[56]

Bloch's work seems to exemplify the contemporary dominance of philosophical types of thinking over the mythological, as Biblical motifs are assimilated into modern concepts of progress. One cultural aspect which has appeared to inform apocalypticism and which Rozanov picks up on is the separation of history from myths, particularly from myths dealing with the Creation. However, it is Rozanov's attempt to merge myth and history, constructed on his willingness to associate essence and energies, that fuels Rozanov's vision that the sacred narratives depicted in the Bible are a historical reality. In particular, his construction of myths and his ability to rely on subjective truths which are given universal relevance is demonstrative and influential in a Russian philosophical culture which has often defined its purpose in challenging the rationalist approach of the West. Rozanov pre-empts to some degree the reconnection presented in twentieth-century social anthropology of myth and meaning. He would probably agree that, although myths narrate events, they do not exist purely in order to tell stories, but fulfil 'the human desire to express the inexpressible or to know the unknowable'.[57] In Voegelin, therefore, myths constitute the means by which humanity reconciles itself to the limited nature of our existence. Human consciousness unravels our own finiteness, and yet this is accompanied by an awareness of the infinitude of the cosmos; myths act as a finite symbol which provides '"transparence" for a transfinite process'.[58] It is this contrast between contemporary, anti-religious modes of thought, and natural, innocent forms of discussing Paradise, which Rozanov plays on.

> Сага, «миф» (как сказал бы неверующий скептик, «материалист» наших дней); но, как «слово», «επος», так ли она призрачна, как и прочие слова поэтов и сказочников? Нет, «рассказ о рае», «вера в рай» составляет до такой степени основной столп религиозного миросозерцания, что даже и материалист всякий, желая посмеяться над верующим, скажет: «неужели вы *верите в религию?* Что же, по-вашему, *есть в самом деле рай?*» Таким образом, «миф» этот, «сага» входит в самое существо и содержание религии: и мы, начиная детей «учить религии» («Закон Божий»), в первый

56 Bloch, *Atheism in Christianity*, pp. 22–3.

57 This quote is taken from Debra A. Moddelmog, *Readers and Mythic Signs: The Oedipus Myth in Twentieth-Century Fiction* (Carbondale: Southern Illinois University Press, 1993), p. 3.

58 Voegelin, *Anamnesis*, p. 21.

же час учения рассказываем им о «рае», т.е. передаем (по эллинской терминологии, как сказали бы они о себе) «священную сагу».

Is the saga, the myth (as the unbelieving sceptic, the 'materialist' of our time, would say), the 'lay', the 'επος', as illusory as the other words spoken by our poets and storytellers? No, 'the tale of Paradise', 'the belief in Paradise' forms the basic pillar of our religious worldview. Any materialist, wishing to mock the believer, will say: 'Do you really *believe in religion? What, in your view, in actual fact is Paradise?*' In this way, this 'myth', this 'saga' enters the very essence and content of religion: and when we begin to teach children religion ('the Law of God'), in the very first lesson we teach them about 'Paradise', that is we teach them as the Greeks would say 'the holy saga'.[59]

For Rozanov, myths are the bearers of the truths humans took from Paradise. This image of Eden and its proper transmission is the foundation of his religion.

Rozanov's realized Apocalypse was a particular example of the works that in the subsequent years struggled to make sense of the Russian Revolution. Zamiatin is a case in point, but one is brought to mind particularly of Bunin and his narration of the events immediately following the fall of the tsarist regime. Bunin sees the Revolution as a burst of primeval energy and savagery unleashed by the failure of the Russian Church to civilize an innately barbaric nation. Here Bunin opposes Christian civilization with what he sees as natural Russian baseness, whilst maintaining a distrust of the institutional Church's ability to carry its message to the people. In marking this contrast, Bunin shares Rozanov's sense of incompatibility between Christianity and the Russian people, though their conclusions could not be more different. Bunin, like Rozanov, looks back to the 'first page' of Russian history in order to explain the events of the Revolution and Civil War, but locates a terrifying pagan wildness within the Russian soul. While also blaming the Orthodox Church for not having civilized the population, Bunin finds the ultimate fault in the people and turns to Christianity for the possibility of salvation. This intrigue with the potential chaos of the Russian masses, the awe of the primeval energy of the Russian people, also comes out in writers such as Pil′niak and Remizov.[60] Rozanov, in contrast to Bunin, lauds the natural

59 'Chto skazal Teziiu Edip?', p. 290.

60 The figure of Rozanov, 'grand phallus bearer' ('velikii fallofor') of Remizov's 'Great and Free Chamber of the Monkeys', casts a long shadow over many aspects of revolutionary and post-revolutionary Russian literature. Naiman discusses Rozanov's 'worship of sex' and its transformation into a 'violent,

qualities of the people and explains the Revolution through Christianity's dismantling of these facets. Rozanov also achieves this through his merging of Biblical, mythological and historical depictions, which are not so much stylized as brought back to Earth. Whereas Bunin narrates real contemporary events in a natural, diary-like style, Rozanov employs a merging of Biblical, mythical and historical events which produces a way of understanding the world that has a basis in life. This syncretism is an impediment to Rozanov being considered a true Christian thinker; Zen´kovskii argued that the pagan elements in Solov´ev's thought meant that he could not be considered truly Orthodox, and the reader is compelled at least to consider a similar conclusion for Rozanov.

This primal focus has implications for Rozanov's epistemology. Rozanov believes that the Revelation of God was given to humans at the start of history, not through the Tree of Knowledge, but through the Tree of Life. This negates the requirement for a final Apocalypse of salvific knowledge. Rozanov's thought is also a rejection of the Hegelian sense of knowledge as progressive. Rozanov opposes Berdiaev's idea of Creation which emerges from necessity, limiting the freedom of God; Berdiaev consequently ties knowledge to necessity, likewise placing limitations on human freedom.[61] Hence Berdiaev, for all his attention to human creativity, perpetuates the ontological and epistemological division in Russian culture which Rozanov is intent on overcoming.[62] (Rozanov

---

transformative force in Pil´niak. Naiman, pp. 60–1. Cavendish provides a highly-detailed examination of the literary manipulation of Russian folk themes in Zamiatin, as well as contextualizing aspects of Russian modernism within the heritage of its speculative religious thought. See Philip Cavendish, *Mining for Jewels: Evgenii Zamiatin and the Literary Stylization of Rus´* (London: Modern Humanities Research Association, 2000), pp. 190–1. For Rozanov's induction into the Obezvelvolpal (and amusing suggestions of his envy over superiority), see *Kukkha*, pp. 38–9. Here Rozanov's inauguration is juxtaposed with Remizov's composition of his *Tragediia o lude*; the common revolt against Christ appears more than coincidence.

61 N.A. Berdiaev, *Smysl tvorchestva* (Moscow: Izdatel´stvo 'Pravda', 1989), p. 254.

62 Berdiaev presents a highly complex salvific scheme which acknowledges the Gospel's lack of focus on creativity but which relies on an anthropological soteriology. In some ways this is close to Rozanov, but Berdiaev proceeds to found this on a human creativity which is revealed prophetically and which rests on a transfiguration through Christ and His Crucifixion. Like many of his peers, Berdiaev accepts a link between sex and creativity, but this is contingent on the transfiguration of sex. Berdiaev, *Smysl tvorchestva*, pp. 324–9.

was generally critical of Berdiaev and the abstraction in his thought, much preferring Sergii Bulgakov; Rozanov insisted that Berdiaev did not realize that it was the duty of religious thinkers to study the sanctity of this Earth, and not to examine the holiness of Heaven.[63])

Rozanov reached the peak of his powers as Russia entered a new century, a time where the leaps forward in progress were a cause for both intense optimism and despair. The pessimists' worst fears were confirmed as Europe plunged into a century of devastating wars and social turmoil. Many thinkers have discussed the crisis of hope pervading our age; mid-way through the twentieth century Faulkner talked powerfully of a world paralyzed by fear, of man labouring under the curse of grief. To a large degree, these fears appear to be a deficiency of Christianity, its inability – and, historically speaking, often its unwillingness – to reassure its believers of the meaning of earthly existence. In any case, apocalypticism appears to be a persistent trend in human thought, in particular in Christian thinking, but also in other cultures which have their roots in the major monotheistic religions. Modern fears over climate change (Rozanov's environmentalism, founded in a reverence of the Earth as God's child, was centred on the Volga), international terrorism, or the extinction of the bees, only appear to support this view. The Western human seems to have an obsession with their own demise, to the detriment of their origins. In the context of humanity's morbid fixation, a work such as Vidal's 1981 novel *Creation* brings a very rare message of hope. (Vidal, like Rozanov, uses the Creation of the world to attack Western civilization's reliance on Hellenistic philosophy and, like Rozanov's contemporary Dmitrii Merezhkovskii, uses Julian the Apostate to attack modern Christianity.)

Questions of hope are intrinsically linked with interpretations of history. In Russian thought, where historicity has played a dominant role, apocalyptic motifs have been highly prominent. Berdiaev astutely distinguishes active from passive apocalypticism, where humanity has varying degrees of responsibility in bringing about the end of time. Throughout the history of Russian thought, its protagonists have battled over the varying relationship between history and its eschaton, but Berdiaev identifies Fedorov for changing the character of Russian apocalypticism, from a hope in the eventual transfiguration of matter, to a fearful identification of the end of human time with the victory of the Antichrist. Following on from him, Rozanov likewise separates

63 'Nikolai Berdiaev. Smysl tvorchestva.', p. 487.

history from eschatology, focusing his attention on maintaining the links between human activity and this world. Rozanov is an eternal optimist in both senses; he understands the world as essentially good, but also sees in the ever-lasting divinity of matter the basis for hope against the forces which threatened to destroy his country.

It is this intimate relationship between the creative work of God and the activity of humanity which provides the basis for Rozanov's emphasis on writing. Writing is for Rozanov an essentially sexual act, inseparable from the activities of the home and the juices of the body. Just as the demands of history weighed heavily on Rozanov's Russia, he also understood the vital role literature was playing in turning man away from his origins. Consequently, Rozanov was certain of the need to reconnect literature with the Creation, with family joys and with tenderness. Despite his destructive engagement with literature, Rozanov was at times optimistic that he could, phoenix-like, preside over its rebirth. Faulkner expressed the hope that the poet would secure man's immortality by helping him forget fear and remember love. Likewise, Rozanov believed that literature would provide a route from despair. Rozanov may have lost sight of this hope in his final work and died in tragic circumstances, but thanks to the rebirth of Russian religious thought the message of his writings has also been resurrected. It is this simple and undying hopefulness which is Rozanov's greatest contribution to us: his Edenic vision, his faith in the Creation and his assurance that we are loved.

# Selected Bibliography

## Primary sources

### 1. Books written in Rozanov's lifetime, including contemporary republications of these books, in chronological order of composition (date of original publication given in brackets).


*O ponimanii: Opyt issledovaniia prirody, granits i vnutrennego stroeniia nauki kak tsel'nogo znaniia* (Moscow: Tanias, 1996) [1886].

*Legenda o velikom inkvizitore F.M. Dostoevskogo* (Moscow: Respublika, 1996) [published in sections 1891; first complete edition 1894].

*Sumerki prosveshcheniia: Sbornik statei po voprosam obrazovaniia* (Moscow: Pedagogika, 1990) [1899].

*V mire neiasnogo i nereshennogo* (Moscow: Respublika, 1995) [1901].

*Semeinyi vopros v Rossii* (Moscow: Respublika, 2004) [1903].

*Okolo tserkovnykh sten* (Moscow: Respublika, 1999) [1905].

*Ital'ianskie vpechatleniia* (St Petersburg, no given publisher, 1909) [1909].

*Kogda nachal'stvo ushlo...* (Moscow: Respublika, 2005) [1910].

*Liudi lunnogo sveta: Metafizika khristianstva* (St Petersburg: Prodolzhenie zhizni, 2003) [1911].

*V temnykh religioznykh luchakh* (Moscow: Respublika, 1994) [1911].

*Smertnoe* (Moscow: Russkii Put', 2004) [1913].

*Sredi khudozhnikov* (Moscow: Respublika, 1994) [1913].

*Literaturnye izgnanniki: N.N. Strakhov, K.N. Leont'ev* (Moscow: Respublika, 2001) [1913].

*Sakharna* (Moscow: Respublika, 1998) [written 1913; complete edition not published until 1998].

*Mimoletnoe* (Moscow: Respublika, 1994) [written 1915; first published in full 1994].

*Apokalipsis nashego vremeni* (Moscow: Respublika, 2000) [first sections published 1917–1918; complete edition not published until 2000].


### 2. Collections of Rozanov's works, in alphabetical order


*Chernyi ogon'* (Paris: YMCA Press, 1991).

*Esteticheskoe ponimanie istorii*, ed. by A.N. Nikoliukin (Moscow: Respublika, 2010).

*Iudaizm: Stat'i i ocherki 1898–1901 gg.*, ed. by A.N. Nikoliukin (Moscow: Respublika, 2010).

*Iz zhizni, iskanii, i nabliudenii studenchestva*, ed. by A.F. Malyshevskii (Kaluga: Grif, 2006).

*Literaturnye izgnanniki: P.A. Florenskii, S.A. Rachinskii*, ed. by A.N. Nikoliukin (Moscow: Respublika, 2010).

*Metafizika khristianstva*, ed. by E.V. Vitkovskii and others (Moscow: Folio, 2001).
*Mysli o literature* (Moscow: Sovremennik, 1989).
*Na fundamente proshlogo: Stat'i i ocherki 1913–1915 gg.*, ed. by A.N. Nikoliukin (Moscow: Respublika, 2007).
*Okolo narodnoi dushi: Stat'i 1906–1908 gg.*, ed. by A.N. Nikoliukin (Moscow: Respublika, 2003).
*O pisatel'stve i pisateliakh*, ed. by A.N. Nikoliukin (Moscow: Respublika, 1995).
*O sebe i zhizni svoei* (Moscow: Moskovskii rabochii, 1990).
*Poslednie list'ia*, ed. by A.N. Nikoliukin (Moscow: Respublika, 2000).
*Priroda i istoriia: Stat'i i ocherki 1904–1905 gg.*, ed. by A.N. Nikoliukin (Moscow: Respublika, 2008).
*Priznaki vremeni: Stat'i i ocherki 1911 g. Pis'ma A.S. Suvorina k V.V. Rozanovu. Pis'ma V.V. Rozanova k A.S. Suvorinu*, ed. by A.N. Nikoliukin (Moscow: Respublika, 2006).
*Religiia, filosofiia, kul'tura*, ed. by A.N. Nikoliukin (Moscow: Respublika, 1992).
*Religiia i kul'tura*, ed. by E.V. Vitkovskii et al. (Moscow: Folio, 2001).
*Religiia i kul'tura: Stat'i 1902–1903 gg.*, ed. by A.N. Nikoliukin (Moscow: Respublika, 2008).
*Russkaia gosudarstvennost' i obshchestvo: Stat'i 1906–1907 gg.*, ed. by A.N. Nikoliukin (Moscow: Respublika, 2003).
*Russkaia mysl'* (Moscow: Algoritm-EKSMO, 2006).
*Sochineniia* (Moscow: Sovetskaia Rossiia, 1990).
*Staraia i molodaia Rossiia: Stat'i i ocherki 1909 g.*, ed. by A.N. Nikoliukin (Moscow: Respublika, 2004).
*Terror protiv russkogo natsionalizma: Stat'i i ocherki 1911 g.*, ed. by A.N. Nikoliukin (Moscow: Respublika, 2005).
*V nashei smute: Stat'i 1908 g. Pis'ma k E.F. Gollerbakhu*, ed. by A.N. Nikoliukin (Moscow: Respublika, 2004).
*Vo dvore iazychnikov*, ed. by A.N. Nikoliukin (Moscow: Respublika, 1999).
*Vozrozhdaiushchiisia Egipet*, ed. by A.N. Nikoliukin (Moscow: Respublika, 1999).
*Zagadki russkoi provokatsii: Stat'i i ocherki 1910 g.*, ed. by A.N. Nikoliukin (Moscow: Respublika, 2005).

## Secondary literature

Aristotel', *Metafizika*, trans. and ed. by P.D. Pervov and V.V. Rozanov (Moscow: Institut filosofii, teologii i istorii, 2006) [1890].
Assmann, Jan, *The Search for God in Ancient Egypt*, trans. by David Lorton (Ithaca/London: Cornell University Press, 2001).
Bataille, Georges, *Eroticism*, trans. by Mary Dalwood (London: Penguin, 2001).
Berdiaev, Nikolai, *Russkaia ideia: Osnovnye problemy russkoi mysli XIX veka i nachala XX veka* (Paris: YMCA Press, 1971).
Bethea, David M., *The Shape of Apocalypse in Modern Russian Fiction* (Princeton: Princeton University Press, 1989).

Bibikhin, V.V., 'K metafizike Drugogo', *Nachala*, 3 (1992), 52–65.
Billington, James Hadley, *The Icon and the Axe: An Interpretive History of Russian Culture* (London: Weidenfeld & Nicolson, 1966).
Bloch, Ernst, *Atheism in Christianity*, trans. by J.T. Swann (London: Verso, 2009).
Boldyrev, Nikolai, *Semia Ozirisa, ili Vasilii Rozanov kak poslednii vetkhozavetnyi prorok* (Cheliabinsk: Ural L.T.D., 2001).
Breasted, James Henry, *Development of Religion and Thought in Ancient Egypt* (London: Hodder & Stoughton, 1912).
Breasted, James Henry, *A History of Egypt From the Earliest Times to the Persian Conquest* (London: Hodder & Stoughton, 1945).
Bukharev, A., *Moia apologiia po povodu kriticheskikh otzyvov o knige: o sovremmenykh dukhovnykh potrebnostiakh mysli i zhizni, osobenno russkoi* (Moscow, no given publisher, 1866).
Burns, Gerald L., *Tragic Thoughts at the End of Philosophy: Language, Literature, and Ethical Theory* (Evanston: Northwestern University Press, 1999).
Campbell, Robert Allen, *Phallic Worship* (London: Kegan Paul, 2002).
Camporesi, Piero, *Juice of Life: The Symbolic and Magic Significance of Blood*, trans. by Robert R. Barr (New York: Continuum, 1995).
Clowes, Edith W., *Fiction's Overcoat: Russian Literary Culture and the Question of Philosophy* (Ithaca: Cornell University Press, 2004).
Copleston, Frederick C., *Philosophy in Russia: From Herzen to Lenin and Berdyaev* (Tunbridge Wells: Search Press, 1986).
Copleston, Frederick C., *Russian Religious Philosophy: Selected Aspects* (Tunbridge Wells: Search Press, 1988).
Costlow, Jane T., and others, eds, *Sexuality and the Body in Russian Culture* (Stanford: Stanford University Press, 1993).
Crone, Anna Lisa, *Rozanov and the End of Literature: Polyphony and the Dissolution of Genre in Solitaria and Fallen Leaves* (Würzburg: Jal-Verlag, 1978).
Crone, Anna Lisa, 'Nietzschean, All Too Nietzschean? Rozanov's Anti-Christian Critique', in *Nietzsche in Russia*, ed. by Bernice Glatzer Rosenthal (Princeton: Princeton University Press, 1986), pp. 95–112.
Crone, Anna Lisa, 'Remizov's "Kukkha": Rozanov's "Trousers" Revisited', *Russian Literary Triquarterly*, 19 (1986), 197–211.
Crone, Anna Lisa, 'Mandelstam's Rozanov', in *Stoletie Mandel´shtama: materialy simpoziuma*, ed. by Robin Aizlewood and Diana Myers (Tenafly: Hermitage, 1994), pp. 56–71.
Crone, Anna Lisa, *Eros and Creativity in Russian Religious Renewal: The Philosopher and the Freudians* (Leiden: Brill, 2010).
Davidson, Pamela, ed., *Russian Literature and its Demons* (New York: Berghahn, 2000).
Dowler, Wayne, *Dostoevsky, Grigor´ev and Native Soil Conservatism* (Toronto/London: University of Toronto Press, 1982).
Edoshina, I.A., ed., *Vasilii Rozanov v kontekste kul´tury* (Kostroma: Kostromskoi gosudarstvennyi universitet, 2000).

Eilberg-Schwartz, Howard, *God's Phallus and Other Problems for Men and Monotheism* (Boston: Beacon Press, 1994).

Engelstein, Laura, *The Keys to Happiness: Sex and the Search for Modernity in Fin-de-Siècle Russia* (Ithaca/London: Cornell University Press, 1992).

Englestein, Laura, and Stephanie Sandler, eds, *Self and Story in Russian History* (Ithaca/London: Cornell University Press, 2000).

Epstein, Mikhail, Alexander Genis and Slobodanka Vladiv-Glover, *Russian Postmodernism: New Perspectives on Post-Soviet Culture*, trans. and ed. by Slobodanka Vladiv-Glover (New York: Berghahn, 1999).

Ermichev, A.A., ed., *Religiozno-filosofskoe obshchestvo v Peterburge 1907–1917. Khronika zasedanii* (St Petersburg: Russkii Put´, 2007).

Fateev, Valerii, *S russkoi bezdnoi v dushe: Zhizneopisanie Vasiliia Rozanova* (St Petersburg: Kostroma, 2001).

Fateev, V.A., *V.V. Rozanov: Zhizn´. Tvorchestvo. Lichnost´* (Leningrad: Izdatel´stvo 'Khudozhestvennaia literatura', 1991).

Fateev, V.A., ed., *Vasilii Rozanov: Pro et Contra. Lichnost´ i tvorchestvo Vasiliia Rozanova v otsenke russkikh myslitelei i issledovatelei*, 2 vols (St Petersburg: Izdatel´stvo Russkogo Khristianskogo gumanitarnogo instituta, 1995).

Fateev, V.A., ed., *Slavianofil´stvo: Pro et Contra. Tvorchestvo i deiatel´nost´ slavianofilov v otsenke russkikh myslitelei i issledovatelei* (St Petersburg: Izdatel´stvo Russkogo Khristianskogo gumanitarnoi akademii, 2006).

Fiddes, Paul S., *The Promised End: Eschatology in Theology and Literature* (Oxford: Blackwell, 2000).

Florenskii, Pavel, *Stolp i utverzhdenie istiny: Opyt pravoslavnoi teoditsei* (Moscow: Izdatel´stvo 'AST', 2002).

Florovskii, Georgii, *Puti russkogo bogosloviia*, 2 vols (Paris: YMCA Press, 1937).

Fomin, Sergei, ed., *Rossiia pered vtorym prishestviem (Materialy k ocherku russkoi eskhatologii)* (Tiflis: Bratstvo vo imia blagovernogo kniazia Aleksandra Nevskogo, 1995).

Galkovskii, Dmitrii, *Beskonechnyi tupik*, 2 vols (Moscow: Izdatel´stvo Dmitriia Galkovskogo, 2008).

Gasparov, Boris, Robert P. Hughes, Irina Paperno, and Olga Raevsky-Hughes, eds, *Christianity and the Eastern Slavs*, ed. by, 3 vols (Berkeley/London: University of California Press, 1995), III, *Russian Literature in Modern Times.*

Gasparov, Boris, Robert P. Hughes, and Irina Paperno, eds, *Cultural Mythologies of Russian Modernism: From the Golden Age to the Silver Age* (Berkeley/Oxford: University of California Press, 1992).

Gasparov, Boris, Robert P. Hughes, Irina Paperno, and Olga Raevsky-Hughes, eds, *Russian Literature in Modern Times* (Berkeley/Oxford: University of California Press, 1995).

Giliarov-Platonov, N.P., *Evreiskii vopros v Rossii* (St Petersburg, no given publisher, 1906).

Giliarov-Platonov, N., *Iz perezhitogo: Avtobiograficheskie vospominania* (Moscow: Izdanie tovarishchestva M.G. Kuvshinova, 1886).

Giliarov-Platonov, N.P., *Sbornik sochinenii* (Moscow: Izdanie K.P. Pobedonostseva, 1899).

Glouberman, Emanuel, 'Vasilii Rozanov: The Antisemitism of a Russian Judephile', *Jewish Social Studies*, 38 (1976), 117–44.

Gollerbakh, E.F., *V.V. Rozanov: Zhizn´ i tvorchestvo* (Paris: YMCA Press, 1976).

Gorodetzky, Nadejda, *The Humiliated Christ in Modern Russian Thought* (London: SPCK, 1938).

Goux, Jean-Joseph, *The Coiners of Language*, trans. by Jennifer Curtiss Gage (Norman/London: University of Oklahoma Press, 1994).

Goux, Jean-Joseph, *Oedipus, Philosopher*, trans. by Catherine Porter (Stanford: Stanford University Press, 1993).

Hare, Tom, *ReMembering Osiris: Number, Gender and the Word in Ancient Egyptian Representational Systems* (Stanford: Stanford University Press, 1999).

Hunt, Stephen, ed., *Christian Millenarianism: From the Early Church to Waco* (London: Hurst, 2001).

Hutchings, Stephen C., 'Breaking the Circle of Self: Domestication, Alienation and the Question of Discourse Type in Rozanov's Late Writings', *Slavic Review*, 52 (1993), 67–86.

Hutchings, Stephen C., *Russian Modernism: The Transfiguration of the Everyday* (Cambridge: Cambridge University Press, 1997).

Isupov, K., and I. Savkin, eds, *Russkaia filosofiia sobstvennosti* (St Petersburg: SP Ganza, 1993).

Ivask, George, 'Rozanov', *Slavic and East European Journal*, 5 (1961), 110–22.

Kadloubovsky, E., and G.E.H. Palmer, trans. and eds, *Early Fathers from the Philokalia, together with some writings of St. Abba Dorotheus, St. Isaac of Syria and St. Gregory Palamas* (London: Faber, 1954).

Kartashev, A.V., *Tserkov´, Istoriia, Rossiia: Stat´i i vystupleniia* (Moscow: Izdatel´stvo 'Probel', 1996).

Katsis, L.F., 'Iz kommentariia k iudeiskim motivam V.V. Rozanova', *Nachala*, 3 (1992), 75–78.

Katsis, L., *Russkaia eskhatologiia i russkaia literatura* (Moscow: O.G.I., 2000).

Katsis, L.F., *Vladimir Maiakovskii: Poet v intellektual´nom kontekste epokhi* (Moscow: Rossiiskii gosudarstvennyi gumanitarnyi universitet, 2004).

Kazakova, N.Iu., *Filosofiia igry: V.V. Rozanov – Zhurnalist i literaturnyi kritik* (Moscow: Flinta-Nauka, 2001).

Khanin, Dmitry, 'Beauty and the Beast: Vasilii Rozanov's Aesthetic and Moral Ideal', *Russian Review*, 57 (1998), 72–86.

Khanin, Dmitry, 'What Was Leont´ev to Rozanov?', *Canadian Slavonic Papers*, 41 (1999), 69–84.

Khoruzhii, Sergei, *O starom i novom* (St Petersburg: Aleteiia, 2000).

Kline, George Louis, *Religious and Anti-Religious Thought in Russia* (Chicago: University of Chicago Press, 1968).

Kornblatt, Judith Deutsch, and Richard F. Gustafson, eds, *Russian Religious Thought* (Madison: University of Wisconsin Press, 1996).

Korol´kova, E.L., *Russkaia filosofiia: V. Rozanov i metafizika seksa* (St Petersburg: GUAP, 2006).

Krivonos, V.Sh., ed., *Rozanovskie chteniia: Materialy k respublikanskoi nauchnoi konferentsii* (Elets: Eletskii gosudarstvennyi pedagogicheskii institut, 1993).

Kurganov, E., 'Vasilii Rozanov, Mikhail Lermontov i Pesnia pesnei', *Scando-Slavica*, 46 (2000), 5–16.

Kurganov, Efim, and Genrietta Mondri, *Rozanov i evrei* (St Petersburg: Akademicheskii proekt, 2000).

Lebedev, Iu.V., ed., *Chteniia, posviashchennye 80-letiiu pamiati V.V. Rozanova* (Kostroma: Kostromskoi filial Rossiiskogo fonda kul´tury, 1999).

Lindemann, Albert S., *The Jew Accused: Three Anti-Semitic Affairs (Dreyfus, Beilis, Frank) 1894–1915* (Cambridge: Cambridge University Press, 1991).

Losev, Aleksei Fedorovich, *Mif, chislo, sushchnost´* (Moscow: Izdatel´stvo 'Mysl', 1994).

Losskii, Nikolai, *Istoriia russkoi filosofii* (Moscow: Vysshaia Shkola, 1991).

Lossky, Vladimir, *The Mystical Theology of the Eastern Church*, trans. by the Fellowship of St Alban and St Sergius (New York: St Vladimir's Seminary Press, 2002).

Lossky, Vladimir, *The Vision of God*, trans. by Asheleigh Moorhouse (Crestood, New York: St Vladimir's Seminary Press 1983).

Lotman, Iu.M., *Izbrannye stat'i v trekh tomakh*, 3 vols (Tallinn: Aleksandra, 1992).

Lotman, Yuri M., *Universe of the Mind: A Semiotic Theory of Culture*, trans. by Ann Shukman (London: Tauris, 1990).

Lotman, Yu.M., and A.M. Piatigorsky, 'Text and Function', trans. by Ann Shukman, *New Literary History*, 9 (1978), 233–44.

Masing-Delic, Irene, *Abolishing Death: A Salvation Myth of Russian Twentieth-Century Literature* (Stanford: Stanford University Press, 1992).

Matich, Olga, *Erotic Utopia: The Decadent Imagination in Russia's Fin de Siècle* (Wisconsin: University of Wisconsin Press, 2005).

McGinn, Bernard, John J. Collins, and Stephen J. Stein, eds, *The Encyclopedia of Apocalypticism*, 3 vols (New York: Continuum, 1998).

Merezhkovskii, D., *Taina trekh: Egipet i Vavilon* (Moscow: Respublika, 1999).

Meyendorff, John, *Byzantine Theology: Historical Trends and Doctrinal Themes* (New York: Fordham University Press, 1974).

Miller, Patricia Cox, 'Visceral Seeing: The Holy Body in Late Ancient Christianity', *Journal of Early Christian Studies*, 12 (2004), 391–411.

Mondry, Henrietta, 'Is the End of Censorship in the Former Soviet Union a Good Thing? The Case of Vasily Rozanov', *East European Jewish Affairs*, 32 (2002), 114–20.

Mondry, Henrietta, 'Beyond the Boundary: Vasilii Rozanov and the Animal Body', *Slavic and East European Journal*, 4 (1999), 651–73.

Moseiko, A.N., *Mify Rossii: Mifologicheskie dominanty v sovremennoi rossiiskoi mental´nosti* (Moscow: In-tut Afriki RAN, 2003).

Moser, Charles A., *Esthetics as Nightmare* (Princeton: Princeton University Press, 1989).

Murav, Harriet, 'The Beilis Ritual Murder Trial and the Culture of Apocalypse', *Cardozo Studies in Law and Literature*, 12 (2000), 243–63.

Naiman, Eric, *Sex in Public: The Incarnation of Early Soviet Ideology* (Princeton: Princeton University Press, 1997).

Negrov, Alexander I., *Biblical Interpretation in the Russian Orthodox Church* (Tübingen: Mohr Siebeck, 2008).

Nikoliukin, Aleksandr, *Golgofa Vasiliia Rozanova* (Moscow: Russkii Put´, 1998).
Nikoliukin, Aleksandr, *Nastoiashchaia magiia slova: V.V. Rozanov v literature russkogo zarubezh´ia* (St Petersburg, 2007).
Nikoliukin, Aleksandr, *Rozanov* (Moscow: Rostok, 2001).
Nosov, Sergei, *V.V. Rozanov: Estetika svobody* (St Petersburg: Izdatel´stvo 'Logos', 1993).
Ouspensky, Leonid, *Theology of the Icon*, trans. by Anthony Gythiel, 2 vols (New York: St Vladimir's Seminary Press, 1992).
Ouspensky, Leonid, and Vladimir Lossky, *The Meaning of Icons* (Olton: Urs Graf-Verlag, 1952).
Palamas, Gregory, *The Triads*, trans. by Nicholas Gendle, ed. by John Meyendorff (London: Paulist Press, 1983).
Paperno, Irina, and Joan Delaney Grossman, eds, *Creating Life: The Aesthetic Utopia of Russian Modernism* (Stanford: Stanford University Press, 1994).
Pease, Allison, *Modernism, Mass Culture, and the Aesthetics of Obscenity* (Cambridge: Cambridge University Press, 2000).
Pishun, V.K., and S.V. Pishun, *"Religiia zhizni" V. Rozanova* (Vladivostok: Izdatel´stvo dal´nevostochnogo universiteta, 1994).
Poggioli, Renato, *The Phoenix and the Spider* (Cambridge [Mass.]: Harvard University Press, 1957).
Poggioli, Renato, *Rozanov* (London: Bowes & Bowes, 1962).
Poliakov, Léon, *The History of Anti-Semitism*, trans. by Richard Howard, 4 vols (London: Routledge & Kegan Paul, 1955).
Polovinkin, S.M., ed., *Zapiski peterburgskikh Religiozno-filosofskikh sobranii (1901–1903 gg.)* (Moscow: Respublika, 2005).
Pyman, Avril, *A History of Russian Symbolism* (Cambridge: Cambridge University Press, 1994).
Rahner, Karl, *On the Theology of Death*, trans. by Charles H. Henkey (Freiburg/London: Nelson, 1961).
Remizov, Aleksei, *Kukkha: Rozanovy pis´ma* (New York: Serebrianyi Vek, 1978).
Rolt, C.E., *Dionysius the Areopagite on the Divine Names and the Mystical Theology* (Montana: Kessinger, 1992).
Romanov, Iv.F. (Rtsy), *Chervotochina istorii: Sbornik statei Iv.F. Romanova (Rtsy)* (St Petersburg, no given publisher, 1906).
Rorem, Paul, *Pseudo-Dionysius: A Commentary on the Texts and an Introduction to Their Influence* (New York/Oxford: Oxford University Press, 1993).
Rosenthal, Bernice Glatzer, ed., *The Occult in Russian and Soviet Culture* (Ithaca/London: Cornell University Press, 1997).
Rozanova, Tat´iana, *Bud´te svetly dukhom (Vospominaniia o V.V. Rozanove)*, ed. by A.N. Bogoslovskii (Moscow: Blue Apple, 1999).
Rtsy, *Listopad* (Moscow, no given publisher, 1895).
Sabaneeff, Leonid, 'Religious and Mystical Trends in Russia at the Turn of the Century', *Russian Review*, 24 (1965), 354–68.
Savin, Olga, trans., *The Way of a Pilgrim* (Boston/London: Shambhala, 1996).
Scheibert, Peter, 'Die Petersburger religiös-philosophischen Zusammenkünfte von 1902 und 1903', *Jahrbücher für Geschichte Osteuropas*, 12 (1964), 513–60.

Schmidt, Evelies, *Ägypten und Ägyptische Mythologie: Bilder der Transition im Werk Andrej Belyjs* (Munich: Otto Sagner, 1986).

Sergl, Anton, *Literarisches Ethos* (Munich: Otto Sagner, 1994).

Sharapov, S., ed., *Neopoznannyi genii: Sbornik statei i materialov, posviashchennykh pamiati N.P. Giliarova-Platonova* (no given place or date of publication).

Shell, Marc, *Art and Money* (Chicago/London: University of Chicago Press, 1995).

Shell, Marc, *Money, Language and Thought: Literature and Philosophy in the Economies from the Medieval through to the Modern Era* (Berkeley/London: University of California Press, 1982).

Shell, Marc, *The Economy of Literature* (Baltimore/London: The John Hopkins University Press, 1978).

Shklovskii, Viktor, *Gamburgskii schet* (Moscow: Sovetskii pisatel′, 1990).

Shklovskii, Viktor, *Izbrannoe v dvukh tomakh*, 2 vols (Moscow: Khudozhestvennaia literatura, 1983).

Shklovskii, Viktor Borisovich, *Rozanov* (Letchworth: Prideaux Press, 1974).

Shperk, Fedor, *Dialektika bytiia: Argumenty i vyvody moei filosofii* (St Petersburg, no given publisher, 1897).

Shperk, Fedor Eduardovich, *Literaturnaia kritika*, ed. by T.V. Savina (Novosobirsk: PITs GNU, 1998).

Siniavskii, Andrei, *"Opavshie list′ia" V.V. Rozanova* (Paris: Sintaxis, 1982).

Slobin, Greta N., *Remizov's Fictions 1900–1921* (DeKalb: Northern Illinois University Press, 1991).

Smirnov, M.Iu., *Mifologiia i religiia v rossiiskom soznanii* (St Petersburg: Letnii Sad, 2000).

Solkin, V.V., ed., *Peterburgskie sfinksy: Solntse Egipta na beregakh Nevy* (St Petersburg: Neva, 2005).

Solov′ev, V.S., *Polnoe sobranie sochinenii*, ed. by A.A. Nosov (Moscow: Nauka, 2000).

Spasovskii, M.M., *V.V. Rozanov v poslednie gody svoei zhizni* (New York: Vseslavianskoe izdatel′stvo, 1968).

Stammler, Heinrich A., 'Apocalypse: V.V. Rozanov and D.H. Lawrence', *Canadian Slavonic Papers*, 16 (1974), 221–43.

Stammler, H.A., 'Conservatism and Dissent: V.V. Rozanov's Political Philosophy', *Russian Review*, 32 (1973), 241–53.

Stammler, Heinrich A., *Vasilij Vasil′evič Rozanov als Philosoph* (Giessen: Schmitz, 1984).

Strakhov, N., *Bor′ba s zapadom v nashei literature*, 3 vols (Kiev: Tip. I.I. Chokolova, 1898).

Strakhov, N.N., *Literaturnaia kritika: Sbornik statei* (St Petersburg: Rossiiskii gosudarstvennyi gumanitarnyi universitet, 2000).

Sukach, V.G., ed., *Inaia zemlia, inoe nebo* (Moscow: Tanias, 1994).

Sukach, V.G., ed., *V.V. Rozanov. O sebe i zhizni svoei* (Moscow: Moskovskii rabochii, 1990).

Sukach, V.G., 'O V.V. Rozanove: Interv′iu s V.G. Sukachom', *Nachala*, 1 (1991), 33–43.

Sukach, V.G., *Vasilii Vasil´evich Rozanov: Biograficheskii ocherk* (Moscow: Progress-Pleiada, 2008).

Tager, A.S., ed., *Delo Beilisa: Tsarskaia Rossiia i delo Beilisa* (Moscow: Gesharim, 1995).

Tareev, M.M., *Osnovy khristianstva*, 4 vols (Sergiev Posad, no given publisher, 1903).

Timothey, T., *Dionysius' Mysticism: A Modern Version of the Middle English Translation* (York: 1st Resource, 1990).

Tlif, Irina, *"Koren´ rozhdeniia moego..." (K istorii roda V.V. Rozanova)* (Kostroma: DiAr, 2005).

Trotskii, L., *Literatura i revoliutsiia* (Moscow: Gosudarstvennoe izdatel´stvo, 1924).

Tukh, Boris, *Putevoditel´ po Serebrianomu veku: Kratkii populiarnyi ocherk ob odnoi epokhe v istorii russkoi kul´tury* (Moscow: Oktopus, 2005).

Valliere, Paul, *Modern Russian Theology: Bukharev, Solov´ev, Bulgakov: Orthodox Theology in a New Key* (Edinburgh: T&T Clark, 2000).

Vassiliadis, Petros, *Eucharist and Witness: Orthodox Perspectives on the Unity and Mission of the Church* (Geneva [England]: WCC Publications, 1998).

Zen´kovskii, V.V., *Istoriia russkoi filosofii*, 2 vols (Paris: YMCA Press, 1989).

Ziablikov, Aleksei, *Politicheskoe mirovospriiatie khudozhnika (V.V. Rozanov, A.P. Chekhov, P.L. Florenskii)* (Kostroma: KGU, 2003).

Zizioulas, John D., *Being as Communion: Studies in Personhood and the Church* (London: Darton, Longmann and Todd, 1985).

# Index